Authors & Artists for Young Adults

ISSN 1040-5682

Authors & Artists for Young Adults

VOLUME 87

GALE
CENGAGE Learning™

Detroit • New York • San Francisco • New Haven, Conn • Waterville, Maine • London

GALE
CENGAGE Learning

Authors and Artists for Young Adults, Volume 87

Project Editor: Mary Ruby

Permissions: Sheila Spencer

Imaging and Multimedia: John Watkins

Composition and Electronic Capture: Amy Darga

Manufacturing: Rita Wimberley

Product Manager: Meggin Condino

For product information and technology assistance, contact us at
Gale Customer Support, 1-800-877-4253.
For permission to use material from this text or product,
submit all requests online at **www.cengage.com/permissions.**
Further permissions questions can be emailed to
permissionrequest@cengage.com

Since this page cannot legibly accommodate all copyright notices, the acknowledgments constitute an extension of the copyright notice.

While every effort has been made to ensure the reliability of the information presented in this publication, Gale, a part of Cengage Learning, does not guarantee the accuracy of the data contained herein. Gale accepts no payment for listing; and inclusion in the publication of any organization, agency, institution, publication, service, or individual does not imply endorsement of the editors or publisher. Errors brought to the attention of the publisher and verified to the satisfaction of the publisher will be corrected in future editions.

EDITORIAL DATA PRIVACY POLICY. Does this product contain information about you as an individual? If so, for more information about our editorial data privacy policies, please see our Privacy Statement at www.gale.cengage.com.

Gale
27500 Drake Rd.
Farmington Hills, MI, 48331-3535

LIBRARY OF CONGRESS CATALOG CARD NUMBER 89-641100

ISBN-13: 978-0-7876-9480-7
ISBN-10: 0-7876-9480-0

ISSN 1040-5682

Printed in Mexico
1 2 3 4 5 6 7 16 15 14 13 12

Contents

Introduction

Authors and Artists for Young Adults is a reference series designed to serve the needs of middle school, junior high, and high school students interested in creative artists. Originally inspired by the need to bridge the gap between Gale's *Something about the Author,* created for children, and *Contemporary Authors,* intended for older students and adults, *Authors and Artists for Young Adults* has been expanded to cover not only an international scope of authors, but also a wide variety of other artists.

Although the emphasis of the series remains on the writer for young adults, we recognize that these readers have diverse interests covering a wide range of reading levels. The series therefore contains not only those creative artists who are of high interest to young adults, including cartoonists, graphic naovelists, photographers, music composers, bestselling authors of adult novels, media directors, producers, and performers, but also literary and artistic figures studied in academic curricula, such as influential novelists, playwrights, poets, and painters. The goal of *Authors and Artists for Young Adults* is to present this great diversity of creative artists in a format that is entertaining, informative, and understandable to the young adult reader.

Entry Format

Each volume of *Authors and Artists for Young Adults* will furnish in-depth coverage of approximately thirty authors and artists. The typical entry consists of:

—A detailed biographical section that includes date of birth, marriage, children, education, and addresses.

—A comprehensive bibliography or filmography including publishers, producers, and years.

—Adaptations into other media forms.

—Works in progress.

—A distinctive essay featuring comments on an artist's life, career, artistic intentions, world views, and controversies.

—References for further reading.

—Extensive illustrations, photographs, movie stills, cartoons, book covers, and other relevant visual material.

A cumulative index to featured authors and artists appears in each volume.

Compilation Methods

The editors of *Authors and Artists for Young Adults* make every effort to secure information directly from the authors and artists through personal correspondence and interviews. Sketches on living authors and artists are sent to the biographee for review prior to publication. Any sketches not personally reviewed by biographees or their representatives are marked with an asterisk (*).

Contact the Editor

We encourage our readers to examine the entire *AAYA* series. Please write and tell us if we can make *AAYA* even more helpful to you. Give your comments and suggestions to the editor:

BY MAIL: The Editor, *Authors and Artists for Young Adults,* 27500 Drake Rd., Farmington Hills, MI 48331-3535.

BY TELEPHONE: (800) 347-GALE

Authors and Artists for Young Adults Product Advisory Board

The editors of *Authors and Artists for Young Adults* are dedicated to maintaining a high standard of excellence by publishing comprehensive, accurate, and highly readable entries on writers, artists, and filmmakers of interest to middle and high school students. In addition to the quality of the entries, the editors take pride in the graphic design of the series, which is intended to be orderly yet appealing, allowing readers to utilize the pages of *AAYA* easily, enjoyably, and with efficiency. Despite the success of the *AAYA* print series, we are mindful that the vitality of a literary reference product is dependent on its ability to serve its readers over time. As critical attitudes about literature, art, and media constantly evolve, so do the reference needs of students and teachers. To be certain that we continue to keep pace with the expectations of our readers, the editors of *AAYA* listen carefully to their comments regarding the value, utility, and quality of the series. Librarians, who have firsthand knowledge of the needs of library users, are a valuable resource for us. The *Authors and Artists for Young Adults* Product Advisory Board, made up of school, public, and academic librarians, is a forum to promote focused feedback about *AAYA* on a regular basis, as well as to help steer our coverage of new authors and artists. The advisory board includes the following individuals, whom the editors wish to thank for sharing their expertise:

- **Eva M. Davis,** Youth Department Manager, Ann Arbor District Library, Ann Arbor, Michigan

- **Joan B. Eisenberg,** Lower School Librarian, Milton Academy, Milton, Massachusetts

- **Susan Dove Lempke,** Children's Services Supervisor, Niles Public Library District, Niles, Illinois

- **Robyn Lupa,** Head of Children's Services, Jefferson County Public Library, Lakewood, Colorado

- **Caryn Sipos,** Community Librarian, Three Creeks Community Library, Vancouver, Washington

- **Stephen Weiner,** Director, Maynard Public Library, Maynard, Massachusetts

David Almond

■ Personal

Born May 15, 1951, in Newcastle upon Tyne, England; son of James Arthur and Catherine Almond; married Sara Jane Palmer; children: Freya Grace Almond-Palmer. *Education:* University of East Anglia, B.A. (with honors). *Hobbies and other interests:* Walking, listening to music, traveling, spending time with family.

■ Addresses

Home—Northumberland, England. *E-mail*—dalmond@lineone.net.

■ Career

Writer and educator. Teacher in primary, adult, and special-education schools in England; *Panurge* (fiction magazine), editor, 1987-93; creative writing tutor for Arvon Foundation, beginning 1987, and Open College of the Arts, 1995-99; Huntington School, York, England, visiting writer, 1996-98; Hartlepool Schools, writer-in-residence, spring, 1999; visiting speaker and course leader.

■ Awards, Honors

Northern Arts Writers Award; Hawthornden fellowship, 1997; Whitbread Book Award, 1998, Lancashire Children's Book of the Year, Stockton Children's Book of the Year, *Guardian* Children's Fiction Prize shortlist, and Carnegie Medal, British Library Association, all 1999, Michael L. Printz Honor Book, American Library Association, 2000, and shortlist for Sheffield Children's Book of the Year, all for *Skellig;* British Arts Council Award for outstanding literature for young people, 1998, Smarties Silver Award, 1999, and Michael L. Printz Award, 2001, all for *Kit's Wilderness;* Smarties Gold Award, 2003, Carnegie Medal shortlist, 2003, Whitbread Book Award shortlist, 2003, and *Boston Globe/Horn Book* Award for fiction and poetry, 2004, all for *The Fire-eaters;* Coventry Inspiration Book Award, for *My Dad's a Birdman;* Hans Christian Andersen Award, International Board on Books for Young People, 2010; *Guardian* Children's Fiction Prize shortlist, 2011, for *My Name Is Mina.*

■ Writings

JUVENILE FICTION

Skellig, Hodder Children's Books (London, England), 1998, Delacorte Press (New York, NY), 1999.

Kit's Wilderness, Hodder Children's Books (London, England), 1999, Delacorte Press (New York, NY), 2000.

Heaven Eyes, Hodder Children's Books (London, England), 2000, Delacorte Press (New York, NY), 2001.

Counting Stars (short stories), Hodder Children's Books (London, England), 2000, Delacorte Press (New York, NY), 2002.

Secret Heart, Hodder Children's Books (London, England), 2001, Delacorte Press (New York, NY), 2002.

The Fire-eaters, Hodder Children's Books (London, England), 2003, Delacorte Press (New York, NY), 2004.

Kate, the Cat, and the Moon (picture book), illustrated by Stephen Lambert, Random House (New York, NY), 2005.

Clay, Delacorte Press (New York, NY), 2006.

The Savage, illustrated by Dave McKean, Candlewick Press (Cambridge, MA), 2008.

My Dad's a Birdman (picture book), illustrated by Polly Dunbar, Candlewick Press (Cambridge, MA), 2008.

Jackdaw Summer, Hodder Children's Books (London, England), 2008, published in America as *Raven Summer,* Delacorte Press (New York, NY), 2009.

The Boy Who Climbed into the Moon, illustrated by Polly Dunbar, Candlewick Press (Somerville, MA), 2010.

Slog's Dad (graphic novel), illustrated by Dave McKean, Walker Books (London, England), 2010, Candlewick Press (Somerville, MA), 2011.

My Name Is Mina, Delacorte Press (New York, NY), 2011.

The True Tale of the Monster Billy Dean, Viking (London, England), 2011.

OTHER

Mickey and the Emperor (play for children), produced at Washington Arts Center, 1984.

Sleepless Nights (short stories), Iron Press (North Shields, England), 1985.

A Kind of Heaven (short stories), Iron Press (North Shields, England), 1997.

Skellig: A Play (first produced on BBC Radio 4, 2000; also see below), Hodder Children's Books (London, England), 2002.

Wild Girl, Wild Boy: A Play (first produced in London, England, 2001; also see below), Hodder Children's Books (London, England), 2002.

Clay Boy (radio play), produced on BBC Radio 4, 2002.

Two Plays (contains *Wild Girl, Wild Boy* and *Skellig*), Delacorte Press (New York, NY), 2005.

My Dad's a Birdman (play), produced at the Edinburgh Fringe, 2005.

Also contributor to *Click: One Novel, Ten Authors,* Arthur A. Levine Books, 2007. Contributor to *London* and *Critical Quarterly.* Author's works have been published in twenty languages; short stories have been broadcast on BBC Radio 4.

■ Adaptations

Clay was adapted for film, British Broadcasting Corporation (BBC), 2008; *Skellig* was adapted for a radio play, a stage play, an opera, and a film, starring Tim Roth as Skellig, 2009.

■ Sidelights

"I never planned to be a children's writer," British author David Almond noted in his acceptance speech for the 2010 Hans Christian Andersen Award, the world's most prestigious prize in children's literature. Almond further noted in his acceptance speech, quoted on the *International Board on Books for Young People* Web site: "I thought, I'm a sensible grown up so I'll write sensible grown up books for sensible grown ups. And then I was walking along the street one day and a new story, *Skellig,* started to tell itself in my mind. When I started to write it down I knew straight away that it was one of the most special things I'd ever done, that it was somehow the culmination of everything I'd written before and I realised with amazement that it was a book for the young."

That 1998 tale of a boy's discovery of a possibly supernatural creature in his own backyard was unanimously praised by reviewers, sold out its first printing in four days, and went on to win Britain's Whitbread Book Award and the Carnegie Medal. It also inaugurated a career for Almond as a writer of juvenile and young adult novels as well as picture books, each of them lauded by critics and fans alike, and honored by some of the top prizes in children's literature. Almond received the Michael L. Printz Award for *Kit's Wilderness,* for instance, and the *Boston Globe/Horn Book* Award as well as another Whitbread Children's Book Award and England's Smarties Award for *The Fire-eaters.* Reception of the Hans Christian Andersen Award capped off a career notable, as that award jury noted, for a body of work that "captures his young readers' imagination and motivates them to read, think and be critical." As quoted in the *Guardian Online* by Alison Flood, the award jury further praised Almond's "unique voice" as a "creator of magical realism for children . . . whose use of language is sophisticated and reaches across the ages." On the *British Council* Web site, Elizabeth O'Reilly noted of the author's work: "Almond combines a variety of influences: most of his fiction is set in his home territory of north-east England, poignantly capturing its landscape, people and mythologies; other influences include magic realist literature, Arthurian legend and the work of

William Blake. The result is an infusion of thought-provoking, philosophical ideas and magical elements, all rooted in a realistic and detailed evocation of place."

Dreams of Writing

Like the hero in *Skellig*, Almond grew up on the fringes of a Northern English city, a landscape that offered great imaginative possibilities for him as a youth. In an interview with Joseph Pike for *Jubilee Books*, Almond remarked that he considered pursuing a career in the literary arts at a young age: "I was probably about 6 or 7 when I first started to think consciously about it. . . . I loved reading." Speaking with Anthony Hill on the *Female First* Web site, the author noted familial influences in his deci-

Almond was nominated for the prestigious Whitbread Book Award for *The Fire-eaters*, a novel set during the Cuban Missile Crisis.

sion to become a professional writer: "I had an uncle who wrote poetry—he was never published—and I remember being really charged by the fact that I had an uncle who was a poet. He was also a printer; he printed the local newspaper, so I think my attachment to print was there from a young age." Almond also remarked to Pike about the importance of the northeast of England in his works. "I use the landscape that was around me when I was growing up," he stated, adding that "my childhood in a small town on Tyneside, and the way people spoke, the stories they told, the different kinds of characters that were walking around the streets are really important to me. The history of the North East, the local landscape, North Eastern mythology and folklore, it's all very, very important to me."

After earning a degree from the University of East Anglia, Almond became a teacher. In 1982, he quit a full-time job, sold his house, and moved to a commune in order to devote himself to writing. The result was a collection of stories, *Sleepless Nights*, published by a small press in 1985. As Almond once commented: "I began to write properly after university, after five years of teaching. Short stories appeared in little magazines. A couple were broadcast on Radio 4. A small press collection, *Sleepless Nights*, appeared to a tiny amount of acclaim and a vast amount of silence. I ran a fiction magazine, *Panurge*, that excited and exhausted me for six years. I wrote The Great English Novel that took five years, went to thirty-three publishers and was rejected by them all. I went on writing. More stories, more publications, a few small prizes. Another novel, never finished. Another story collection was published, *A Kind of Heaven*, twelve years after the first. Then at last I started writing about growing up in our small, steep town: a whole sequence of stories, half-real, half-imaginary, that I called *Stories from the Middle of the World*. They took a year to write."

Achieves Breakthrough with *Skellig*

It was the act of finishing the Newcastle stories that inexplicably led Almond to the opening lines of *Skellig*: "I found him in the garage on Sunday afternoon," recalls the book's narrator, ten-year-old Michael—an opening line that, Almond said, simply came to him as he was walking down the street. As he explained in an interview with *Publishers Weekly*: "When I wrote the last of these stories, I stuck them into an envelope, and as soon as I'd posted away the book to my agent, the story of *Skellig* just flew into my head, as if it had just been waiting there." The Sunday on which *Skellig* begins, Michael and his family have just taken possession of an old, run-down house; also new to them is a newborn infant sister for Michael, who initially arrives home from the hospital but soon must return for heart surgery.

In the garage, behind a great deal of clutter, Michael discovers a man covered in dust and insects. At first he believes it is an old homeless man, but he finds that Skellig, who communicates with Michael but does not reveal much by way of explanation, has odd wing-like appendages. It seems Skellig has come there to die. As he begins his new school, while his mother is away with his sister at the hospital and his father is understandably preoccupied, Michael begins to bring Skellig food and medicine. He also befriends his new neighbor, a girl name Mina who is an intelligent, independent thinker. Mina explains to Michael a few of her interests, such as ornithology and the poetry of early nineteenth-century Romantic writer William Blake. She also shows him a nest of rare owls, which may have something to do with Skellig's presence.

As Perri Klass noted, writing about *Skellig* for the *New York Times Book Review,* the book's charm lies in its author's courage for allowing some things to remain a mystery: "In its simple but poetic language, its tender refusal to package its mysteries neatly or offer explanations for what happens in either world, it goes beyond adventure story or family-with-a-problem story to become a story about worlds enlarging and the hope of scattering death." As the story progresses, Michael shares the secret of Skellig with Mina, and as they both visit him in the garage, his health improves considerably. As a result, however, the mysterious occupant becomes even more secretive and mystical before he vanishes.

Michael feels his baby sister's heart beating one day, and he realizes that love can achieve miracles that science cannot. Klass praised Almond's talent for weaving in the more prosaic details of life such as soccer practice and the daily school-bus ride with larger questions involving the metaphysical world. "Its strength as a novel is in its subtlety, its sideways angles," observed Klass. "It is a book about the business of everyday life proceeding on a canvas suddenly widened to include mystery and tragedy, although not everyone has eyes to see."

Other reviews were similarly positive. Cathryn M. Mercier, writing for *Five Owls,* called *Skellig* a "novel of faith and hope," and "a book of rare spirituality for young adults." *Reading Time* contributor Howard George described it as "a haunting story" whose impact lies in "the deep emotions evoked by the family crisis and the love given out to Skellig."

Playing Dead

Almond had already completed his second young adult novel, *Kit's Wilderness,* before *Skellig* won several literary prizes in Britain, including the Whitbread and the Carnegie Medal. The focus of this second book is a game of pretend death that its characters play. "In my primary school—a spooky turreted place down by the river where the ancient coal mines had been—a bunch of kids used to play a fainting game in the long grass beyond the school yard wall," wrote Almond in *Carousel.* The story is far less insular than the secretive plot of *Skellig,* and Almond has noted that as a work of fiction it took him far longer to develop coherently. "At times I was scared stiff by what was happening in the tale," Almond admitted in *Carousel.* "Scared that it might all end dreadfully, scared that the darkness would gain the upper hand." But *Kit's Wilderness* would prove as successful as its predecessor. It is a tale that is "very linked to the scenery of my childhood and the stories and history of the place where I grew up," the author told *Booklist* interviewer Ilene Cooper.

In the novel, thirteen-year-old Kit Watson moves with his family to the old British coal-mining town of Stoneygate, where they will care for Kit's widowed grandfather. A troubled, enigmatic classmate named John Askew befriends Kit and introduces him to a bizarre game called "Death" that is played in the abandoned mines. Participants lie alone in the dark mines in an attempt to connect with the spirits of their ancestors, who died there as young boys in a terrible accident. Though several of the players treat the game as a lark, "Kit senses something far more profound and dangerous, and the connection he forges with the ancient past also circuitously seals a deeper bond with Askew," noted a critic writing for *Publishers Weekly.* When John disappears, Kit determines to locate his friend and reunite him with his family. At the same time, Kit discovers an artistic side to his personality through his relationship with his grandfather, a storyteller who inspires Kit to write his own tale, one that mirrors the events of Kit's life.

According to *School Library Journal* contributor Ellen Fader, the author "brings these complicated, interwoven plots to a satisfying conclusion as he explores the power of friendship and family, the importance of memory, and the role of magic in our lives." In her review of *Kit's Wilderness, Booklist* contributor Ilene Cooper remarked that "the story's ruminations about death and the healing power of love will strike children in unsuspected ways."

In *Raven Summer*, Almond tells the story of a British youth who befriends a Liberian refugee with a dark and violent past. (Jacket cover copyright 2008 by Delacorte Press. Used by permission of Delacorte Press, an imprint of Random House Children's Books, a division of Random House, Inc.)

Tales of Outcasts

In 2000 Almond published his third novel for teens. *Heaven Eyes* blends everyday adventure with a dalliance in the netherworld; its characters are escapees from a juvenile home who flee on a raft to an old printing plant on the River Tyne. The autobiographical story collection *Counting Stars* followed, and in 2001 the author produced *Secret Heart*, "a thought-provoking allegory," wrote Daniel L. Darigan for *School Library Journal*. *Secret Heart* focuses on Joe Maloney, a lonely misfit who dreams of tigers and finds himself curiously drawn to a ragged traveling circus that arrives in his town. "Almond fans, who relish the author's skill at creating surreal landscapes and otherworldly images, will not be disappointed by this tale," remarked a *Publishers Weekly* contributor.

Almond's 2003 novel, *The Fire-eaters*, was shortlisted for both the Carnegie Medal and the Whitbread Award and received the Smarties Gold Award. Set in 1962 during the Cuban Missile Crisis, the book concerns twelve-year-old Bobby Burns, who lives with his family in a small English seaside village. Accepted into an elite private school, Bobby must deal with a cruel teacher who practices corporal punishment, his evolving relationships with a pair of old friends, and a strange illness that befalls his father. Overshadowing everything is the threat of nuclear war; according to a *Publishers Weekly* contributor: "Bobby's reflections . . . convey the young protagonist's uncertainties and a sense of the world itself being on the cusp of change." "The apocalyptic atmosphere is personified by the tragic character McNulty, a fire-eating exhibitionist whose torturous feats raise" another significant theme, observed *Horn Book* contributor Lauren Adams, "the human capacity for pain—giving it, accepting it, bearing it for another." A contributor to *Kirkus Reviews* deemed *The Fire-eaters* "breathtakingly and memorably up to Almond's best."

Set in Felling, England, in the 1960s, Almond's novel *Clay* features fourteen-year-old David, an altar boy at a Catholic church, who befriends the troubled Stephen Rose, who has been thrown out of the seminary. A gifted sculptor, Stephen possesses the mystical power to bring his creations to life. Stephen recognizes that David also has the same power and convinces David, with the help of communion wafers, to bring to life a life-size figure the two have created. Clay is born innocent in nature but willing to obey the commands of his masters, and Stephen has destructive goals in mind for their creation. "This book will certainly fascinate readers, pulling them completely into the remarkable world Almond has created, leaving them reluctant to look up from this novel and force themselves back into the real world," wrote Jocelyn Pearce in a review for the *Curled Up with a Good Kid's Book* Web site. "David Almond shows, in this book, a rare gift for creating stories that literally will take your breath away." Hazel Rochman, writing for *Booklist*, commented that "this story will grab readers with its gripping action and its important ideas."

Of Savages, Birdmen, and Ravens

The Savage, illustrated by Dave McKean, features Blue Baker, who tries to come to terms with his father's death by writing a journal, as suggested by his counselor. Before long, Blue is making up a story about a savage who lives in the woods. As Blue continues to write, the line between reality and fantasy blurs. Noting that "there has always been a

> *"Writing can be difficult, but sometimes it really does feel like a kind of magic. I think that stories are living things—among the most important things in the world."*
>
> —David Almond, in his book *Counting Stars.*

fear on the part of humankind that words could carry this power" to become real, *Fuse #8 Production* contributor Elizabeth Bird added: "Almond touches on this fear. If you could create a living breathing danger by simply writing about it, would you?" In Blue's case, he describes a confrontation between one of his classmates, a bully, and the savage. The next day, the bully appears at school displaying prominent bruises. "The art ramps up the intensity of this provocative outing," wrote a *Kirkus Reviews* contributor of *The Savage*. Jonathan Hunt, writing for *Horn Book*, referred to *The Savage* as "a welcome addition to Almond's body of work." Similarly, *Booklist* reviewer Ian Chipman found that this "illuminating book captures the staggering power of raw emotions on young minds, and demonstrates the ways expression can help transform and temper them."

Raven Summer, published in England as *Jackdaw Summer,* tells the story of Liam, who, along with his friend, Max, follows a jackdaw, or raven, into the country and eventually finds an abandoned baby in an old farmhouse. Along with the child is a jar filled with money and a note that reads "Please look after her rite. This is a childe of God." Initially, the discovery is a big news event, but eventually the public forgets about the little girl after she is placed in foster care. When Liam and his family visit the girl, Liam ends up meeting two other foster children in the house. One, a young girl named Crystal, is a troubled orphan who appears to want to harm herself. Oliver is a refugee from Liberia who was forced to join the army at the age of ten after witnessing soldiers kill his entire family. In the meantime, Liam's friendship with Max falls apart while Liam's self-absorbed father decries the war in Iraq.

Noting that "all the ingredients are here for a worthy, socially conscious novel," London *Independent Online* contributor Nicholas Tucker went on his review to write that Almond also reveals "the darker side of his imagination," pointing out that the author's "good characters cannot escape the knowledge of their failings" and that the "villains have a way of saying . . . things containing a kernel

of truth." A *Write Away* Web site contributor commented: "Credible, beautifully drawn characters and a sparse, exquisite prose which sparkles off the page take the reader into different territory."

Almond has also produced books for middle-grade readers and children. Almond's short novel, *My Dad's a Birdman*, illustrated by Polly Dunbar, began as a play and was produced at the Edinburgh Fringe in 2005. "Afterwards, the script lay in my drawer," the author told a *Books for Keeps* Web site contributor. The author went on to note in the same interview: "I tried reducing it to a picture book text, but I couldn't get the story to fit." The author set aside the project but took it up again after the publication of his novel *Clay*. In his interview for the *Books for Keeps* Web site, the author commented that he wrote down the book's first line and "the whole thing burst into life. I couldn't stop. Within four days I had the first draft of a short novel."

The story revolves around young Lizzie's father, Jackie, who is trying to win Mr. Poop's Great Human Bird Competition. Intent on making wings that will help him win, Jackie first eats bugs to try to grow wings. Before long, Lizzie joins her father in his quest as the two realize that they need faith and togetherness just as much as, if not more than, wings. As usual with works by Almond, the book includes dark undertones concerning the death of Lizzie's mother and her father's possible madness. "As always . . . Almond writes beautifully, and . . . this novel is a tribute to the human spirit," wrote Ilene Cooper in a review for *Booklist*.

Working again with Dunbar, Almond produced another allegorical tale for young readers with *The Boy Who Climbed into the Moon*. "Roald Dahl meets Antoine de Saint-Exuépry in this delightfully improbable tale," wrote a *Kirkus Reviews* contributor of this story about an English boy, Paul, who plans to prove that the moon is simply a hole in the sky. Daniel Kraus, reviewing the tale in *Booklist*, noted: "Urban daily life meets magical realism in this quirky tale of a boy overcoming shyness." Further praise for *The Boy Who Climbed into the Moon* came from *Horn Book* contributor Sarah Ellis, who observed: "Paul's adventure, beautifully illustrated in full color, reveals a new dimension to Almond's particular brand of magic realism."

Skellig Redux

Almond returns to an important character from *Skellig* in *My Name Is Mina*. This work serves as a prequel to that earlier novel, introducing the reader to the nine-year-old girl who lives opposite Michael's house and who is a devotee of the work of poet

Winner of the 2010 Hans Christian Andersen Award for his contributions to children's literature, Almond makes an appearance at the Pen World Voices Festival.

William Blake. In *Skellig*, the reader first meets Mina as she sits in a tree writing in a notebook. That journal, which forms the core of this novel, offers insights into episodes from Mina's life as well as her thoughts on a host of subjects, including the death of her father, whose loss she is still grieving. Home-schooled, Mina is creative and lonely, intelligent and an outsider. She also displays, as Nicholas Tucker noted in the London *Independent Online*, "relentless positivity." Teachers think she is a misfit and her schoolmates have dubbed her crazy. She is happy to learn at home, as her inquisitive mind is not a good fit in the traditional school system. Yet Mina is not totally closed off; when Michael, the new boy, arrives in the neighborhood, she is curious enough to approach him and join in his adventure with Skellig. Thus, by the end of her journal, Mina has decided to come down out of her tree and join the family of man.

"Even by David Almond's standards this is a truly remarkable book," wrote *School Librarian* reviewer Peter Hollindale of *My Name Is Mina*. Hollindale further noted: "Each of Almond's children is completely individual and unique, and none more so than Mina. She, and her journal, and the book, are wholly original and marvellous." The reviewer concluded by calling this an "extraordinary masterpiece." Similar praise came from Tucker, who felt that Almond is a "canny as well as a considerable writer." Tucker went on to explain that remark by noting: "At a time when general negativism is riding high in teenage fiction, it is good to have an author coming out with a more uplifting view." London *Guardian Online* contributor Marcus Sedgwick noted that though it is a prequel to *Skellig*, Almond's *My Name Is Mina* is a "wonderful book in its own right." Sedgwick added: "Through the delightful Mina, Almond covers many subjects: big stuff such as death and loss; mundane stuff like the appropriate nature of schooling. And, while the school system works fine for the vast majority of children, he reminds us that there has to be a place for alternative schooling for boys and girls like Mina." London *Observer* reviewer Geraldine Brennan also had a positive assessment of *My Name Is*

Mina, commenting that "this account of how [Mina's] zest for living overcomes her temporary isolation and lingering sadness at the loss of her father is . . . a tale that will draw in young readers of her age and above." Further praise for the novel came from a contributor for the online *Bookbag,* who observed: "It's beautiful, of course. Everything David Almond writes is beautiful. There is lyrical language, themes of love and loss, philosophical musing and a big dollop of love."

Almond once again teams up with McKean, the illustrator from *The Savage,* for his first graphic novel *Slog's Dad.* As in *My Name Is Mina,* a parent's death plays a pivotal role in the work. Adapted from a short story, the graphic novel tells the story of a young boy, Slog, who believes that his deceased father has come back to visit him, just as the man vowed to do. Narrated by Slog's young friend, Davie, the story focuses on an event from the spring after the death of Slog's dad, when the pair come across a stranger sitting on a bench. Slog swears that it is his father returned from the dead, though Davie continues to have his doubts. "With understated and uncommon wisdom, Almond and McKean wring a bit of hope out of the toughest of emotions," noted *Booklist* contributor Ian Chipman. *Voice of Youth Advocates* writer Paula Gallagher was also impressed with this work, calling it "emotionally touching and affective yet mysterious and somewhat creepy." Writing in *School Library Journal,* Benjamin Russell similarly termed *Slog's Dad* a "strangely incomplete, but fascinating work." Much higher praise came from a *Publishers Weekly* reviewer who found it "haunting and beautiful," and a "pitch-perfect story."

With his second title from 2011, *The True Tale of the Monster Billy Dean,* Almond presents a novel geared for both young adult and adult readers. In fact, Almond's publisher, Viking, released two editions of the book, one for the adult market and one under the Puffin imprint for younger readers, and also mounted dual publicity campaigns. A post-apocalyptic tale, the story takes place in the fictional town of Blinkbonny and centers on the young Bill Dean, born out of an illicit relationship between his mother and a priest. The very day he is born, a deadly bombing occurs, and Billy is hidden away from the world for years, his parents believing that he has a sacred future ahead of him. There Billy remains, barely literate and supremely unworldly until the day that his father disappears. Thereafter his mother allows him out into the world, but when it appears that he has the ability to heal, he soon becomes the center of a messianic cult, thought of as a prophet. Then Billy is confronted with his ultimate challenge, a mysterious figure from his past.

If you enjoy the works of David Almond, you may also want to check out the following books:

Neil Gaiman's award-winning *The Graveyard Book* (2008), which follows the adventures of an orphaned boy raised by ghosts.
Rick Yancey's *The Monstrumologist* (2010), a gothic thriller set in late-nineteenth-century New England.
A Monster Calls (2011), a haunting tale of grief and loss by Patrick Ness, based on an idea by the late Siobhan Dowd.

Almond writes in the voice of young, unschooled Billy, introducing himself at the opening of the story: "I wos a secrit shy and tungtied emptyheded thing. I wos tort to read and rite and spell by my tenda littl muther & by Mr McCaufrey the butcha & by Missus Malone and her gosts. So I am not cleva, so please forgiv my folts and my mistayks. I am the won that glares into your harts & that prowls insyde yor deepist dremes. Wonce I was The Anjel Childe. Now I am The Monster. Just read and lissen and take note. Let the words enter yor blud & boans." A contributor for *Bookbag* Web site found this a "lovely story of the aftermath of war, of sin and of redemption."

The Writing Life

In Almond's works for young readers and adults, the author presents characters about whom readers feel deeply, and he places those characters in situations that stretch a reader's imagination and view of the world. Speaking with Judith Ridge on the *Misrule* blog, Almond noted a difference between the juvenile and adult audiences: "Kids don't have this need to know everything. As adults we think, if I don't know something I've got to make sure that I do know it. But kids live in this sort of area where they know that they don't know everything, so that's there sort of natural way of being." In his story collection *Counting Stars,* Almond had this to say about the craft of writing: "Writing can be difficult, but sometimes it really does feel like a kind of magic. I think that stories are living things—among the most important things in the world."

Almond practices his craft, as he has noted in numerous interviews, in a business-like way, starting at nine in the morning, taking a break for lunch, and then continuing on into the late afternoon. Speaking with Hill on the *Female First* Web site, Almond remarked on this aspect of being an author: "As well as being work, it's also play. I think it's really important to recognise that it's hard work and can be very dure but it's fun as well." He further commented to Hill on what he hopes to achieve in his writing: "Oh I have some outrageous goals, but the predominant one really is just to keep on writing good books."

■ Biographical and Critical Sources

BOOKS

Almond, David, *Skellig,* Hodder Children's Books (London, England), 1998.

Almond, David, *Counting Stars,* Hodder Children's Books (London, England), 2000, Delacorte Press (New York, NY), 2002.

Almond, David, *Raven Summer,* Delacorte Press (New York, NY), 2009.

Almond, David, *The True Tale of the Monster Billy Dean,* Viking (London, England), 2011.

PERIODICALS

Book, May, 2001, Kathleen Odean, review of *Kit's Wilderness,* p. 80.

Booklist, January 1, 2000, Ilene Cooper, "The *Booklist* Interview: David Almond," p. 898, and review of *Kit's Wilderness,* p. 899; April 1, 2001, Ilene Cooper, "The *Booklist* Interview," interview with Almond, p. 1464; February 1, 2002, Hazel Rochman, review of *Counting Stars,* p. 934; October 1, 2002, Michael Cart, review of *Secret Heart,* p. 322; March 15, 2004, Ilene Cooper, review of *The Fire-eaters,* pp. 1297-1298; July 1, 2005, Ilene Cooper, review of *Kate, the Cat, and the Moon,* p. 1929; October 1, 2005, Hazel Rochman, review of *Two Plays,* p. 51; June 1, 2006, Hazel Rochman, review of *Clay,* p. 74; September 15, 2007, Lynn Rutan, review of *Click: One Novel, Ten Authors,* p. 57; March 15, 2008, Ilene Cooper, review of *My Dad's a Birdman,* p. 54; September 15, 2008, Ian Chipman, review of *The Savage,* p. 49; January 1, 2010, Daniel Kraus, review of *The Boy Who Climbed into the Moon,* p. 79; March 15, 2011, Ian Chipman, review of *Slog's Dad,* p. 62.

Bookseller, September 30, 2005, Benedicte Page, "Through Almond's Eyes: David Almond's New Book Brings the Frankenstein Myth to the Northeast," p. 20; February 17, 2006, review of *Clay,* p.

42; May 9, 2008, "Watch the Birdie," p. 9; September 12, 2008, Caroline Horn, "Cracking Ahead: David Almond Talks to Caroline Horn about Being a Regional Writer and the Need for Constant Re-invention," p. 21; May 20, 2011, Charlotte Williams, "Penguin Planning Dual Campaign for New David Almond Novel," p. 28.

Carousel, summer, 1999, David Almond, "Writing for Boys," p. 29.

Five Owls, May-June, 1999, Cathryn M. Mercier, review of *Skellig,* p. 110.

Horn Book, May, 1999, review of *Skellig,* p. 326; March-April, 2002, Gregory Maguire, review of *Counting Stars,* pp. 207-208; November-December, 2002, Christine M. Heppermann, review of *Secret Heart,* pp. 745-746; May-June, 2004, Lauren Adams, review of *The Fire-eaters,* p. 324; January-February, 2006, Deirdre F. Baker, review of *Two Plays;* July-August, 2006, Vicky Smith, review of *Clay;* January-February, 2007, review of *Clay;* November-December, 2007, Vicky Smith, review of *Click;* May-June, 2008, Deirdre F. Baker, review of *My Dad's a Birdman;* September-October, 2008, Jonathan Hunt, review of *The Savage;* May-June, 2010, Sarah Ellis, review of *The Boy Who Climbed into the Moon,* p. 79.

Journal of Adolescent & Adult Literacy, October, 2007, James Blasingame, review of *Click,* p. 191.

Kirkus Reviews, March 15, 2002, review of *Counting Stars,* p. 404; September 1, 2002, review of *Secret Heart,* p. 1300; April 1, 2004, review of *The Fire-eaters,* p. 323; September 1, 2005, review of *Kate, the Cat, and the Moon,* p. 967; October 15, 2005, review of *Two Plays,* p. 1133; June 1, 2006, review of *Clay,* p. 567; September 15, 2007, review of *Click;* March 15, 2008, review of *My Dad's a Birdman;* September 15, 2008, review of *The Savage;* March 1, 2010, review of *The Boy Who Climbed into the Moon.*

Kliatt, November, 2002, Paula Rohrlick, review of *Secret Heart,* p. 5; January, 2004, Nola Theiss, review of *Counting Stars,* p. 26; July, 2006, Paula Rohrlick, review of *Clay,* p. 7; May, 2008, Paula Rohrlick, review of *Clay,* p. 26.

Los Angeles Times, April 8, 2001, "Books for Kids," includes review of *Heaven Eyes,* p. 6.

New York Times Book Review, June 6, 1999, Perry Klass, review of *Skellig,* p. 49.

Observer (London, England), October 3, 2010, Geraldine Brennan, review of *My Name Is Mina,* p. 42.

Publishers Weekly, June 28, 1999, Elizabeth Devereaux, "Flying Starts," profile of Almond, p. 25; January 3, 2000, review of *Kit's Wilderness,* p. 77; November 6, 2000, "Best Children's Books 2000," review of *Kit's Wilderness,* p. 43; April 1, 2002, review of *Counting Stars,* p. 85; July 1, 2002, "The British Invasion: *PW* Speaks to Five Authors Who Have Crossed the Atlantic and Found American

Readers," pp. 26-29; August 19, 2002, review of *Secret Heart*, p. 90; May 3, 2004, review of *The Fire-eaters*, p. 192; September 5, 2005, review of *Kate, the Cat, and the Moon*, p. 61; May 29, 2006, review of *Clay*, p. 60; March 29, 2010, review of *The Boy Who Climbed into the Moon*, p. 59; March 7, 2011, review of *Slog's Dad*, p. 66.

Reading Time, May, 1999, Howard George, review of *Skellig*, p. 25.

Resource Links, December, 2007, Myra Junyk, review of *Click*, p. 37.

School Librarian, winter, 2010, Peter Hollindale, review of *My Name Is Mina*, p. 238.

School Library Journal, March, 2000, Ellen Fader, review of *Kit's Wilderness*, p. 233; April, 2001, Kathleen Odean, review of *Mystic Man*, p. 48; March, 2002, William McLoughlin, review of *Counting Stars*, p. 225; October, 2002, Daniel L. Darigan, review of *Secret Heart*, p. 54; May, 2004, Joel Shoemaker, review of *The Fire-eaters*, p. 140; September, 2005, Maura Bresnahan, review of *Kate, the Cat, and the Moon*, p. 164; December, 2005, Nancy Menaldi-Scanlan, review of *Two Plays*, p. 160; August, 2006, Joel Shoemaker, review of *Clay*, p. 113; October, 2006, review of *Two Plays*, p. 71; May, 2008, Margaret A. Chang, review of *My Dad's a Birdman*, p. 92; December, 2008, Johanna Lewis, review of *The Savage*, p. 118; May, 2010, Susan Hepler, review of *The Boy Who Climbed into the Moon*, p. 78; May, 2011, Benjamin Russell, review of *Slog's Dad*, p. 105.

Voice of Youth Advocates, April, 2000, Bette Ammon, review of *Kit's Wilderness*, p. 42; June, 2011, Paula Gallagher, review of *Slog's Dad*, p. 155.

ONLINE

Achuka Web site, http://www.achuka.co.uk/ (October 19, 2001), interview with Almond.

American Library Association Web site, http://www.ala.org/ (February 9, 2001), "David Almond Wins Printz Award."

Australian Online, http://www.theaustralian.news.com.au/ (March 28, 2009), review of *Jackdaw Summer*.

Birmingham Post Online, http://www.birminghampost.net/ (October 6, 2008), Terry Grimley, "Author David Almond Happy at Last with *Skellig* Success," interview with author.

Bookbag Web site, http://www.thebookbag.co.uk/ (August 13, 2011), review of *My Name Is Mina*; review of *The True Tale of the Monster Billy Dean*.

BookLoons Web site, http://www.bookloons.com/ (June 19, 2009), J.A. Kaszuba Locke, reviews of *Clay*, *Two Plays*, and *Kate, the Cat, and the Moon*.

Books for Keeps Online, http://www.booksforkeeps.co.uk/ (June 19, 2009), David Almond, "*My Dad's a Birdman*: David Almond on His New Novel."

British Council Web site, http://www.britishcouncil.org/new/ (August 13, 2011), Elizabeth O'Reilly, "David Almond."

Columbus Dispatch Online, http://www.dispatch.com/ (June 11, 2008), Nancy Gilson, "Father-Daughter Story a Tender, Funny Tale," review of *My Dad's a Birdman*.

Curled Up with a Good Kid's Book Web site, http://www.curledupkids.com/ (June 19, 2009), Jocelyn Pearce, review of *Clay*.

David Almond Home Page, http://www.davidalmond.com (November 1, 2011).

Evansville Courier & Press Online, http://www.courierpress.com/ (December 21, 2008), Charles Sutton, "Tales of Graphic Novels Paint Pictures for All Ages," review of *The Savage*.

Female First Web site, http://www.femalefirst.co.uk/ (April 20, 2009), Anthony Hill, "David Almond Interview."

Fortean Times Online, http://www.forteantimes.com/ (June 19, 2009), Gordon Rutter, "A Fortean at the Fringe—Part I," review of *Clay*.

Fuse #8 Production Blog, http://blog.schoollibraryjournal.com/afuse8production/ (July 13, 2007), Elizabeth Bird, review of *Click*; (December 6, 2008), Elizabeth Bird, review of *The Savage*.

Guardian Online, http://www.guardian.co.uk/ (March 23, 2010), Alison Flood, "David Almond Wins 2010 Hans Christian Andersen Medal;" (September 4, 2010), Marcus Sedgwick, review of *My Name Is Mina*; (October 3, 2010), Geraldine Brennan, review of *My Name Is Mina*.

International Board on Books for Young People Web site, http://www.ibby.org/ (September 11, 2010), David Almond, "Acceptance Speech by David Almond: 2010 Hans Christian Andersen Award Winner."

Independent Online, http://www.independent.co.uk/ (November 6, 2005), Benedicte Page, "David Almond: Frankenstein Goes to Tyneside," review of *Clay*; (November 17, 2008) Nicholas Tucker, review of *Jackdaw Summer*; (September 8, 2010), Nicholas Tucker, review of *My Name Is Mina*.

Irish Independent Online, http://www.independent.ie/ (December 7, 2008), Celia Keenan, "Tales of Love and Death with a Little Bit of Gore," review of *The Savage*.

Jubilee Books Web site, http://www.jubileebooks.co.uk/ (March 1, 2002), Joseph Pike, "Author Interview: David Almond."

Metro Online, http://www.metro.co.uk/ (March 26, 2002), Fiona MacDonald, "David Almond," interview with author.

Misrule Blog, http://www.misrule.com.au/ (May 1, 2003), Judith Ridge, "An Interview with David Almond."

Scotland on Sunday Online, http://scotlandonsunday. scotsman.com/ (March 16, 2008), Janet Christie, review of *The Savage.*

Scottish Book Trust Web site, http://www.scottish booktrust.com/ (June 19, 2009), "David Almond & Sara Grady," interview with author.

Seattle Post-Intelligencer Online, http://www. seattlepi.com/ (June 19, 2006), Cecelia Goodnow, "Wade into Summer Reading Fun," review of *Clay.*

Star Online, http://www.thestar.com/ (November 26, 2006), Deirdre Baker, "Just the Right Read for Every Single Kid," review of *Clay.*

Teen Reads Web site, http://www.teenreads.com/ (October 19, 2001), interview with Almond.

Telegraph Online, http://www.telegraph.co.uk/ (October 24, 2008), Nicolette Jones, "David Almond: 'Story Is a Kind of Redemption,'" interview with author.

Time Out London Web site, http://www.timeout. com/ (April 11, 2008), review of *The Savage;* (December 2, 2008) review of *Jackdaw Summer.*

Times Online, http://www.timesonline.co.uk/ (October 24, 2004), Nicolette Jones, review of *Kate, the Cat, and the Moon;* (October 21, 2007) Nicolette Jones, review of *My Dad's a Birdman.*

Write Away Web site, http://www.writeaway.org. uk/ (March 14, 2008), review of *My Dad's a Birdman;* (September 28, 2008) review of *Jackdaw Summer.**

Mary Jane Beaufrand

■ Personal

Married; children: two. *Education:* Wellesley College, earned degree; Bennington College, M.F.A. (creative writing).

■ Addresses

Home—Seattle, WA. *Agent*—Steven Chudney, The Chudney Agency, 72 North State Rd., Ste. 501, Briarcliff Manor, NY 10510.

■ Career

Writer. Also teaches writing.

■ Awards, Honors

Edgar Allan Poe Award nomination for best young adult fiction, Mystery Writers of America, 2011, for *The River.*

■ Writings

Primavera, Little, Brown (New York, NY), 2008.
The River, Little, Brown (New York, NY), 2010.

Contributor to *Toddler: Real-life Stories of Those Fickle, Irrational, Urgent, Tiny People We Love*, edited by Jennifer Margulis, Seal Press (Berkeley, CA), 2003, and *How to Fit a Car Set on a Camel and Other Misadventures Traveling with Kids*, edited by Sarah Franklin, Seal Press (Berkeley, CA), 2008.

■ Sidelights

Mary Jane Beaufrand features perceptive and resilient female narrators in her highly regarded young adult novels, *Primavera* and *The River*. In the former, a work of historical fiction that takes place during the Florentine Renaissance, the unassuming daughter of an Italian merchant finds herself at the center of a bloody struggle between warring families. The latter title, a contemporary thriller, focuses on a despondent teen's search for her young neighbor's killer in rural Oregon. Beaufrand noted that the decision to write such vastly different novels was motivated primarily by her interest in the books' settings, telling Trisha Murakami on the *Ya Ya Yas Blog* that "it seems to me that instead of thinking of deliberately switching genres, I thought in terms of beauty. The beauty of Florence and the central Cascades are completely different, but they both acted on my imagination the same way in creating *Primavera* and *The River*."

From a young age, Beaufrand seemed destined to become an author. "I totally fit the profile of a writer's childhood," she recalled in an online interview with Becky Laney. "I was asthmatic growing up and spent a lot of the school year wheezing on the living room sofa, getting through sick days with the help of *The Secret Garden* and *The Chronicles of Narnia*." Beaufrand's mother, an English major in college who once studied with esteemed novelist and short story writer Bernard Malamud, also served as an important role model for the budding author.

Art Inspires Art

Beaufrand, a graduate of Wellesley College who has also earned a master of fine arts degree in creative writing from Bennington College, began writing *Primavera*, her debut novel, in 2004. Her interest in the Renaissance began at Wellesley, when a lecturer in her introductory art class showed the students a picture of the Basilica di Santa Maria del Fiore, a stunning Gothic cathedral in Florence known familiarly as the Duomo. Beaufrand also frequented the Isabella Stewart Gardner Museum in Boston, Massachusetts, where she first encountered Sandro Botticelli's *Virgin and Child with an Angel*, an allegorical painting by the celebrated artist dating from the 1470s. Botticelli plays a key role in the novel, which draws its title from his 1482 masterpiece, a celebration of love and the return of spring.

"It was early 1478 when my family's fortunes ebbed. Those who still speak of the April Rebellion say how sudden it was, how no one had any idea things were so bad in our city of flowers."

—protagonist Flora Pazzi in *Primavera*.

Primavera begins, in fact, as Botticelli enters the home of Maestro Orazio, a goldsmith in Florence, the Italian city-state under the control of Lorenzo de Medici, known as *Il Magnifico*. Medici has ruled the region since the brutal, blood-soaked April Rebellion of 1478, just four years earlier, in which members of the rival Pazzi family conspired to murder him. Botticelli brings word from his patron, Lucrezia de Medici, Lorenzo's wife, that Girolamo

Riorio, one of the leaders of the uprising, has been caught and executed for his crimes, thus ending the Medici's pursuit of their enemies. Bearing witness to the conversation is the goldsmith's apprentice, Lorenza Pazzi, who, disguised as a boy and calling herself Emilio, recognizes that Botticelli's message is actually intended for her ears. As Botticelli departs, Lorenza begins recalling the events of the April Rebellion, which signaled the demise of her once-powerful family.

The youngest daughter of Jacopo Pazzi, a greedy merchant, and Maddelena, his power-hungry spouse, Lorenza—known to everyone as Flora—spends her days in relative anonymity, tending the garden in the family's elegant *palazzo*, slaving in the kitchen with Nonna, her beloved grandmother who works as a healer, and playing second fiddle to her beautiful older sister, Domenica. Though her mother plans to send Flora to Our Lady of Fiesole, a convent, the fourteen year old has grander plans for her future, and she has been pilfering gems from her father to finance her escape. After journeying to Venice, Flora schemes, "I would book passage on a ship to the Holy Lands, battle infidels, and rescue the bones of some saint. From there I would ride on a camel through the mountains and have tea with a Chinese lord with a moustache so long it dragged to the ground. When I came back, I would stand at the altar during high mass at our *duomo*. I would slit open my robes as Marco Polo did, and say: *See, Papa? Is this enough? Do you love me now?*"

When a scrawny, youthful member of her father's guard appears one day, bearing a message from Pope Sixtus IV, a friend of the Pazzis, Flora escorts him to her father's library, where her parents are plotting an alliance with the increasingly influential Medici family. The Pazzis decide to hire Botticelli to paint a dazzling portrait of Domenica, hoping that her beauty will snare the attention of Giuliano de Medici, Lorenzo's younger brother, and lead to marriage. After reading the missive from Sixtus IV, Jacopo sends the young guard, named Emilio, to the town of Forli with a message for Count Riorio, the Pope's nephew.

Days later, Emilio returns with Riorio, a sinister-looking and arrogant man, who is accompanied by several members of his brutish entourage. Under Jacopo's orders, they soon attempt to turn Flora's garden into a training area for the soldiers, only to be stopped by Botticelli, who has arrived to begin work on Domenica's picture, and Nonna. Flora then overhears her father admit to Nonna that the Pope, who is greatly in debt to *Il Magnifico*, hopes that Jacopo and Riorio can wrest control of the city from Medici, by any means necessary. As her father tells Flora, "We will be joined to the Medici, or we will destroy them and take their place. It is that simple."

Nonna, realizing the gravity of the situation, enlists Captain Umberto, the head of Jacopo's guard, to teach Flora how to wield a sword and staff. As Flora trains with Emilio, she finds herself drawn to his courageous but sensitive nature, and they stand guard together over the *palazzo* when the soldiers face quarantine after one perishes in a suspicious manner. After the soldiers are released, however, Flora learns that the quarantine resulted from a secret alliance between Nonna and Captain Umberto, who share a distrust of Riorio's thugs.

Murderous Intentions

As Easter approaches, Maddelena Pazzi decides to host a grand party, at which time Botticelli will unveil his portrait, which portrays Domenica as the Madonna holding the Christ child. Meanwhile, Riorio, who suspects that the Pazzis are attempting to gain favor with the Medicis, pressures Jacopo to uphold his promise to the Pope by assassinating *Il Magnifico*. After the Pazzi's feast, when Lucrezia announces that Giuliano will join the priesthood instead of marrying Domenica, Jacopo makes a fateful decision, and Riorio's men attack the Medicis at Easter mass, killing Giuliano and injuring Lorenzo, who is saved by Flora and Emilio.

With the Medici army advancing on the Pazzi's home, Flora sends Emilio to Porta Romana, where the Pope's army supposedly awaits, though he never returns. To disguise her looks, Flora cuts her hair and enters her home through a secret passage, rescuing Domenica and retrieving the body of Nonna, who has committed suicide, as the other members of her family are rounded up. Returning once again to the city, Flora attempts to work through an angry mob that has gathered to watch the brutal revenge murder of Jacopo, but she is wisely halted by Orazio, the goldsmith, who takes her into his home in gratitude to Nonna, who once helped his terminally ill son.

As time passes, Flora learns to craft fine jewelry under Orazio's tutelage, keeping herself hidden from the public eye until Botticelli's unexpected visit years later. When she goes to see her jailed brother, Flora is recognized by the sheriff, a former Medici soldier who spares her life for saving *Il Magnifico*. Later, while delivering a ring to Botticelli, he unveils one of his grandest works, *Primavera*, inspired by Flora's strength and determination, and he further surprises the young woman by reintroducing her to an old friend.

Discussing her novel in a *Damsels in Regress* interview with Emilie Bishop, Beaufrand stated, "I was drawn to the Pazzi Rebellion because I loved the contrast of the beauty and the brutality. We tend to think of the Florentine Renaissance as this great flowering of ideas, when all these wonderful thinkers and artists appeared. And yet, here was this bloody spectacle which was anything but enlightened. I thought it was really interesting that Lorenzo de Medici, the great patron of the arts, was behind both." According to Jill Heritage Maza in *School Library Journal*, "Political, historical, and art historical details provide a canvas on which this tale of murder, intrigue, and young romance is played out," and a *Kirkus Reviews* critic noted that Beaufrand's "story does propel the reader along to its gentle epilogue."

Displaced and Distressed

Beaufrand's next novel, *The River*, concerns Veronica "Ronnie" Severance, a high school student living in

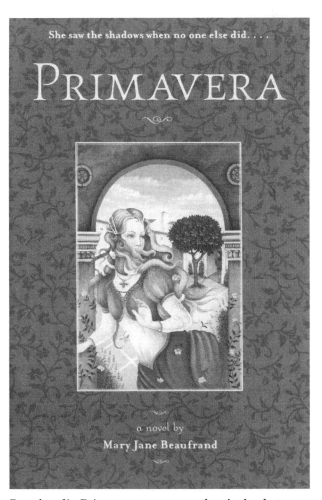

Beaufrand's *Primavera* centers on the rivalry between two powerful families during the Florentine Renaissance. (Cover art by Joyce Patti. Copyright © 2008 Reproduced by permission of Hachette Book Group USA. All rights reserved.)

the small town of Hoodoo, Oregon, with her mother, Claire, a celebrity chef, and father, Paul, a former public defender. They share their home with Gloria Inez and her children, Tomàs and Esperanza, who joined the Severance clan after Gloria's husband, once a client of Paul's, was arrested for hoarding an arsenal of weapons. Seeing her husband overwhelmed with guilt, Claire suggests that the entire group spend some time renovating an old inn she inherited, and after they arrive, the rustic atmosphere proves so appealing that Claire and Paul decide to relocate and serve as the proprietors of the Patchworks Inn, located on the banks of the Santiam River.

To Ronnie, however, Hoodoo feels stifling, a far cry from the hustle and bustle of cosmopolitan Portland, and she alleviates her frustrations with weekend runs along the rural roads. One summer day, while jogging past a neighbor's home, she tends to a frightened girl who took a spill from a trampoline. Having earned the trust of the girl's parents, Mr. and Mrs. Armstrong, Ronnie becomes a frequent babysitter for young Karen, an adventurous sort who fancies herself a modern-day Sacagawea, always intent on exploring the woods. In the months that follow, Karen helps Ronnie learn about nature's simple pleasures, and the teen begins to develop an appreciation for her new surroundings.

All that changes on a rainy February morning, however, when Ronnie spies something unusual in the Santiam River during her run. After scrambling down the embankment, she discovers Karen's lifeless body snagged on a branch, and rushes to alert Ranger Dave, a member of the U.S. Forest Service, who in turn summons Santiam County Sheriff McGarry and her deputy. After returning home, Ronnie is comforted by her parents as well as Gretchen, a friend and classmate who waitresses at the inn; the "two Brads," snowboard enthusiasts who are visiting the area; and Keith Spady, her abrasive but attractive chemistry partner who offers a bouquet of lupine, the same flowers Karen favored, as a consolation for her loss. Ronnie also receives a cautionary warning from the sheriff, who suggests that the child's drowning may not have been an accident.

As Ronnie recalls Karen's desire to explore deep in the woods, where Ronnie refused to venture, she begins feeling responsible for the youngster's death and decides to search the muddy riverbank for clues, assisted by Tomàs, a quiet, brawny teenager. Though the pair have no luck, their time together helps Ronnie better understand her gruff protector, who suffered abuse at the hands of his father. Later, while searching alone against her family's wishes,

Ronnie finds a mastiff roaming loose in the woods, and she reluctantly adopts the dog, naming the smelly beast Petunia. While on a walk with Petunia—and with Tomàs close by—Ronnie discovers a cigarette package in the woods, which turns out to be a crucial piece of evidence.

A few days later, at a party thrown by Gretchen and Keith, events spiral out of control. A fight breaks out between Keith and Tomàs, who has a crush on Ronnie, and Gretchen is discovered passed out in the bathroom, having overdosed on crystal meth. Gretchen and Tomàs, who broke his collarbone, are rushed to the hospital, where Ronnie is met by a pair of special agents from the Drug Enforcement Agency investigating the region's meth epidemic. Ronnie begins to make connections between seemingly unrelated events, and risks her life in her attempt to find those responsible for Karen's death.

The River was nominated for an Edgar Allan Poe Award for best young adult fiction. *Horn Book*'s Tanya D. Auger commented, "Beaufrand has a knack for scene-setting, and her characters are nicely realized," while a *Kirkus Reviews* contributor credited the author for "insightful and often surprisingly funny prose." "Beaufrand does a nice job of building suspense," observed *Booklist* critic Michael Cart, and Deborah Stevenson, writing in the *Bulletin of the Center for Children's Books*, maintained that *The River* "will be a favorite with fans of mysteries that tug the heartstrings." According to *School Library Journal* reviewer Terri Clark, the novel's "real strength and beauty come from the healing nature of family and unexpected friendships."

If you enjoy the works of Mary Jane Beaufrand, you may also want to check out the following books:

The Girl with the Pearl Earring (1999), Tracy Chevalier's bestselling work that offers a fictional account of the model who appears in Dutch master Johannes Vermeer's painting of the same title.

Donna Jo Napoli's *The Smile* (2008), a novel set in Renaissance Florence that explores the identity of the woman who posed for Leonardo da Vinci's *Mona Lisa*.

Please Ignore Vera Dietz, a 2010 work by A.S. King that centers on a teenager's remorse following the death of her best friend.

Beaufrand remarked to Murakami in the *Ya Ya Yas* interview that although *Primavera* required more research than *The River*, "in both cases the reward wasn't the research itself but the deep writing that came out of it. When given a choice, I'm more interested in the emotions than puttering around in footnotes, although puttering is a lot of fun."

■ **Biographical and Critical Sources**

BOOKS

Beaufrand, Mary Jane, *Primavera*, Little, Brown (New York, NY), 2008.

Beaufrand, Mary Jane, *The River*, Little, Brown (New York, NY), 2010.

PERIODICALS

Booklist, January 1, 2008, Anne O'Malley, review of *Primavera*, p. 61; December 15, 2009, Michael Cart, review of *The River*, p. 36.

Bulletin of the Center for Children's Books, February, 2010, Deborah Stevenson, review of *The River*, p. 235.

Horn Book, May-June, 2010, Tanya D. Auger, review of *The River*, p. 176.

Kirkus Reviews, January 1, 2008, review of *Primavera*; February 15, 2010, review of *The River*.

Kliatt, March, 2008, Janis Flint-Ferguson, review of *Primavera*, p. 8.

School Library Journal, February, 2008, Jill Heritage Maza, review of *Primavera*, p. 111; February, 2010, Terri Clark, review of *The River*, p. 104.

Seattle Times, April 26, 2008, Stephanie Dunnewind, "Fairy Tales and Tales of Teen Angst," p. D3.

Voice of Youth Advocates, April 1, 2008, Laura Woodruff, review of *Primavera*, p. 58; April, 2010, Judith Brink-Drescher, review of *The River*, p. 54.

ONLINE

Becky's Book Reviews Blog, http://blbooks.blogspot.com/ (May 5, 2008), Becky Laney, "Interview with Mary Jane Beaufrand."

Damsels in Regress Blog, http://damselsinregress.wordpress.com/ (August 11, 2010), Emilie Bishop, "Interview: Mary Jane Beaufrand."

Hachette Book Group Web site, http://www.hachettebookgroup.com/ (October 14, 2008), author profile.

Readergirlz Blog, http://readergirlz.blogspot.com/ (November 25, 2010), "November Feature: *The River* by Mary Jane Beaufrand."

Ya Ya Yas Blog, http://theyayayas.wordpress.com/ (May 18, 2010), Trisha Murakami, "Summer Blog Blast Tour: Mary Jane Beaufrand."*

Don Calame

■ Personal

Surname is pronounced "Cal-uh-may"; born October 10, 1968, in New York, NY; married to Meg Tilly (an actress); children: a son. *Education:* Adelphi University, B.A. (communications). *Hobbies and other interests:* Reading, watching hockey, collecting hockey memorabilia, listening to music.

■ Addresses

Home—British Columbia, Canada. *Agent*—(Literary) Jodi Reamer, Writer's House, 21 West 26th St., New York, NY 10010; (film) Caren Bohrman, 8899 Beverly Blvd., Ste. 811, Los Angeles, CA 90048. *E-mail*—don@doncalame.com.

■ Career

Screenwriter and novelist. Served as assistant to a talent agent in Los Angeles, CA; Motion Picture & Television Fund Foundation, Woodland Hills, CA, staff member; elementary school teacher in Los Angeles, for four years. Has also worked as a bike mechanic, musical instrument salesman, and supermarket cashier.

■ Awards, Honors

Awarded Los Angeles Unified School District Intern Golden Apple Award; Los Angeles Education Partnership Grant; Thumbs Up! Award honor book, Michigan Library Association, Pacific Northwest Booksellers Association Book Award nomination, Best Books for Young Adults designation, American Library Association (ALA), Nevada Young Readers Award nomination, 2011, and White Pine Award nomination, Ontario Library Association, 2011, all for *Swim the Fly;* Best Fiction for Young Adults designation, ALA, for *Beat the Band.*

■ Writings

NOVELS

Swim the Fly, Candlewick Press (Somerville, MA), 2009.
Beat the Band, Candlewick Press (Somerville, MA), 2010.

SCREENPLAYS

(With Chris Conroy) *Hounded,* Disney Channel, 2001.

(With Chris Conroy and Greg Coolidge) *Employee of the Month*, Lionsgate Films, 2006.

Author of *The Lie*, with Chris Conroy. Also author of *Saturday Afternoon Madness, Always a Bridesmaid, Damage Control*, and *Prime*.

▪ Adaptations

Swim the Fly and *Beat the Band* were adapted as audio books, Brilliance Audio, 2010.

▪ Sidelights

"Movies don't count," Cooper says. "The Internet doesn't count. Magazines don't count. A real, live naked girl. That's the deal. That's our goal for the summer."

Thus begins *Swim the Fly*, Don Calame's debut novel for young adults, which follows the adventures of three sex-crazed fifteen year olds over the course of one wild summer. Raucous humor is a trademark of Calame's work, which includes *Beat the Band*, a companion volume to *Swim the Fly*, and *Employee of the Month*, a motion picture starring Dane Cook and Jessica Simpson. "Growing up I was a huge fan of Monty Python, Woody Allen and Douglas Adams," Calame remarked in an online interview with Steph Su. "I love things that are bizarrely comic and absurd."

Drawn to the Page

Born in New York City, Calame grew up in Hicksville, a small community on Long Island. Calame's love of all things literary began at an early age; his mother and grandmother, who were avid readers, often gave him books as birthday and Christmas presents. "My passion for reading started when I was very young with books by Dr. Seuss and Richard Scarry," he recalled in a London *Guardian* essay. "That foundation was built upon by the likes of Roald Dahl, C.S. Lewis, Lloyd Alexander, and George Selden. But what really cemented my love of books (my wife might call it an obsession, and my aching bookshelves would probably agree) were the novels I read as a teenager."

During his adolescent years, Calame developed a taste for horror, science fiction, and courtroom dramas, and he devoured works such as *The Shin-*

ing and *Salem's Lot* by Stephen King, *Jurassic Park* and *The Andromeda Strain* by Michael Crichton, and *Presumed Innocent* by Scott Turow. "But the book I attribute most with teaching me that reading could be extraordinarily fun (as opposed to drudgery, toil, and homework) was *The Hitchhiker's Guide to the Galaxy* by Douglas Adams," he remarked in the *Guardian*. "Why? Because it was just plain hilarious. Completely absurd silliness that had me rolling on the floor with laughter way before there ever was ROTFWL or even ROTFLMAO."

Calame also delighted in creating his own tales and decided to pursue a career as a writer at the tender age of nine. His first attempt at a serious work focused on a conflict between Earthlings and Martians. "Many of the characters and storylines were borrowed from *Star Wars* and *Star Trek*. . ., he stated in an essay on the Candlewick Press Web site. "Upon reading the tale, a friend of the family suggested I try making up my own stories and, oddly enough, it completely freed up my imagination. I haven't stopped writing since. . . ."

After graduating from Hicksville High School, Calame briefly toyed with the idea of becoming a professional jazz guitarist before attending Adelphi University in Long Island, graduating with a bachelor's degree in communications. He then moved to Los Angeles, California, where he tried his hand at penning screenplays while working as an assistant to a talent agent and, later, for the Motion Picture & Television Fund Foundation. When his screenplays failed to sell, Calame earned a teaching certificate from the Los Angeles Unified School District's Intern Program and spent four years in the classroom, working with third-, fourth-, and fifth-grade students.

Calame's big break finally arrived when, after several years of effort, he sold his first screenplay; *The Lie*, co-written with Chris Conroy, was purchased by Universal Studios. Since that time Calame has written for Paramount Pictures and Marvel Studios, among others. In 2001 *Hounded*, another project done in collaboration with Conroy, was produced by the Disney Channel, and their first feature film, *Employee of the Month*, reached the big screen in 2006. Directed by Greg Coolidge, who also had a hand in the screenplay, *Employee of the Month* features popular standup comedian Cook as Zack Bradley, a lazy but amiable box boy at a warehouse retailer. When gorgeous Amy Renfro (Simpson) is hired as a cashier, word quickly spreads that she will only date those who have earned "Employee of the Month" status, a title currently held by Zack's nemesis, Vince Downey (played by Dax Shepard), an arrogant checkout clerk who has received the honor seventeen straight times. Soon, the two men are engaged in a heated battle to capture the coveted award, as well as Amy's affections. *Village Voice* critic Luke Y. Thompson offered praise for the screenplay, calling it "witty and peppered with good laughs," and *Variety* reviewer Robert Koehler also complimented the film, noting that the competition between Vince and Zack "is unexpectedly funny and involving."

"Growing up I was a huge fan of Monty Python, Woody Allen and Douglas Adams. I love things that are bizarrely comic and absurd."

—Don Calame, in an interview with Steph Su.

An X-Rated Quest

Swim the Fly, Calame's first novel, was inspired in part by his own experiences as a teenager. The work began as a short essay Calame penned at a writing workshop, in which the author recalled the summer he was asked by his swim coach to enter the one-hundred-yard butterfly, a particularly grueling event. "It was more of a rhetorical question when my coach asked me so, really, I had no choice," Calame told Su in their blog interview. "One of the guys I was swimming against was this huge, muscle-bound kid who looked like he was twenty-five instead of fourteen." At the urging of his wife, Calame expanded the piece into a novel, which was released in 2009.

Swim the Fly introduces Matt Gratton, who has just finished his freshman year at Lower Rockville High School, and his lifelong friends Sean Hance and Cooper "Coop" Redmond. Each summer the trio set a goal for themselves, to be accomplished before the new school year; past escapades have included obtaining a copy of *Playboy* magazine and finding a password to a pornographic Web site. At Coop's urging, the virginal threesome decides to up the ante, challenging themselves to catch a glimpse of a girl's naked body, a task that Matt, the book's narrator, sees as hopeless, telling his friends: "Maybe we'd better set a more realistic goal for the summer. Like finding Atlantis."

Matt's dark mood brightens, however, when he discovers that Kelly West, a stunning brunette, has joined the Lower Rockville Razorbacks, his swim team. Hoping to impress the newcomer, Matt boldly offers to fill an empty slot on his club's roster, surprising his teammates and his tyrannical coach, Ms. Luntz, by volunteering to swim the butterfly, a difficult stroke that he has failed to master: "It's up with the arms and head, suck in a breath, and back under again. A hard kick with feet together. Weaving in and out of the water. You're supposed to look like a dolphin. Smooth and graceful. You're not supposed to look like a palsied whippet struggling for its life. Which is exactly what I feel like. I am all splash and very little momentum."

While Matt comes to grip with the consequences of his impulsive decision, Coop devises his own wildly impetuous scheme: Knowing that the voluptuous Mandy Reagan takes tae kwon do lessons at the local community center, he proposes that the boys dress up in women's clothing, sneak into the ladies' locker room, and wait for Mandy to undress and shower after her session. When Coop's older sister, Cathy, catches the trio in her bedroom, fully attired, she blackmails them into taking a nude photograph of Mandy, which she will post online to embarrass the girl, who seduced Cathy's boyfriend. Once at the community center, the boys' disguises get them past the front desk clerk, much to their surprise, but just minutes before Mandy arrives in the locker room, Matt experiences severe intestinal discomfort, and his panicked trip to the bathroom, which results in an overflowing toilet, ruins the plan.

As the summer progresses, Matt, Coop, and Sean bungle every opportunity they have to spy on a naked girl. Hoping to catch a glimpse of Mandy having sex with Tony Grillo, Kelly's ex-boyfriend, at a house party, they hide in a bedroom closet, only to tumble out when Sean loses his balance. Later, after spotting Kelly and her friend, Valerie Devereaux, trying on bikinis in the mall, Coop and Sean head to the changing rooms and occupy the adjacent stalls, peering over the walls until a store employee spots them. That embarrassing episode represents a turning point for Matt, who helped prevent his friends from attaining their hormone-driven goal by protecting Valerie, whose sweet demeanor and casual confidence proves more appealing than Kelly's narcissistic personality.

Matt's efforts to improve his technique in the pool fare as poorly as his friends' attempts to see naked flesh until he meets Ulf, a stern and enigmatic swim instructor from Germany who heads an advanced lifesaving course at a ritzy country club. Although Ulf discovers that Matt has snuck into the club's pool, he allows the teen to stay in his class, and during their time together he imparts valuable life lessons while strengthening Matt's body in some unconventional ways, including having Matt pluck hundreds of coins from the bottom of the pool while fully clothed. At the annual swimming championships, where Matt competes in the one-hundred-yard butterfly against the muscular Grillo, he turns in a most surprising performance, aided by Coop and Sean, who resort to some chicanery to spoil Grillo's race.

Swim the Fly garnered strong reviews from the critics, earning comparisons to the work of Judd Apatow, a writer and director known for *The Forty Year Old Virgin, Knocked Up,* and other films. According to a contributor in *Publishers Weekly,* Matt, Coop, and Sean's "pursuits make for a hilarious, if raunchy, what-I-did-last-summer narrative," and

★ "Hilarious.... This one will spread like athlete's foot in a locker room." — *Publishers Weekly* (starred review)

Swim the Fly, **Calame's debut novel, follows the adventures of a trio of oversexed high school students.** (Cover photographs by pixhook/iStockphoto (goggles) and Konstantin Tavrov/iStockphoto (girl). Copyright © 2009 Don Calame. Reproduced by permission of Candlewick Press, Somerville, MA.)

Daniel Kraus, writing in *Booklist,* noted that Calame's background as a screenwriter is apparent, stating that "his hilarious debut resembles nothing so much as the crude-yet-insightful comedies of . . . Apatow." In the *New York Times Book Review,* John Schwartz observed that the novel "is punctuated with all of the predictable gross-out scenes, involving vomiting, flatulence and diarrhea," adding, "*Swim the Fly* occupies the low ground of offensive, knuckleheaded fun. Which is to say, boys will probably love it. This one did."

A Study in Musical Ineptitude

Cooper Redmond takes center stage in *Beat the Band* a sequel of sorts to *Swim the Fly.* Calame's second young adult novel finds Coop, Matt, and Sean entering their sophomore year of high school, which begins on an inauspicious note. After Mrs. Turris, their health instructor, assigns them a semester-long project that must be completed with a partner, Coop finds himself paired with social pariah Helen Harriwick, nicknamed "Hot Dog Helen" in reference to a bizarre sexual practice. Their topic: contraception. The normally cocky and confident Cooper (who is immediately saddled with the nickname "Corn Dog Coop"), realizing that his own reputation will suffer simply by being associated with Helen, tries to sabotage the partnership (once by punishing Helen with excessive flatulence), though Mrs. Turris, infuriated by the teen's uncooperative attitude, forces the pair to continue working together by assigning them to detention.

Desperate to salvage his image, Coop convinces Matt and Sean, his partners in a hapless garage band named "Arnold Murphy's Bologna Dare," to try out for the school's "Battle of the Bands." As Coop relates: "Here is my miracle. Win the battle of the bands and the Hot Dog Helen taint will be obliterated by my rock-and-roll awesomeness." When their jam session reveals the trio's lack of talent, however, Coop's father comes to the rescue, creating a demo CD—featuring songs from an obscure, unsigned, Canadian band—that fools the judges, who choose "Arnold Murphy's Bologna Dare" for the competition.

During one of his detention sessions with Helen, Coop is approached by Prudence, Bronte, and Gina, three of the hottest girls in his school and members of The Wicked, a rival band. When they tell an adoring Coop that Helen has been spreading vicious rumors about him, he vows to seek revenge, agreeing to covertly gather personal information about Helen as part of Prudence's devious plan to humiliate the girl. But as Coop spends more time with Helen and learns about her difficult home environment, he comes to admire her courage, and he begins having second thoughts about the subterfuge. While visiting Coop's home one day during band practice, Helen takes over as lead vocalist at the urging of Coop's father, stunning everyone with her range and artistry, and the boys come to believe that they can contend for the "Battle of the Bands" crown with Helen fronting the group.

Already feeling guilty over his role in the plot to discredit Helen, Coop tries to convince Prudence to put a stop to the shenanigans. She refuses, and during Coop and Helen's health class presentation, they are pelted by hot dogs. Later, comforting a forlorn Helen, Coop learns that she and Prudence were once best friends whose relationship ended because of lies told by Prudence's unfaithful ex-boyfriend, who claimed that Helen pursued him. An embarrassed Coop cannot bring himself to admit his mistakes, and on the night of the contest, after Prudence and her allies witness an amazing rehearsal by "Arnold Murphy's Bologna Dare," they

reveal Coop's involvement in their plot, which threatens to destroy his relationship with Helen as well as his band's chances to win the competition.

Like Calame's first novel, *Beat the Band* earned plaudits from the critics. A *Kirkus Reviews* contributor described the novel as a "side-splitting sequel," and Angelina E. Barnard, writing in *Voice of Youth Advocates,* stated that "Calame provides a very entertaining, laugh-out-loud read." According to *School Library Journal* reviewer Amy Pickett, "Messages about bullying and consequences of teen sex (included via the health project) add just the right note of gravitas to this rockin' romp."

Calame notes that the demands of writing for the big screen and the page are very different. "As a screenwriter you are sketching out a story that will be filled in later by the director, the actors, the musical composer, the set designer and a million other people," he remarked on his home page. "Movie making is extremely collaborative. Sometimes for the better, sometimes for the worse. As a novelist

A screenwriter as well as a novelist, Calame cowrote *Employee of the Month,* a workplace comedy featuring Dane Cook (left) and Dax Shepard. (Copyright © Lionsgate/Kobal Collection/Picture Desk Inc./Art Resource. All rights reserved. Reproduced by permission.)

you are all those people. The writer, the director, the actor, the costume designer, etc. You are creating the complete work; a complete world."

"You were in class. They were like a pack of hungry cheetahs on a downed ibex. And now I'm the ibex's partner. The rest of my high-school days are cursed."

—protagonist Cooper "Coop" Redmond in *Beat the Band.*

Though he initially found success as a screenwriter, Calame says that he prefers penning books. "Right now I enjoy writing novels more," he commented on his home page. "But that might change. I wrote for film and television for around 15 years and I was getting tired/bored/frustrated with it. It's just the nature of the movie industry. Things get bought, rewritten and never made. Or things get bought, rewritten and made in a way you don't like. Doesn't mean I won't ever write movies again." The important thing, he noted, is to keep writing. "I get depressed when I haven't written something for several days," Calame remarked in a *TRT Book Club* interview with Jen Wardrip. "Writing keeps my mood level. Actually boosts my mood. Usually. When it's going well. When it's not going well, it can drag me down to the pits of Hell. Even then, I'd still write."

■ Biographical and Critical Sources

BOOKS

Calame, Don, *Swim the Fly*, Candlewick Press (Somerville, MA), 2009.

Calame, Don, *Beat the Band*, Candlewick Press (Somerville, MA), 2010.

PERIODICALS

Booklist, March 15, 2009, Daniel Kraus, review of *Swim the Fly*, p. 55; September 1, 2010, Daniel Kraus, review of *Beat the Band*, p. 101.

Bulletin of the Center for Children's Books, July-August, 2009, Karen Coats, review of *Swim the Fly*, p. 437.

Guardian (London, England), June 14, 2011, "Don Calame's Top 10 Funny Teen Boy Books."

Kirkus Reviews, March 1, 2009, review of *Swim the Fly*; August 15, 2010, review of *Beat the Band*.

New York Times Book Review, August 16, 2009, John Schwartz, "What Teenagers Want," review of *Swim the Fly*, p. 13.

Publishers Weekly, April 20, 2009, review of *Swim the Fly*, p. 49.

School Library Journal, April, 2009, Diane P. Tuccillo, review of *Swim the Fly*, p. 129; December, 2010, Amy Pickett, review of *Beat the Band*, p. 104.

Variety, October 2, 2006, Robert Koehler, review of *Employee of the Month*, p. 118.

Village Voice, October 3, 2006, Luke Y. Thompson, review of *Employee of the Month*.

Voice of Youth Advocates, April, 2009, Ria Newhouse, review of *Swim the Fly*, p. 221; December, 2010, Angelina E. Barnard, review of *Beat the Band*, p. 446.

ONLINE

Bri Meets Books Blog, http://brimeetsbooks. wordpress.com/ (May 3, 2009), Brianna Ahearn, "Interview: Don Calame."

Candlewick Press Web site, http://candlewick.com/ (October 1, 2011), "Don Calame: About Me."

Don Calame Home Page, http://www.doncalame.com (October 1, 2011).

Steph Su Reads Blog, http://stephsureads.blogspot. com/ (April 6, 2009), Steph Su, interview with Calame.

TRT Book Club Blog, http://trtbookclub.blogspot. com/ (October 13, 2010), Jen Wardrip, "Visit with Don Calame."*

(Photographer Bob Boyd. Copyright © Caroline Cooney. All rights reserved. Reproduced by permission.)

Caroline B. Cooney

■ Personal

Born May 10, 1947, in Geneva, NY; daughter of Dexter Mitchell (a purchasing agent) and Martha (a teacher) Bruce; married (divorced); children: Louisa, Sayre, Harold. *Education:* Attended Indiana University, 1965-66, Massachusetts General Hospital School of Nursing, 1966-67, and University of Connecticut, 1968. *Hobbies and other interests:* Playing the piano and organ, singing.

■ Addresses

Home—SC. *Agent*—Curtis Brown Ltd., 10 Astor Pl., New York, NY 10003. *E-mail*—cbc@carolinebcooney books.com.

■ Career

Writer and author, 1978—.

■ Member

Authors Guild, Authors League of America, Mystery Writers of America.

■ Awards, Honors

Award for Juvenile Literature, American Association of University Women, North Carolina chapter, 1980, for *Safe as the Grave*; Romantic Book Award, Teen Romance category, 1985, for body of work; International Reading Association/Children's Book Council Choice designation, Pacific States Award, and Iowa Teen Award, all for *The Face on the Milk Carton*; Best Young-Adult Fiction Books citation, *Booklist*, 1993, for *Flight Number 116 Is Down*; Notable Children's Book designation, American Library Association (ALA), 1990, for *The Face on the Milk Carton*, 2001, for *The Ransom of Mercy Carter*, and 2002, for *Goddess of Yesterday*; National Science Teachers award for *Code Orange*; Church and Synagogue Library Association Award, for *A Friend at Midnight*; Edgar Allen Poe Award nomination, Mystery Writers of America, Quick Picks for Reluctant Young Adult Readers, ALA, and Christopher Award, all 2008, all for *Diamonds in the Shadow*.

■ Writings

YOUNG-ADULT FICTION

Safe as the Grave, illustrated by Gail Owens, Coward, McCann (New York, NY), 1979.
The Paper Caper, illustrated by Gail Owens, Coward, McCann (New York, NY), 1981.
An April Love Story, Scholastic (New York, NY), 1981.

Nancy and Nick, Scholastic (New York, NY), 1982.

He Loves Me Not, Scholastic (New York, NY), 1982.

A Stage Set for Love, Archway (New York, NY), 1983.

Holly in Love, Scholastic (New York, NY), 1983.

I'm Not Your Other Half, Putnam (New York, NY), 1984.

Sun, Sea, and Boys, Archway (New York, NY), 1984.

Nice Girls Don't, Scholastic (New York, NY), 1984.

Rumors, Scholastic (New York, NY), 1985.

Trying Out, Scholastic (New York, NY), 1985.

Suntanned Days, Simon & Schuster (New York, NY), 1985.

Racing to Love, Archway (New York, NY), 1985.

The Bad and the Beautiful, Scholastic (New York, NY), 1985.

The Morning After, Scholastic (New York, NY), 1985.

All the Way, Scholastic (New York, NY), 1985.

Saturday Night, Scholastic (New York, NY), 1986.

Don't Blame the Music, Putnam (New York, NY), 1986.

Saying Yes, Scholastic (New York, NY), 1987.

Last Dance, Scholastic (New York, NY), 1987.

The Rah Rah Girl, Scholastic (New York, NY), 1987.

Among Friends, Bantam (New York, NY), 1987.

Camp Boy-meets-Girl, Bantam (New York, NY), 1988.

New Year's Eve, Scholastic (New York, NY), 1988.

Summer Nights, Scholastic (New York, NY), 1988.

The Girl Who Invented Romance, Bantam (New York, NY), 1988, reprinted, Delacorte Press (New York, NY), 2006.

Camp Reunion, Bantam (New York, NY), 1988.

Family Reunion, Bantam (New York, NY), 1989, reprinted, Delacorte Press (New York, NY), 2004.

The Fog, Scholastic (New York, NY), 1989.

The Face on the Milk Carton, Bantam (New York, NY), 1990.

Summer Love, Mammoth (London, England), 1990.

The Snow, Scholastic (New York, NY), 1990.

The Fire, Scholastic (New York, NY), 1990.

The Party's Over, Scholastic (New York, NY), 1991.

The Cheerleader, Scholastic (New York, NY), 1991.

Twenty Pageants Later, Bantam (New York, NY), 1991.

The Perfume, Scholastic (New York, NY), 1992.

Operation: Homefront, Bantam (New York, NY), 1992.

Freeze Tag, Scholastic (New York, NY), 1992.

The Return of the Vampire (sequel to *The Cheerleader*), Scholastic (New York, NY), 1992.

Flight Number 116 Is Down, Scholastic (New York, NY), 1992.

The Vampire's Promise (sequel to *The Return of the Vampire*), Scholastic (New York, NY), 1993.

Whatever Happened to Janie? (sequel to *The Face on the Milk Carton*), Scholastic (New York, NY), 1993.

Forbidden, Scholastic (New York, NY), 1993.

The Stranger, Scholastic (New York, NY), 1993.

Twins, Scholastic (New York, NY), 1994.

Emergency Room, Scholastic (New York, NY), 1994.

Driver's Ed, Bantam (New York, NY), 1994.

Unforgettable, Point (New York, NY), 1994.

Flash Fire, Scholastic (New York, NY), 1995.

Night School, Scholastic (New York, NY), 1995.

The Voice on the Radio (sequel to *What Ever Happened to Janie?*), Delacorte Press (New York, NY), 1996.

The Terrorist, Scholastic (New York, NY), 1997.

Wanted!, Scholastic (New York, NY), 1997.

What Child Is This? A Christmas Story, Delacorte Press (New York, NY), 1997.

Burning Up, Delacorte Press (New York, NY), 1999.

Tune in Anytime, Delacorte Press (New York, NY), 1999.

Hush Little Baby, Scholastic Paperbacks (New York, NY), 1999.

What Janie Found (sequel to *The Voice on the Radio*), Delacorte Press (New York, NY), 2000.

Mummy, Scholastic (New York, NY), 2000.

The Ransom of Mercy Carter, Delacorte Press (New York, NY), 2001.

Fatality, Scholastic (New York, NY), 2001.

Goddess of Yesterday, Delacorte Press (New York, NY), 2002.

Mercy, Macmillan Children's Books (London, England), 2002.

On the Seas to Troy, Macmillan Children's Books (London, England), 2004.

Code Orange, Delacorte Press (New York, NY), 2005.

Hit the Road, Delacorte Press (New York, NY), 2005.

A Friend at Midnight, Delacorte Press (New York, NY), 2006.

Enter Three Witches: A Story of Macbeth, Scholastic (New York, NY), 2007.

Diamonds in the Shadow, Delacorte Press (New York, NY), 2007.

If the Witness Lied, Delacorte Press (New York, NY), 2009.

They Never Came Back, Delacorte Press (New York, NY), 2010.

Three Black Swans, Delacorte Press (New York, NY), 2010.

The Lost Songs, Delacorte Press (New York, NY), 2011.

"VAMPIRE'S PROMISE" SERIES; FOR YOUNG ADULTS

Evil Returns, Topeka Bindery (Topeka, KS), 2003.

The Fatal Bargain, Topeka Bindery (Topeka, KS), 2003.

Deadly Offer, Topeka Bindery (Topeka, KS), 2003.

"TIME-TRAVEL" NOVEL SERIES; FOR YOUNG ADULTS

Both Sides of Time (also see below), Delacorte Press (New York, NY), 1995.

Out of Time (also see below), Delacorte Press (New York, NY), 1996.

Prisoner of Time (also see below), Delacorte Press (New York, NY), 1998.

For All Time (also see below), Delacorte Press (New York, NY), 2001.

Time Travelers, Volume One (contains *Both Sides of Time* and *Out of Time*), Laurel Leaf (New York, NY), 2006.

Time Travelers, Volume Two (contains *Prisoner of Time* and *For All Time*), Laurel Leaf (New York, NY), 2006.

NOVELS

Rear View Mirror (adult), Random House (New York, NY), 1980.

Sand Trap (adult), Berkley (New York, NY), 1983.

Personal Touch, Silhouette (New York, NY), 1983.

Contributor of stories to periodicals, including *Seventeen, American Girl, Jack and Jill, Humpty Dumpty,* and *Young World.*

■ Adaptations

Rear View Mirror was adapted as a television movie starring Lee Remick, Warner Bros., 1984; *The Face on the Milk Carton* and *Whatever Happened to Janie?* were adapted as a television movie broadcast by CBS in 1995. Many of Cooney's books have been adapted as audiobooks.

■ Sidelights

Known for her "reluctant-reader-friendly titles," as *School Library Journal* reviewer Jennifer Barnes stated, Caroline B. Cooney is a prolific and versatile writer for young adults. With her first novel appearing in 1979, Cooney has more than eighty works to her credit. One of her most popular novels, *The Face on the Milk Carton,* has sold over three million copies since its publication in the early 1990s and was made into a popular television movie. Cooney is praised by critics for her ability to entrance readers, and she has received a host of literary honors, including the Christopher Award.

Cooney has become known for her teen romances as well as for writing more edgy novels that explore the ways that the horrors of the world at large can infiltrate even the most mundane life of the average American adolescent. Cooney's books feature young protagonists struggling to come to terms with a wide range of concerns, from troubles in school to problems of identity, all told in a fast-paced, entertaining style. Shelly Shaffer noted in the *Journal of Adolescent & Adult Literacy* that many of Cooney's books "deal with secret identities and issues from the past." A *Kirkus Reviews* contributor similarly remarked of Cooney's themes: "Cooney has long been intrigued by the subject of familial loss and the messy, ungovernable feelings that are its emotional aftermath." This motif is also commented on by another *Kirkus Reviews* writer who felt that Cooney's interests as a writer are focused on "families pushed to the edge by anomalous situations." In an interview with a *Charlotte Mecklenburg Library Reader's Club* contributor, Cooney further remarked on her prime topic: "I like to write about families. Plain old happy families, where everybody's doing fine and everybody gets along, are wonderful, and I'm lucky enough to have one. But they don't make terrific books."

Although she began her writing career focusing on adult readers, Cooney quickly learned that she had a gift for connecting with young adults, and this led her to "the type of writing that I could both be successful at and enjoy," as she once recalled. In addition to winning the respect of critics for their likeable protagonists, fast-moving plots, and relevant topical focus, her novels *The Face on the Milk Carton, The Ransom of Mercy Carter, Diamonds in the Shadow, If the Witness Lied,* and *Three Black Swans* have proven to be popular with teen audiences.

The Making of a Writer

Cooney had a happy childhood growing up during the 1950s in Greenwich, Connecticut, as the author noted on her home page: "Sometimes my days at school were rough, and some years I had few friends and few successes. But at home, we had a sunny childhood. My brother said once that we two were the only people he knew without a single unhappy childhood story to tell." These were the early years of television, and Cooney was not allowed to watch it after school. Instead, she indulged in books from the local library and in creating fantasy stories of her own. By the time she was twenty, she had already written a number of novels and short stories. She studied nursing and music in college but didn't earn a degree in either field. Writing was always there, beckoning.

"I don't worry about what kids are wearing right now, or what the slang is. It dates the story. Everything that really matters in a story (or in life) is just the same: do I honor my parents, am I popular, what will I do with my life, am I doing the right thing?"

—Caroline B. Cooney, in a *Teenreads.com* interview.

Cooney began writing seriously when she was a young homemaker raising three children. "Sitting home with the babies," she once commented, "I had to find a way to entertain myself. So I started writing with a pencil, between the children's naps—baby in one arm, notebook in the other." She had difficulty marketing her novel-length historical novels for adults but found that the short stories she wrote for a young-adult readership were quickly accepted by magazines such as *Seventeen*. "Having already written eight books with no luck," Cooney once recalled, "I wasn't interested in wasting my time writing another unpublishable novel. So instead I wrote an outline [of a teen mystery novel] and mailed it along with my short story-resumé to a number of publishers, saying: 'Would you be interested in seeing this'—knowing, of course, that they wouldn't. Naturally, when they all said 'yes,' I was stunned; the only thing to do was to quick write the book." That book was published in 1979 as *Safe as the Grave*.

Safe as the Grave, in which a young girl encounters a secret in the family cemetery, was followed up by Cooney with the adult suspense novel *Rear View Mirror*, the story of a young woman who is kidnapped and forced to drive two killers in her car. Michele Slung, reviewing Cooney's second novel for the *Washington Post*, called *Rear View Mirror* "so tightly written, so fast-moving, that it's easy not to realize until the last paragraph is over that one hasn't been breathing all the while." Cooney returned to young-adult fiction with *An April Love Story*, a romance novel published in 1981. Except for one more adult novel—1983's *Sand Trap*—her focus has been exclusively on a young-adult readership.

Dramatic, Propulsive Narratives

Though Cooney enjoys penning teen romances and stories of strong friendships such as the 2006 cross-generational novel *Hit the Road*, many of her books deal with serious topical issues that affect teens directly. In *Operation: Homefront*, a wife and mother with three children is called up for National Guard duty and shipped off to Saudi Arabia during the Gulf War, while *Family Reunion* focuses on a teen dealing with her parents' separation and divorce, as well as with her dad's remarriage. In *A Friend at Midnight* a teen must decide whether to betray a confidence when her older sister insists on inviting their abusive father to her wedding, while *Burning Up* finds an affluent Connecticut adolescent coming face to face with prejudice after the inner-city church where she volunteers is torched by an arsonist. As Stephanie Zvirin noted in her *Booklist* review of *Burning Up*, Cooney excels at portraying both "the tentative boy-girl relationship between" her teen protagonists, and the "questioning and fervor that propels some teens to look beyond themselves and their families to larger issues."

While teens encounter divorce, prejudice, and separation within their own families and personal interactions, other more abstract issues are made equally personal in several of Cooney's timely works of fiction. In *The Terrorist*, for example, she deals with the sobering subject of international terrorism, and, in the opinion of a *Publishers Weekly* contributor, "combines heartpounding suspense with some sobering reflections on the insular attitude characteristic of many Americans both at home and abroad."

Terrorism of a different kind is the focus of *Code Orange*, a novel written in response to the nation's state of heightened vigilance following the September 11, 2001 terrorist attacks. While conducting research for a school paper on smallpox, slacker prep-school student Mitty Blake discovers an old envelope tucked into a book that contains hundred-year-old smallpox scabs. As the Manhattan teen researches the highly contagious infectious disease, he realizes that he may have infected himself; in fact, he may be a danger to everyone he has contacted since first opening the envelope. Panic turns into a bumbling attempt to solve the problem as Mitty contacts Federal authorities and inadvertently attracts the notice of a terrorist group that has far darker motives. Praising *Code Orange* in *Horn Book*, Jeannine M. Chapman noted that Mitty's growing resourcefulness "is believably conveyed," as the "lighthearted tone" at the beginning of the novel builds to a "thrilling climax (with a twist)." A *Publishers Weekly* wrote that the author's "rat-a-tat delivery and hairpin turns keep the pages turning," and *Booklist* contributor John Peters lauded the novel's "profoundly disturbing premise" and "its likable, ultimately heroic slacker protagonist."

Perhaps Cooney's most widely read novel, the critically acclaimed *The Face on the Milk Carton*, deals with the topic of child abduction. Janie Johnson is kidnapped when she is three years old by Hannah, a teenaged cult member; unaware of her past, she is raised by Hannah's parents. Janie's picture, displayed on a milk carton as that of a missing child, leads her to uncover her past. Cooney continues Janie's story in the novels *Whatever Happened to Janie?*, *The Voice on the Radio,* and *What Janie Found,* which follow the efforts of Cooney's determined young heroine to discover the truth about her family and her real identity. Citing Cooney's "skilled writing," a *Publishers Weekly* contributor noted of *The Face on the Milk Carton* that the book's likeable protagonist and "suspenseful, impeccably-paced action add to this novel's appeal" among teen readers. "Cooney seems to have a special radar for adolescent longings and insecurities," noted another critic in the same periodical during a review of *The Voice on the Radio.* While the *Publishers Weekly* contributor also noted the plot's lack of believability, this quality is more than outweighed by the novel's "psychological accuracy and well-aimed, gossipy views of teens," according to the reviewer.

Somewhat of a departure from her other books, Cooney's *Among Friends* features a unique structure. Six students have been given an assignment to write in journals during a three-month period. The entries from those journals, providing a variety of points of view, make up the novel. This approach, stated Mitzi Myers in the *Los Angeles Times,* provides "a more rounded interpretation than any single character could supply." Myers concluded: "It is a pleasure to find a book for young readers that not only individualizes characters through their writing but also has wise words to say about how writing offers very real help in coping with the problems of growing up."

Imaginative Teen Thrillers

Cooney mixes romance with science fiction in her "Time-Travel" novel series, which includes *Both Sides of Time, Out of Time, Prisoner of Time,* and *For All Time.* In *Both Sides of Time* readers meet high school graduate Annie Lockwood, whose romantic perspective would have made her better suited for life in the past. When Annie gets her wish and winds up in 1895, however, her twenty-first-century attitudes and expectations make her realize that living in the past means dealing with far more than long gowns, lavish balls, and dapper, respectful young gentlemen. However, when she falls in love with Strat, her link with the past is forever cemented, and she must learn to balance both her worlds. After revealing Annie's secret to his father in *Out of Time,* Strat is dismissed as insane and sent

to a mental asylum. Despite the family problems in her modern life, Annie must now risk everything to return through time and bring her beloved to safety in her (for him) futuristic world. The series takes a new twist in *Prisoner of Time,* as Strat's sister Devonny finds herself betrothed to an unpleasant English noble and requires her brother's help in breaking the engagement. Surprise turns to romance when Annie's brother, Tod Lockwood, answers the call back through time. The series concludes in *For All Time,* as Annie's effort to control her travel through time misfires, and she winds up in the right place at the wrong time. Transported back into ancient times, Annie finds herself trapped in an Egyptian city. Meanwhile, her beloved Strat awaits her in the same city, three thousand years in the future, unaware of his time-traveling girlfriend's fate. In a review of *Both Sides of Time* for *Horn Book,* Sarah Guille deemed Cooney's story "suspenseful and poignant," noting that her heroine matures while learning an important lesson: "That real love has consequences and obligations that fantasies don't." Dubbing the series "a breathlessly romantic whirl through the centuries," a *Publishers Weekly* contributor noted that readers will be carried along by Cooney's "characteristically breezily, intimate style."

Cooney is also the author of a series of horror novels sometimes referred to as the "Vampire's Promise" series. In *Evil Returns,* young Devenee wants to be pretty and popular. A vampire offers her the chance to be both, in exchange for a price that may be too high. *The Fatal Bargain* features a group of teens who must choose who to leave behind in an old house so that the vampire who lives there will let the others leave. In *Deadly Offer,* Althea must agree to an evil deal to gain the popularity in school that she desires and that a vampire guarantees to provide.

Exploring the Past

In *The Ransom of Mercy Carter,* Cooney offers readers another departure from her contemporary novels: a historical fiction based on the 1704 raid on the English settlement at Deerfield, Massachusetts, when Kahnawake Mohawks destroyed the village and took more than one hundred captives back to Canada. The novel focuses on young Mercy, a captive whose growing respect for the Native American culture into which she is forced ultimately causes her to question her loyalty to her own family. Calling *The Ransom of Mercy Carter* a "gripping and thought-provoking account," a *Publishers Weekly* contributor added that, though Cooney oversimplifies some historical elements, "the immediacy of

Mercy's dilemma comes through." In her *Kliatt* review, Sally M. Tibbetts praised the author's detailed research, calling the novel "a great story about a young girl who learns to adapt and survive." Noting that Cooney raises "excellent questions" about how different cultures view what it means to be civilized or savage, *Booklist* contributor Gillian Engberg deemed *The Ransom of Mercy Carter* a "vivid, dramatic novel."

Another travel back through time is offered in *Goddess of Yesterday*, which transports readers back to the classical world and the years leading up to the Trojan War. When readers meet Anaxandra, the six year old is living on an island in the Aegean sea until she is sent as a hostage to the King of Siphnos. Six years later, her life is again thrown into turmoil when the king's palace is attacked and all are killed. By assuming the identity of the king's daughter, Callisto, Anaxandra is accepted at the palace of Sparta's King Menelaus, whose young wife is destined to become the fabled Helen of Troy. Charged with caring for the king's two-year-old son, Callisto/Anaxandra soon learns of the clandestine romantic affair between the boy's mother and Paris, prince of Troy. As the political tensions between Sparta and Troy mount, Helen's jealousy of her grows, forcing Callisto/Anaxandra to navigate the shifting allegiances in order to survive. Her destiny alters once again when she is ordered to accompany Helen and her young son on the deceitful queen's pivotal journey to Troy. There, in the company of her lover, the ill-fated Trojan prince Paris, one of the most dramatic battles of the ancient world will play out. Reviewing the novel for *Horn Book*, Kristi Elle Jemtegaard described *Goddess of Yesterday* as "by turns gruesome, dramatic, and tenderly domestic." In *Booklist*, Frances Bradburn praised Cooney for the "fresh perspective" from which she spins her "exciting, complex adventure story," although the critic added that the plot might confuse teens unfamiliar with the history of the Trojan War. In the opinion of *Kliatt* contributor Claire Rosser, *Goddess of Yesterday* stands as one of Cooney's "most ambitious" books for teen readers. Through the book's likeable fictional heroine, the novel "will make the ancient Greek world" come alive for teens, Rosser added, especially the actual men and women who figure in the tragedies preserved through the literary works of "Homer and the Greek dramatists." Noting that Cooney refashions the classic tale as a "grand adventure with a heroic girl at the center," Angela J. Reynolds predicted in *School Library Journal* that her "fine-tuned adventure . . . may leave middle-schoolers asking to read Homer."

History again mixes with literature in *Enter Three Witches: A Story of Macbeth*, which a *Publishers Weekly* contributor dubbed a "compulsively readable, behind-the-scenes peek into the rise and fall of Lord and Lady Macbeth." In bringing the Shakespearean drama to life for teens—revealing portions of the bard's text begin each chapter—Cooney mixes the play's characters with fictional ones such as Lady Mary, the fourteen-year-old ward of Lady Macbeth, until her father falls from grace and she is promised in marriage to a ruthless friend of the Scottish king. In her "engaging" retelling of the tragic story of how the lust for power can destroy lives and torment the soul, Cooney crafts prose with what *School Library Journal* contributor Nancy Menaldi-Scanlan described as an "elevated tone." "While it may be difficult at first," the critic hastened to add, Cooney's text is "interesting and appropriate" enough to sustain reader interest. Although noting that fans of the original drama can most fully appreciate Cooney's "fascinating, humanizing" insight into each familiar character, Carolyn Phelan added in *Booklist* that the likeable teen at the center of *Enter Three Witches* will engage fans of historical fiction and even inspire some to seek *Macbeth* in its original text.

Families in Distress

In *Hit the Road* the author features another complex topical issue, namely the problems associated with growing old. Brittany is sent to stay with her grandmother, Nannie Scott, while her parents go on vacation. Before long, she is caught up in an adventure featuring Nannie and three friends driving off to their college reunion despite the fact that they no longer have drivers' licenses. To make matters worse, another friend has been sent to a nursing home against her will. Janis Flint-Ferguson, writing for *Kliatt*, noted that the author "delivers with humor the poignant interaction between young and old."

A Friend at Midnight finds Lily living with her mother while her eight-year-old brother, Michael, goes to live with her father following their parents' divorce. Before long, Lily realizes that her father has abandoned her brother. Lily, who turned all her inner anger towards her father, finds the renewed feelings becoming too much to bear.

In *Diamonds in the Shadow*, Cooney once again takes on a topical issue as she tells the story of an American family who agree to take in refugees from Liberia, which has undergone a civil war. "This tense thriller has more heart, and depth, than some of Cooney's others," wrote Paula Rohrlick in a review for *Kliatt*. When the Finches arrive at the

Four orphaned children discover that their media-obsessed guardian wants them to star in a reality television show in Cooney's *If the Witness Lied*. (Jacket cover copyright © 2009 by Delacorte Press. Used by permission of Delacorte Press, an imprint of Random House Children's Books, a division of Random House, Inc.)

airport, they greet Andre Amabo, who lost his arms in the war, his wife Celestine, and their children. Although the refugee family has a harrowing story to tell, teenaged Jared Finch is mostly unsympathetic and grows increasingly discontent with his new roommate, Mattue, as well as the Amabo family in general. Jared is suspicious of the family's tale of suffering and begins to investigate their background, thinking that the Amabos may not be a family at all. When he snoops into the cremated remains the Amabos brought with them, he finds a stash of diamonds. His discovery soon puts both families in danger, possibly from another refugee who arrived with the Amabos. The book includes an afterword in which Cooney recounts her experiences hosting a family of refugees from Africa; the author also provides statistical information on Darfur, which

has endured a civil war and refugee crisis. *Horn Book* contributor Lauren Adams noted: "The satisfying thriller introduces the complex issues of African civil war and violence with compassion."

Stories Taken from the Headlines

Cooney's tales have been lauded for their thrilling, "ripped-from-the-headlines" narratives. In *If the Witness Lied,* she creates a "a mystery with a touch of realistic fiction," according to Mary Lynch, writing in the *Journal of Adolescent & Adult Literacy*. Here the author examines a family ripped apart under horrific circumstances. When Laura Fountain is diagnosed with cancer while she is pregnant, she refuses chemotherapy until she can deliver the baby. Laura dies not long after giving birth to a baby boy named Tris. Now the strain of parenting and a career prove too much for her husband, Reed, so Aunt Cheryl agrees to help raise Reed's daughters, Madison and Smithy, and his son, Jack. A sense of normalcy returns until tragedy strikes again: Tris, now two, inadvertently releases the handbrake on the family's car, and Reed is accidentally killed. Aunt Cheryl becomes the guardian for the family, but the girls decide to move away while Jack stays behind to take care of his little brother. As the anniversary of his father's death approaches, Jack discovers that Aunt Cheryl has decided that the Fountains will become the stars of a reality television show, prompting his sisters to return home. Madison, especially, has always wondered how it would be possible for little Tris to have released an emergency brake. The siblings finally are reunited and try to solve the mystery of what really happened to their father. As they gather clues, the children conclude that their father's death could not have been an accident.

"Anchored by a poignant sibling reunion," *Horn Book* reviewer Claire E. Gross noted, "this family-drama-turned-thriller will have readers racing, heart in throat, to reach the conclusion." Similarly, Lynch thought that the "readers will be able to identify with the Fountain family in this novel in their disappointment with each other but also, finally, in realizing that family is there in times of need." *School Library Journal* reviewer Rhona Campbell, on the other hand, was less impressed with *If the Witness Lied,* writing: "Fans of previous Cooney offerings will enjoy this, but most others can pass on it." Other reviewers, however, found more to like in the novel. A *Kirkus Reviews* contributor dubbed it a "psychologically penetrating page-turner," and a "fast-paced thriller" that deals with the theme of family "solidarity." Likewise, *Booklist* reviewer Ilene Cooper found that "readers will be enthralled" with this tale of "creepy (if one-dimensional) villains, page-turning action, and kids taking charge," while a *Publishers Weekly* reviewer concluded: "Cooney masterfully ratchets up the tension in each scene and delivers fully in the exhilarating conclusion."

Another contemporary drama takes place in *They Never Came Back,* in which the Lymans, a wealthy couple accused of embezzling millions of dollars in investment funds, flee the United States, leaving behind their ten-year-old daughter, Murielle. Now, five years later, the girl has changed her name to Cathy Ferris and is living with a foster family in Greenwich, Connecticut. While attending summer school, Cathy is surprised to be recognized by her cousin, Tommy, and shocked when the FBI contacts her, asking the teen to coax her parents back to the United States. The book alternates between the events of five years ago, narrated in Murielle's voice, and the present, narrated by Cathy.

Barnes, writing in *School Library Journal,* called *They Never Came Back* an "interesting . . . adaptation of a complex fraud story for this age group." *Booklist* reviewer Kimberly Garnick offered a mixed assessment of the novel, calling it an "accessible read for reluctant readers, if not quite a must for devotees of suspenseful thrillers." A much higher evaluation came from a *Publishers Weekly* contributor who felt that the author "expertly plumbs the lingering emotional aftereffects of the Lymans' actions, raising difficult questions about family, loyalty; and self."

In her *Three Black Swans,* Cooney again presents a complex family saga. Things backfire for high school sophomore Missy when she calls her cousin Claire to help with an unusual school assignment: to perpetrate a hoax. Missy wants her cousin, who looks very similar to her, to come on a school news broadcast as her long-lost twin. Remarkably, it turns out that the girls really are identical twins, a fact that the family has been trying to keep secret. Soon the broadcast is picked up on YouTube and goes viral on the Internet, attracting the attention of another girl, Genevieve, who also appears to be a double for both Claire and Missy. Now three families are drawn into the mystery to sort out the secret of these triplets.

Debbie Carton, writing in *Booklist,* felt that "the entwined stories of the three sisters and their families will attract and hold Cooney's many loyal fans." *School Library Journal* reviewer Suzanne Gordon similarly noted that the experiences of all the characters involved "delve into the nature of love, family, parenting, and the bond of siblings," and a *Publishers Weekly* contributor dubbed *Three Black Swans* an "exhilarating investigation of displacement, regret, and the bonds of sisterhood."

A Writer's Toolbox

When Cooney started her literary career, she wrote in a spontaneous fashion, though that process has changed over time. "I never used to know what was going to happen in the story until I wrote it," she once observed. "Then I began doing paperbacks for Scholastic and they required outlines, largely just to ensure that two writers didn't waste time and effort on similar ideas. Before, I'd always allowed the story to develop out of the characters, but the outlines demanded that the plot and characters evolve together at the same time. Now I wouldn't do it any other way."

Cooney's decision to create novels with compelling, high-energy stories, interesting protagonists, and strong, upbeat resolutions has been prompted by her observation that young people want stories that end on an upbeat note and a future that looks positive. "They want hope," she explained, "want things to work out, want reassurance that even were they to do something rotten, they and the people around them would still be all right. No matter what it is that they're doing, I don't think they want to have to read about it. Teenagers looking for books to read don't say, 'Oh, good, another depressing story.'"

If you enjoy the works of Caroline B. Cooney, you may also want to check out the following books:

Killing Mr. Griffin (1978), Lois Duncan's thriller about a kidnapping plot gone awry.
Dana Reinhardt's *Harmless* (2007), a gripping tale about three teens who tell a lie that spins out of control.
What Happened to Goodbye (2011), Sarah Dessen's tale of a young woman's attempt to reinvent her life after a scandal involving her parents.

In a career that has lasted more than thirty years, Cooney has had no problems keeping her works fresh and exciting. As she remarked in a *Teenreads. com* interview, "Luckily, I love writing and it comes easily. I don't worry about what kids are wearing right now, or what the slang is. It dates the story.

Everything that really matters in a story (or in life) is just the same: do I honor my parents, am I popular, what will I do with my life, am I doing the right thing?"

■ Biographical and Critical Sources

BOOKS

Beacham's Guide to Literature for Young Adults, Gale (Detroit, MI), Volume 10, 2000, Volume 11, 2000.

Carroll, Pamela Sissi, *Caroline Cooney: Faith and Fiction* ("Scarecrow Studies in Young-Adult Literature" series), Scarecrow Press (Metuchen, NJ), 2002.

Drew, Bernard A., *The One Hundred Most Popular Young Adult Authors*, Libraries Unlimited (Englewood, CO), 1996.

St. James Guide to Young-Adult Writers, 2nd edition, St. James Press (Detroit, MI), 1999.

PERIODICALS

Booklist, March 15, 1993, review of *Flight Number 116 Is Down*, p. 89; June 1, 1994, Stephanie Zvirin, review of *Driver's Ed*, p. 1809; November 1, 1995, Susan Dove Lempke, review of *Flash Fire*, p. 464; February 15, 1996, Sally Estes, review of *Out of Time*, p. 1004; July, 1997, Anne O'Malley, review of *The Terrorist*, p. 1810; June 1, 1998, Sally Estes, review of *Prisoner of Time*, p. 1745; December 1, 1998, Stephanie Zvirin, review of *Burning Up*, p. 661; April 1, 2001, Gillian Engberg, review of *The Ransom of Mercy Carter*, p. 1481; September 15, 2001, Debbie Carton, review of *For All Time*, p. 215; June 1, 2002, Frances Bradburn, review of *Goddess of Yesterday*, p. 1704; September 1, 2005, John Peters, review of *Code Orange*, p. 124; March 15, 2006, review of *Hit the Road*, p. 46; December 15, 2006, Jennifer Mattson, review of *A Friend at Midnight*, p. 44; March 1, 2007, Carolyn Phelan, review of *Enter Three Witches: A Story of Macbeth*, p. 73; September 1, 2007, Hazel Rochman, review of *Diamonds in the Shadow*, p. 104; May 1, 2009, Ilene Cooper, review of *If the Witness Lied*, p. 39; November 15, 2009, Kimberly Garnick, review of *They Never Came Back*, p. 35; July 1, 2010, Debbie Carton, review of *Three Black Swans*, p. 54.

Books, November 10, 2007, Mary Harris Russell, review of *Diamonds in the Shadow*.

Bulletin of the Center for Children's Books, July-August, 1986, review of *Don't Blame the Music*, p. 205; April, 1991, review of *The Party's Over*, p. 187; December, 1992, review of *Operation: Homefront*, p. 108; September, 1994, review of *Driver's Ed*, p. 10; October, 1995, review of *Both Sides of Time*, p. 50; May, 1996, review of *Out of Time*, p. 296; November, 1999, review of *Tune in Anytime*, p. 87; March, 2000, review of *What Janie Found*, p. 241; November, 2001, review of *For All Time*, p. 97; July, 2002, review of *Goddess of Yesterday*, p. 397; June, 2006, Deborah Stevenson, review of *Hit the Road*, p. 448; September, 2007, Deborah Stevenson, review of *Diamonds in the Shadow*, p. 3.

Christian Century, December 14, 2010, Nancy L. Hull, review of *If the Witness Lied*, p. 26.

Horn Book, November-December, 1995, Sarah Guille, review of *Both Sides of Time*, p. 745; November-December, 2003, Kristi Elle Jemtegaard, review of *Goddess of Yesterday*, p. 774; September-October, 2005, Jeannine M. Chapman, review of *Code Orange*, p. 574; November-December, 2007, Lauren Adams, review of *Diamonds in the Shadow*; July-August, 2008, "Christopher Award," p. 477; May-June 2009, Claire E. Gross, review of *If the Witness Lied*, p. 294.

Journal of Adolescent & Adult Literacy, February, 2010, Mary Lynch, review of *If the Witness Lied*, p. 431; September, 2010, Shelly Shaffer, review of *They Never Came Back*, p. 72

Kirkus Reviews, September 1, 2005, review of *Code Orange*, p. 970; March 1, 2007, review of *Enter Three Witches*, p. 218; September 1, 2007, review of *Diamonds in the Shadow*; April 15, 2009, review of *If the Witness Lied*; December 15, 2009, review of *They Never Came Back*; July 15, 2010, review of *Three Black Swans*.

Kliatt, March, 2003, Sally M. Tibbetts, review of *The Ransom of Mercy Carter*, p. 21; September, 2003, Barbara McKee, review of *For All Time*, p. 24; January, 2004, Claire Rosser, review of *Goddess of Yesterday*, p. 16; September, 2005, Paula Rohrlick, review of *Code Orange*, p. 6; September, 2007, Paula Rohrlick, review of *Diamonds in the Shadow*, p. 8; March, 2008, Francine Levitov, review of *Enter Three Witches*, p. 44; March, 2008, Janis Flint-Ferguson, review of *Hit the Road*, p. 23.

Los Angeles Times, February 6, 1988, Mitzi Myers, "High Schoolers Learn about the Meaning of Friendship."

Publishers Weekly, August 25, 1989, review of *The Fog*, p. 65; January 12, 1990, review of *The Face on the Milk Carton*, p. 62; March 23, 1992, review of *Flight Number 116 Is Down*, p. 73; June 14, 1993, review of *Whatever Happened to Janie?*, p. 72; July 4, 1994, review of *Unforgettable*, p. 65; July 10, 1995, review of *Both Sides of Time*, p. 59; July 22, 1996, review of *The Voice on the Radio*, p. 242; July 28, 1997, review of *The Terrorist*, p. 75; October 6, 1997, review of *What Child Is This? A Christmas Story*, p. 57; December 7, 1998, review of *Burning*

Up, p. 61; July 26, 1999, review of *Tune in Anytime*, p. 92; January 3, 2000, review of *What Janie Found*, p. 77; February 12, 2001, review of *The Ransom of Mercy Carter*, p. 213; October 22, 2001, review of *For All Time*, p. 77; July 8, 2002, review of *Goddess of Yesterday*, p. 50; September 5, 2005, review of *Code Orange*, p. 63; May 22, 2006, review of *Hit the Road*, p. 54; November 6, 2006, review of *A Friend at Midnight*, p. 62; April 2, 2007, review of *Enter Three Witches*, p. 58; September 17, 2007, review of *Diamonds in the Shadow*, p. 55; May 4, 2009, review of *If the Witness Lied*, p. 51; January 11, 2010, review of *They Never Came Back*, p. 49; August 16, 2010, review of *Three Black Swans*, p. 54.

St. Petersburg Times (St. Petersburg, FL), March 24, 2008, "*Code Orange* Red Hot among Middle School Readers," p. 3.

School Library Journal, February, 1990, Tatiana Castleton, review of *The Face on the Milk Carton*, p. 109; February, 1992, review of *Flight Number 116 Is Down*, p. 107; November, 1992, Kenneth E. Kowen, review of *Operation*, p. 88; June, 1993, Jacqueline Rose, review of *Whatever Happened to Janie?*, p. 126; August, 1994, Susan R. Farber, review of *Driver's Ed*, p. 168; July, 1995, Connie Tyrrell Burns, review of *Both Sides of Time*, p. 168; February, 1999, Claudia Moore, review of *The Voice on the Radio*, p. 69; August, 2001, Renee Steinberg, review of *The Ransom of Mercy Carter*, p. 213; June, 2002, Angela J. Reynolds, review of *Goddess of Yesterday*, p. 134; August, 2005, Blair Christolin, review of *The Ransom of Mercy Carter*, p. 48; October, 2005, Courtney Lewis, review of *Code Orange*, p. 156; November, 2006, Marie Orlando, review of *A Friend at Midnight*, p. 132; May, 2007, Nancy Menaldi-Scanlan, review of *Enter Three Witches*, p. 130; September, 2007, Lillian Hecker, review of *Diamonds in the Shadow*, p. 194; May, 2009, Rhona Campbell, review of *If the Witness Lied*, p. 102; January, 2010, Jennifer Barnes, review of *They Never Came Back*, p. 98; September, 2010, Suzanne Gordon, review of *The Three Black Swans*, p. 214.

Social Education, May-June, 2008, review of *Diamonds in the Shadow*.

Times Literary Supplement, May 20, 1988, review of *The Girl Who Invented Romance*.

Voice of Youth Advocates, February, 1990, review of *The Face on the Milk Carton*, p. 341; October, 1992, review of *Operation*, p. 222; December, 1992, review of *The Return of the Vampire*, p. 291; April, 1993, review of *The Perfume*, pp. 20-21, 38; August, 1993, Samantha Hunt, review of *The Vampire's Promise*, p. 162; April, 1994, review of *The Stranger*, p. 36; August, 1994, review of *Emergency Room*, pp. 143-144; August, 1995, review of *Both Sides of Time*, p. 168; October, 1997, review of *The Terrorist*, p. 242; June, 1998, review of *What Child Is This?*, p. 128; February, 1999, review of *Burning Up*, p. 431; April, 2000, review of *What Janie Found*, p. 33; April 1, 2001, review of *The Ransom of Mercy Carter*, p. 36; June, 2001, review of *The Voice on the Radio*, p. 97; August, 2002, review of *Goddess of Yesterday*, p. 200; October, 2005, review of *Code Orange*, p. 298; December, 2006, review of *A Friend at Midnight*, p. 421; June, 2007, Laura Panter, review of *Enter Three Witches*, p. 158.

Washington Post, June 1, 1980, Michele Slung, review of *Rear View Mirror*.

ONLINE

Caroline B. Cooney Home Page, http://www.caroline bcooneybooks.com (July 15, 2011).

Charlotte Mecklenburg Library Reader's Club, http://www.cmlibrary.org/readers_club/ (August 1, 2009), "Meet the Author: Caroline B. Cooney."

Mid-Ohio Valley Parent Magazine Web site, http://www.movparent.com/ (May 22, 2009), "Interview with Author Caroline B. Cooney."

Teenreads.com, http://www.teenreads.com/ (July 28, 2000), interview with Cooney; (April 24, 2011), Audrey Marie Danielson, interview with Cooney.

Alison Croggon

■ Personal

Born 1962, in South Africa; immigrated to Australia at age seven; daughter of a geologist father; married Daniel Keene (a playwright); children: three.

■ Addresses

Home—Melbourne, Victoria, Australia. *Agent*—Jenny Darling & Associates Property Limited, P.O. Box 413, Toorak, Victoria 3142, Australia. *E-mail*—ajcroggon@gmail.com.

■ Career

Writer, poet, playwright, editor, and critic. *Melbourne Herald*, Melbourne, Victoria, Australia, until 1985; *Bulletin*, Sydney, New South Wales, Australia, Melbourne theater reviewer, 1989-92; poetry editor for *Overland Extra*, 1992, *Modern Writing*, 1992-94, and *Voices*, 1996; *Masthead* (literary arts journal), founding editor, 1998—; *Australian*, Sydney, Melbourne theater reviewer, 2007-10. Board member, Keene/Taylor Theatre Project, 1997-2002; Pembroke College, University of Cambridge, Australia Council writer-in-residence, 2000; Australian Poets against the War, organizer, 2003; Malthouse Theatre, member of artistic counsel, 2005-06; Green Room Awards,

2007-08; Helpmann Awards panelist, 2009-10; member of programming advisory group for the Melbourne Writers Festival.

■ Awards, Honors

Anne Elder and Dame Mary Gilmore Prizes, 1991, for *This Is the Stone*; Highly Commended, Vogel/Australian National Literary Award, 1995, for *Navigatio*; Victorian Premier's Poetry Prize shortlist, for *The Blue Gate*; Kenneth Slessor Prize for Poetry shortlist, NSW Premier's Literary Awards, and Pushcart Prize nomination, 2003, both for *Attempts at Being*; Aurealis Awards nominations, 2002, and Notable Book citation, Children's Book Council of Australia, 2003, all for *The Naming*; Pascall Prize, Geraldine Pascall Foundation, 2009, for Australian critic of the year; grants and fellowships from Australia Council, Victorian Ministry for the Arts, and Victorian Council for the Arts.

■ Writings

"*BOOKS OF PELLINOR*" *QUARTET*

The Gift, Penguin Books (Camberwell, Victoria, Australia), 2002, published as *The Naming*, Candlewick Press (Cambridge, MA), 2005.

The Riddle, Penguin Books (Camberwell, Victoria, Australia), 2004, Candlewick Press (Cambridge, MA), 2006.

The Crow, Penguin Books (Camberwell, Victoria, Australia), 2006, Candlewick Press (Cambridge, MA), 2007.

The Singing, Penguin Books (Camberwell, Victoria, Australia), 2008, Candlewick Press (Somerville, MA), 2009.

Novels have been published in Spanish and German.

POETRY

This Is the Stone (published with *Pharaohs Returning,* by Fiona Perry), Penguin Books (New York, NY), 1991.

The Blue Gate, Black Pepper (North Fitzroy, Victoria, Australia), 1997.

Mnemosyne, Wild Honey (County Wicklow, Ireland), 2002.

Attempts at Being, Salt Publishing (Great Wilbraham, Cambridge, England), 2002.

The Common Flesh: New and Selected Poems, Arc (Todmorden, England), 2003.

November Burning, Vagabond Press (Newton, New South Wales, Australia), 2004.

Ash, Cusp Books (Los Angeles, CA), 2006.

Theatre, Salt Publishing (Great Wilbraham, Cambridge, England), 2009.

Contributor of poetry to numerous anthologies, chapbooks, and periodicals.

OTHER

(Author of text) *The Burrow* (produced at Perth Festival, Sydney, New South Wales, Australia, 1994), published as *The Burrow: Opera in Prologue and Five Scenes,* introductory note by Elliot Gyger, plot synopsis by Alison Jones, Pellinor (Sydney, New South Wales, Australia), 1994.

(Author of text, with Daniel Keene and Jacintale Plastrier) *Skinless Kiss of Angels* (audio CD), score by Michael Smetanin, ABC Classics, 1995.

Navigatio (novella), Black Pepper (North Fitzroy, Victoria, Australia), 1996.

Lenz (play based on novella by Georg Buchner), produced in Melbourne, Victoria, Australia, 1996.

(Author of lyrics) *Confidentially Yours* (musical), produced at the Playbox Theatre, 1998.

(Author of libretto) *Gauguin,* music by Michael Smetanin, produced at Melbourne International Festival of the Arts (Melbourne, Victoria, Australia), 2000.

Blue (play), produced in Canberra, Australian Capital Territory, Australia, 2001.

Monologues for an Apocalypse (play), ABC Radio, 2001.

Specula (play), ABC Radio, 2006.

Also author of plays *Samarkand* and *The Famine.* Member of editorial advisory board for *Meanjin* (literary journal).

■ **Adaptations**

Poems have been adapted for music.

■ **Sidelights**

An Australian poet, playwright, critic, editor, and novelist, Alison Croggon is known to young adult audiences for her "Books of Pellinor" quartet, a fantasy series that has drawn comparisons to J.R.R. Tolkien's classic *The Lord of the Rings.* The "Books of Pellinor," which includes *The Gift* (published in the United States as *The Naming*), *The Riddle, The Crow,* and *The Singing,* follows the life-altering journey of a young woman who finds herself at the center of an epic battle between the forces of good and evil. "These books are about things that I think matter— what it means to grow up and find out who you are, what it means to be part of a society, to love, to hate, to encounter difference," Croggon stated on the *Books of Pellinor* Web site. "Most of all, I think they're about the struggle to be humane in a world that is too often inhumane. And I hope that if those things matters to me, they might matter to others too."

Born in 1962 in South Africa, where her father worked as a mining engineer, Croggon moved with her parents to Cornwall, England, when she was four. Three years later, the family settled in Australia. An avid reader as a youngster, Croggon devoured works by such celebrated writers as Lewis Carroll, Ursula K. Le Guin, Alan Garner, Rosemary Sutcliffe, Rudyard Kipling, and C.S. Lewis. She also developed an interest in the Greek myths. "I loved them," she related in a *Scribble City Central* interview with Lucy Coats. "Maybe because they were beautiful and strange and ancient: they are about being human, but they are also about the world that is not us, and that we can't control."

Exquisite Versatility

At the age of ten, Croggon first discovered the joys of Tolkien's literary masterpiece. "It was all my parents' fault," she recalled in an essay on her home page. "One night I couldn't sleep because they were fighting, and after they finally went to bed I crept into the empty kitchen. On the table was a single volume paperback edition of *The Lord of the Rings* which my father had left there, and I started reading it out of idle curiosity. I sat up all that night reading and read it all the next day, until I had finished it. Then I started reading it again."

Inspired by Tolkien's work, Croggon decided to write her own fantasy novel, though she put those dreams on hold for almost three decades. After leaving school, Croggon pursued a career in journalism, writing for the *Melbourne Herald*, and after a stint as a theater critic, she began crafting poetry. Her first volume of poems, *This Is the Stone*, won the 1991 Anne Elder and Dame Mary Gilmore Prizes, and *Attempts at Being*, a 2002 collection, was nominated for a Pushcart Prize. Croggon has also served as the poetry editor for *Overland Extra*, among other publications, and was the founding editor of *Masthead*, a literary arts journal. In addition, her writings include the plays *Lenz* and *Blue*, as well as libretti for the operas *Gauguin* and *The Burrow*. "Croggon's work is full of depth as well as range; her work is particularly rich because, in whatever mode she writes, there is an intersection of preoccupations . . .," observed *Drunken Boat* contributor Rebecca Seiferle. "For it's not just that she writes this and writes that, but that any particular work is difficult to limit and contain; her meditations extend in so many directions and yet are vertical in sensibility, a diving into or a flight out of, so that in any mode we see the deep originality and fluidity of genius."

Croggon returned to fantasy after her oldest child began reading *The Lord of the Rings*. Remembering her childhood desire to pen a fantasy tale, in 2000 she started *The Gift*, her translation of the *Naraudh Lar-Chanë* (or *Riddle of the Treesong*), one of the most important legends from the lost (and entirely fictional) civilization of Edil-Amarandh. For a poet like Croggon, writing a prose narrative proved to be quite a challenge. As she recalled in a speech delivered at a conference for the International Federation for the Teaching of English (and reprinted on her home page): "I found one of the most demanding aspects of writing fantasy was the necessity to precisely imagine every moment: if a character was inside a room, it wasn't enough to know that she was sitting down. I had to know where she was sitting in the room, the dimensions and colours of the room, and where she was in relation to any other characters. If she was eating, I had to know what she was eating, and what it tasted like, and it had to reflect the culture she was inhabiting."

"The kind of emotional catharsis fantasy can provide is a more profound human need than mere escapism. It may be the most fleeting of experiences, but it does indeed provide a glimpse of possibility, and it is moving because it is a possibility which in fact exists within our own realities. If fantasy isn't true, it is also, most certainly, not a lie."

—Alison Croggon, in a 2003 speech to the International Federation for the Teaching of English.

Undiscovered Powers

In *The Gift*, the first work in the "Books of Pellinor" quartet, Croggon introduces Maerad of Pellinor, a sixteen year old enslaved in the grim mountain hamlet of Gilman's Cot, in the kingdom of Annar. One day a mysterious stranger appears and, recognizing that Maerad possesses special powers known as the Gift, arranges her escape. After her rescue by Cadvan of Lirigon, a great Bard and a keeper of the Light, Maerad learns that Edil-Amarandh is threatened by the Nameless One, a soulless being who seeks dominion over the land. As Cadvan and Maerad embark on a journey to Norloch, the center of high learning where Cadvan hopes to have the young woman instated as a Bard, they come under attack from vicious wers, a sign that forces of the Dark have entered the region.

Arriving first at Innail, the site of a great School, Maerad commences training as a Bard under the tutelage of Dernhil, who instructs her in the basics of the literary arts, and Indik, a master of horse riding and swordcraft. Though she has yet to come into the Speech, a potent language central to the Bards' learnedness, Maerad proves to be a quick study, and her lyre, which is inscribed with cryptic runic symbols, becomes a source of great interest to her teachers. After Cadvan and Maerad depart from Innail, they learn that the School was invaded by Hulls, corrupt Bards who are now devoted to the dark arts. Convinced that his young charge is in grave danger, Cadvan confesses to Maerad his belief that she is the Foretold who, according to an ancient prophecy, will defeat the Nameless One.

During their travels, Maerad demonstrates her vast but undisciplined powers by destroying a terrifying Kulag, and the duo encounters Ardina, a forest queen who, curiously, speaks to Maerad in the language of the Elidhu, a race of immortal, elemental creatures. They also find the lone survivor of a Hull attack, a boy named Hem who, to their astonishment, turns out to be Maerad's long-lost brother. Arriving in Norlach, the trio is greeted by Nelac, Cadvan's former teacher, whose attempts to have Maerad instated are opposed by Enkir, a traitorous Bard in league with the Dark. As Norlach falls under Enkir's control, Hem ventures south with Saliman, a Bard from Turbansk, while Cadvan and Maerad escape to the north.

The Gift earned solid reviews. According to *Sydney Morning Herald* critic Peter Pierce, "Croggon has crafted an elaborate and beguiling world of legend," and Lesley Farmer, writing in *Kliatt,* remarked that the "characters are well developed, and the plot twists keep the reader engaged." *Booklist* reviewer Carolyn Phelan cited Croggon's background as a poet, stating that she "makes good use of imagery in her writing," and Rachelle Bilz in *Voice of Youth Advocates* noted that the work "is evocative of both the Arthurian legend and *The Lord of the Rings* trilogy with the added twist of a female protagonist."

In the Lair of the Winterking

The Riddle, the second work in Croggon's fantasy quartet, finds Cadvan and Maerad journeying to Zmarkan, driven by the young woman's prescient dreams of locating the Treesong, which lies at the root of the Speech and which appears to be central to the prophesy of the Foretold. Instated as a Bard in a secret ceremony, Maerad continues her education, including lessons in High Magery, at the School of Busk, and she also learns of the Split Song, a legend describing a conflict between the Nameless One and the Elidhu. As news spreads of Enkir's shocking actions to consolidate power in Norlach, there are also rumors of a massive army forming in Dén Raven, a region to the south that is the stronghold of the Nameless One, and that the soldiers plan to advance on Turbansk.

Nearing Lirhan, a region of North Annar, Cadvan and Maerad are met by a pair of Bards who accuse them of rebelling against Enkir, and in her anger Maerad slays one of them, an unconscionable act that prompts her mentor to admit that he senses a darkness surrounding her. The rift between them weakens their defenses, and when they are attacked by frost giants, Cadvan disappears in an avalanche, presumed dead. Maerad must then travel alone to Murask, where relatives prepare her for a trek through the arctic to visit the Wise Kindred, who

have knowledge of the Treesong. Taken to Inka-Reb, a wolf spirit, she discovers that her lyre contains half of the Treesong, and she is warned that uniting the halves could be disastrous.

En route back to Murask, Maerad is captured by Jussack warriors who take her to Arkan-Da, where she is imprisoned in the Ice Palace of the Winterking, an Elidhu who demands the return of the Treesong. Offering to make Maerad his queen, the Winterking also informs her that she must perform the song to unlock its secrets. Though she almost falls prey to his spells, Maerad decides to liberate herself from the Winterking's fortress, using her own magic to decipher his numerous illusions, and once outside, she meets Ardina, who aids in her escape. She makes her way to the ruins of Pellinor, finding Cadvan alive and well there, and they agree to restore the Treesong, the other half of which

The Naming, the first work in Croggon's "Books of Pellinor" fantasy series, introduces Maerad, a slave girl who possesses hidden gifts, and her powerful mentor, Cadvan. (Copyright © 2002 Alison Croggon. Jacket illustration copyright © 2005 Matt Mahurin. Reproduced by permission of Candlewick Press, Somerville, MA. on behalf of Walker Books, London.)

belongs to the Nameless One. "Deep currents of sorrow, loneliness, and love run through this haunting epic fantasy," Cristi Voth observed in her *School Library Journal* review of *The Riddle,* and Cameron Woodhead, writing in the *Age,* noted that "Croggon's novel cycle is intensely imagined and extraordinary in its level of detail."

The Nameless One Strikes

With *The Crow,* her third "Pellinor" title, Croggon returns to the story of Hem, Maered's younger brother. Now studying in Turbansk under the care of Saliman, a fierce but compassionate Bard, Hem displays talents as a healer, skills that are much in need. Refugees from Baladh, a nearby town, stream daily into Turbansk, having fled the Black Army, a mighty force under the direction of Imank, a monstrous Hull allied with the Nameless One. One survivor, a youngster named Zelika, reports that the Black Army has enlisted children to fight alongside Hulls and dogsoldiers, beasts of metal and flesh that breathe liquid fire.

As the citizens of Turbansk prepare for war, Hem forms a strong bond with Irc, a white crow that he saved from destruction. When the Black Army unleashes flocks of deathcrows on the city, Hem commands Irc to rally the birds of Turbansk against their enemies, destroying them. As Imank's forces continue to lay siege to the city, Juriken, an illustrious Bard, sacrifices his life to slow the Black Army, and Saliman, a captain of the harbor forces, opens an escape route by sea, fleeing with Hem, Irc, and Zelika. Reaching the underground city of Nak-Al-Burat, they join with Hared, another Bard, and learn of a rivalry brewing between Imank and the Nameless One. Hem also receives visits from Nyanar, an Elidhu, who suggests that the youngster will play a vital role in solving the riddle of the Treesong.

Trained as spies by Hared, Hem and Zelika attempt to gather information on the child soldiers, who are camped near the Glandugir Hills of Dén Raven. Though Zelika is killed, Hem infiltrates their ranks, living and working with members of the savage Blood Block and communicating his findings to Hared through Irc. After a forced march to Dagra, the industrial center for the Black Army, Hem takes possession of a golden tuning fork from Irc, who stole it during a confrontation between Imank and the Nameless One. Escaping the city, Hem and Irc locate Saliman, who recognizes that the runes engraved on the tuning fork belong to the Treesong, and that Hem must be reunited with Maerad. "This serious penultimate epic, filled with Tolkien-like images, is emotionally astute and brimming with vivid detail," a contributor in *Kirkus Reviews* maintained. Woodhead, reviewing *The Crow,* reported that Croggon displays "a highly immersive imagination," and Farmer commented that the author's "messages of loyalty and self-identity ring true."

The Song That Saved the World

Croggon ends her "Pellinor" saga with *The Singing,* a "complex and gripping tale," according to *School Library Journal* critic Beth L. Meister. Sensing that she must find Hem, Maerad treks with Cadvan to Innail, which is under attack from the Landrost, an Elidhu abetting the forces of the Dark. Tapping into both her Bardic and Elemental powers, Maerad turns back the assault, using knowledge gained from the Winterking. Meanwhile, Hem and Saliman, hoping to conceal their identities, join a caravan of actors traveling through the countryside, though floods, the deadly White Sickness, Hulls, and soldiers of the Black Army pose constant threats to their safety.

While traveling through the desolate Hollow Lands, Maerad seeks help from Ardina, who counsels the young woman to explore her powers to the fullest, assuring her that she will remain a force of the Light. By doing so, she mindtouches Hem, summoning him to join her, and when they finally meet, both her lyre and the tuning fork glow with life. The young Bards and their mentors decide the riddle of the Treesong can only be solved in the ancient city of Afinil, where the runes were created, yet when they reach the Hutmoors, Maerad is mindtouched by the Nameless One, who offers to share his power if she refuses to perform. Resisting his advances, she joins Hem in the Singing, opening a door to the Elidhu world that changes her—and the war-torn land of Edil-Amarandh—forever. "Croggon splinters the narrative perspective . . ., creating a sense of unease as the climax builds," a critic observed in *Kirkus Reviews,* and Carolyn Phelan, writing in *Booklist,* noted that the author "creates a fitting conclusion to this epic high-fantasy series."

Croggon believes the role of fantasy literature is an essential one. Fantasy, she remarked in her conference speech, "answers a profound and ancient need within human beings, who need some way to explore and understand their darkest fears. In the grip of terror, we do not understand what it is: we can only experience it. Fantasy offers us a way of perceiving and dealing with the shadows within and outside us." Writing for a young adult audi-

Alison Croggon was influenced by these writers while growing up in Australia:

J.R.R. Tolkien, author of *The Hobbit; or, There and Back Again* (1937) and *The Lord of the Rings* (1954-55).
C.S. Lewis, author of *The Lion, the Witch, and the Wardrobe* (1950), and other works in his "Chronicles of Narnia" series.
Ursula K. Le Guin, author of the Hugo- and Nebula Award-winning *The Left Hand of Darkness* (1969).

ence also serves an important need, she told Coats in her *Scribble City Central* interview. "We all have an endless appetite for stories, and myths are a bottomless source of stories that resonate deeply within us," Croggon observed. "Everyone plunders them because they give us narrative and symbolic shapes in which to speak about basic human mysteries—birth, death, change. And like all good stories, they give us pleasure. Why should young people miss out on all that richness?"

■ Biographical and Critical Sources

PERIODICALS

Age, January 15, 2005, Cameron Woodhead, review of *The Riddle,* p. 4; April 29, 2006, Cameron Woodhead, review of *The Crow,* p. 24.
Booklist, May 1, 2005, Carolyn Phelan, review of *The Naming,* p. 1579; November 1, 2006, Carolyn Phelan, review of *The Riddle,* p. 41; February 1, 2008, Carolyn Phelan, review of *The Crow,* p. 40; March 1, 2009, Carolyn Phelan, review of *The Singing,* p. 46.
Bookseller, January 16, 2004, Claudia Mody, review of *The Gift,* p. 37.
Bulletin of the Center for Children's Books, September, 2005, Timnah Card, review of *The Naming,* p. 12; January, 2007, April Spisak, review of *The Riddle,* p. 208; January, 2008, April Spisak, review of *The Crow,* p. 206.

Drunken Boat, winter, 2003, Rebecca Seiferle, "An Interview with Alison Croggon."
Kirkus Reviews, June 1, 2005, review of *The Naming,* p. 634; August 15,2006, review of *The Riddle,* p. 838; September 1, 2007, review of *The Crow;* February 15, 2009, review of *The Singing.*
Kliatt, July, 2005, Lesley Farmer, review of *The Naming,* p. 10; September, 2006, Lesley Farmer, review of *The Riddle,* p. 8; November, 2007, Lesley Farmer, review of *The Crow,* p. 8.
School Library Journal, October, 2005, Beth L. Meister, review of *The Naming,* p. 157; January, 2007, Cristi Voth, review of *The Riddle,* p. 126; February, 2008, Amy J. Chow, review of *The Crow,* p. 112; May, 2009, Beth L. Meister, review of *The Singing,* p. 102.
Sydney Morning Herald, October 19, 2002, Peter Pierce, "As Old as Odysseus," review of *The Gift,* p. 12.
Voice of Youth Advocates, August, 2005, Rachelle Bilz, review of *The Naming,* p. 232; December, 2007, Rachelle Bilz, review of *The Crow,* p. 442; Rachelle Bilz, review of *The Singing,* p. 61.

ONLINE

Alison Croggon Blog, http://alisoncroggon.blogspot.com/ (October 1, 2011).
Alison Croggon Home Page, http://www.alisoncroggon.com (October 1, 2011).
Books of Pellinor Web site, http://booksofpellinor.com/ (October 1, 2011).
Cordite Poetry Review Online, http://cordite.org.au/ (September 23, 2011), "Kate Middleton interviews Alison Croggon."
Jenny Darling & Associates Web site, http://jd-associates.com.au/ (October 1, 2011), "Alison Croggon."
Scribble City Central Blog, http://scribblecitycentral.blogspot.com/ (May 21, 2010), Lucy Coats, "Mythic Interview Friday: Number 8—Alison Croggon."
Theatre Notes Blog, http://theatrenotes.blogspot.com/ (October 1, 2011).
Walker Books Web site, http://www.walkerbooks.co.uk/ (October 1, 2011), autobiographical essay by Croggon.*

■ Personal

Born in New York, NY; married to Leslie Tarbell Donovan (president of Donovan Design). *Education:* Queens College, B.A. (fine arts), 1974.

■ Addresses

E-mail—donovandesign@optonline.net.

■ Career

Designer, artist, and curator. Donald Deskey Associates, New York, NY, senior designer and head illustrator, 1980-90; Donovan Design, Southampton, NY, designer 1990—; Sage Marine (premium lighting company), Sag Harbor, NY, founder and designer, 2010—. Hamptons Antique Galleries, Bridgehampton, NY, curator of steampunk exhibition, 2008; Museum of the History of Science, University of Oxford, England, curator of "Steampunk: Devices + Contraptions Extraordinaire" exhibition, 2009-10.

■ Writings

The Art of Steampunk: Extraordinary Devices and Ingenious Contraptions from the Leading Artists of the Steampunk Movement, Fox Chapel Publishing (East Petersburg, PA), 2011.

■ Sidelights

For three decades, designer Art Donovan has worked to create unique, handmade light fixtures. But it was his casual discovery of the art and literary movement known as "steampunk" that brought new radiance to his career.

Searching for design inspiration on the internet, Donovan—who also works in marine and commercial lighting design—found existing work from artists who meld Victorian-era aesthetics and materials into beautiful and strange objects with often fantastic utility. "I was awestruck," Donovan told a contributor for the online design magazine *MoCoLoco* in 2008. "For me, it was the most exciting new style that I had seen in over 30 years as a designer."

That excitement has vaulted Donovan to the center of the Steampunk scene, making him, according to Oliver Peterson in the *Southhampton Patch*, "one of the genre's most admired designers and perhaps its greatest ambassador." His intricate work has gained

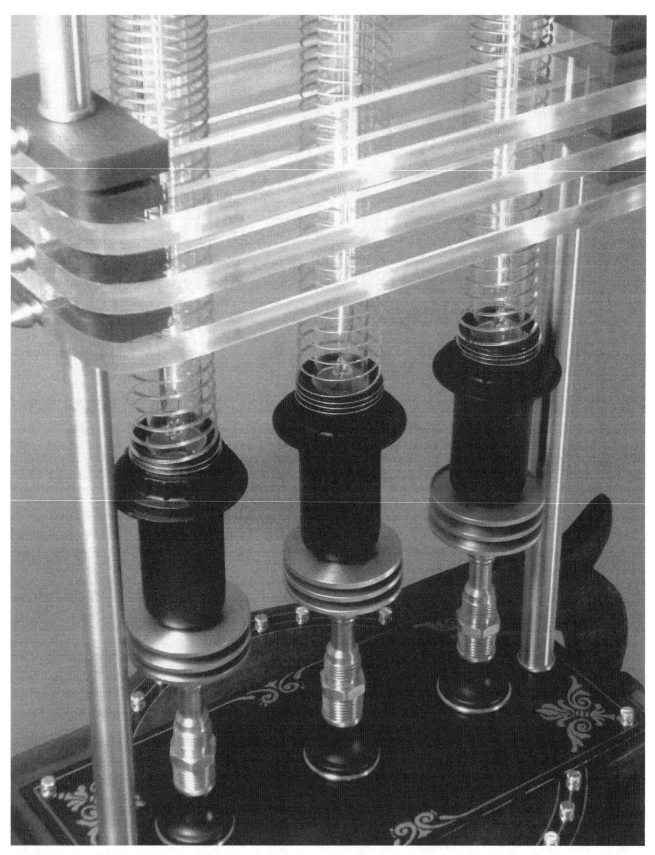

Handcrafted in solid mahogany and brass, Donovan's *Siddhartha Pod Lantern* reflects his interest in Victorian-era styling and technology. (From *The Art of Steampunk*, Fox Chapel Publishing. Copyright © Fox Chapel Publishing. All rights reserved. Reproduced by permission.)

international notoriety and his connections and knowledge of Steampunk's visual art led him to curate a show of the movement's definitive works at Oxford University's Museum of the History of Science in 2009.

What is Steampunk?

According to an essay on *Steampunk Lighting Master*, Donovan's personal blog about Steampunk design, the artist believes there are several characteristics that define the genre. First, and perhaps most importantly, is an eye for evocative design, which includes "defining visual references to the antique sciences or 19th century sci-fi novels that so critically inform the genre."

This view of design often reveals itself in imagined pseudo-scientific utility, intricate exposed mechanics, use of vintage raw materials, and a reliance on low-tech industrial tools—all references to the Victorian era Donovan deems critical to the Steampunk aesthetic. In 2008, Donovan told Eileen Casey of *Hamptons.com* that "the prerequisites of Steampunk design are the 'humane' and natural materials of 19th century technology, such as solid hardwoods, brass, hand-applied rivets and exposed gears and workings that are understandable and self-evident in their operation and function."

The artifacts that result from this aesthetic and technical approach appear to be products of an alternate future, where mass production and modern materials have no place in handiwork. This is also critical to Donovan's view of Steampunk, which he elaborated on in a 2011 interview with Mark Keenan in the *London Sunday Times*. "When you buy a computer, do you notice that this fantastic modern device, which does such incredible and wonderful things, comes encased in bland homogenous plastic? Why is this? Why do all modern and exciting things in our lives have to be made so soullessly?"

It's in the way that Steampunk is out-of-step with the modern world that Donovan sees the promise of creative invention. In his *MoCoLoco* interview he said, "I think that most of us believe that our past 2 decades are the pinnacle of science, illumination and discovery, but actually it doesn't come close to the sheer scope and diversity of disciplines that engaged the Victorian scientist, author and artist."

This view also yields a diversity of artistic objects. An article titled "What's With Steampunk" by Gary Moskowitz, published on the *More Intelligent Life* Web site, listed an odd menagerie of retro-futuristic

"Steampunk is a mash-up of traditional materials and crafts as applied to modern technologies and uses. The true steampunk wants to modify the modern device with rich and beautiful materials and components."

—Art Donovan, in a London *Sunday Times* interview with Mark Keenan.

works by Steampunk artists. "Old clocks, gas lamps, dirigibles, submersibles, goggles, helmets, compasses and small machines are common items" are objects found in the Steampunk workshop, according to the story.

All this culminates in a simple Steampunk mantra for Donovan. "It's a celebration of antique and traditional sciences given a delightful physical form," he told *North Fork Patch* contributor Sandy Martocchia in 2011.

Full Steam Ahead

Donovan translated this view of the Steampunk aesthetic into several of his key works. Consistent with his commercial design efforts, Donovan makes signature use of light and lighting elements in his Steampunk art. For example, *Arc Light,* a representative example of Steampunk lighting, suspends a glowing filament in a glass sphere, attached to a decorated golden brass fitting and a spiral-carved maple fixture. This assembly is pinched between two points of an aggressively rusted semicircle, which is reminiscent of a riveted iron girder. In total, the piece suggests an arcane machine designed to imprison the magic of light in an intentional collection of simple, crafted materials.

Another Donovan work, *Steampunk Clock,* is made of darkened and distressed solid brass and features the exposed internal mechanics common in Steampunk art. A large gear is positioned just above the square clockface and electrical wiring is anchored simply with brass screws, revealing the basics of the work's simple circuitry. But the most striking aspect of the *Steampunk Clock* is the large, adjustable magnifying glass suspended by two brass arms in front of the dial, exaggerating the modest face of the clock to match the scale of the rest of the piece.

The Shiva Mandala is a work that Donovan describes as his "Steampunk masterpiece." The work is defined by five circular aspects—at the center, a

Donovan's *Steampunk Clock*, made of weathered brass, features exposed internal mechanics and an adjustable magnifying lens on its face. (From *The Art of Steampunk*, Fox Chapel Publishing. Copyright © Fox Chapel Publishing. All rights reserved. Reproduced by permission.)

replica of an ornate twelfth-century Persian astrolabe anchors the work. Radiating from the astrolabe at each compass point lies another handmade machine of symbolic import; to the north, a brass clock with Masonic references indicates time; to the south, a nineteenth-century phrenological tool called the Craniometer measures and contains a human skull and symbolizes mortality; at the eastern point, a flickering blue plasma disc represents the electric life force of the physical sciences; and to the west, a rotating image of the Indian god Nataraja Shiva indicates the constant cycle of death and rebirth. In total, *The Shiva Mandala* is overwhelming in its craft and intricacy.

Oxford Victorian

The astrolabe at the center of the *Shiva Mandala* is modeled after an original found in Oxford University's Museum of the History of Science. In 2009, Donovan approached the museum with the idea of doing a Steampunk exhibit among the original Victorian-era artifacts that are part of the museum's permanent collection and have inspired Donovan and other Steampunk artists. "This is the pre-

eminent location for such an exhibition," Donovan told Julie Webb in the *Oxford Times* in 2009.

That same year, the exhibition opened featuring work from eighteen Steampunk artists from around the world, including Steampunk jewelry, time pieces, goggles, ray guns, and unique mechanical contraptions. It was an instant sensation. In his *Southhampton Patch* interview, Donovan reported the Oxford show "ended up being the most popular exhibit they ever had. There were lines around the block."

Following the exhibit, Donovan assembled a book called *The Art of Steampunk: Extraordinary Devices and Ingenious Contraptions from the Leading Artists of the Steampunk Movement* that served as a kind of retrospective of the Oxford show. A review by James Floyd Kelly on the *Geekdad Blog* noted that beyond the expected artist biographies and photos of artwork, Donovan's book included "bits of fiction scattered here and there, giving the objects in question a bit of history and mystique."

This attaching of a backstory or narrative to the artwork is consistent with statements Donovan has made about the role fiction plays in the Steampunk

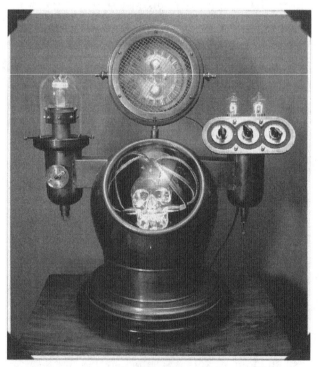

Donovan served as the curator for the "Steampunk: Devices + Contraptions Extraordinaire" exhibition at the University of Oxford, which included this work, titled *The Electric Skull*. (From *The Art of Steampunk*, Fox Chapel Publishing. Copyright © Fox Chapel Publishing. All rights reserved. Reproduced by permission.)

"Steampunks revere the creative renegade and have a special fondness for all those who were considered 'mad' scientists in their own times."

—Art Donovan, in an interview with Eileen Casey of *Hamptons.com.*

movement. He told Casey about "the all important, 'What If?' of science fiction that has been so influential in the creation of real world technologies. Steampunk creatively re-imagines the past to provide an alternative visual image and attitude that can work with contemporary life." This suggests Donovan regards his aesthetics as a visual language from which he constructs speculative fiction.

Steampunk Influence on Young Adult Fiction

This link to fiction has become more explicit in past years, with more and more (particularly young adult) writers picking up on Steampunk to create their fictional worlds. Donovan underscored the history of that link in the interview with Webb: "The term 'Steampunk' was coined by an American science fiction writer, K.W. Jeter, as a tongue-in-cheek response to the 'cyberpunk' literature of the 1980s, in which dystopian futures were depicted, with punks—young renegades outside normal society—battling the forces of oppression using mashed-together devices."

Indeed, Donovan's own description of Steampunk underscores a theme of independence—a subject that is sure to resonate with young adults: "Steampunk represents the age of individual innovation," he told Casey. "It's a rekindling of the age of wonder, new sciences and accomplishments—an age where great innovation could be achieved by dedicated, private individuals. . . ."

■ Biographical and Critical Sources

BOOKS

Donovan, Art, *The Art of Steampunk: Extraordinary Devices and Ingenious Contraptions from the Leading* *Artists of the Steampunk Movement,* Fox Chapel Publishing (East Petersburg, PA), 2011.

PERIODICALS

Oxford Times (Oxford, England), October 23, 2009, Julie Webb, "Weird and Truly Wonderful."

Sunday Times (London, England), August 7, 2011, Mark Keenan, "Get into Steampunk: It's Modern Technology Encased In Victorian Materials—and the Best of All Possible Worlds," p. 14.

ONLINE

Donovan Design Blog, http://donovandesign.blog spot.com/ (August 15, 2011).

Donovan Design Web site, http://www.donovan design.com/ (August 15, 2011).

Geekdad Blog, http://www.wired.com/geekdad/ (June 15, 2011), James Floyd Kelly, "Amazing Creations in *The Art of Steampunk.*"

Hamptons.com http://www.hamptons.com/ (August 1, 2008), Eileen Casey, "Steampunk Art and Design Exhibits in the Hamptons."

MoCoLoco Web site, http://mocoloco.com/ (June 19, 2008), "2 (or 3) Questions for Art Donovan."

More Intelligent Life Web site, http://www.more intelligentlife.co.uk/ (July 6, 2010), Gary Moskowitz, "What's with Steampunk?: A Bizarre Subculture That Romanticises Victorian-era Machines and Jules Verne Is Steadily Entering the Mainstream."

North Fork Patch Web site, http://northfork.patch. com/ (July 27, 2011), Sandy Martocchia, "Artist of the Week: Art Donovan Introduces North Fork to Steampunk."

Number One of One Blog, http://www.number1of1. blogspot.com/ (August 15, 2011).

Southhampton Patch Web site, http://southampton. patch.com/ (July 18, 2011), Oliver Peterson, "Art Donovan Brings Mainstream Attention to Steampunk."

Steampunk Art and Design Blog, http://steampunk museumexhibition.blogspot.com/ (August 15, 2011).

Steampunk Lighting Master, Art Donovan Blog, http:// artdonovan.typepad.com/ (August 15, 2011).*

Kathryn Erskine

■ Personal

Born in the Netherlands; married; children: Fiona. *Hobbies and other interests:* Traveling, exploring, walking, spending time with family and friends, playing games, fencing.

■ Addresses

Home and office—Charlottesville, VA. *E-mail*—kathy@kathrynerskine.com.

■ Career

Writer. Formerly worked as an attorney for fifteen years, including a trademark attorney for the U.S. Department of Commerce.

■ Member

Society of Children's Book Writers and Illustrators.

■ Awards, Honors

Best Books for Young Adults selection, and Quick Picks for Reluctant Young Adult Readers selection, both American Library Association (ALA), both 2008, both for *Quaking;* Best Books for Young Adults selection, ALA, National Book Award for Young People's Literature, 2010, and Children's award, Southern Independent Booksellers Alliance, 2011, all for *Mockingbird.* Erskine's books have also received honors from state reading associations.

■ Writings

NOVELS

(As D.K. Erskine) *Ibhubesi: The Lion,* PublishAmerica, 2004.
Quaking, Philomel Books (New York, NY), 2007.
Mockingbird, Philomel Books (New York, NY), 2010.
The Absolute Volume of Mike, Philomel Books (New York, NY), 2011.

■ Adaptations

Quaking and *Mockingbird* were adapted as audiobooks.

■ Sidelights

Kathryn Erskine is the author of a number of well-recieved coming-of-age novels, most notably *Mockingbird*, which won the 2010 National Book Award. Her characters and plots are varied—*Quaking* focuses on a foster child living with a Quaker family while *Mockingbird* is narrated by a girl with Asperger's Syndrome—but she says all her books share a common theme: "I guess I'd have to say that my stories all seem to be about tolerance and understanding," Erskine told Margaret Ann Abrahams of the the *On Beyond Words and Pictures* blog. "Isn't it wonderful that there are so many different ways to tell a story?"

Erskine was born in the Netherlands and spent her childhood in many different countries, including Israel, South Africa, Scotland, and Canada. She developed a love of literature at an early age and began reading mature books as a youngster. "I tended to pull books off our shelves at home, so I read Nevil Shute and Graham Greene when I was 10 and 11," she remarked in a *Scholastic Book Box Daily* interview. "We were allowed to read anything, encouraged to, actually. That's why I read *To Kill a Mockingbird* at 8. I don't think any of the books scarred me; in fact, they helped me look at the world from viewpoints I'd never imagined. . . ."

Erskine came to writing after a fifteen-year career as a lawyer. "I worked in international trade and then as a trademark attorney for the U.S. Department of Commerce," she told *On Beyond Words and Pictures* blogger Margaret Ann Abrahams. "I can't say the subject matter informs my writing but the research and analytical skills I used for years are a definite help. I'm critical of my writing, wanting everything to be logical or supported by the facts, and I do a tremendous amount of research to ensure accuracy."

When her mother—who had also dreamed of publishing a novel—passed away, Erskine decided that she needed to pursue her own literary career. "I intended to wait until I retired to start writing but after that I thought, I better start now," she remarked to Sue Corbett in a *Publishers Weekly* interview. "I liked being a lawyer but I didn't feel real passion about it. It wasn't hard to give up."

Raising Awareness

For her novels, Erskine draws upon a variety of sources, including current news stories and her own personal background and experiences. Her first novel, *Ibhubesi: The Lion*, was based on her early life

---

"Mrs. Brook always wants me to look in her eyes. She says we can see emotion in people's eyes. I can't. Eyes always look the same to me."

—Caitlin in *Mockingbird.*

---

in South Africa, where, according to her Web site, she got her "first taste of politics, the terrible policy of apartheid." In the book (written under the name D.K. Erskine), a white boy befriends a black servant, defying his father and the apartheid system.

Erskine's next novel, *Quaking,* was inspired by her concern over the Iraq war and, she told blogger Jessica Burkhart, a desire "to relate the issue of violence in war to a more personal level." It took Erskine a little more than a year to write the story, which focuses on a foster child, Matilda (who goes by the nickname "Matt"). Since her abusive father murdered her mother when she was just six years old, Matt has been shuttled from one relative's home to another. Now fourteen, Matt lives with Sam and Jessica Fox, a Quaker couple in Pennsylvania. The teen soon learns that the peace-loving Foxes are not universally admired by members of their small community, many of whom support the U.S. military's efforts in the Middle East.

Having decided that it is far better to withdraw from the world rather than risk confrontation, Matt, too, finds herself at odds with Sam's need to express his views, stating: "I understand his point but I do not understand his desire to act. It does not matter if you are right. What matters is self-preservation. Somewhere along the way, Sam, you missed the raison d'etre, the whole meaning of life: If you will draw negative attention to yourself, it is better to Shut Up." When Matt is targeted by a school bully and a pro-war teacher, however, and learns about threats against local churches, including the Quaker's Meeting House, she must complete what *Horn Book* reviewer Lauren Adams called "her transformation from silent victim to empowered hero."

Quaking was chosen as a Best Books for Young Adults by the American Library Assocation and called "one of the first, if not the first anti-war novel for this generation" by a contributor in *Kirkus Reviews*. Janis Flint-Ferguson, writing in *Kliatt*, also praised the work, stating, "The novel gives a balanced look at the ramifications of violent actions, both on a personal and a national level." Erskine told an interviewer on the *Charlotte Mecklenburg Library* Web site that the most memorable response she had gotten to *Quaking* came from an American Muslim mother whose daughters were being tormented by classmates but who had found comfort in the novel. "It was an awful ordeal they went through," the author remarked, "but I was glad that I was able to give them something that could help them feel just a bit better."

Promoting Empathy

The plot for Erskine's National Book Award-winning novel, *Mockingbird,* was based on two events closer to home: her daughter's diagnosis of Asperger's Syndrome and a 2007 shooting at Virginia Tech during which a mentally disturbed

"**Extraordinary...** [A] moving and insightful masterpiece."
—*Publishers Weekly*

mockingbird
(mok'ing-bûrd)

NATIONAL BOOK AWARD WINNER

KATHRYN ERSKINE

A fifth-grader with Asperger's syndrome grieves for her older brother, the victim of a school shooting, in Erskine's novel *Mockingbird*, winner of the National Book Award. (Cover photograph by Stock4B/Getty Images. Used by permission of Philomel Books, A Division of Penguin Young Readers Group, A Member of Penguin Group (USA) Inc., 345 Hudson Street, New York, NY 10014. All rights reserved.)

gunmen killed 32 people and wounded 25 others, then killed himself." My thoughts went to what it must be like to be related to one of the victims and to how a kid like mine who sees the world so differently, who doesn't feel heard or understood, how frustrated she gets and how frustrated other people get with her because they don't understand how her mind works," she told Corbett. "Those two ideas gelled in my mind."

In the book, Caitlin Smith, a fifth-grader with Asperger's syndrome, has to learn to translate life for herself when the older brother she has always depended on is murdered in a school shooting. "Caitlin's condition allows her to understand things literally," Betsy Taylor observed in the *St. Louis Post-Dispatch,* "but she doesn't get the more nuanced and hard-to-define methods of communication and understanding, from idioms to empathy." As Caitlin's father, a widower, falls once again into despair, the youngster discovers how to express herself with the help of Mrs. Brook, a patient and compassionate counselor at her school. Through these efforts, Faith Brautigam noted in *School Library Journal,* Caitlin "begins to come to terms with her loss and makes her first, tentative steps toward friendship."

Erskine says that while Caitlin shares some characteristics with her daughter, Fiona, they are not identical. "A few of the experiences are similar, but mostly I did a lot of research—reading, going to workshops, talking to people affected by Asperger's—because I wanted to make the story as universal as possible," she said in an interview with Eisa Ulen on the *National Book Foundation* Web site. "Every kid is different, just like every kid with Asperger's is different, although there are certainly traits that are similar and are used to define the condition, such as (over) reactions to noise or touch, lack of eye contact, difficulty in social situations, etc."

Erskine hopes that *Mockingbird* promotes understanding and empathy, much like Harper Lee's classic novel *To Kill a Mockingbird,* which Erskine's book references. A critic in *Kirkus Reviews* observed that both works address a similar theme—the death of an innocent person—calling *Mockingbird* a "heartbreaking story," and Cindy Dobrez, writing in *Booklist,* maintained that a highlight of Erskine;s work is her "portrayal of a whole community's healing process. . . ." In *Publishers Weekly,* a contributor similarly remarked that "this novel is not about violence as much as about the ways in which a wounded community heals."

A Lighter Touch

The fourteen-year-old protagonist of Erskine's next novel, *The Absolute Value of Mike,* struggles with dyscalculia, a wide range of learning disabilities involving mathematics. Complicating matters even more, Mike's dad is a math and engineering genius who wants his son to attend a magnet high school. To develop Mike's engineering skills, his father sends him to help elderly relatives build what they call an "artesian screw," a type of pump used to transfer water. Mike has a different reason for going: "If I could ace this artesian screw, maybe Dad would be satisfied that I'd 'mastered math and engineering at an acceptable level.' Then I could show him how I could take care of myself and not end up on the street. And maybe he'd let me just go to a regular high school."

But there's been a misunderstanding—the offbeat members of the town where Mike's octogenarian relatives, Moo and Poppy, live are actually assembling an 'artisan's crew" to make and sell wooden boxes; the money they raise will help the local minister adopt a Romanian child. Mike must use his own talents, including his computer skills, to help with the townspeople's effort, in the process coming to a greater understanding of his own worth.

Erskine told Holly Schindler on the *Novel Anecdotes* blog that, with *The Absolute Value of Mike*, she started out trying to write a funny book but "with every revision it became more serious and poignant. My sister read the final draft and called me in tears— from some highway in the middle of Montana where she finally found a cell signal—to tell me how beautiful and heartfelt it was. I thought, 'Well, shoot, that was supposed to be my funny one.'"

In the *The New York Times Book Review*, Gary D. Schmidt called *The Absolute Value of Mike* a "comedy about deadly serious things. It is also decidedly more comic than either of . . . Erskine's two earlier books, mostly because of its quirky cast and authentic 14-year-old voice." The critic added that the novel "shares with the author's previous books one technique in particular: Erskine puts her characters into intensely uncomfortable circumstances, ones bound to create oppositional relationships." A writer in *Kirkus Reviews* described the work as a "satisfying story of family, friendship and small-town cooperation in a 21st-century world," and a *Publishers Weekly* critic, even while noting the book's "many contrivances" stated that "the wacky cast, rewarding character growth, and ample humor make this an effortless read."

A True Comfort

Erskine believes that addressing complex and difficult themes in her novels is essential to her success. "When I choke up at the subject matter," she told Burkhart, "I know it's incredibly important to me, which means both that I have something I really have to put into words and that I will probably write about it fairly well because I feel so strongly. The subjects tend to be weighty, and I know others are dealing with these issues, too. I want to give hope and encouragement. . . ."

"It's so exciting to see a story being born. That whole creative blitz, and the neurons firing with new ideas and characters, that's the best part. I sometimes feel that I'm just a conduit and the story is pouring out and I'm the scribe."

—Kathryn Erskine, in an interview with Holly Schindler.

Erskine enjoys writing for a young adult audience. As she told a contributor on the *Charlotte Mecklenburg Library* Web site, "I admire teenagers and how they handle their lives, which are fast paced, complicated, and fraught with high expectations. I hope my books give some comfort, hope, and maybe a few laughs, too."

■ Biographical and Critical Sources

BOOKS

Erskine, Kathryn, *Quaking* Philomel Books (New York, NY), 2007.
Erskine, Kathryn, *The Absolute Volume of Mike*, Philomel Books (New York, NY), 2011.

PERIODICALS

Booklist, May 1, 2007, Francisca Goldsmith, review of *Quaking*, p. 82; February 15, 2010, Cindy Dobrez, review of *Mockingbird*, p. 78.
Denver Post, April 11, 2010, Claire Martin, review of *Mockingbird*, p. E-11.
Horn Book, July-August, 2007, Lauren Adams, review of *Quaking*, p. 393; March-April, 2010, Betty Carter, review of *Mockingbird*, p. 54; July-August, 2011, Susan Dove Lempke, review of *The Absolute Value of Mike*, p. 148.

Kirkus Reviews, July 1, 2007, review of *Quaking;* March 1, 2010, review of *Mockingbird;* May 1, 2011, review of *The Absolute Value of Mike.*

Kliatt, July, 2007, Janis Flint-Ferguson, review of *Quaking,* p. 14.

New York Times Book Review, June 5, 2011, Gary D. Schmidt, "Figuring Out Dad," review of *The Absolute Value of Mike,* p. 26.

Publishers Weekly, June 4, 2007, review of *Quaking,* p. 50; March 8, 2010, review of *Mockingbird,* p. 57; April 25, 2011, review of *The Absolute Value of Mike,* p. 138.

St. Louis Post Dispatch, November 28, 2010, Betsy Taylor, "Offbeat Narrators Tell the Struggles of Youth," review of *Mockingbird,* p. D10.

School Library Journal, July, 2007, Kathleen Isaacs, review of *Quaking,* p. 101; April, 2010, Faith Brautigam, review of *Mockingbird,* p. 154.

ONLINE

Charlotte Mecklenburg Library Web site, http://www.cmlibrary.org/readers_club/ (July, 2009), "Q&A with Kathryn Erskine."

Jessica M. Burkhart Blog, http://jessicaburkhart.blogspot.com/ (February 22, 2008), "Author Visit: Kathryn Erskine."

Kathryn Erskine Blog, http://kathyerskine.wordpress.com/ (July 15, 2011).

Kathryn Erskine Home Page, http://www.kathrynerskine.com (July 15, 2011).

National Book Award Web site, http://www.nationalbook.org/ (July 15, 2011), Eisa Ulen, interview with Erskine.

Novel Anecdotes Blog, http://hollyschindler.blogspot.com/ (February 9, 2010), Holly Schindler, "Interview with Kathryn Erskine."

On Beyond Words and Pictures Blog, http://www.onbeyondwordsandpictures.com/ (May 25, 2011), Margaret Ann Abrahams, "An Interview with Kathryn Erskine."

Publishers Weekly Online, http://www.publishersweekly.com/ (April 8, 2010), Sue Corbett, "Q & A with Kathryn Erskine: A Second Novel Combines Two Life-changing Events from the Author's Life."

Scholastic Book Box Daily Web site, http://bookboxdaily.scholastic.com/ (January 6, 2011), "Author Interview: Kathryn Erskine."

TeensReadToo.com, http://teensreadtoo.com/ (August 10, 2008), Jennifer Wardrip, interview with Erskine.

TRT Book Club Blog, http://trtbookclub.blogspot.com/ (May 12, 2010), Jen Wardrip, "Visit with Kathryn Erskine."

■ Personal

Born October 28, 1957, in Newport, Wales. *Education:* University of Wales, B.A., 1980.

■ Addresses

Home—Newport, Wales. *Agent*—Lesley Pollinger, Pollinger Ltd., 9 Staple Inn, Holborn, London WC1V 7QH, England.

■ Career

Writer and educator. Worked as a school teacher, archaeologist, broadcaster, and adjudicator. University of Glamorgan, Glamorgan, Wales, visiting lecturer of children's literature; teacher in Newport, Gwent, Wales.

■ Awards, Honors

Welsh Arts Council Young Writers Award, 1988, for *Immrama;* Welsh Arts Council Young Writers' Prize, and Cardiff International Poetry Competition prize,

Catherine Fisher

both 1989, both for poetry; Smarties Award shortlist, for *The Conjuror's Game;* Cardiff International Poetry Prize, 1990; Tir na n'Og Prize, 1995, for *The Candle Man;* Whitbread Prize shortlist, 2003, for *The Oracle;* Mythopoeic Society Children's Fiction Award, 2007, for *Corbenic;* London *Times* Children's Book of the Year, and Carnegie Medal longlist, both 2008, both for *Incarceron.*

■ Writings

NOVELS; EXCEPT AS NOTED

The Conjuror's Game, Bodley Head (London, England), 1990.

Fintan's Tower, Bodley Head (London, England), 1991.

Saint Tarvel's Bell, Swift Children's (London, England), 1992.

The Hare and Other Stories, Pont Books (Llandysul, Wales), 1994.

The Candleman, Bodley Head (London, England), 1994.

Belin's Hill, Bodley Head (London, England), 1997.

Scared Stiff: Stories, Dolphin Books (London, England), 1997.

Magical Mystery Stories, Red Fox (London, England), 1999.

The Lammas Field, Hodder Children's Books (London, England), 1999.

Darkwater Hall, Hodder Children's Books (London, England), 2000.

Old Enough and Other Stories, Cló Iar-Chonnachta, (Indreabhán, Conamara, Wales), 2002.

The Glass Tower (contains *The Conjuror's Game, Fintan's Tower,* and *The Candleman*), Red Fox (London, England), 2004.

Corbenic, Greenwillow Books (New York, NY), 2006.

Darkhenge, Greenwillow Books (New York, NY), 2006.

The Weather Dress, Pont Books (Llandysul, Wales), 2006.

Incarceron, Hodder Children's Books (London, England), 2007, Dial Books (New York, NY), 2010.

Sapphique (sequel to *Incarceron*), Hodder Children's Books (London, England), 2008, Dial Books (New York, NY), 2011.

The Pickpocket's Ghost (novella), Barrington Stoke (London, England), 2008.

Crown of Acorns, Hodder Children's Books (London, England), 2010.

The Magic Thief (novella), illustrated by Peter Clover, Barrington Stoke (London, England), 2011.

The Ghost Box (novella), illustrated by Peter Clover, Barrington Stoke (London, England), 2012.

"SNOW-WALKER" TRILOGY

The Snow-walker's Son, Bodley Head (London, England), 1993.

The Empty Hand, Bodley Head (London, England), 1995.

The Soul Thieves, Bodley Head (London, England), 1996.

The Snow-walker Trilogy (includes *The Snow-walker's Son, The Empty Hand,* and *The Soul Thieves*), Red Fox (London, England), 2003, published as *Snow-walker,* Greenwillow Books (New York, NY), 2004.

"BOOK OF THE CROW" SERIES; PUBLISHED AS "RELIC MASTER" SERIES IN U.S.

The Relic Master, Bodley Head (London, England), 1998, published as *The Dark City,* Dial Books (New York, NY), 2011.

The Interrex, Bodley Head (London, England), 1999, published as *The Lost Heiress,* Dial Books (New York, NY), 2011.

Flain's Coronet, Bodley Head (London, England), 2000, published as *The Hidden Coronet,* Dial Books (New York, NY), 2011.

The Margrave, Red Fox (London, England), 2001, Dial Books (New York, NY), 2011.

"ORACLE PROPHECIES" SERIES

The Oracle, Hodder Children's Books (London, England), 2003, published as *The Oracle Betrayed,* Greenwillow Books (New York, NY), 2004.

The Archon, Hodder Children's Books (London, England), 2004, published as *The Sphere of Secrets,* Greenwillow Books (New York, NY), 2005.

The Scarab, Hodder Children's Books (London, England), 2005, published as *Day of the Scarab,* Greenwillow Books (New York, NY), 2006.

POETRY

Immrama, Seren (Bridgend, Wales), 1988.

The Unexplored Ocean, Seren (Bridgend, Wales), 1994.

Altered States, Seren (Bridgend, Wales), 1999.

Folklore, Smith/Doorstep Books (Wakefield, England), 2003.

Contributor to poetry anthologies, including *Twentieth-Century Anglo-Welsh Poetry,* Seren (Bridgend, Wales); *Oxygen,* Seren (Bridgend, Wales), and *The Forward Book of Poetry, 2001.*

■ Sidelights

Catherine Fisher is, according to London *Times Online* reviewer Amanda Craig, "a writer who has thought deeply not just about realizing the supernatural, but about the extreme loneliness of being different." In her works, which include *Snow-walker,* the "Book of the Crow" and the "Oracle" series, and *Corbenic,* she has explored fantasy realms from an icy world that is structured on Norse legends, a desert kingdom grounded in ancient myth, and a living, sentient prison. She has revamped the Holy Grail legend, traveled into Welsh legend, and made readers look over their shoulders with chilling tales of government surveillance. As Craig noted, Fisher's protagonists are often "children whose devastating gift of magic is matched by vulnerability, needing support from a cast of fierce heroines, shrewd bards and semi-corrupt officials." Craig added that Fisher is "far from the sword and sorcery of cliché" further noting that she is "closer to SF, imagining a place where science and magic overlap."

Speaking with Steph Su of the online *Steph Su Reads,* Fisher remarked of her fiction: "I don't really categorize what I write as fantasy, or dystopian or anything really," adding, "I just like to write stories with a strong element of the metaphysical, the strange, the unearthly, and that manifests in various ways—ghosts, sci-fi, elemental beings, gods. I think such stories have a consistent readership because they, like myths, appeal to some very deep need in us." Since the publication of her first novels for young adults, Fisher "has been one to watch both for her remarkable imagination and a pared-down prose style," according to Craig. Readers and critics alike have concurred with that judgment. Short-listed for the Whitbread Children's Prize in 2003, Fisher won the Mythopoeic Society Children's Fiction Award in 2007. She has also won awards for her poetry as well as the Welsh Tir na n'Og Prize in 1995 for fiction.

An Early Love of Fantasy and Poetry

Fisher was born in Newport, Wales, the daughter of a painter and decorator. Books definitely were a major part of Fisher's youth. "My favourite writers were often experts at fantasy," she remarked to I.E. Johnson in a *Totally YA* interview. These authors included Alan Garner, J.R.R. Tolkien, Ursula Le Guin, and Arthur Machen. Fisher continued, "I was the sort of teenager who is always reading or out walking in the courtyard. I had a feeling I would be a writer but didn't really know, so I studied English." Fisher attended the University of Wales in Caerleon, outside of her native Newport. After graduation she took part in a year-long archaeological dig in the town's Roman ruins and held various other jobs. But, as Fisher explained to Johnson, "I was always writing poems and stories and gradually I began to try and get them published."

Fisher began her publishing career with the 1988 poetry collection, *Immrama*, which won the Welsh Arts Council Young Writers Award that year. She has continued to write poetry along with fiction, publishing three further collections: *The Unexplored Ocean, Altered States,* and *Folklore.* Welsh history and mythology inform much of Fisher's poetry. A *Publishers Weekly* reviewer felt that *The Unexplored Ocean* "conveys a reverence for the physical world," while *Booklist* contributor Patricia Monaghan, writing about *Altered States,* commended the "classic dignity" in Fisher's verse, concluding, "Fisher's is a sterling presence in poetry."

Fisher's first novel for young readers is *The Conjuror's Game,* from 1990, about a young, six-fingered boy with healing powers. Shortlisted for England's Smarties Award, this debut was followed by other tales blending magic and myth, such as *Fintan's Tower* and *The Candleman.* These three early works were collected in the 2004 title, *The Glass Tower.* However, Fisher is better known for another early work, the "Snow-walker" trilogy, inaugurated in 1993 and including *The Snow-walker's Son, The Empty*

"I just like to write stories with a strong element of the metaphysical, the strange, the unearthly, and that manifests in various ways—ghosts, sci-fi, elemental beings, gods. I think such stories have a consistent readership because they, like myths, appeal to some very deep need in us; they try to explain the workings of the world, and they give readers the ability in some way to control fate and nature."

—Catherine Fisher, in an interview with Steph Su.

Hand, and *The Soul Thieves.* This trilogy was later reprinted in the United States in the one-volume *Snow-walker.* Set in a frozen world and infused with Norse myth, the novels in this cycle deal with the efforts of a small and dedicated band of youth to overthrow the magical tyranny of Gudrun, the Snow-walker, who has come from the icy edges of the world to rule the Jarl's people through fear and sorcery. Though Gudrun has absolute power over the Jarlshold, she still had a weak spot: her son, Kari, whom she banished to the far north. Rumors have long mentioned his magical powers, and when the girl Jessa is also banished to the north, she encounters Kari, who, she discovers, is also a Snow-walker possessing great powers. Together with Jessa, a bard named Skapti, and Kari's long-time caregiver Brochael, the banished youth ultimately defeats his mother and returns the Jarlshold to the people.

Reviewers responded warmly to this work. A *Kirkus Reviews* contributor called it a "supremely satisfying one-volume trilogy [that] combines snow and ice with loyalty, love, trust, and adventure." *Booklist* reviewer Cindy Dobrez similarly noted: "It's the description of the icy back-drop and the mythological beings in the cast, most notably the predatory rune creature, that reveals the beauty of Fisher's prose." Likewise, a *Publishers Weekly* writer felt that "the author creates an atmospheric setting, and fans of Norse myths and magic may be swept up in this frosty tale," and *School Library Journal* contributor Margaret A. Chang believed that "fantasy readers will happily follow the adventures of Jessa, Kari, and their brave companions."

The World of the Relic Masters

Fisher blends science fiction and fantasy in a quartet of novels that were originally published in England between 1998 and 2001, and that were published in

An inmate with no memories tries to escape from a sentient prison with the help of the warden's daughter in Fisher's *Incarceron*. (Cover art by SY Design. Used by permission of Dutton Children's Books, A Division of Penguin Young Readers Group, A Member of Penguin Group (USA) Inc., 345 Hudson Street, New York, NY 10014. All rights reserved.)

the United States in 2011. Originally called the "The Book of the Crow" series, the novels were re-titled the "Relic Master" series for U.S. publication. The books are set in the land of Anara, a planet once terraformed by the mysterious Makers, who are now considered to be semi-divine by their descendants. The planet was never properly developed, however, and has devolved into a "grim, dark, medieval world, connected by a portal to a more advanced civilization" ruled by the omniscient Watch, according to *Voice of Youth Advocates* contributor Walter Hogan. The ancient Order attempts to maintain the ancient technologies, which are found emanating from relics.

In the series opener, *The Relic Master* (titled *The Dark City* in its U.S. edition), the Relic Master Galen and

his apprentice, Raffi, have been entrusted with the job of preserving the ancient technology of the Makers, but Galen has lost his mystical powers. Now he and Raffi travel to the devastated city of Tasceron, where Galen may find sufficient magical power to heal himself. At the same time, the Watch is tracking them, and when they are joined by a young woman, Carys, who claims to be in search of her father, the danger level is increased, for she has been assigned by the Watch to spy on Raffi and Galen. However, in the course of their journey to the dark city, Carys's allegiances begin to shift. A *Kirkus Reviews* contributor praised Fisher's "mastery of detailed and exotic worldbuilding," in this first series installment, calling the work a "tale redolent with humor, wonder and suspense." A *Publishers Weekly* reviewer also commended the novel, calling it a "gritty and enjoyable tale of adventure, poised on the dividing line between science fiction and fantasy," while *School Library Journal* contributor Eric Norton dubbed it a "moody book full of mist, swamps, and darkness."

In the second book of the series, *The Interrex* (also published as *The Lost Heiress*), Galen and Raffi are still fugitives from the Watch, and now they must set out on another quest. This time they are in search of the Interrex, the granddaughter of the former emperor. They must summon all the magic and power they have to free the Interrex and bring her to safekeeping on the isle of Sarres, accompanied by their alien Sekoi companion (one of the seven-fingered, catlike creatures that once had the planet to themselves and want to reclaim it) and by Carys, who is still working out her loyalties. This second series installment also elicited praise from reviewers. For example, a *Kirkus Reviews* contributor noted Fisher's "flair for fantastical worldbuilding," and Hogan lauded the book's "colorful secondary characters."

The third work in the series, *Flain's Coronet* (*The Hidden Coronet*), finds Galen and young Raffi on yet another quest, this time to save a fellow Relic Master from the Watch. Meanwhile, the land of Anara continues to deteriorate geologically and environmentally; even the seasons have shifted. Raffi and his companions realize only a magical Coronet of the Makers can save their world, but they neither know the object's location nor its specific use. "The climactic integration of visionary mysticism and gee-whiz gadgetry, rendered bittersweet by all-too-human failures, leads directly to a cliffhanger ending," wrote a *Kirkus Reviews* contributor of this third installment.

The concluding volume, *The Margrave*, features Galen's efforts to destroy the leader of the Watch, the mysterious Margrave. Here Raffi is captured by the

Watch, and as the others try to save him, he is able to get to the center of the mystery surrounding the deterioration of Anara by using compassion rather than intellect and power. This final volume "leaves open most of the mysteries of the world and the Makers, while providing emotional closure to each character's narrative arc," according to a *Kirkus Reviews* contributor.

Trouble in the Two Lands

Fisher's first true international success was her "Oracle" series (published as the "Oracle Prophecies" in the United States), set in the desert-like world of the Two Lands, an amalgam of ancient Egypt and Greece. Fisher described the inspiration for this series on her home page: "I wanted to write something a little exotic here. I'd been reading a lot of Greek myth and history, and decided to mix it with the death rituals of the ancient Egyptians and a few touches of Aztec, to create the hot desert country of the Two Lands, the living above and the dead below." The first work in the series, *The Oracle* (published as *The Oracle Betrayed* in the United States), finds the Two Lands faced with a terrible drought. Only the Archon can save the people by serving as an oracle to the gods to seek relief for the lands. However, a plot is afoot led by the Speaker, one of the nine young priestesses who serve the Archon. This woman, in love with an ambitious general, plans to replace the Oracle with an individual that she controls. However, before his death, the Archon secures the assistance of another of the nine priestesses, young and shy Mirany, who quickly takes on the role of powerful conspirator to battle the crafty Speaker. Mirany and the musician of the Archon, Oblek, both recognize the next true Archon: a ten-year-old boy named Alexos. Now, aided by the ambitious scribe, Seth, they must battle to ensure Alexos does in fact become next in line and foil the machinations of the Speaker.

"Action trumps character development in this page-turning fantasy, while an open ending paves the way for subsequent volumes," wrote *School Library Journal* reviewer Chang of this first book in the series. *Horn Book* contributor Anita L. Burkam felt that "Mirany's world is richly imagined, and thoughtful readers will delight in the interplay of the allegorical with the literal." A *Publishers Weekly* reviewer offered further praise for *The Oracle Betrayed*, noting: "A crisp, quick-moving narrative and fully fleshed out characters will keep readers hooked to . . . remaining installments in this trilogy." *Booklist* reviewer Carolyn Phelan similarly felt that Fisher's novel provides a "well-developed world with its own culture, some sharply realized

settings, and several strong, distinctive characters," while *Kliatt* contributor Michele Winship termed it a "fast-paced and intriguing tale."

The Archon (also published as *The Sphere of Secrets*), finds Alexos, Mirany, Oblek, and Seth back in action, attempting to end the ruinous drought of the Two Lands. Recognized by his people as a reborn god, Alexos is still unable to bring rain, and he must journey to the Well of Songs to undo a past wrong. He travels with Seth and Oblek on this quest, as Mirany attempts to protect the Oracle during a siege of the city and to fend off the evil workings of General Argelin and Speaker-for-the-God Hermia.

"Fisher has created an incredible, detailed, and believable setting, and the characterizations are vivid and complex," noted Tasha Saecker in a *School Library Journal* review of *The Sphere of Secrets*.

An award-winning poet as well as a novelist, Fisher signs copies of *Incarceron,* winner of London *Times* **Children's Book Of The Year.**

Burkam, writing again in *Horn Book,* also had a high assessment of this second series installment, writing: "This beautifully set, canny story of politics and religion ends in resounding success but will keep readers hungry for the third installment in the projected trilogy." Similarly, a *Kirkus Reviews* contributor noted the "almost painfully heightened tension right to the end—that will have readers queuing for the concluding volume."

That volume, *The Scarab* (*Day of the Scarab* in its U.S. edition), sees Mirany, Oblek and the boy Archon Alexos still battling General Argelin. The group travels to the underworld to find Hermia, whom Argelin has killed by accident, hoping to use the dead Speaker to bargain with the power-mad general, who is destroying the religion of the Rain Queen. Meanwhile, Seth, the scribe, works above ground, acting as a secretary for the general while passing information to the resistance. *School Library Journal* reviewer Coop Renner noted that despite the fact the book is packed with incident and characters, "most . . . [readers] are likely to be swept along in this entertaining and evocative adventure, eager to keep turning the pages." Similar praise was offered by *Horn Book* contributor Burkam, who wrote: "Vivid, complicated, and thoroughly engrossing, this fast-paced adventure keeps readers avidly turning pages until the majestic conclusion." Winship, again writing in *Kliatt,* also felt that this third installment provides a "satisfying conclusion to the trilogy," as did a contributor for *Kirkus Reviews,* who described the work as a "triumphant finale to a complex and multilayered adventure."

Blending Fantasy, Myth, and Dystopian Visions

Fisher has also written a number of contemporary stand-alone novels featuring youthful protagonists who face harsh realities and even harsher magic. Young Huw in *Belin's Hill,* for example, survives a tragedy only to have his waking life torn asunder by nightmares. He knows he must somehow deal with the myths of Belin's Hill to finally find peace. Similarly, Mick in *The Lammas Field* is being drawn to the Otherworld by a mysterious woman who comes to the festival held annually at the seventeenth-century house and grounds that his father manages. In *Darkwater Hall,* Tom Hughes, a student at the eponymously named school, becomes caught up in a century-old deal with the devil.

Darkhenge blends "Celtic lore, fairy-tale archetypes, and family tragedy," according to *Booklist* reviewer Jennifer Matson. Here, teenager Rob and his family are in great distress after Chloe, Rob's younger sister, is left in a coma following a riding accident. When Rob takes a job documenting a local archaeological dig by sketching it, he discovers a link to his sister's coma. A henge, or circular prehistoric enclosure, at the dig appears to provide a portal into an alternate world, Anwyn, where he learns that Chloe's coma is actually self-inflicted; she is withdrawing from the world as a result of long unsettled sibling problems with Rob. While Mattson felt that this theme of sibling rivalry does not work "as the plot's psychological lynchpin," she still believed many readers would "thrill to the magical, atmospheric setting." Higher praise came from *Horn Book* reviewer Burkam, who called the novel a "complex fantasy that resonates with strangeness, mysticism, and magic." *School Library Journal* reviewer Sharon Grover similarly found the book a "challenging read, but one that is ultimately very satisfying." Likewise, a *Kirkus Reviews* contributor noted that "the portrayal is delicate and poetic, the journey frightening, with suspense that builds as young, bitter Chloe decides whether or not to return to life," while a *Publishers Weekly* writer dubbed *Darkhenge* a "haunting tale."

Another mythic tale finds contemporary resonance in *Corbenic,* in which the author revamps the "Fisher King," a tale from Arthurian legend. Cal's mother is an alcoholic and schizophrenic. The teen travels to live with his uncle but detrains at the wrong stop, which leads him to a roadside inn, the Castle Hotel Corbenic, which in fact turns out to be the castle Corbenic, part of the legend of the Holy Grail. The castle is ruled by Alain Bron, the wheelchair-bound Fisher King who recognizes Cal as Percival, there to restore his realm. But failing a test by the king, Cal is banished back to the dreadful reality of modern England and to his uncle's suburban home, where he learns about the Grail legend. Cal begins to worry that he is becoming afflicted by his mother's schizophrenia but nonetheless begins to search again for Corbenic, which now appears as if it never existed. Two Arthurian re-enactors, who claim not to be actors at all, help Cal in his search, and when his mother commits suicide after Cal fails to return home for a promised Christmas visit, his guilt drives him on in his Grail-like quest. "The blurring of fantasy and reality is sometimes confusing but helps to sustain the mood of wonder and mystery," noted Johanna Lewis in *School Library Journal.* Burkam similarly wrote in *Horn Book:* "Playing with our perceptions, Fisher purposefully blurs the line between supernatural occurrences and mental illness" *Kliatt* writer Claire Rosser also noted the ambiguity in the narrative, observing: "The delicious success of this story is the ambiguity of it, looking at it rationally or with the suspension of disbelief." A *Kirkus Reviews* contributor remarked that "Fisher ably splices the Arthurian legend into

Cal's very modern quest for self-determination." Still higher praise came from a *Publishers Weekly* reviewer who called *Corbenic* an "elegiac, mature modern fantasy."

Fisher again blends fantasy with science fiction in her dystopian pair of novels, *Incarceron* and *Sapphique*. These are set in the distant future on a world whose technologies were artificially halted at medieval stages in order to save humanity. At that time a huge, sentient prison, Incarceron, was created as a social engineering experiment: all malcontents and undesirables would be housed there, and the enclosed society would be transformed into a utopia. Instead, in the centuries since, the prison has become self-aware, and the incarcerated have split into numerous factions, while the outside world has remained stagnant. Incarceron's mission has also evolved dramatically: the prison prevents individuals from the outside from entering and captives from escaping. But young prisoner Finn and his unlikely lover, Claudia, the warden's daughter, have different plans. Just as Finn desperately wants to escape from Incarceron, Claudia wants to escape from an arranged marriage and the rigid norms of society. *Booklist* reviewer Krista Hutley called this novel a "gripping futuristic fantasy [that] has breathless pacing, an intelligent story line, and superb detail in rendering both of the stagnating environments." Similarly, a *Publishers Weekly* writer felt that Fisher "scores a resounding success in this beautifully imagined science fantasy," while a *Kirkus Reviews* contributor termed it a "far-future thriller [that] combines riveting adventure and masterful world-building with profound undertones." London *Times Online* contributor Craig also had praise for this work's "imaginative scale and gob-smacking finale." For *School Library Journal* reviewer Karen E. Brooks-Reese, this novel is a "a tour de force," that is "on the surface . . . a fast-paced if dense adventure," but on a deeper level is also a novel about the "philosophy of imprisonment and the development of society."

The sequel, *Sapphique,* finds Finn—two months after his escape from Incarceron—still feeling guilty for leaving friends behind in the prison and hardly fitting in with courtly life, where he is disguised as Prince Giles. Claudia also begins to wonder about Finn's true identity, even as Finn's prison-bound friends believe they have found a means of escape in the fabled Glove of Sapphique. These two books create a "high-intensity, mind-bending duology," according to *Booklist* reviewer Hutley. Reviewing the work in *Voice of Youth Advocates,* Judy Brink-Drescher felt this "well-written, fast-paced novel is quite the page-turner." Similarly, *School Library Jour-*nal writer Jessica Miller termed *Sapphique* "a dark, interesting foray into vivid imagery, danger, surprising twists, and intriguing revelations."

In *Crown of Acorns,* Fisher takes the reader into three time periods, all revolving around the English city of Bath. In prehistory, Bladud, the mythical builder of Bath, is a leprous king who is cured by the sacred spring of Sulis. He builds circles as a temple to Sulis's honor, but these only turn out to imprison him. This myth becomes a fetish for an eighteenth-century architect, Jonathan Forrest, a fictional stand-in for the real-life John Wood, architect of the King's Circus in Bath, the first terraced street built in a circle. He and his young apprentice, Zac, struggle with their architectural creation in this second section. In a third subplot, set in contemporary times, an abused teen named Sulis arrives in Bath with a new identity, hoping to escape memories of her horrific childhood. She ends up living in the circle built by Forrest, and in turn helps another teen, Josh, come to terms with events in his own past. The manner in which these three tales intertwine is "masterfully accomplished," according to *School Librarian* reviewer Marzena Currie, who further termed *Crown of Acorns* "a sophisticated and beautifully written novel with a brilliant climax."

Catherine Fisher cites these writers as being among her favorites:

Arthur Machen, author of the chilling short stories "The White People" (1904) and "The Bowmen" (1914).

Alan Garner, author of the Carnegie Medal winner *The Owl Service* (1967).

Robert Holdstock, author of *Mythago Wood*, (1984), recipient of the World Fantasy Award.

In an online interview with author Brenna Yovanoff, Fisher offered the following advice for aspiring authors: "My only advice is read, write what you want to, and don't give up. Take advice, but don't always follow it. Read your stuff aloud. Be bold, take risks." She concluded, "Above all, don't think you have to know everything in the story at the start—I never do. Just begin, and see where it leads you. Amazing places, very often."

■ Biographical and Critical Sources

PERIODICALS

Booklist, June 1, 2000, Patricia Monaghan, review of *Altered States,* p. 1839; February 15, 2004, Carolyn Phelan, review of *The Oracle Betrayed,* p. 1059; September 1, 2004, Cindy Dobrez, review of *Snow-walker,* p. 106; March 15, 2005, Carolyn Phelan, review of *The Sphere of Secrets,* p. 1292; January 1, 2006, Jennifer Mattson, review of *Darkhenge,* p. 81; May 15, 2006, Carolyn Phelan, review of *Day of the Scarab,* p. 61; August 1, 2006, Holly Koelling, review of *Corbenic,* p. 65; January 1, 2010, review of *Incarceron,* p. 80; October 1, 2010, Krista Hutley, review of *Sapphique,* p. 81.

Horn Book, March-April, 2004, Anita L. Burkam, review of *The Oracle Betrayed,* p. 181; September-October, 2004, Anita L. Burkam, review of *The Snow-walker,* p. 581; March-April, 2005, Anita L. Burkam, review of *The Sphere of Secrets,* p. 200; March-April, 2006, Anita L. Burkam, review of *Darkhenge,* p. 187; May-June, 2006, Anita L. Burkam, review of *Day of the Scarab,* p. 315; September-October, 2006, Anita L. Burkam, review of *Corbenic,* p. 582; January-February, 2010, Anita L. Burkam, review of *Incarceron,* p. 86; January-February, 2011, Anita L. Burkam, review of *Sapphique,* p. 93.

Kirkus Reviews, February 1, 2004, review of *The Oracle Betrayed,* p. 132; July 15, 2004, review of *Snow-walker,* p. 684; February 1, 2005, review of *The Sphere of Secrets,* p. 176; February 1, 2006, review of *Darkhenge,* p. 131; May 1, 2006, review of *Day of the Scarab,* p. 457; August 1, 2006, review of *Corbenic,* p. 785; January 15, 2010, review of *Incarceron;* October, 2010, review of *Sapphique;* April 15, 2011, review of *The Dark City;* May 1, 2011, review of *The Lost Heiress;* June 1, 2011, review of *The Hidden Coronet;* June 15, 2011, review of *The Margrave.*

Kliatt, March, 2004, Michele Winship, review of *The Oracle Betrayed,* p. 10; September, 2004, Michele Winship, review of *Snow-walker,* p. 10; March, 2005, Michele Winship, review of *The Oracle Betrayed,* p. 26; November, 2005, Michele Winship, review of *Snow-walker,* p. 20; March, 2006, Lesley Farmer, review of *Darkhenge,* p. 10; May, 2006, Michele Winship, review of *Day of the Scarab,* p. 8; September, 2006, Claire Rosser, review of *Corbenic,* p. 11; May, 2007, Lesley Farmer, review of *Darkhenge,* p. 30.

Publishers Weekly, June 26, 1995, review of *The Unexplored Ocean,* p. 102; January 19, 2004, review of *The Oracle Betrayed,* p. 77; November 15, 2004, review of *Snow-walker,* p. 61; April 10, 2006, review of *Darkhenge,* p. 73; November 6, 2006, review of *Corbenic,* p. 62; December 7, 2009, review of *Incarceron,* p. 49; November 8, 2010, review of *Incarceron,* p. 34.

School Librarian, fall, 2010, Marzena Currie, review of *Crown of Acorns,* p. 176.

School Library Journal, March, 2004, Margaret A. Chang, review of *The Oracle Betrayed,* p. 210; November, 2004, review of *Snow-walker,* p. 143; March, 2005, Tasha Saecker, review of *The Sphere of Secrets,* p. 210; March, 2006, Sharon Grover, review of *Darkhenge,* p. 220; July, 2006, Coop Renner, review of *Day of the Scarab,* p. 101; November, 2006, Johanna Lewis, review of *Corbenic,* p. 134; February, 2010, Karen E. Brooks-Reese, review of *Incarceron,* p. 110; December, 2010, Jessica Miller, review of *Sapphique,* p. 113; June, 2011, Tricia Melgaard, review of *Sapphique,* p. 60; July, 2011, Eric Norton, review of *The Dark City,* p. 97.

Times (London, England), February 21, 2004, Amanda Craig, "Mad Magician in Search of Rain," p. 17.

Voice of Youth Advocates, December, 2010, Judy Brink-Drescher, review of *Sapphique,* p. 468; August, 2011, Walter Hogan, review of *Dark City,* p. 287.

Western Mail (Cardiff, Wales), November 14, 2003, Karen Price, "Welsh Writer Shortlisted for Book Award," p. 8.

ONLINE

Amanda Craig Blog, http://www.amandacraig.com/ (September 9, 2011), "Catherine Fisher Interview."

Book Smugglers Web site, http://thebooksmugglers.com/ (June 14, 2011), "Relic Master Blog Tour & Giveaway: A Chat with Catherine Fisher."

Brenna Yovanoff Live Journal, http://brennayovanoff.livejournal.com/ (December 17, 2010), interview with Catherine Fisher.

Catherine Fisher Home Page, http://www.catherine-fisher.com/ (November 1, 2011).

Eternal Ones Blog, http://theeternalones.wordpress.com/ (December 8, 2010), Kirsten Miler, "My Interview with Author Catherine Fisher."

Steph Su Reads Blog, http://stephsureads.blogspot.com/ (August 9, 2011), Steph Su, "Blog Tour Interview: Catherine Fisher."

Times Online, http://entertainment.timesonline.co.uk/ (April 27, 2007), Amanda Craig, "Scared? You Will be Soon"; (December 7, 2007), Amanda Craig, review of *Incarceron.*

Totally YA Blog, http://fictionforyoungadults.blogspot.com/ (May 5, 2010), E.I. Johnson, "Interview: Catherine Fisher—New York Times Bestseller and Award-Winning Welsh Children's Fantasy Author of 'Incarceration.'"*

Becca Fitzpatrick

■ Personal

Born February 3, 1979, in Ogden, UT; married, 2000; husband's name Justin; children: two sons. *Education:* Brigham Young University, B.A. (community health), 2001. *Hobbies and other interests:* Running, gardening, reading.

■ Addresses

Home—Timnath, CO. *Agent*—Catherine Drayton, InkWell Management, 521 5th Ave., 26th Fl., New York, NY 10175. *E-mail*—becca@beccafitzpatrick. com.

■ Career

Novelist. Formerly worked in an alternative high school in Provo, UT.

■ Member

Sisters in Crime.

■ Awards, Honors

Young Adults' Choices, International Reading Association, for *Hush, Hush;* has also received honors from state reading associations.

■ Writings

"HUSH, HUSH" SERIES

Hush, Hush, Simon & Schuster Books for Young Readers (New York, NY), 2009.
Crescendo, Simon & Schuster Books for Young Readers (New York, NY), 2010.
Silence, Simon & Schuster Books for Young Readers (New York, NY), 2011.

Author's works have been translated into several languages, including French, Italian, Polish, Spanish, and Swedish.

OTHER

Contributor to *Kiss Me Deadly: Thirteen Tales of Paranormal Love,* edited by Tricia Telep, Running Press Kids, 2010.

■ Sidelights

In a world of fantasy fiction seemingly dominated by werewolves and vampires, Becca Fitzpatrick's "Hush, Hush" series, about a mortal girl's love for a fallen angel, offers a refreshing break from the norm. Fitzpatrick's debut novel, *Hush, Hush,* made the *New York Times* bestseller list in 2009, and was followed by a sequel, *Crescendo,* the next year.

"Everyone can relate to fallen angels," Fitzpatrick remarked to *Albuquerque Journal* contributor Matt Andazola, "because we all make mistakes big or small, and we all want back on the right path."

Fitzpatrick was born in Ogden, Utah, in 1979. An avid reader as a child, she developed a love of mysteries, in particular the "Nancy Drew" series. "She was such a role model to me: brave, independent, unconventional, and smart," Fitzpatrick noted in a *Barnes & Noble* online interview. "She planted in my heart the desire to have the same kind of adventures in my own life." At age eight, Fitzpatrick realized that she wanted to be a writer, choosing her career path after viewing the popular film *Romancing the Stone,* an adventure-romance starring Kathleen Turner and Michael Douglas. "I thought all authors flew to Colombia to rescue their sister from Bad Guys, hunted for treasure, and fell in love with a sexy dangerous guy in crocodile boots," she remarked on her home page.

The Gift That Led to a Career

While attending high school in Idaho, Fitzpatrick attempted a few short stories, although they "never made it past fifteen pages," she told a *Teens Writing for Teens* interviewer. Fitzpatrick added, "I wish I'd written more as a teen. Teens writing for teens don't have to remember what it feels like to be in high school, to fall in love for the first time, to fight for independence—because they're living it in real time." An outstanding student who ran cross-country and played clarinet, Fitzpatrick graduated valedictorian of her class in 1997.

Once in college, she went through a phase where she wanted to be a spy and, according to her home page, sent in "at least a dozen applications" to the CIA. Fitzpatrick married her husband, Justin, in 2000 and graduated from Brigham Young University in 2001 with a degree in community health. She landed a job at an alternative high school in Provo, Utah. She loved working with the students but performing duties outside of her job description, such as "having the principal call me in on Saturdays to operate the copy machine," made the job pale for her.

In 2003, as a present for her twenty-fourth birthday, Fitzpatrick's husband enrolled her in an online writing course. It was in this class that she started writing the story that would become *Hush, Hush.* "I've always been an avid journal writer," she recalled in an online interview with the *Open Book Society,* "but during that writing class, I knew I'd found the one

thing I wanted to spend the rest of my life doing," Fitzpatrick didn't find instant success, however. Five years and close to one hundred rejection slips later, after sending out her fourth revision of the manuscript, Fitzpatrick signed with agent Catherine Drayton, who guided her through another revision until they both were confident that they had something saleable. Simon & Schuster bought the manuscript and, after more revisions, published it in the fall of 2009. "It was a long journey, but worth it a million times over," Fitzpatrick remarked in her *Barnes & Noble* interview, adding, "I wanted to quit, but I love writing so much, I think I would have had to remove my heart first!"

Her publisher's confidence was rewarded when *Hush, Hush* made the *New York Times* bestseller list. "I was in no way prepared for how successful *Hush,*

In Fitzpatrick's debut novel, *Hush, Hush,* a high school sophomore finds herself drawn to a fallen angel with a dark and mysterious agenda. (Simon & Schuster/BFYR, 2009 Jacket photograph copyright © James Porto 2009. Reproduced by permission of the illustrator.)

Hush would be," Fitzpatrick told a *Wondrous Reads* interviewer, "and how many people would fall in love with Patch and Nora's story."

"When I started writing Hush, Hush, *I knew I wanted Patch to be the ultimate bad boy . . . but with a twist."*

—Becca Fitzpatrick, in an *Open Book Society* interview.

The Trouble with Angels

Fitzpatrick's tale centers on Nora Grey, a sixteen year old whose father has been murdered and whose working mother is often traveling, leaving Nora to fend for herself much of the time. In biology class, she is partnered with a transfer student, Patch, who is darkly handsome, aloof, and supremely self-confident. He seems to know much about Nora already. Too much. Yet, despite her suspicions about his true intentions, Nora is attracted to this intriguing stranger. "I wanted Patch to be the ultimate bad boy . . . but with a twist," Fitzpatrick told a *Bitten by Books* contributor. "He hadn't always been bad. In fact, at one point, he'd been really good, and something had caused this big change. While pondering what had caused Patch's fall from grace, the metaphor of 'falling' that I was carrying around in my head became something quite literal—a fallen angel."

As time passes, Nora finds herself in several dangerous situations from which she incredibly and inexplicably emerges unscathed, and she suspects that Patch may be involved somehow. Nora becomes obsessed with and attracted to Patch even as she finds him disturbing and frightening, and she comes to realize that there is more to Patch and his world than she can imagine.

Unbeknownst to Nora, she is in the middle of a battle between ancient beings. Nora, it seems, is a descendent of Chauncey, who is a Nephilim, the offspring of a fallen angel and a human, as well as Patch's sworn vassal. Patch has been protecting Nora from danger only until he can kill her, occupy her body, and transform from a fallen angel into a human. Chauncey intends to murder Nora himself, thus denying Patch the chance to become mortal. When Patch realizes that he has fallen in love with Nora, though, his plan goes awry, and Nora chooses to sacrifice herself, allowing Patch the opportunity to become fully human while destroying Chauncey in the process. Yet Patch rejects her sacrifice, and Nora is returned to the living. The act of saving a human life gives Patch the chance to redeem himself, and he becomes Nora's Guardian Angel.

Hush, Hush earned generally solid reviews. A *Publishers Weekly* critic described the work as "a gripping chiller," adding that "fans of paranormal romance should be rapt." Charles de Lint, writing in the *Magazine of Fantasy and Science Fiction,* stated that he was "was quite taken with the fresh appeal of Fitzpatrick's prose and the whole concept of her fallen angels," and *School Library Journal* contributor Sue Lloyd believed that "the premise of *Hush, Hush* . . . is worthy of contemplation and appealing to teens." Although a *Kirkus Reviews* contributor felt that the end of the novel was "rushed," the same critic praised the "thrilling debut," and Michael Cart in *Booklist* observed that "Fitzpatrick spares no contrivance in her sometimes uneven but always eerie novel of supernatural suspense. . . ."

Heed the Warnings

Crescendo, published in 2010, continues the story of Nora and Patch. In this sequel to *Hush, Hush,* readers learn more about Patch's history, the murder of Nora's father, and the angelic and demonic hierarchy that surrounds them all. *Crescendo* opens with a flashback, as Harrison Grey is warned by a friend he has not seen in fifteen years to get Nora to safety: "Once she turns sixteen, he'll come for her. You need to take her far away." After agreeing to flee with his wife and daughter, though, Harrison is shot to death by a black-haired young man who seeks Nora's whereabouts.

Fourteen months later, Patch and Nora are together. They exchange tokens of affection, but Patch explains to Nora that, as her Guardian Angel, he is forbidden to fall in love with her. Hurt deeply and seeing no future between them, Nora breaks off their relationship and refuses his protection. She begins hanging out with Scott Parnell, an old friend who has just moved back to town and who seems to have secrets of his own, including the ability to project his thoughts.

Nora later discovers sees that Patch is spending time with her childhood nemesis, Marcie Millar. Patch tells Nora that since she dismissed him, the

Fitzpatrick discusses *Crescendo*, **the second installment of her popular "Hush, Hush" series of paranormal romances, at the St. Louis County Library in 2010.**

archangels have reassigned him to be the Guardian Angel of Marcie, whose father, Hank, is a first-generation Nephilim. He also cautions Nora to be on guard against Scott who, he says, is also Nephilim and part of a group, the Black Hand, that plans to resist the Fallen Angels, who possess the Nephilim's bodies for two weeks every year against their will. If the plan succeeds, the fallen angels would then choose to occupy human bodies, resulting in the deaths of countless mortals, since the human body cannot take the strain of being possessed for long.

Then, mysteriously, Nora starts seeing her father in town, but when she follows him, he disappears. Patch enters Nora's dreams, telling her this is the only way they can communicate without the archangels knowing. Nora not only distrusts him but believes that he is the one who killed her father. In spite of Nora's feeling that "everything had come into sharp focus," nothing is as it seems. In fact, Nora learns that Harrison was not her real father, and Patch confesses that he has broken with the archangels by trying to save her: "I'm a private contractor now. I choose my clients, not the other way around."

The final page of *Crescendo* offers a cliffhanger ending that surprised its creator as much as the book's readers. "I wasn't planning on ending [the novel] that way, I was planning to end it the same way as *Hush, Hush*—tying everything up and having a sweet reunion between Patch and Nora," Fitzpatrick recalled in her *Wondrous Reads* interview. "As often happens, I was sitting there writing a little further. Once I'd written those last few paragraphs . . . I kind of smiled in surprise because it was something I didn't see coming."

Though several reviewers felt that *Crescendo* was not as successful as its predecessor, it stayed on the *New York Times* bestseller list for eight weeks after its release. "Fitzpatrick captures the emotional roller coaster of those teen years—while still maintaining her characters (Nora especially) as unique individuals," Sara Gundell remarked in her *Novel Novice* review. Fitzpatrick commented to Gundell that "Nora is a very real sixteen-year-old girl, dealing with first love and betrayal," adding that "she's also dealing with rather evil creatures toying with her mind." While a *Kirkus Reviews* critic described *Crescendo* as "repetitive" and *Voice of Youth Advocates* contributor Lynne Farrell Stover deemed it "overly long," a *Dark Faerie Tales* reviewer observed that "Fitzpatrick dishes up another sexy, gripping read with plenty of danger and thrills. *Crescendo* is a compelling story with clever plot twists, and is sure to have readers riveted."

Fitzpatrick has two more volumes planned in her "Hush, Hush" saga. Her short story, "The Dungeons of Langeais" appeared in the anthology *Kiss Me Deadly: Thirteen Tales of Paranormal Love.* Set 300 years before the events of *Hush, Hush,* the work concerns Patch and Chauncey and sheds some light on their mutual hostility. A graphic novel version of *Hush, Hush* is also in the works.

"As a voracious reader myself, I like to read opening pages that show a character in conflict. I love that wickedly foreboding feeling of sensing that the conflict will escalate into a full-blown crisis over the course of the book."

—Becca Fitzpatrick, in a *First Novels Club* interview.

Fitzpatrick thoroughly enjoys writing for a teen audience. "I love YA—it makes up most of what I read—so I imagine I'll stay here as long as the genre will have me," she remarked to a *Story Siren* contributor. Asked if she had any advice for aspiring writers, Fitzpatrick told a *Galleysmith* inter-

viewer, "Keep a journal and write in it daily. It's practice in getting in touch with your emotions. It's practice in writing first-person. It's practice in writing in general. Plus, you never know when your own life experiences will inspire a story!"

■ Biographical and Critical Sources

BOOKS

Fitzpatrick, Becca, *Crescendo,* Simon & Schuster Books for Young Readers (New York, NY), 2010.

PERIODICALS

Albuquerque Journal (Albuquerque, NM), August 22, 2010, Matt Andazola, "Where Mortals Want to Tread: Angels Fall to Earth as People Look for Hope in Tough Economic Times."

Booklist, October 15, 2009, Michael Cart, review of *Hush, Hush,* p. 60.

Bulletin of the Center for Children's Books, December, 2009, Kate Quealy-Gainer, review of *Hush, Hush,* p. 152.

Houston Chronicle (Houston, TX), January 17, 2010, Tara Dooley, "Light vs. Dark: Vampires and Werewolves, Step Aside—the Angels Are Here," p. 1.

Kirkus Reviews, September 1, 2009, review of *Hush, Hush;* September 15, 2010, review of *Crescendo.*

Magazine of Fantasy and Science Fiction, September-October, 2010, Charles de Lint, review of *Hush, Hush,* p. 49.

Publishers Weekly, October 12, 2009, review of *Hush, Hush,* p. 51.

School Librarian, spring, 2010, Alison A. Maxwell-Cox, review of *Hush, Hush,* p. 47.

School Library Journal, December, 2009, Sue Lloyd, review of *Hush, Hush,* p. 116; March, 2011, Rival Pollard, review of *Crescendo,* p. 160.

Voice of Youth Advocates, December, 2009, Lynne Farrell Stover, review of *Hush, Hush,* p. 419; October, 2010, Lynne Farrel Stover, review of *Crescendo,* p. 346.

ONLINE

Barnes & Noble Web site, http://www.barnesand noble.com/ (September 1, 2011), interview with Fitzpatrick.

Becca Fitzpatrick Blog, http://proudtobeya.blogspot. com/ (September 1, 2011).

Becca Fitzpatrick Home Page, http://beccafitzpatrick. com (September 1, 2011).

Bitten by Books Web site, http://www.bittenbybooks. com/ (December 8, 2009), "Interview, Chat and Contest with Author Becca Fitzpatrick."

Dark Faerie Tales Web site, http://darkfaerietales. com/ (October 12, 2009), "Author Interview: Becca Fitzpatrick."

Falcata Times Blog, http://falcatatimes.blogspot. com/ (November 2, 2009), "Interview: Becca Fitzpatrick."

First Novels Club Web site, http://www.firstnovels club.com/ (July 26, 2009), "Becca Fitzpatrick Interview."

Galleysmith Web site, http://www.galleysmith.com/ (November 16, 2010), "Interview: Becca Fitzpatrick."

Novel Novice Web site, http://novelnovice.com/ (November 17, 2010), Sara Gundell, "Exclusive Q&A w/*Crescendo* Author Becca Fitzpatrick: Part 1"; (November 18, 2010), Sara Gundell, "Exclusive Q&A w/*Crescendo* Author Becca Fitzpatrick: Part 2."

Open Book Society Web site, http://openbooksociety. com/ (December 23, 2009), "OBS Exclusive Interview: Becca Fitzpatrick."

Story Siren Web site, http://www.thestorysiren.com/ (October 13, 2009), "Author Interview: Becca Fitzpatrick."

Teens Writing for Teens Blog, http://teenswritingfor teens.wordpress.com/ (March 26, 2009), "Interview with Author Becca Fitzpatrick."

Wondrous Reads Web site, http://www.wondrous reads.com/ (April 28, 2011), "Author Interview: Becca Fitzpatrick."

Gayle Forman

■ Personal

Born c. 1971, in Brooklyn, NY; married Nick Tucker (a librarian); children: Willa. *Education:* University of Oregon, B.A. (journalism), 1995.

■ Addresses

Home—New York, NY. *E-mail*—info@gayleforman. com.

■ Career

Freelance journalist and author. *Seventeen* magazine, New York, NY, began as senior writer, became contributing writer, 1997-2000; Collins Literary Agency, New York, NY, writer, 2003-08; Mediabis-tro, New York, NY, writing instructor, 2005—. Judge, Amazon Breakthrough Novel Award, 2011.

■ Awards, Honors

Hearst Journalism Award, Association of Schools of Journalism and Mass Communication/William Ran-dolph Hearst Foundation, and Gold Circle Award, Columbia Scholastic Press Association, both 1995, both for article "Denying History"; Harry Chapin Media Award, 1998, for article "All Work No Play"; Book of the Year, New Atlantic Independent Book-sellers Association, 2009, Indie Choice Honor Award, and Best Fiction for Young Adults designa-tion, American Library Association, both 2010, all for *If I Stay.*

■ Writings

You Can't Get There from Here: A Year on the Fringes of a Shrinking World (travel memoir), Rodale Press (Emmaus, PA), 2005.
Sisters in Sanity (young adult novel), HarperTeen (New York, NY), 2007.
If I Stay (young adult novel), Dutton (New York, NY), 2009.
Where She Went (sequel to *If I Stay*), Dutton (New York, NY), 2011.

Contributor of articles to periodicals, including *New York Times Cosmopolitan, Nation, Glamour, Elle, Details, Travel & Leisure, Jane,* and *Budget Travel.*

■ Adaptations

If I Stay was adapted as an audio book, Listening Library, 2009, and has been optioned for film by Summit Entertainment.

■ **Sidelights**

Gayle Forman didn't set out to be a young adult novelist. After working as a globe-trotting journalist and publishing a travel memoir, she made the transition to fiction writing, inspired largely by necessity. As Forman remarked in an interview with Frankie Diane Mallis of the *First Novels Club:* "I had a baby and suddenly I couldn't gallivant around the world and travel to report stories anymore and suddenly we couldn't pay our mortgage and you know how in life when one door closes, another one opens? Well, I was freaking out, thinking I'd have to abandon writing and someone suggested I write a YA novel and this light bulb went on."

Though *Sisters in Sanity,* her debut work of fiction, appeared in 2007, it was actually Forman's second title that lit up the YA literary world. *If I Stay,* about a Julliard-bound cellist who is in a devastating car crash, earned rave reviews and a host of honors, including the New Atlantic Independent Booksellers Association Book of the Year.

Writing for young adults was a revelation for Forman. As she told Michelle Pauli in the *Guardian Online,* "It is a fantastic audience to write for—they are so engaged. They will respond passionately to an article they like and if they hate it they'll let you know. The same is true for fiction and now they can start a blog or Facebook page and get the word out. I would much prefer to have my books published as teen books than adult books."

A Global Citizen

Forman worked as a journalist for ten years before writing fiction, but her love of storytelling began in childhood. In an interview with Jen Wardrip of *Authors Unleashed,* she recalled, "I have been writing, or maybe I should say composing, stories, since before I could write. And I of course wrote lots of Very Deep Poetry in my teens and then short stories in my teens and twenties. But it wasn't until I started college (in my twenties; I took a few years off in between high school and college to travel) when I started studying journalism (this after pre-med didn't pan out) that I started thinking about becoming a writer."

In 1995 Forman graduated with a degree in journalism from the University of Oregon, and as a senior writer for *Seventeen* magazine, she covered stories about children struggling as they grew up in violent, war-torn nations such as Sierra Leone and Northern Ireland. "I met some incredible young people who inspired me to no end," Forman stated in a *View from Here* conversation with Mike French. "People outside of the magazine were constantly shocked and amazed at the stories we did, and dubious that teenagers cared about such things, but of course teenagers did. They were passionate about these stories. When they heard about some young person being mistreated, it didn't matter where this person lived, the reader was incensed, wanted to do something about it. I was constantly grateful to write for a readership that was so engaged."

"What would you do if something catastrophic happened to your family and you yourself were hovering between life and death and were aware of what had happened. If you could choose to go with your family or stay alive, what would you do?"

—Gayle Forman, in an *First Novels Club* interview with Frankie Diane Mallis.

After freelancing for a number of magazines, from *Glamour* and *Cosmopolitan* to the *Nation,* Forman decided in 2002 to spend the year traveling the world with her husband. They journeyed to places such as Tonga, where she spent time with transvestites, and Kazakhstan, where she met role-playing Tolkien fans. Her offbeat travels—and her relationship struggles along the way—inspired her memoir, *You Can't Get There From Here: A Year on the Fringes of a Shrinking World,* a work that Margaret Flanagan in *Booklist* described as "a transglobal attempt to catalog a series of offbeat locales and colorful experiences." "Forman writes breezily and pleasantly," a critic in *Kirkus Reviews* observed, and a *Publishers Weekly* contributor stated, "Armchair travelers will be sated by these smart, well-written tales."

Forman's first novel, *Sisters in Sanity,* also grew out of her journalism work, namely a story she wrote for *Seventeen* about behavior modification boot camps for teens. The book focuses on Brit Hemphill, a rebellious teen who, against her will, is placed in a Utah reform school where she is diagnosed with oppositional defiance disorder. As Brit is introduced to Red Rock Academy's controversial therapies, which include hurling insults at distraught girls and perform exhausting labor in the desert heat, she forms a fierce bond with a quartet of her fellow "inmates," V, Bebe, Martha, and

Cassie, and the four vow to expose the treatment center's abusive practices. Ginny Gustin, writing in *School Library Journal,* noted that "Forman does a good job of capturing teen friendship and angst," and a critic in *Kirkus Reviews* maintained that the author "tackles a usual teen issue—seeking respect and acknowledgment from adults—and puts a new slant on it." "Well written, edgy, powerful," *Kliatt* reviewer Claire Rosser noted.

The Ultimate Choice

Forman admitted to Mallis in the *First Novels Club* interview that her "ideas percolate for a long time and then they sort of erupt when they're ready."

A talented cellist faces a momentous decision after a tragic car accident takes the lives of her parents and brother in Forman's *If I Stay.* (Cover photograph by Brooke Pennington/ Flickr/Getty Images. Used by permission of Dutton Children's Books, A Division of Penguin Young Readers Group, A Member of Penguin Group (USA) Inc., 345 Hudson Street, New York, NY 10014. All rights reserved.)

"If you stay, I'll do whatever you want. I'll quit the band, go with you to New York. But if you need me to go away, I'll do that, too."

—Adam to Mia, in *If I Stay.*

After all, she had written the article that sparked *Sisters in Sanity* a decade before the book's publication. Her second novel, *If I Stay,* emerged in a similar way. There was a question, she told Isabel Wilkinson in the *Daily Beast,* that "haunted" her for a number of years: "What would you do if the rest of your family had died, and you were cognizant of this, and you could choose to go with them? What would you do, if you had to choose? And one day out of the blue, Mia arrived—a totally fictional, fully formed 17-year-old cello player—to answer it."

If I Stay opens as the members of the Hall family— high schooler Mia, her parents, and her younger brother Teddy—plan a drive through the Oregon countryside to celebrate an unexpected snow day. In an instant, however, everything changes, tragically and horribly, as a pickup truck plows into their car, severely injuring Mia and killing her parents and sibling. Though comatose, Mia is acutely aware of her surroundings, able to view the chaos through an out-of-body experience: "I edge closer and now I know that it's not Teddy lying there. It's me. The blood from my from my chest has seeped through my shirt, skirt, and sweater, and is now pooling like paint drops on the virgin snow. One of my legs is askew, the skin and muscle peeled away so that I can see white streaks of bone. My eyes are closed, and my dark brown hair is wet and rusty with blood."

As she drifts between life and death, Mia narrates the day's events, describing the medical team's efforts to save her life; the arrival at the hospital of her paternal grandmother, who encouraged her musical skills and first suggested that she audition for the Juilliard School in New York City; and the frantic prayers of her best friend, Kim. Interspersed with the real-time narrative are flashbacks detailing Mia's memories of her parents and brother, her growing love of classical music, and her complex relationship with her boyfriend, Adam Wilde, a rocker whose band is on the verge of stardom.

As the enormity of the day's events sink in, Mia realizes that she must make a choice: fight for survival and live without her family, or let go. After an impassioned plea from Adam, in which he asks

Forman, here signing copies of *If I Stay*, **notes that teenagers are "a fantastic audience to write for—they are so engaged. They will respond passionately to an article they like and if they hate it they'll let you know."**

her to stay, even if it means she must rebuild her life without him, Mia makes her decision: "Adam is crying and somewhere inside of me I am crying, too, because I'm feeling things at last. I'm feeling not just the physical pain, but all that I have lost, and it is profound and catastrophic and will leave a crater in me that nothing will ever fill. But I'm also feeling all that I have in my life, which includes what I have lost, as well as the great unknown of what life might still bring me."

Drawing comparisons to Alice Sebold's celebrated 2002 novel *The Lovely Bones* because of Mia's out-of-body narration, *If I Stay* was praised by reviewers. Lynn Rashid in *School Library Journal* described the work as "a compelling story that will cause [readers] to laugh, cry, and question the boundaries of family and love," and a critic in *Publishers Weekly* remarked that the novel "will force readers to take stock of their lives and the people and things that make them worth living." According to Elle Wolterbeek in the *Journal of Adolescent and Adult Literacy,* "Mia is a strong and extremely likeable narrator

who engages the reader." Sonja Bolle, writing in the *Los Angeles Times*, also commended Forman's portrayal of Mia, stating that a thoughtful protagonist was necessary "to turn the despair of this beautiful novel into the discovery that, orphaned or not, every child goes on into adult life alone and has to find the strength to leave family behind."

Next Up . . . Heartbreak

With the success of *If I Stay*, many readers wanted to know what would happen next to Mia and Adam, but Forman hadn't considered the possibility of a sequel. As she recalled to Mallis, "When I sat down and started writing *If I Stay*, I wasn't even thinking about it being a published book. . . . I didn't know how it would end and I certainly wasn't thinking about a second book. But once I finished . . . I started thinking a lot about Adam and Mia and where I'd left them. I mean, it certainly is a hopeful ending but the way I see it, they both have some rough times ahead of them."

From this sense of duty to her characters came *Where She Went*, published in 2011. Forman told an interviewer on the *Fluttering Butterflies* blog that *Where She Went* "felt like an entirely new book because this is Adam's story. The book takes place three years later, it is told from Adam's point of view, and while readers will learn what happened to Mia in the intervening three years, it is very much about Adam's own journey. And very much a story about the price of unconditional love."

Forman's third young adult novel again takes place over the course of twenty-four hours. Though he has achieved fame and fortune with his band, Shooting Star, Adam wallows in misery, chain-smoking and gobbling prescription medications to help him combat anxiety, frequently tussling with the media, and dreading his upcoming world tour. The morose rocker still pines for Mia, who he nursed back to health after the near-fatal automobile accident. Upon recovering from her injuries, however, Mia left for Julliard and, quite suddenly and without warning, ended their relationship; the two haven't seen each other or even spoken for three years. "The thing I can't wrap my head around is *how* she did it," Adam states. "I've never dumped a girl with such brutality."

Thanks to the success of *Collateral Damage*, the hit record composed in the painful aftermath of the breakup, Adam and Shooting Star soar to national attention, and for a time Adam embraces the limelight, moving to Los Angeles, hobnobbing with celebrities, and enjoying the company of groupies. He soon tires of the rigors of the music industry, though, and begins feeling disconnected from his fans and band mates, even finding it difficult to rekindle his love of songwriting.

While preparing to tour behind Shooting Star's new album, Adam stops over in New York City and decides to take in Mia's Carnegie Hall debut. After the show, they reconnect, touring several of Mia's favorite haunts, and as the night unfolds, the duo's "awkward reunion sparks a night of painful reminiscing, heartbreaking closure, and hopeful discoveries," in the words of *School Library Journal* contributor Rashid. Like its predecessor, *Where She Went* garnered solid reviews. "Told from Adam's point of view—one laced with cynicism, desperation, and exhaustion—Forman's tale is pitch-perfect," according to *Voice Of Youth Advocates* critic Lauri J. Vaughan. Gillian Engberg, writing in *Booklist*, commented that the author explores "the infinite ways that grief of all kinds permeates daily life," and a contributor in *Kirkus Reviews* stated that the characters' "pain-filled back story and current realities provide depth and will hold readers fast."

Despite the fact that music plays a significant role in two of her novels, Forman doesn't play any instruments. "The thing about novels is that they're like a culmination of your whole life," she told French. "Bits fly in from here and there. So the influences were from all over the place. The years I lived in Oregon were hugely influential, in part because that was a time and a place when music was very influential (this was the Pacific Northwest in the early to mid 1990s when the music scene was just exploding)." Deciding to center two novels around a performer of classical music? "That was a mystery," she admitted to a *Wondrous Reads* interviewer. "Mia arrived as a cellist and I had to go out and listen to a lot of classical music and learn about the cello to do her justice."

Forman's path from journalist to novelist may not be traditional, but it's a logical one, she observed in her *First Novels Club* interview, telling Mallis that "the thing with doing journalism, especially long-form magazine pieces, is that it teaches you how to write a narrative and dialogue and a lot about structure." And while she notes that new projects are coming, she also tells readers not to expect any more sequels to *If I Stay*. Adam and Mia are "happy now," she wrote on her blog. "They're quiet now. I'm happy for them now."

■ Biographical and Critical Sources

BOOKS

Forman, Gayle, *If I Stay*, Dutton (New York, NY), 2009.

Forman, Gayle, *Where She Went*, Dutton (New York, NY), 2011.

PERIODICALS

Booklist, February 15, 2005, Margaret Flanagan, review of *You Can't Get There from Here: A Year on the Fringes of a Shrinking World*, p. 1053; December 15, 2008, Francisca Goldsmith, review of *If I Stay*, p. 50; April 15, 2011, Gillian Engberg, review of *Where She Went*, p. 57.

Horn Book, July-August, 2009, Lauren Adams, review of *If I Stay*, p. 422; May-June, 2011, Lauren Adams, review of *Where She Went*, p. 89.

Journal of Adolescent and Adult Literacy, April, 2010, Elle Wolterbeek, review of *If I Stay*, p. 616.

Kirkus Reviews, January 15, 2005, review of *You Can't Get There from Here*, p. 99; August 1, 2007, review of *Sisters in Sanity*; April 1, 2009, review of *If I Stay*; March 1, 2011, review of *Where She Went*.

Kliatt, September 1, 2007, Claire Rosser, review of *Sisters in Sanity*, p. 12.

Library Journal, February 1, 2005, Alison Hopkins, review of *You Can't Get There from Here*, p. 106.

Los Angeles Times, April 5, 2009, Sonja Bolle, "Let's Hear It For The Good Girls," review of *If I Stay*.

Newsweek, May 9, 2005, Lorraine Ali, "Snap Judgement: Books," review of *You Can't Get There from Here*, p. 57.

Publishers Weekly, February 7, 2005, review of *You Can't Get There from Here*, p. 50; October 8, 2007, review of *Sisters in Sanity*, p. 56; March 2, 2009, review of *If I Stay*, p. 64; February 28, 2011, review of *Where She Went*, p. 59.

School Library Journal, December 1, 2007, Ginny Gustin, review of *Sisters in Sanity*, p. 128; May, 2009, Lynn Rashid, review of *If I Stay*, p. 106; March, 2011, Lynn Rashid, review of *Where She Went*, p. 161.

USA Today, April 16, 2009, Carol Memmott, "Roundup," review of *If I Stay*, p. 7D.

Voice of Youth Advocates, June, 2011, Lauri J. Vaughan, review of *Where She Went*, p. 162.

ONLINE

Authors Unleashed Blog, http://authorsunleashed.blogspot.com/ (August 21, 2009), Jen Wardrip, "Interview with Gayle Forman.

Daily Beast, http://www.thedailybeast.com/ (March 19, 2009), Isabel Wilkinson, "The Next *Twilight?*," review of *If I Stay*.

First Novels Club, http://www.firstnovelsclub.com/ (August 5, 2009), Frankie Diane Mallis, "Interview with Gayle Forman."

Fluttering Butterflies Blog, http://www.flutteringbutterflies.com/ (April 6, 2011), "Interview with Gayle Forman."

Gayle Forman Home Page, http://www.gayleforman.com (July 15, 2011).

Guardian Online, http://www.guardian.co.uk/ (July 24, 2009), Michelle Pauli, "Gayle Forman: Sixteen Inside" (interview).

View from Here Online, http://www.viewfromheremagazine.com/ (February 13, 2010), Mike French, "Interview with Gayle Forman."

Wondrous Reads, http://www.wondrousreads.com/ (May 5, 2009) "Author Interview: Gayle Forman."*

Keith Gray

■ Personal

Born 1972, in Grimsby, England; partner of Jasmine.

■ Addresses

Home—Edinburgh, Scotland. *Agent*—Jenny Brown Associates, 33 Argyle Pl., Edinburgh EH19 1JT, Scotland. *E-mail*—keith@keith-gray.com; keithsg@live.co.uk.

■ Career

Writer. Virtual writer-in-residence for Scottish Book Trust, 2008—. Worked variously as a waiter, truck driver, bartender, clerk, and theme park character. Has served as judge for the Blue Peter Book Award, the Guardian Fiction Prize, and the Kathleen Fiedler Award.

■ Awards, Honors

London *Guardian* Fiction Prize shortlist, for *Creepers*; Smarties Silver Award and special mention, Sankei Prize for Children's Cultural Publishing (Japan), both for *The Runner*; Angus Book Award, 2003, for *Warehouse*; Booktrust Teenage Prize shortlist, 2003, and South Lanarkshire Book Award, 2004, for *Malarkey*; Costa Children's Book Award shortlist, 2008, Booktrust Teenage Prize shortlist, Carnegie Medal shortlist, and *Royal Mail* Scottish Children's Book Awards, all 2009, all for *Ostrich Boys*.

■ Writings

Creepers (young adult), Putnam (New York, NY), 1996.

Hunting the Cat (young adult), Mammoth (London, England), 1997.

Dead Trouble (juvenile), illustrated by Clive Scruton, Mammoth (London, England), 1997.

From Blood: Two Brothers (young adult), Mammoth (London, England), 1997.

Happy (young adult), Mammoth (London, England), 1998.

The Runner (juvenile), illustrated by Clive Scruton, Mammoth (London, England), 1998.

£10,000 (juvenile), illustrated by Mark Edwards, Mammoth (London, England), 2001.

Warehouse (young adult), Red Fox (London, England), 2002.

Mourn Home, Mammoth (London, England), 2002.

Malarkey (young adult), Red Fox (London, England), 2003.

Jonathan Patrick: Poltergeist, Mammoth (London, England), 2003.

Before Night Falls (young adult), Barrington Stoke (London, England), 2003.

The Fearful (young adult), Bodley Head (London, England), 2005.

The Chain (young adult), Barrington Stoke (London, England), 2006.

Ostrich Boys (young adult), Definitions/Bodley Head (London, England), 2008, Random House (New York, NY), 2010.

Ghosting (young adult), Barrington Stoke (London, England), 2008.

The Return of Johnny Kemp (young adult), Barrington Stoke (London, England), 2009.

Hoodlum, Definitions/Bodley Head (London, England), 2010.

(Editor and contributor) *Losing It*, Andersen Press (London, England), 2010.

Contributor of reviews to the London *Guardian* and to the *Scotsman*. Contributor to anthologies, including *Reading Round Edinburgh*, Floris Books, 2007; *Our City*, Polygon Books, 2008.

■ Adaptations

Warehouse was optioned for a television movie; *Ostrich Boys* was adapted for audiobook, Listening Library, 2010, and for a stage play, Birmingham Repertory Theatre, England, 2011.

■ Sidelights

At one time, British author Keith Gray was the unlikeliest of candidate to become a writer. Well into adolescence he avoided books. "I had a big label on my back saying 'reluctant reader,'" Gray noted to *Birmingham Post Online* contributor Diane Parkes. "I saw reading books as a chore. . . . It wasn't until I was a teenager and a friend gave me a book to read, Robert Westall's *The Machine Gunners*, that I realised reading was an adventure." And from that moment, he was hooked on books and reading. "I am writing for the boy I used to be," Gray told Parkes. As a result, Gray's fiction, targeted mostly at boys, has, as the author further noted to Parkes, "lots of adventure and a story that feels a little rebellious." Gray remarked to online *Vulpes Libris* contributor Eve Harvey, "I'm trying to write books . . . that can hook-in reluctant readers. And keep them reading."

In works such as *Creepers*, *Malarkey*, and *Ostrich Boys*, Gray does just that, giving young adult readers a story that hits the ground running—novels that have a message, but that put the action first. Gray's winning formula has been recognized by awards committees: his novels have won England's Smarties Silver Award and a Scottish Children's Book Award, and they have been shortlisted for such prestigious prizes as the Costa Children's Award and the Carnegie Medal. Though initially published in England, the author's works have also found a welcome audience in the United States.

From Reluctant Reader to Writer

Born in the early 1970s in the seaport and fishing village of Grimsby, England, Gray did not excel as a student. "I was an eager rebel and a particularly enthusiastic pain-in-the-backside, but a reluctant reader," Gray noted in a profile he wrote for the

Three teens steal an urn containing the ashes of their best friend and begin a wild journey to Scotland in *Ostrich Boys*, **Gray's award-winning novel.** (Cover art by Ellice M. Lee. copyright © 2010 by Random House Children's Books. Used by permission of Random House Children's Books, a division of Random House, Inc.)

Scottish Book Trust Web site. Speaking with Kieran Fanning in an *Inis Magazine Online* interview, Gray further explained: "There were no books in my house. My parents valued education but they're not particularly well educated themselves and so they didn't read." However, Gray's father did enjoy telling stories, and the author credits that early experience with storytelling as being influential in his ultimate decision to become a writer.

"I attempted suicide when I was 18. Ostrich Boys *isn't about me, it's not particularly autobiographical, but my own experiences have obviously added a lot to the book."*

—Keith Gray, in a *Vulpes Libris* interview with Eve Harvey.

Once bitten by the reading bug, though, Gray underwent a stunning transformation. He recalls coming home from school one day when he was thirteen and, while waiting for his afternoon tea, writing down a story of his own. It was less than a page in length, but it was the beginning of his ambition to become a professional writer. Thereafter, he continued to write longer and longer stories and pass them out among his friends. One of these friends would draw a cover for the stories; Gray then photocopied the pages of the story and sold these at school. He submitted some of his stories to magazines, with little success, and when he decided to try for a degree in English, his poor grades held him back. Instead, he started a program in business at a local school; a dismal score on an accounting exam, however, let him know that this was not his dream career. Gray quit school and began working a variety of jobs to support himself, finding employment in a record shop and even as a mascot in a theme park. All the while he was writing stories and novels in his spare time. Then came the call to let Gray know that his first young adult novel, *Creepers,* was accepted for publication.

Novels of Friendship, Courage, and Loss

The "creeping" of Gray's debut title, *Creepers,* refers to an unofficial youth sport in England in which teens attempt to prowl through a neighborhood at night without being caught. They climb fences, cut through private property, and make their way quickly through backyards without being detected by the homeowners. There are strict rules to this dangerous game, as well as a very specific vocabulary to describe events. One of the most important caveats is that one never goes on a creep without a buddy. Thus, when the nameless shy loner who narrates the tale meets Jamie, a new student at his school, the stage is set for action. The narrator's older brother, Carl, has been the only person to be able to complete the most challenging creep of all: Derwent Drive. What makes this so difficult is the lack of cover, the security lights at various homes, and worst of all, the Alsatian guard dogs at house number 50. Jamie and the narrator decide to take the challenge and almost make it, but at the last minute Jamie is caught by a homeowner, Mr. Doberman. Meanwhile, the narrator panics and runs away.

At school, the narrator now has the reputation of being a coward who will leave a buddy in the lurch. The only good thing to come out of it all, it seems, is that the narrator meets Mr. Doberman's engaging daughter, Ruth. Soon, however, things take on a darker mood when it is learned that Jamie has died in a fire. The narrator refuses to believe it, though, and is seemingly vindicated when Jamie shows up one night and the pair again takes on the challenge of Derwent Drive, successfully completing this hardest of all creeps. The narrator feels empowered, and his feelings of having deserted Jamie on their last creep are put to rest. However, from clues in the text, the reader is left to wonder if Jamie really did die in the fire after all and whether it was the ghost of Jamie that accompanied the narrator on his creep. Gray's first novel was shortlisted for the London *Guardian* Fiction Prize and won praise from reviewers. *Horn Book* contributor Nancy Vasilakis felt that "themes of courage and betrayal are explored within an unusual context; the elements of suspense are skillfully manipulated." Vasilakis also thought that this work "should lure plenty of readers." Similarly, *Booklist* reviewer Frances Bradburn found that readers will respond to the "psychological suspense of an outcast teen trying desperately to salvage his tarnished, albeit slim, reputation." Further praise came from a *Junior Bookshelf* writer who termed *Creepers* "a brillant first novel." The same reviewer added: "The complex culture of creeping makes a convincing background for the interplay of schoolboy loyalties and rivalries."

Gray again examines friendship and includes a supernatural twist with his novel, *From Blood: Two Brothers.* When Chris and Paul use a razor blade to cut their skin and mix their blood, they think they are becoming blood brothers. But the process also fashions a telepathic link; the question lingers if the

A reluctant reader as a child, Gray (left) poses with Lari Don and John Fardell at the 2009 Royal Mail Awards at Queen's Hall in Edinburgh, Scotland. (Copyright © David Cheskin/Associated Press. All rights reserved. Reproduced by permission.)

pair is ready for the unintended consequences of their action. Writing in *School Librarian*, Sandra Bennett said that the book's "treatment of friendship is comic and moving, and the plot is skillfully handled to reveal character and maintain suspense." Written for slightly younger readers, *Dead Trouble* takes on the issue of guns and the danger of firearms. Jarrod and Sean find a loaded revolver and hide it so that they can play with it later. This leads, ultimately, to the shooting of a deer. *School Librarian* reviewer Gillian Cross termed this work "memorable."

Besides wanting to be a writer when he was a youth, Gray also had dreams of becoming a guitarist in a rock band. *Happy*, from 1998, is the author's "attempt to merge together my two loves of writing and music," as he noted in an *Achuka* interview. In this work, seventeen-year-old Will and his pal, Danny, form a band called Happy. Will wants desperately to make a success of the band and follow in the footsteps of his musician father. The group, with two other musicians in attendance, gets

its first gig, but when a fire at the venue cuts their performance short, Will is bitterly disappointed. He retreats more and more into himself, even cutting off his girlfriend, Beth. Ultimately, Beth and Danny find comfort in each other, and Will, having rejected his friends and band mates, decides to live with his father in London, where he hopes to achieve his dream. Alexandra Fouracres, a reviewer for the online *Chicklish*, found this novel "lively and passionate at times." A contributor for *Reading Matters* Web site also thought that Gray's book deals with a serious teen issue, that is how to know "whether your dream is just a dream, or whether you can take it further and make it your life."

Misfits Aplenty

Gray's award-winning 2002 novel, *Warehouse*, is set in a small northern English town, where a community of runaways have sought shelter at a derelict dockside warehouse. Less a novel than a collection of interlinked stories, the work presents a rather hopeful picture of a makeshift community. London *Guardian* reviewer Kevin Crossley-Holland felt like the novel "reads as if it actually happened." Crossley-Holland added: "It's a wonderfully convincing, funny, hurtful, pulsing account of a society within a society—a group of young outcasts living together, . . . bound by loyalties, riven by betrayal. It's foul and grim yet warm and moral." A contributor for the online *Reading Matters* also had a high assessment of this "brilliant" work, noting that "everyone [at the warehouse] understands about having problems, and needing a little time and space to work them out for yourself." Similarly, Fouracres called *Warehouse* "a very original novel" as well as an "intriguing read."

Malarkey, Gray's 2003 novel, takes its title from the book's protagonist, John Malarkey, who is the new kid at a tough school, Brook High. Malarkey had a difficult time of it at his previous high school, and he vows to keep a low profile at Brook. He forgets this resolution, however, when he helps a girl named Mary Chase, who is in a difficult and embarrassing situation. But his bid at helpfulness blows up in Malarkey's face, for now he is accused of a scam involving stolen report cards. The teacher who accuses Malarkey of this crime gives the new student just twenty-four hours to prove his innocence.

Malarkey is at a loss; he must track down Mary so that she can corroborate his story, but soon it becomes apparent to Malarkey that the chance meeting with her was not so accidental after all. In fact, he has been set up to take the fall for this illicit operation, one of many run by a sinister and dangerous underground "mafia" of students at the school, recognized by their black Adidas sneakers.

An advocate for literacy, Gray often travels to schools and libraries in the United Kingdom, including the St. Ninians Community Library in Scotland. (Copyright © 2010 St. Ninians Library, Stirling Council Libraries and Archives. All rights reserved. Reproduced by permission.)

He soon learns that the head of this band of student criminals is a boy named Freddie Cloth, and that Mary is Freddie's girlfriend. Cloth and his gang get wind of Malarkey's investigation and threaten him, but with the deadline looming, Malarkey knows that he cannot back off his pursuit of the truth. This novel earned praise from numerous reviewers. Writing in the *Guardian Online,* Julia Eccleshare found the work "compelling," further terming it a "tense thriller founded on convincing psychology." Kit Spring, reviewing the novel for the London *Observer,* felt it is a "fast-paced read" that is at once "ingenious and exciting."

Rites of Passage

In *The Fearful,* Gray devises a metaphorical tale about faith and the difficulty of believing in the unseen in the modern world. The roots of the novel begin in 1699 when William Milmullen, a resident of Moutonby, takes several of his pupils to a nearby lake, only to see them—so he later declares—devoured by a horrible creature that rose from the depths of the lake. Ever since that time, the Milmullen family has devoted itself to being the guardians of the creature called the Mourn; every Milmullen son becomes a Mourner at age sixteen, throwing livestock into the lake to appease the monster below. Centuries later, the Milmullen family still practices its ancient rite, but residents of Moutonby are embarrassed by the ritual and believe that the William Milmullen simply killed the six students and used the lie of a monster to cover up for his crimes. Tim Milmullen is soon to turn sixteen, but he is no longer sure he believes in this ritual nor in his father's guarantees about its veracity. Tim is caught between his desire to end the practice and his fear that the town may be in danger without a Mourner. An *Achuka* reviewer called *The Fearful* a "dense, thoughtful and thought-provoking novel that demands careful reading providing ample reward through its sociological and implicit religious comment as well as its lithe determination to avoid the condemnation of any systems of belief or world views." Further praise came from *Bookseller* reviewer Anna Gibbons, who noted that this work is "more than just an intelligent piece of writing, it's also an incredibly brave one." Similarly, a *Kirkus Reviews* writer found this book "an unusual and entertaining read."

Ostrich Boys expands Gray's reach into gritty realism. After attending a funeral for their friend, Ross, three teens—Blake, Kenny, and Sim—kidnap the dead boy's ashes in order to bury him in the town of Ross, Scotland, where their pal had always talked of traveling one day. Though it is believed that Ross was run over by a car, his death might not have been an accident after all. In fact, he might have committed suicide by riding his bike into the traffic, and his friends have simply blinded themselves to this glaring truth. Such a revelation comes toward the finale of this "smart, touching novel with an ending that packs an emotional wallop," as *School Library Journal* reviewer Geri Diorio described it.

"The scariest times are when the light that had been your only Cover is switched off. Anybody inside can see perfectly then. And you don't know whether they're watching or not. This is quite simply known as a Nastie. They're not the best of situations to be in."

—From the opening chapter of *Creepers.*

A *Kirkus Reviews* contributor felt that Gray's cast of characters "strut, preen, pose and fret in a way that will instantly be recognized by any teenage boy." A *Publishers Weekly* reviewer dubbed this novel an "unusual twist on the road trip trope and a touching story of teenage friendship," while *Booklist* contributor Michael Cart thought that the boys' "adventures en route are often diverting, and the big reveal invites some rethinking of the meaning of hypocrisy." A *Bookbag* Web site reviewer termed the novel a "a wonderful book, beautifully written, cleverly written, humorously written, humanely written." Online *Vulpes Libris* reviewer Harvey dubbed it an "exhilarating book . . . full of humour and banter and arguments and mishaps." Harvey added that this novel is a "finely crafted piece of literature, the writing is truly outstanding and the build up of tension as the problems the boys encounter mount up leads to frantic page turning."

Books Are for Life, Not Just for Homework

Explaining his writing process in his *Achuka* interview, Gray commented: "I seem to get my best writing done during the night. I like to get the day out of the way and then stay up till the early hours of the morning with a big pot of coffee and some good music in the background. I listen to a lot of music when I write. I use it to help influence my mood depending on what kind of scene I'm writing. Aggressive music for a fight scene, romantic music for a romantic scene." Speaking with Fanning in his interview for *Inis Magazine Online*, Gray further explained his writing technique and his goals as a writer: "I write about teenagers for teenagers. I am standing shoulder to shoulder with the young person, looking forward, whereas he is looking back over his shoulder at the teenager. So when I say I don't patronise my audience, I mean I try to be a ventriloquist. I put my feet in my character's shoes and write as if I was that character." The author added to Harvey: "I never plan my books. I like to surprise myself along the way. And I've rarely got a clue how a book is going to finish until I actually get there."

Discussing the importance of literature with Fanning, Gray stated, "Books are for life, not just for homework." In his 2006 novel *The Chain*, Gray has his young character Kate, speak for him in this regard, as well: "She knew that books could make you laugh, or make you cry. They could be thrilling, or romantic, or scare you. They could take you all around the world, and beyond. They could make you see things from someone else's point of view. They could challenge you. They could help you understand. They could bring comfort. So much. So very much. Kate thought that books could be shared."

■ Biographical and Critical Sources

BOOKS

Gray, Keith, *The Chain*, Barrington Stoke (London, England), 2006.

PERIODICALS

Booklist, February 1, 1998, Frances Bradburn, review of *Creepers*, p. 911; February 1, 2010, Michael Cart, review of *Ostrich Boys*, p. 38.

Books, April, 1996, review of *Creepers*, p. 26; summer, 1998, review of *Happy*, p. 19.

Bookseller, February 18, 2005, review of *The Fearful*, p. 37; May 19, 2006, Anna Gibbons, review of *The Fearful*, p. 22.

Books for Keeps, July, 1996, review of *Creepers*, p. 13; March, 1997, review of *Creepers*, p. 27; January, 2003, review of *Warehouse*, p. 27; May, 2003, review of *Happy*, p. 26.

Bulletin of the Center for Children's Books, January, 1998, review of *Creepers*, pp. 160-161.

Children's Book Review Service, November, 1997, review of *Creepers*, p. 34.

Guardian (London, England), October 12, 2002, Kevin Crossley-Holland, review of *Warehouse*.

Horn Book, September-October, 1997, Nancy Vasilakis, review of *Creepers*, p. 570.

Junior Bookshelf, October, 1996, review of *Creepers*, pp. 201-202.

Kirkus Reviews, September 15, 1997, review of *Creepers*, p. 1457; July 1, 2008, review of *The Fearful*; February 15, 2010, review of *Ostrich Boys*.

Observer (London, England), May 25, 2003, Kit Spring, review of *Malarkey*.

Publishers Weekly, February 8, 2010, review of *Ostrich Boys*, p. 52.

School Librarian, November, 1996, review of *Creepers*, p. 170; August, 1997, Sandra Bennett, review of *From Blood: Two Brothers*, p. 158, Susan Hamlyn, review of *Hunting the Cat*, p. 158; summer, 1998, Gillian Cross, review of *Dead Trouble*, pp. 78-79; autumn, 2002, review of *Warehouse*, p. 27; summer, 2003, review of *Happy*, p. 99; winter, 2003, review of *Malarkey*, p. 210; summer, 2005, review of *The Runner*, p. 99, and Gerry McSourley, review of *The Fearful*, p. 102; autumn, 2006, Sophie Smiley, review of *The Chain*, p. 154; winter, 2006, review of *The Fearful*, p. 207; spring, 2009, Janet Sims, "Our City," p. 42.

School Library Journal, February, 2010, Geri Diorio, review of *Ostrich Boys*, p. 110.

Times Educational Supplement (London, England), June 20, 1997, review of *From Blood*, p. 7; March 18, 2005, Jan Mark, "Boys to Men," review of *The Fearful*, p. C19.

ONLINE

Achuka Web site, http://www.achuka.com/ (January 3, 2003), interview with Gray; (September 9, 2006), review of *The Fearful*.

Birmingham Post Online, http://www.birminghampost.net/ (July 8, 2011), Diane Parkes, "Keith Gray's Words Are Given Life with *Ostrich Boys*."

Bookbag Web site, http://www.thebookbag.co.uk/ (September 12, 2011), review of *Ostrich Boys*.

Chicklish Blog, http://keris.typepad.com/ (September 12, 2011), Alexandra Fouracres, reviews of *Malarkey*, *Warehouse*, and *Happy*.

Chronicle Live, http://www.chroniclelive.co.ik/ (November 10, 2009), Dean Golden, review of *The Fearful*.

Contemporary Writers Web site, http://www.contemporarywriters.com/ (September 12, 2001), Jasmine Fassl, "Keith Gray."

Guardian Online, http://books.guardian.co.uk/ (September 12, 2011), Julia Eccleshare, review of *Malarkey.*

Inis Magazine Online, http://www.inismagazine.ie/ (September 12, 2011), Kieran Fanning, "Books Are for Life, Not Just for Homework."

Jenny Brown Associates Web site, http://www.jennybrownassociates.com/ (September 12, 2011), "Keith Gray."

Random House Group Web site, http://www.randomhouse.co.uk/ (September 12, 2011), "Author: Keith Gray."

Reading Matters Web site, http://www.readingmatters.co.uk/ (November 10, 2009), review of *Warehouse;* review of *Happy.*

Scottish Book Trust Web site, http://www.scottishbooktrust.com/ (September 12, 2011), "Keith Gray."

Vulpes Libris Blog, http://bulpeslibris.wordpress.com/ (July 5, 2008), Eve Harvey, review of *Ostrich Boys;* (July 30, 2008), Eve Harvey, "Interview with Keith Gray."

Write Away! Teachers' Centre Web site, http://improbability.ultralab.net/writeaway/ (February 6, 2003), interview with Gray.

Writers Online, http://www.literacytrust.org.uk/ (February 6, 2003), interview with Gray.*

Laura Hillenbrand

■ Personal

Born May 15, 1967, in Fairfax, VA; married Borden Flanagan (a professor), 2008. *Education:* Attended Kenyon College.

■ Addresses

Home—Washington, DC. *Agent*—Tina Bennett, Janklow & Nesbit Associates, 445 Park Ave., New York, NY 10022.

■ Career

Writer. *Equus*, contributing editor/writer, 1989—. Cofounder, Operation Iraqi Children (now Operation International Children); consultant, PBS documentary on Seabiscuit, 2002. Has appeared in *Remembrance* (video short), 2002, and on television, including *The American Experience* and ESPN.

■ Awards, Honors

Eclipse Awards for magazine writing, 1998 and 2001; Booksense Nonfiction Book of the Year, 2001, William Hill Sports Book of the Year, 2001, National Book Critics Circle Award finalist, 2001, *Los Angeles Times* Book Prize finalist, and second prize, Barnes & Noble Discover Award, all for *Seabiscuit: An American Legend*; National Magazine Award, 2004, for "A Sudden Illness" (a *New Yorker* article).

■ Writings

Seabiscuit: An American Legend, Random House (New York, NY), 2001, special illustrated collector's edition, 2003.

Unbroken: A World War II Story of Survival, Resilience, and Redemption, Random House (New York, NY), 2010.

Contributor to anthologies, including *Bloodlines,* edited by Maggie Estep and Jason Start, Vintage (New York, NY), 2006. Contributor to periodicals, including *American Heritage, New Yorker, Blood-Horse, Thoroughbred Times, Backstretch, Turf, Sport Digest, Washington Post, Los Angeles Times,* and *USA Today.*

■ Adaptations

Hillenbrand served as consultant on the Universal Studios movie based on the book, *Seabiscuit: An American Legend,* 2003, and the adapted screenplay by Garry Ross was published as *Seabiscuit: The*

Screenplay, Ballantine Books, 2003. An audiobook version of *Seabiscuit* was released by Random AudioBooks, 2001. *Unbroken: A World War II Story of Survival, Resilience, and Redemption* has been optioned for film by Universal Studios.

■ Sidelights

In her bestselling nonfiction titles, *Seabiscuit: An American Legend* and *Unbroken: A World War II Story of Survival, Resilience, and Redemption*, Laura Hillenbrand offers stirring tales of courageous individuals triumphing against great odds. Hillenbrand writes from experience. Despite suffering from chronic fatigue syndrome (CFS), a debilitating malady that leaves her homebound for months at a time, she has forged a successful career as a writer, earning a host of honors for her highly regarded works. Described as "a modern-day Emily Dickinson" by *USA Today* critic Deirdre Donahue, Hillenbrand feels a personal connection to the protagonists of her books. As she told *Wall Street Journal* contributor Steve Oney, "I'm attracted to subjects who overcome tremendous suffering and learn to cope emotionally with it."

Losing Control of Life

Hillenbrand was born May 15, 1967, in Fairfax, Virginia. A competitive swimmer who also loved horseback riding and tennis, she fell ill at the age of nineteen, during her sophomore year at Kenyon College. While driving home from spring break with her then-boyfriend (and now-husband) Borden Flanagan, she became chilled and nauseated, and after arriving on campus, she was diagnosed with food poisoning. Her condition worsened after several days, however, and she found it difficult to rise from her bed in the morning, much less attend class. Three weeks later, Hillenbrand was forced to drop out of college, and she returned to her mother's home in Maryland, where she experienced fever, joint pain, swollen lymph nodes, forgetfulness, and exhaustion. As she recalled in "A Sudden Illness," her award-winning *New Yorker* essay that chronicled her struggle, "A walk to the mailbox on the corner left me so tired that I had to lie down. Sometimes I'd look at words or pictures but see only meaningless shapes. I'd stare at clocks and not understand what the positions of the hands meant."

Over the next several months, Hillenbrand visited a series of doctors, none of whom lessened her symptoms (one internist even suggested her prob-

lems were psychological). Cared for by her mother and Flanagan, who had taken a job in the area and moved into the house, Hillenbrand sought advice from an expert at Johns Hopkins University, who told her she had CFS, a mysterious and frustrating medical disorder that has no cure. When her condition improved slightly, Hillenbrand moved to Chicago, Illinois, with Flanagan, who was attending graduate school, and she began earning regular work as a freelance writer, focusing on the thoroughbred industry and equine medicine for such publications as *Equus* magazine.

"I have an illness I cannot defeat, so I'm interested to see how other people have endured great hardship."

—Laura Hillenbrand, discussing her battle with chronic fatigue syndrome.

In the summer of 1991, while visiting her mother, Hillenbrand decided she was well enough to visit the Saratoga Race Course in New York, ten hours away. During the trip, however, she became seriously ill; back in Maryland, she found herself virtually confined to her bedroom. As she wrote, "The smallest exertion plunged me into a 'crash.' First, my legs would weaken and I'd lose the strength to stand. Then I wouldn't be able to sit up. My arms would go next, and I'd he unable to lift them. I couldn't roll over. Soon, I would lose the strength to speak. Only my eyes were capable of movement." A long bout with vertigo made it impossible to read or write, and it wasn't until 1995, with the help of an infectious-disease specialist who helped manage her symptoms, that Hillenbrand began working again, primarily for *Equus*.

Hillenbrand and Flanagan settled in Washington, DC, in 1996, and during the fall of that year she came across a set of documents about the wondrous Depression-era racehorse Seabiscuit and his hardscrabble jockey, John "Red" Pollard. Fascinated by their tale, Hillenbrand started writing a magazine article that blossomed into a book, a project that took nearly four years to complete and required her to adjust her research and writing methods. "At the local library, I pored over documents and microfilm I requisitioned from the Library of Congress," she stated in her *New Yorker* essay. "If I looked down at my work, the room spun, so I perched my laptop on a stack of books in my office, and [Flanagan] jerry-rigged a device that held documents vertically. When I was too tired to sit at my desk, I set the laptop up on my bed. When I was too dizzy to read, I lay down and wrote with my eyes closed. Living in my subjects' bodies, I forgot about my own."

The Unlikeliest of Champions

Released in 2001, *Seabiscuit* became a literary sensation, spending forty-two weeks at the top spot on the *New York Times* bestseller list, and it was adapted as an Academy Award-nominated 2003 film starring Tobey Maguire and Jeff Bridges. In the work, Hillenbrand scrupulously weaves together the tale of three men—Charles Howard, Tom Smith, and Pollard—who shared little in common beyond their love of horses, as well as the undersized thoroughbred that drew them together. Speaking to *Publishers Weekly* interviewer Lynn Andriani, Hillenbrand stated, "I've tried to write this book for a general audience and I think its biggest appeal is not the sports angle; it's the human angle. I think these people are absolutely fascinating—and would have been even if I didn't care about horse racing."

Howard, an Easterner who developed his riding skills in the cavalry, arrived in San Francisco, California, in 1903 with twenty-one cents in his pocket, seeking wealth and adventure. A consummate salesman and shameless self-promoter, he soon opened a Buick dealership and within twenty years had amassed a fortune, using his money to purchase a working ranch, construct a hospital, and indulge his love of horseracing, with an eye on winning the Santa Anita Handicap, which offered the richest purse in the world, $100,000. In 1935, he opened his own racing stable, casting his lot with bargain-basement-priced yearlings.

Through a series of coincidences, Howard met Smith, a skilled trainer, and hired him for his barn. A taciturn individual known as the "Lone Plainsman," Smith grew up on the American prairie, driving cattle, tracking mountain lions, and taming mustangs. After a twenty-year stint as a ranch foreman, he joined a traveling Wild West show and racing stable, developing a reputation as a patient and nurturing handler of horses, particularly ones that other men considered useless. It was Smith's stellar work with a racehorse named Oriley that brought him to the attention of George Giannini, a close friend of Howard's, who arranged their introduction. In short time, Howard's eye for overlooked racehorses, coupled with Smith's unorthodox training methods, proved to be an unbeatable combination.

In June 1936, while touring Suffolk Downs in Boston, Massachusetts, Smith spotted a hardheaded colt that piqued his interest. A descendent of the powerful and charismatic Man o' War, Seabiscuit certainly didn't look the part of a champion. As Hillenbrand writes, "His stubby legs were a study in unsound construction, with squarish, asymmetrical 'baseball glove' knees that didn't quite straighten all the way, leaving him in a permanent semicrouch. Thanks to his unfortunate assembly, his walk was an odd, straddle-legged motion that was often mistaken for lameness. Asked to run, he would drop low over the track and fall into a comical version of what horsemen call an egg-beater gait, making a spastic sideways flailing motion with his left foreleg as he swung it forward, as if he were swatting at flies." Still, Smith recognized that the creature had heart, and Howard bought the horse for $8,000. Then, Smith and Howard began their search for the perfect jockey for Seabiscuit.

By the time he met Smith, Pollard was on the downside of his riding career. Born in Canada in 1909, Pollard delivered groceries aboard his pony as a youngster, and during his teens he became a fixture at the local stables. At the age of fifteen, determined to join the racing circuit, he ventured to Montana; his guardian, a family friend, deserted him. Pollard persevered, though, working his way through the bush leagues and gaining notice as a deft rider who gained the confidence of nervous, troubled horses. Pollard had his greatest success in Tijuana, Mexico, in the late 1920s and early 1930s, but during this time he also suffered an injury that blinded his right eye; amazingly, he managed to keep this a secret from jockeys and trainers alike. As his fortunes fell, Pollard drifted around the United States, ending up at the Detroit Fair Grounds in August 1936, where Smith was prepping Seabiscuit for a race. Pollard's instant connection with the horse impressed Smith, and the trainer knew he had his man.

With Smith and Pollard working to overcome Seabiscuit's lazy habits and harness his competitive instincts, Howard brought the colt back to California, and his incredible performances there drew national attention in an economically ravaged nation yearning for escapism. In 1938, in fact, the horse was the biggest newsmaker of the year, ahead of U.S. President Franklin Delano Roosevelt and German Chancellor Adolf Hitler. At the height of Seabiscuit's fame, however, tragedy struck: Pollard was involved in a devastating accident that nearly killed him, and Howard was forced to switch jockeys, with George Wolff guiding Seabiscuit to a victory in a long-awaited match race against his East Coast rival, War Admiral. During Pollard's long recuperation, Seabiscuit also pulled up lame a

The 2003 film adaptation of *Seabiscuit*, starring Tobey Maguire, earned seven Academy Award nominations. (Copyright © Universal/The Kobal Collection. All rights reserved. Reproduced by permission.)

number of times, rupturing a ligament in one race, and rumors circulated that he was finished. Both horse and jockey made miraculous recoveries, though, culminating in a victory at the 1940 Santa Anita Handicap, one of the fastest ten-furlong races in American history. "In telling the Cinderella story of Seabiscuit and his devoted trainer, owner and jockey," Michiko Kakutani observed in the *New York Times*, ". . . Hillenbrand, has written an absorbing book that stands as the model of sportswriting at its best."

Seabiscuit garnered the William Hill Sports Book of the Year and a National Book Critics Circle Award nomination, among other honors. Writing in the *New York Times Book Review,* Jim Squires called the book "a flawless trip, with the detail of good history, the blistering pace of Biscuit himself and the charm of grand legend." A contributor in the *Economist* maintained that Hillenbrand's "research is meticulous, the writing elegant and concise, so that every page transports you back to the period," and a *Publishers Weekly* critic noted that the author "unearths the rarefied world of thoroughbred horse racing in this captivating account of one of the sport's legends." According to Kakutani, "Hillenbrand gives us a visceral appreciation of that sport as refracted through the tumultuous lives of Seabiscuit and his human companions, while at the same time creating a keenly observed portrait of a Depression-era America bent on escapism and the burgeoning phenomenon of mass-media-marketed celebrity."

Remarkable Resilience

Nine years after the release of *Seabiscuit,* Hillenbrand presented readers with *Unbroken,* "a meticulous, soaring and beautifully written account of an extraordinary life," reported Monica Hesse in the *Washington Post.* The biography concerns Louie Zamperini, a 1936 U.S. Olympian who survived incredibly harsh treatment at the hands of Japanese soldiers during World War II. Hillenbrand encountered her subject while researching her first book, she told *Newsweek*'s Malcolm Jones: "Louie and Seabiscuit were famous runners at the same time in the '30s. They were both at their peak and both in California." She continued, "Eventually I came across things from later—his war saga—and I wrote his name down. I thought, when I'm done with Seabiscuit, I'm calling this guy."

Interestingly, though Hillenbrand interviewed Zamperini some seventy-five times for the book, the pair never met, due to the author's ongoing battle with CFS; in 2007 she suffered a relapse and was unable to leave her house for two years. Still, Hillenbrand and Zamperini managed to form a close friendship through their phone conversations. "One of the fascinating things about Louie," she told Oney, "is that he never allowed himself to be a passive participant in his ordeal. It's why he survived. When he was being tortured, he wasn't just lying there and getting hit. He was always figuring out ways to escape emotionally or physically."

Born in Olean, New York, in 1927, Zamperini was raised in a blue-collar neighborhood in Torrance,

California. A true hell-raiser, he began smoking at the age of five and drinking at eight. "Thrilled by the crashing of boundaries," Hillenbrand writes in *Unbroken*, "Louie was untamable." After a number of scrapes with the law, he redirected his energies into running, becoming one of the top milers in the country as a high school student and earning a scholarship to the University of Southern California. In 1936, at the age of nineteen, the former juvenile delinquent qualified for the U.S. Olympic team at 5,000 meters, finishing eighth in the event, held in Berlin, Germany, and earning a special audience with Hitler. He also stole a Nazi flag from the Reich Chancellery.

Though Zamperini entertained dreams of winning a gold medal at the 1940 Olympics, the games were canceled—World War II had begun. In 1941, he enlisted in the Army Air Corps, training as a bombardier. Flying out of Hawaii in May 1943, a B-24 carrying Zamperini crashed in the Pacific Ocean; he was one of only three men to survive.

Adrift in a rubber life raft for forty-seven days, Zamperini and his crew members (one of whom died after a few weeks), were attacked by sharks, strafed by Japanese pilots, and scorched by the sun; they subsisted on rain water and the occasional bird or fish they caught. After seven weeks, the emaciated men landed in the Marshall Islands, where they were captured by the Japanese.

Zamperini spent the next two years in a series of Japanese prisoner-of-war camps, which were notorious for their brutality. Zamperini suffered tremendously; he was starved, beaten, and tortured both physically and psychologically. Because of his stature as a former Olympian, as well as his defiant and prideful nature, Zamperini was singled out for punishment by a psychopathic guard, Mitsuhiro Watanabe, nicknamed "the Bird" by the prisoners, who became one of Japan's most wanted war criminals. Liberated in 1945, Zamperini returned to the States, though he was haunted by memories of his abuse and descended into alcoholism. After a

The cofounder of Operation Iraqi Children (now Operation International Children), Hillenbrand (second from left) poses with U.S. President George W, Bush at the White House in 2006. (Copyright © Chip Somodevilla/Getty Images. All rights reserved. Reproduced by permission.)

chance meeting with evangelist Billy Graham, however, Zamperini became a missionary to Japan, and in 1998 he carried the Olympic torch into the host city of Nagano. Now in his nineties and recovered from his post-traumatic stress disorder, he works as a motivational speaker.

Like Hillenbrand's first book, *Unbroken* earned strong reviews. In the words of *Weekly Standard* critic Noemie Emery, "Hillenbrand's master theme is the battle of will and adversity, and here she rachets the idea of adversity up to its most extreme heights." Emery notes that when the author begins describing conditions in "the Japanese prison camps, we are moved into a realm of pure evil, which makes the story not . . . the struggle of will and misfortune but the battle of malice and good. This gives it a grandeur as stark as a Greek myth or biblical epic, and a stature few modern stories achieve." *Spectator* critic Ian Birrell described the work as "an astonishing tale of fortitude in the face of scarcely believable adversity, a cruel odyssey that descends from battling the elements into the darkest hell of human depravity," and Janet Maslin, writing in the *New York Times,* called it "a celebration of gargantuan fortitude, that of both Ms. Hillenbrand (whose prose shatters any hint of her debilitating fatigue) and Mr. Zamperini's." In *Publishers Weekly,* Sarah F. Gold observed that "Hillenbrand's triumph is that in telling Louie's story . . ., she tells the stories of thousands whose suffering has been mostly forgotten. She restores to our collective memory this tale of heroism, cruelty, life, death, joy, suffering, remorselessness, and redemption."

"Seabiscuit's story is one of accomplishment. Louie's is one of survival. Seabiscuit's story played out before the whole world. Louie dealt with his ordeal essentially alone."

—Laura Hillenbrand, remarking on the subjects of her books *Seabiscuit* and *Unbroken.*

Hillenbrand struggles daily with CFS, but she finds that her writing helps sustain her. As she told Jones, "I can't imagine not having this one thing that I still have. Other than my husband, I've lost just about everything else. It is tremendously important to my emotional health that I be able to write. I can't be social, I can't be out there. The books are my way of communicating with everyone else."

■ Biographical and Critical Sources

BOOKS

Hillenbrand, Laura, *Seabiscuit: An American Legend,* Random House (New York, NY), 2001, special illustrated collector's edition, 2003.
Hillenbrand, Laura, *Unbroken: A World War II Story of Survival, Resilience, and Redemption,* Random House (New York, NY), 2010.

PERIODICALS

Atlanta Journal-Constitution, May 3, 2001, Eleanor Ringel Gillespie, review of *Seabiscuit: An American Legend,* p. D4.
Booklist, September 1, 2001, Bill Ott, review of *Seabiscuit,* p. 35; January 1, 2001, Dennis Dodge, review of *Seabiscuit,* p. 900; November 1, 2010, Roland Green, review of *Unbroken: A World War II Story of Survival, Resilience, and Redemption,* p. 14.
Boston Herald, August 10, 2001, review of *Seabiscuit,* p. 42.
Business Week, March 26, 2001, review of *Seabiscuit,* p. 27.
Christian Century, January 11, 2011, review of *Unbroken,* p. 42.
Economist, February 24, 2001, "Three Men and a Pony: America's Seabiscuit," p. 4; November 27, 2010, "Born to Live; War Heroes," p. 94.
Entertainment Weekly, March 26, 2001, review of *Seabiscuit,* p. 62; November 19, 2010, Benjamin Svetkey, review of *Unbroken,* p. 101.
Forbes, March 5, 2001, Mark Rotella, review of *Seabiscuit,* p. 116.
Guardian (London, England), August 4, 2001, Stephen Moss, review of *Seabiscuit,* p. 9; February 19, 2011, Kevin Rushby, "Run to Ground," review of *Unbroken,* p. 7.
Houston Chronicle, November 21, 2010, "POW's Shocking Stories Make *Unbroken* Riveting," p. 15.
Kirkus Reviews, September 1, 2010, review of *Unbroken.*
Library Journal, April 1, 2001, Patsy E. Gray, review of *Seabiscuit,* p. 106; June 15, 2010, review of *Unbroken,* p. 13.
London Review of Books, October 4, 2001, Marjorie Garber, review of *Seabiscuit,* p. 35.
Los Angeles Times, March 18, 2001, Susan Salter, review of *Seabiscuit,* p. 11.
Military History, May, 2007, "Entertainment Industry Sets Sights on WWII Bombardier," p. 8.
New American, March 6, 2006, "Helping Iraqi Children," p. 32.

Newsweek, November 22, 2010, Malcolm Jones, "Amazing Race," p. 51.

New York, November 22, 2010, Sam Anderson, "Nowhere to Run; an Insane Tale of WWII Survival Starring an Olympian and an Ungodly Number of Sharks."

New Yorker, July 7, 2003, Laura Hillenbrand, "A Sudden Illness"; December 1, 2010, Jon Michaud, "The Exchange: Laura Hillenbrand."

New York Review of Books, July 19, 2001, Elizabeth Hardwick, review of *Seabiscuit,* p. 4.

New York Times, March 6, 2001, Michiko Katutani, "No Beauty, but They Had the Right Horse There," p. B7; November 15, 2010, Janet Maslin, "Enduring All Tests, Time Included," p. 1.

New York Times Book Review, March 11, 2001, Jim Squires, "Can Do! Once upon a Time There Was a Knock-kneed, Mud-colored Runt of a Horse. His Name Was Seabiscuit . . .," p. 12; November 21, 2010, David Margolick, "Zamperini's War," p. 20.

Publishers Weekly, January 1, 2001, Lynn Andriani, "*PW* Talks with Laura Hillenbrand," p. 75, and review of *Seabiscuit,* p. 75; March 26, 2001, Daisy Maryles, review of *Seabiscuit,* p. 24; August 16, 2004, "Hillenbrand to Tell Hero's Tale," p. 14; October 11, 2010, Sarah F. Gold, review of *Unbroken,* p. 34.

School Library Journal, November, 2001, Peggy Bercher, review of *Seabiscuit,* p. 194.

Spectator, January 22, 2011, Ian Birrell, "Hell or High Water," p. 37.

Time, April 2, 2001, Jesse Birnbaum, review of *Seabiscuit,* p. 72; November 22, 2010, "The Man Who Couldn't Stop Running."

Times Literary Supplement, July 20, 2001, Alan Lee, review of *Seabiscuit,* p. 10.

USA Today, November 10, 2010, Deirdre Donahue, "Writing Sets Her Free," p. 1.

US Weekly, May 7, 2001, Phoebe Hoban, review of *Seabiscuit,* p. 48; April 2, 2001, Sarah Goodyear, review of *Seabiscuit,* p. 74.

Wall Street Journal, March 9, 2001, Frederick C. Klein, review of *Seabiscuit,* p. W9; November 12, 2010, Steve Oney, "The Defiant Ones: In Her New Book, the Author Of *Seabiscuit* Turns to the Unimaginable Ordeal of an Olympic Athlete and WW II Hero."

Washington Post, March 9, 2001, Jennifer Frey, "Against the Odds: Laura Hillenbrand Surmounts Illness to Cross the Finish Line with *Seabiscuit,*" p. C1; November 28, 2010, Monica Hesse, "Laura Hillenbrand Releases New Book While Fighting Chronic Fatigue Syndrome."

Washington Post Book World, March 18, 2001, Jane Smiley, "Track Star," p. T5.

Weekend Edition Saturday, July 17, 2010, "Horse Racing's Zenyatta Puts the Boys to Shame;" November 20, 2010, "*Seabiscuit* Author's New Hero *Unbroken* by War."

Weekly Standard, June 20, 2011, Noemie Emery, "Staying Alive: The Limits of Endurance in Enemy Hands."

ONLINE

Laura Hillenbrand Home Page, http://laurahillenbrandbooks.com (October 1, 2011).

National Public Radio Web site, http://www.npr.org/ (October 20, 2010), "*Seabiscuit* Author's New Hero *Unbroken* by War."

Seabiscuit: An American Legend Web site, http://www.seabiscuitonline.com (October 1, 2011).*

A.S. King

■ Personal

Full name Amy Sarig King; born March 10, 1970, in Reading, PA; daughter of Lynn and Lynne Sarig; married, husband's name Topher (a cabinet maker); children: Gracie, Livy. *Education:* Art Institute of Philadelphia, earned degree in photography, 1991.

■ Addresses

Home—Robesonia, PA. *E-mail*—asking@as-king.com.

■ Career

Author. Worked variously as a photographer, master printer, and electrician; Word Aid, literacy teacher in Dublin and Tipperary, Ireland, 1996-2004; self-sufficient farmer and poultry breeder in Tipperary, 1996-2004. Presenter at schools.

■ Member

Assembly on Literature for Adolescents, Society of Children's Book Writers and Illustrators.

■ Awards, Honors

Washington Square Fiction Contest runner-up, 2007; *Glimmer Train* Very Short Fiction Award finalist, 2007; Best Books for Young Adults designation, American Library Association (ALA), Cybil Award finalist, and Indie Next List selection, all 2009, all for *The Dust of One Hundred Dogs;* Best New American Voices nomination, 2010; Edgar Allen Poe Award nominee, Mystery Writers of America, Indie Next List selection, Best Fiction for Young Adults designation, ALA, Junior Library Guild selection, 2010, Quick Picks for Reluctant Young Adult Readers designation, ALA, 2011, Choices selection, Cooperative Children's Book Center, 2011, and Michael L. Printz Honor Book, ALA, 2011, all for *Please Ignore Vera Dietz;* Junior Library Guild selection, 2011, for *Everybody Sees the Ants.*

■ Writings

The Dust of One Hundred Dogs, Flux (Woodbury, MN), 2009.

Please Ignore Vera Dietz, Knopf (New York, NY), 2010.

Everybody Sees the Ants, Little, Brown (New York, NY), 2011.

Contributor to *Dear Bully: Seventy Authors Tell Their Stories,* edited by Megan Kelley Hall and Carrie Jones, HarperTeen (New York, NY), 2011. Contributor of poetry and articles to periodicals, including the Dublin *Sunday Tribune, Natural Bridge, Mélange, Kilkenny Poetry Broadsheet,* and *Quality Women's Fiction.*

■ Sidelights

Amy Sarig King, who writes under the name A.S. King, has published three complex and dramatic young adult novels that blend gritty subject matter with a bit of magic. She is perhaps best known for her second title, *Please Ignore Vera Dietz*, a Michael L. Printz Honor Book that concerns a teenager's reaction to the untimely death of her best friend. "I write my books blindly—without knowing where they will take me, so that can be difficult," the author stated in a *YA Bibliophile* interview. "But when it comes to subject matter, I think it makes my life easier knowing that I can help kids get through things that I know many of them will face. Sometimes a kid doesn't have to read about the specific thing that he or she is experiencing in order to relate to it or draw something useful from it. Some subjects are universal. So writing tough topics is a relief to me in many ways because I know it helps."

King was born in Reading, Pennsylvania, in 1970, the youngest of three daughters. She remembers staying up late as a child to read in her bedroom closet, after the rest of the family had gone to bed. "I'd read anything. The weirder, the better. Once I found Paul Zindel, my early teen life was complete," she told Cynthia Leitich Smith in a *Cynsations* interview.

"Is it okay to hate a dead kid? Even if I loved him once? Even if he was my best friend? Is it okay to hate him for being dead?"

—Vera in *Please Ignore Vera Dietz*.

After graduating from Exeter High School, King majored in photography at the Art Institute of Philadelphia, telling Bruce R. Posten in the *Reading Eagle* that she "became instantly obsolete with the beginning of digital photography." King began writing when she moved to Ireland with her husband, Topher, whom she met at the age of seventeen while working as a camp counselor. After two years in Dublin, Topher's hometown, the couple moved to a small farm in a rural area. King wrote short fiction and poetry, raised chickens, gardened, and taught adult literacy classes. "Eventually, I discovered that my stories mirror my life," she told James Blasingame in the *Journal of Adolescent & Adult Literacy*. "They are not linear, they can be surprising, and

they often do not follow rules. I also realized that self-sufficiency and writing toward publication require a similar stubbornness. A lot of people laugh at you and think you're being silly. But you have to keep believing because you're the only person who really understands what you're working toward.

King attempted her first novels while living in Ireland, but she did not have success selling her work. "They were good ideas, bad execution," she recalled to Posten. In 2004 King returned to Pennsylvania with her husband and their two daughters, Gracie and Livy, and continued writing in the basement of the family's rural home. She completed a short story in 2006 that was nominated for an award, and, inspired by this success, she went on to sell some fifteen other tales. "It's amazing how concentrating on the short form for a year made my novel-length fiction more immediate and fresh," she remarked to Smith.

High Seas and Hard Times

King's first published novel, *The Dust of One Hundred Dogs*, was inspired by her time in Ireland. "My exploration of what the Irish endured, especially during [English political and military leader Oliver] Cromwell's time, stirred feelings about the things women have endured throughout history," she told Smith.

The work focuses on Emer Morrisey, an Irish girl whose family is slaughtered during an attack on their village by Cromwell's army in 1650. After escaping the violence, Emer settles in the impoverished region of Connacht, where she lives with her aunt and uncle and falls in love with Seanie Carroll, a youth whose family has also fled the fighting. On her fourteenth birthday, Emer is strapped to a wagon by her uncle, who has sold her into marriage, and taken to the coast, where she is placed aboard a ship headed for France. Arriving in Paris, Emer slips away from her captors and boldly decides to risk her life by sailing to Tortuga, a Caribbean republic known as a haven for pirates.

Once there, however, Emer becomes the property of a mysterious, lovesick Frenchman, but she cannot tolerate her surroundings and stows away on a supply ship, earning the admiration of the captain—and the reward of her own vessel—when she proves her courage during a pirate attack. Her loyal first mate, David, convinces Emer that her talents as a commander can best be used plundering other ships, and she soon develops a reputation as a fierce, bloodthirsty buccaneer.

Pursued relentlessly by the authorities as well as the enigmatic Frenchman, Emer is arrested in the Bahamas and spends nearly a year in a filthy prison.

When the Frenchman again takes possession of her, David comes to her rescue with a fleet of heavily armed ships, and she is reunited with Seanie, who has been serving as a marine. After a highly profitable raid on a fleet of Spanish galleons, Emer and Seanie hope to return to Europe, but the Frenchman hunts them down again, killing Seanie as the Frenchman's first mate places a curse on Emer: she will be reincarnated as a dog 100 times before she can return to human form.

Interspersed with this narrative is the story of Saffron Adams, a Pennsylvania youngster who, from the day she was born in 1972, miraculously recalls every moment from the past three centuries, including events from her canine existences. At the age of eight, Saffron, still holding strongly to her previous life as Emer, declares, "I forged my plan to return to the Caribbean Sea. . . . Finally done with my one hundred lives as a dog, I would one day reclaim my jewels and gold, hold them close to my heart, and live happily ever after." Free to leave her dead-end town and dysfunctional family after graduating from high school, Saffron ventures to the Caribbean, where her plans to recover buried treasure are stymied by a crazed stranger, Fred Livingstone, who is driven by his own powerful memories.

The Dust of One Hundred Dogs was named a Best Book for Young Adults by the American Library Association and garnered solid, if uneven, reviews. According to Blasingame in the *Journal of Adolescent & Adult Literacy*, "Several narrative devices and innovative plot twists make this a novel unlike any other and a literary delight." *Booklist* contributor Ian Chipman described *The Dust of One Hundred Dogs* as "an undeniably original book that overreaches, yes, but only as a byproduct of its ambition," and *Voice of Youth Advocates* reviewer Catherine Gilmore-Clough described the work as a "remarkable and compelling story for readers seeking something out of the ordinary." The novel's mature passages, which include graphic descriptions of battle and sexual abuse, was also noted by reviewers.

Your Secrets Make You Sick

Please Ignore Vera Dietz, King's second young adult novel, was published to even greater acclaim, being named a Michael L. Printz Honor Book by the American Library Association. "When I got the news (of the honor), I just freaked out and started to cry," King said in an interview with Posten for the *Reading Eagle*. "I worked 17 years to get the right words in the right order to say the right things, and to find out that it actually worked I greatly appreciate it."

In King's *Please Ignore Vera Dietz*, a Michael L. Printz Honor Book, a teen is haunted by visions of her best friend, who died under mysterious circumstances. (Cover photograph by Shutterstock. copyright © 2010 by Alfred A. Knopf. Used by permission of Alfred A. Knopf, an imprint of Random House Children's Books, a division of Random House, Inc.)

In King's breakthrough work, the titular protagonist, a sensitive and intelligent high school senior, begins having outlandish visions of her best friend, Charlie Khan, who died, tragically and mysteriously, just months earlier. The apparitions come as Vera wrestles with feelings of guilt and anguish over the loss of her longtime confidante, knowing that she could clear his name of a terrible crime committed on the night of his death.

Inseparable since childhood, Vera and Charlie shared each other's deepest secrets: she has been raised by her dad, a recovering alcoholic, ever since her mother, a former stripper, abandoned their family, while Charlie, whose thuggish father terrorizes his wife and son, entered a disturbing and possibly dangerous relationship with a man known as John, a sexual deviant. During Vera and Charlie's junior year of high school, however, their once close-knit relationship fractures as Charlie, always impulsive and rebellious, begins hanging with a rougher crowd that includes Jenny Flick, a volatile and jealous teen who spreads embarrassing rumors about Charlie to the student body and blames them on Vera, hoping to drive a wedge between the pair. After falling for Jenny's lies, Charlie betrays Vera's trust by broadcasting news of her mother's past to the school.

Vera manages to recover from the shock of losing her friend by making plans for college and landing a job delivering pizza, and when Charlie approaches her just before senior year begins, warning that Jenny plans to harm animals at a local pet store where Vera once volunteered, she turns him away. Vera's suspicions are aroused, however, and that night she catches Jenny setting fire to the store. When Charlie is found dead the next morning, Vera, still angered by his betrayal, tells no one what she witnessed, and townsfolk suspect Charlie's involvement in the incident. Guilt-ridden, Vera starts binge drinking, even keeping a bottle of vodka in her car, enters a relationship with an older coworker, and begins having her strange visions. Instead of being frightened by the apparitions, though, Vera finds the sight of thousands of Charlies appearing at once to be surprisingly cathartic, and she vows to right a horrible wrong.

In addition to the Printz honor, *Please Ignore Vera Dietz* was an Edgar Award nominee and an American Library Association Best Fiction for Young Adults pick. A number of reviewers praised King's use of flashback and her employments of multiple narrators, including Vera's father, Charlie's spirit, and a sentient town landmark. Laura Lehner wrote in her *Voice of Youth Advocates* review, "It's hard to describe how deeply affecting this story is," adding, "The writing is phenomenal, the characters unforgettable." A contributor in *Publishers Weekly* called the work "suspenseful and profoundly human," and a *Kirkus Reviews* critic dubbed it as a "harrowing but ultimately redemptive tale of adolescent angst gone awry."

King told a contributor on the *BermudaOnion Blog* that she hopes her story inspires readers. "I suppose I hope readers of *Please Ignore Vera Dietz* will remember the book when times call for them to act and not be silent, or when times call for them to be brave and help another person rather than turning their back. It's hard to change the world. (Both your small world and the big world, outside.) The only way to do it is to speak up. And the only way to speak up is to face harsh or sometimes uncomfortable things."

Hope and Misery

In a more recent work, *Everybody Sees the Ants*, King again offers readers a narrative featuring a touch of the supernatural. The work centers on Lucky Linderman, a teenager whose life is marked by a series of decidedly unfortunate circumstances. Lucky is targeted at school by Nader McMillan, an unrelenting bully; he finds himself in hot water after devising a controversial survey on suicide for a class project; and his ineffectual parents, busy with their own causes, fail to provide the support he needs. In his dreams, however, Lucky becomes a hero, leading rescue missions in Vietnam to find his grandfather, a prisoner of war who never returned home. The teen also discovers that his thoughts are encapsulated by a Greek chorus of tiny ants, "which adds welcome doses of humor and pathos," a critic noted in *Publishers Weekly*.

Everybody Sees the Ants earned a warm critical reception. In the words of *Voice of Youth Advocates* reviewer Paula Gallagher, "King remarkably channels fifteen-year-old Lucky, creating one of the most believable teen male characters in young adult fiction." "Blending magic and realism, this is a subtly written, profoundly honest novel," Krista Hutley remarked in *Booklist*, and a *Kirkus Reviews* critic described King's third novel a "resonant, uplifting story about not just getting through, but powering through, the tough times."

Discussing the elements of magical realism that appear in her works, King told *Presenting Lenore* interviewer Lenore Appelhans that "in almost all of these situations, those magical elements could be in the main character's head, and not real at all. I don't mean to do this—it's just the way my brain works. I'm not a very boxed-in or literal person. I believe that anything is possible because no one has proved to me beyond a reasonable doubt that this is untrue."

A self-described "pantser" who doesn't extensively plan her novels in advance, preferring to write from "the seat of her pants," King notes that one of her greatest literary influences is Kurt Vonnegut, the celebrated author of *God Bless You, Mr. Rosewater* and *Slaughterhouse-Five*. "He's the one who taught me that, in a way, I can think out of the box," she told a *Montgomery County Public Libraries* interviewer, adding, "He was always difficult to put on a shelf—no one was quite able to figure it out." Despite her seemingly nonchalant approach to writing, King gives serious thought to her characters and plot. "I think themes and messages and the general feeling of a book are a lot like bands and songs," she told a *Greater Rochester Teen Book Festival* blogger. "There are melodies and harmonies and a rhythm section and a percussionist and maybe a horn section and they all work together to make a killer song. So all the themes in a book are of equal value and they all work together to make a great book. None can be more important than the others, and they all help illuminate each other."

"Younger characters tend to have genuine innocence, and can explore certain themes and subjects that adult characters can't approach realistically. I feel this type of character has the potential to change (or at least, challenge) minds—and that will attract me every time."

—A.S. King, in a *Cynsations* interview.

King explained to Smith in her *Cynsations* conversation that she connects well to her "young heroes and heroines" as a writer. "Younger characters tend to have genuine innocence, and can explore certain themes and subjects that adult characters can't approach realistically," she said. "I feel this type of character has the potential to change (or at least, challenge) minds—and that will attract me every time."

■ Biographical and Critical Sources

BOOKS

King, A.S., *The Dust of One Hundred Dogs*, Flux (Woodbury, MN), 2009.

PERIODICALS

Booklist, February 15, 2009, Ian Chipman, review of *The Dust of One Hundred Dogs*, p. 71; November 15, 2010, Courtney Jones, review of *Please Ignore Vera Dietz*, p. 37; August 1, 2011, Krista Hutley, review of *Everybody Sees the Ants*, p. 43.
Bulletin of the Center for Childrens Books, November, 2010, Deborah Stevenson, review of *Please Ignore Vera Dietz*, p. 136.
Journal of Adolescent & Adult Literacy, November, 2010, James Blasingame, review of *The Dust of One Hundred Dogs*, p. 611, and "Interview with A.S. King about *The Dust of One Hundred Dogs*," p. 612.

Kirkus Reviews, January 1, 2009, review of *The Dust of One Hundred Dogs*; September 15, 2010, review of *Please Ignore Vera Dietz*; September 15, 2011, review of *Everybody Sees the Ants*.
Publishers Weekly, February 15, 2009, review of *The Dust of One Hundred Dogs*, p. 129; October 11, 2010, review of *Please Ignore Vera Dietz*, p. 46; September 19, 2011, review of *Everybody Sees the Ants*, p. 62.
Reading Eagle (Reading, PA), October 10, 2010, Bruce R. Posten, "N. Heidelberg Woman Becomes Successful Author of Young Adult Fiction"; January 13, 2011, Bruce R. Posten, "Young-adult Author Wins Silver Medal for 2nd book."
School Library Journal, May, 2009, Mara Alpert, review of *The Dust of One Hundred Dogs*, p. 110; December, 2010, Diane P. Tuccillo, review of *Please Ignore Vera Dietz*, p. 116.
Voice of Youth Advocates, April, 2009, Catherine Gilmore-Clough, review of *The Dust of One Hundred Dogs*, p. 64; October, 2010, Laura Lehner, review of *Please Ignore Vera Dietz*, p. 352; October, 2011, Paula Gallagher, review of *Everybody Sees the Ants*, p. 385.

ONLINE

A.S. King Blog, http://www.as-king.info (August 1, 2011).
A.S. King Home Page, http://www.as-king.com (August 1, 2011).
BermudaOnion's Weblog, http://bermudaonion.net/ (January 18, 2011), "Author Interview: A.S. King."
Compulsive Reader Web site, http://www.thecompulsivereader.com/ (October 9, 2011), Tirzah Price, "Interview with A.S. King!"
Cynsations Blog, http://cynthialeittichsmith.blogspot.com/ (March 12, 2009), Cynthia Leitich Smith, "Author Interview: A.S. King on *The Dust of One Hundred Dogs*."
Dust of One Hundred Dogs Web site, http://www.TheDustof100Dogs.com/ (August 1, 2011).
Greater Rochester Teen Book Festival Blog, http://carlyreads.blogspot.com/ (April 16, 2011), "Interview Marathon Day 4—A.S. King."
Montgomery County Public Libraries Web site, http://montgomerycountymd.libguides.com/ (April 16, 2011), "Interview with A.S. King."
Presenting Lenore Blog, http://presentinglenore.blogspot.com/ (October 13, 2011), Lenore Appelhans, "A.S. King Discusses *Everybody Sees the Ants*."
YA Bibliophile Blog, http://www.yabibliophile.com/ (October 10, 2011), "Author Interview: A.S King."
Yalitchat.org, http://yalitchat.ning.com/ (January 24, 2011), Adrienne Gelbart, "An Interview with A.S King, Author of 2011 Printz Honor Book *Please Ignore Vera Dietz*."*

Jean Kwok

■ Personal

Born c. 1968 in Hong Kong; immigrated to the United States at the age of five; daughter of Shun and Shuet King Kwok; married Erwin Kluwer (a psychologist); children: Stefan, Milan. *Education:* Harvard University, B.A.; Columbia University, M.F.A.

■ Addresses

Home—Netherlands. *Agent*—Suzanne Gluck, William Morris Endeavor Entertainment, 1325 Avenue of the Americas, New York, NY 10019.

■ Career

Writer and translator. Worked as an English teacher at Leiden University, professional ballroom dancer, a reader for the blind, a housekeeper, a dishwasher, and a computer graphics specialist.

■ Writings

Girl in Translation, Riverhead Books (New York, NY), 2010.

■ Sidelights

Jean Kwok garnered international attention with her debut novel, *Girl in Translation*. Published in 2010, the story recounts the journey of a Chinese girl named Kimberly Chang who emigrates with her mother from Hong Kong to the United States in the 1980s. Part coming-of-age story and part tribute to a mother's love and sacrifices, the book portrays the immigrant experience and the differences in it for those of differing ages and talents. In an interview with Amanda Cardo for the online magazine *Sampsonia Way*, Kwok explained the rationale behind the creation of *Girl in Translation*: "It was my hope to put the reader into the head and heart of a Chinese person and to give English-speaking readers a unique experience: to actually become a Chinese immigrant for the course of my book."

Although a work of fiction, *Girl in Translation* has autobiographical touches. Kwok explained to *Access Atlanta* blogger Jennifer Brett that "the storyline and characters are not real. However, it was certainly inspired by my own life, and by the worlds I had seen." Kwok was a five-year-old child who arrived in the United States with not much more than potential, but grew into a multitalented (scholar, dancer, writer) and multilingual (Chinese, English, Dutch) adult. However, the author gives credit to others who helped her reach her goals: she told Jen Betterley of the *Seattlest* Web site that "at every turn, I was helped by people who believed in me and knew what I was capable of better than I did." The author, who now lives in Holland with her husband and two sons, seems to have the knack for flourishing in any setting. In her interview with Betterley, Kwok revealed, "Especially when I was younger, I always felt I had to translate myself from one world into the other. However, I see this as a great gift, because I can now see the world from many different perspectives."

Coming to America

Kwok immigrated to the United States in the early 1970s with her mother, father, and three older brothers. Her older sister already lived in the United States, while another brother and sister were unable to get visas and stayed in Hong Kong with their grandmother for several years before reuniting with

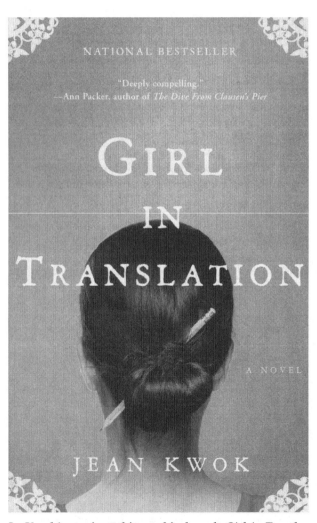

In Kwok's semi-autobiographical work *Girl in Translation,* an immigrant girl from Hong Kong excels in school while toiling in a Manhattan sweatshop at night. (Cover photograph by plainpicture/ballyscanlon. Copyright © Penguin Putnam Inc. All rights reserved. Reproduced by permission.)

the rest of the family. In an autobiographical article for England's *Daily Mail,* Kwok divulged that her family was successful in Hong Kong—"we'd lived in a warm, neat apartment, where I'd had a nanny and my parents owned a general store"—but that her parents were concerned with the political situation there and chose to emigrate. In a feature on the *Time Out Hong Kong* Web site, the author told Clarissa Sebag-Montefiore that her parents "wanted to give us opportunities and freedom, knowing that they would sacrifice themselves in the process." She pointed out in the *Daily Mail* how this decision meant starting over: "Having exhausted all our money in the immigration process, we were burdened by debt: plane tickets, immigration fees and years of lawyers' fees all had to be repaid." The Kwok family lived in a run-down apartment, and the parents took factory jobs.

Like her protagonist, Kimberly, Kwok attended school and then took the subway to the factory to help her parents. In her *Daily Mail* essay, she described how "the combination of the factory dust, the freezing cold at home and the exhaustion from late bedtimes meant that I was always ill with colds." What saved her from a lifetime of menial labor was, as she acknowledged in her conversation with Betterley, the fact that she "was born with the ability to be good at school." Her academic skills earned her a place at Manhattan's Hunter College High School, a school for gifted students where admission depends on both high standardized test scores and passing an entrance exam. Conversely, home economics was not her forte. In a discussion with Jen Chung on the *Gothamist* Web site, Kwok acknowledged that "although I did quite well in school, I was a disaster as a Chinese daughter at home. I burned and spilled everything in the kitchen, took apart appliances I wasn't supposed to, and was (and still am) the worst housekeeper anyone had ever seen. My family didn't think I was smart, because I was dreamy and impractical. My parents were absolutely stunned when I got into Harvard, especially since it was by early admissions."

Kwok observed that most immigrant children who do well in school pursue technical occupations that are well compensated. That was her plan, too. She told Betterley, "My background was so difficult that I never considered doing anything as risky as trying to become a writer. It was only at Harvard that I realized I would never have to go back to the factory, and that I could do what I truly wanted: to become a writer." Buoyed by a full scholarship, she majored in English and American literature while working several jobs to help with expenses. After graduating from Harvard with honors, she spent three years as a ballroom dancer. Kwok explained this apparent detour to Chung by saying, "I've always loved to dance and I think that if I'd been trained when I was younger, I might have become a professional dancer."

Writing proved a stronger calling, however, and the initial spark came from Kwok's older brother Kwan, who nudged her to develop that talent. She recalled in the *Daily Mail* that, when he was sixteen (and already working two jobs), Kwan bought her a diary, saying, "'Whatever you write in this will belong to you.'" The author noted that because of the family's financial situation, "any kind of possession was a luxury. I don't know how he managed to save enough or how—rather than buying sweets or a toy—he'd known to choose something that would nourish my soul. I wrote in it every day. When it was full, I progressed to any paper I could get my hands on. I learned that my own inner world was the most precious possession of all."

Kwok continued that pursuit when she returned to academia, earning a master's in fine arts from Columbia. She told Chung, "The Columbia Graduate Writing Division taught me to be a professional. It was wonderful to have those years mainly to write, although I held other jobs as well to support myself. I learned so much there about craft, language, and passion." While at Columbia, Kwok's talent was recognized and some of her stories were published in a literary journal. Kwok wanted to write a novel, though. She commented in an interview posted on the *Maurice on Books* blog, "I'd received recognition as a writer quite early on in my career . . . but I hit a wall when I tried to write a compelling, well-structured story that would carry the reader effortlessly from beginning to end. It took years to train myself and to find my own process."

Describing her struggles to create what would become *Girl in Translation,* Kwok explained to Cardo that "to make the book a compelling read, I needed to experiment with language and structure in ways that are not possible in a memoir." The author added, "It took me ten years to develop the skills necessary to write this book." Beyond skill development, the time to devote to the work was an issue. She told Betterley, "It was such an uphill struggle to get this novel finished because I had two little children and was also teaching at the university at the same time. I barely slept for years so that I could find the time to write this novel. The reception that *Girl in Translation* has received so far is more than I ever dared to hope for. It is really a dream come true."

Indeed, critics praised Kwok for drafting an intriguing story and creatively using language to mimic an immigrant's struggle to understand the U.S. lan-

Kwok, who moved to the United States when she was five years old, delivers a speech at the American Book Center in Amsterdam, Netherlands, in 2010. (Copyright © 2010 The American Book Center. All rights reserved. Reproduced by permission.)

guage and customs. In a review for the *Irish Examiner,* Afric McGlinchey deemed *Girl in Translation* an "evocative debut" and added, "Kwok's quiet narrative voice steals up on you and captures your heart." Writing in *Booklist,* Hazel Rochman credited the author for her "simple, searing, richly detailed prose." A *Publishers Weekly* contributor judged that "the portrayal of Kimberly's relationship with her mother that makes this more than just another immigrant story." And *Library Journal*'s Shirley N. Quan concluded, "Kwok adeptly captures the hardships of the immigrant experience and the strength of the human spirit to survive."

Depicting the Immigrant Experience

The back story for *Girl in Translation* is the political situation in 1960s China under Mao Zedong. As the book's narrator, Kimberly, recounts, her maternal grandparents "had been landowners and intellectuals, and for that, they'd been unfairly sentenced to death during the Cultural Revolution." Before their deaths, they had spent the family fortune to protect their daughters by sending them to Hong Kong. The younger sister, who played the piano and violin, had fallen in love and married the principal of the school where she taught music. The couple had a baby named ah-Kim. Pa, who was sixteen years older than his wife, died of a stroke when the child was three years old. The older sister, Paula, married a Chinese-American businessman who had come to Hong Kong looking for a wife. Later she would help bring her widowed sister and eleven-year-old niece to America, find them housing, and arrange for Ma to work in the clothing factory she and her husband owned in New York 's Chinatown.

"The road we could follow in Hong Kong was a dead one. The only future I could see for us, for you, was here, where you could become whatever you wanted. Even though this isn't what we'd imagined back home, we will be all right."

—Ma in *Girl in Translation.*

The New York that the mother-daughter duo is confronted with is not the "Min-hat-ton" that young ah-Kim dreamed about—the one with the skyscrapers, bright lights, and the Statue of Liberty (or "Liberty Goddess") welcoming newcomers. Instead, Ma and ah-Kim (soon to be known by the more American-sounding name, Kimberly) live in an apartment that should be condemned: they are the only tenants in the dark building with rickety stairs, broken windows, and no heat, but with plenty of cockroaches, mice, and rats. The factory is a sweatshop, employing both illegal and documented workers. It also skirts labor laws by paying by the piece (at a rate that does not meet minimum wage), not recognizing overtime work, having unsafe air conditions, and allowing children under the age of fourteen to work. Ma and the other workers at the factory need their children to help out in order to meet their quotas. Every day after school, Kimberly must make her way to the shop and assist her mother at the workstation where they sort and finish—belting (if needed), hanging, tagging, and covering the clothing in plastic. Each payday, money is deducted from Ma's check for rent and utilities as well as the principal and interest for the loans her older sister extended to her for medical care, plane tickets, and their visas.

Despite the conditions at the factory, Kimberly feels comfortable there, surrounded by Chinese people. She becomes friends with Matt Wu, a boy a few years older than her who is the unofficial leader of the kids at the shop. Kimberly also revels in the familiarity of Chinatown, with its shops, haggling customers and merchants, and recognizable food. Kimberly's culture shock mostly asserts itself at school. Students slump in their seats, as opposed to folding their hands behind their backs when the teacher is talking; the cafeteria not only seems like a zoo to her, but also the food is truly mysterious; and the students don't stay after class to clean the floors and chalkboards. The English she learned in school in Hong Kong doesn't sound anything like what she hears in her Brooklyn school. Her teacher is more hindrance than help. There is no support for her transition to English, and she fails almost of all her assignments and tests until she grasps the language. Her first success is when she recognizes math problems; she says, "It was like unexpectedly running into old friends."

School becomes bearable when a classmate named Annette shows her kindness. Annette becomes her best friend, sharing her snacks and teaching Kimberly all the things an American sixth-grader should know. The relationships has its constraints, though. When Kimberly confides in Annette that she works in a factory after school, Annette proceeds to tell her dad, who dismisses the idea. The reaction is instructive. Kimberly says, "Annette's friendship was the best thing that had happened to me in America and I was grateful to her for teaching me many things, but that day, I began to understand that there was a part of my life that should remain hidden."

As her language skills improve, Kimberly's keen intelligence becomes evident. When the results of her standardized test scores arrive, the school's stern but kindly principal helps her apply to a prestigious private school for junior-high and high-school students. She aces the entrance exam and is given a life-changing break when the school alters its normal policy by giving her a full scholarship. Even better is that Annette is also a student there. During her six years at the school, Kimberly blossoms. Not only is she a top student, but she does a better job at blending into her surroundings. Her hair has grown out, she is stylishly thin, and she manages to make her clothing seem less cheap than it is. While Kimberly becomes friendly with other kids in her classes, she never socializes with them outside of school. Not only is such behavior frowned upon for good Chinese girls, but she knows she doesn't fit in with them. Also, to visit their homes means she has to repay the hospitality by inviting them to hers, and she is too embarrassed by her living conditions to have anyone see their apartment. Regardless, she becomes popular with the opposite sex, earning special attention from both an American and Chinese boy.

Although she plays the role of an All-American teenager at school, Kimberly has adult obligations and worries in her personal life. She becomes the interpreter for her mother and handles any interactions and responsibilities outside of Chinatown, such as completing tax returns and speaking with store clerks. Ma has tried to learn English, but finds the task too difficult: "I saw her looking through my books sometimes, attempting to sound out a word here or there, but she kept trying to read from right to left. . . . Ma had always been bad at languages. And the two languages were so different, it was as if I were asking her to change her eye color." Kimberly is under constant pressure to hide the facts about her home life, help her mom at the factory, and succeed academically. She is desperate to improve the family's situation and comes to a realization: "School was my only ticket out and just being in this privileged school wasn't enough; I still needed to win a full scholarship to a prestigious college, and to excel there enough to get a good job." The closing chapters of *Girl in Translation* recount the end of Kimberly's high-school experience and then move twelve years into the future, depicting the results of her decisions about school, career, and love.

Writers that Kwok admires include:

Kazuo Ishiguro, best known for his Booker Prize-winning novel *The Remains of the Day* (1989).
Margaret Atwood, and particularly her best-selling novel *Blind Assassin* (2000).
Chang-rae Lee, who published *The Surrendered* in 2010.

Kwok told an interviewer for Portland's *Reading Local* Web site, "I was inspired to write this book because of my mother. I wanted people to know how much a mother could sacrifice for her children because no matter how difficult my own youth may have been, my mother's life was much harder." Using her family's real-life experiences as the basis for *Girl in Translation* in some small way altered them. In an interview with Laura Castellano for *Publishers*

Weekly, the author remarked, "What I think is wonderful about writing and fiction is that you can take something that was difficult, and writing about it transforms it into something positive." Kwok's personal transition is equally inspiring. She told Chung, "The idea that someone can be a child working in a factory one day and a successful novelist a number of years down the road is a powerful one, and in America, we're not afraid to believe in it."

■ Biographical and Critical Sources

BOOKS

Kwok, Jean, *Girl in Translation*, Riverhead Books (New York, NY), 2010.

PERIODICALS

Booklist, April 1, 2010, Hazel Rochman, review of *Girl in Translation*, p. 22; September 1, 2010, Annie McCormick, review of *Girl in Translation*, p. 57.

Christian Science Monitor, May 18, 2010, "Jean Kwok: 'How Very Lonely an Immigrant Girl Can Feel'."

Entertainment Weekly, May 7, 2010, Leah Greenblatt, review of *Girl in Translation*, p. 77.

Guardian (London, England), July 31, 2010, "Review: Fiction First Novels: Catherine Taylor's Choice: *Girl in Translation*, by Jean Kwok," p. 9.

Independent (London, England), October 8, 2010, Emma Hagestadt, review of *Girl in Translation*.

Kirkus Reviews, March 15, 2010, review of *Girl in Translation*.

Library Journal, February 15, 2010, Shirley N. Quan, review of *Girl in Translation*, p. 90.

Publishers Weekly, March 15, 2010, review of *Girl in Translation*, p. 34; March 15, 2010, Laura Castellano, "PW Talks with Jean Kwok: A Girl Gets off a Boat," p. 35; July 26, 2010, review of *Girl in Translation*, p. 68.

St. Louis Post-Dispatch, May 12, 2010, "Chinese Girl Goes from Factory to Harvard."

USA Today, May 6, 2010, Korina Lopez, "'Translation' Speaks Eloquently," p. 4.

ONLINE

Access Atlanta, http://www.blogs.ajc.com/thebuzz/ (April 27, 2010), Jennifer Brett, "Interview with Jean Kwok, author of *Girl in Translation*."

Daily Mail Online, http://www.dailymail.co.uk/ (December 26, 2010), Jean Kwok, "The Sweatshop Was My Second Home: How One Woman Escaped the Poverty Trap."

Gothamist, http://gothamist.com/ (April 28, 2010), Jen Chung, "Jean Kwok, Author of *Girl in Translation.*"

Irish Examiner, http://www.irishexaminer.com/ (June 5, 2010), Afric McGlinchey, review of *Girl in Translation.*

Jean Kwok Home Page, http://jeankwok.net (September 26, 2011).

Maurice on Books, http://www.mauriceonbooks. wordpress.com/ (December 1, 2010), "Author Interview With Jean Kwok."

Melody's Reading Corner, http://www.mel-reading-corner.blogspot.com/ (November 23, 2011), "Guest Post: Jean Kwok's Biking through Life."

New York Daily News, http://www.nydailynews. com/ (May 9, 2010), Jean Kwok, "Our Mothers, Ourselves: A Mother's Day Appreciation by an Immigrant's Daughter."

Reading Local Portland, http://www.portland. readinglocal.com/ (May 5, 2011), Gabe Barber, "On Tour Interview: Jean Kwok presents *Girl In Translation* at Barnes & Noble."

Sampsonia Way, http://www.sampsoniaway.org/ (November 23, 2011), Amanda Cardo, "Jean Kwok and the Girl in Translation."

Seattlest, http://www.seattlest.com/ (May 6, 2010), Jen Betterley, "Debut Novelist Jean Kwok on What it Means to be a Girl in Translation."

Time Out Doha, http://www.timeoutdoha.com/ (October 27, 2010), "Girl in Translation Jean Kwok."

Time Out Hong Kong, http://www.timeout.com.hk/ (June 23, 2010), Clarissa Sebag-Montefiore, "Jean Kwok Interview."

Where and Now, http://www.whereandnow.com/ (November 23, 2011), "Celebrity Travel: Jean Kwok."*

Saci Lloyd

■ Personal

Born December 18, 1967, in Manchester, England; first name pronounced "Sach-ee." *Education:* Attended University of Manchester.

■ Addresses

Home—London, England. *Agent*—Veronique Baxter, David Higham Associates, 5-8 Lower John St., Golden Sq., London W1F 9HA, England. *E-mail*—sacilloyd@gmail.com.

■ Career

Writer, educator, and activist. Newham Sixth Form College, London, England, media studies teacher, 2002—. Previously worked as a cartoonist, as a motorcycle courier, in a band touring the United States, as the head of an interactive team for an advertising agency, and as a script editor for Camouflage Films.

■ Awards, Honors

Grand prize, Green Book Festival Awards, 2009, and Costa Children's Award shortlist, 2010, both for *The Carbon Diaries 2015;* Guardian Children's Fiction prize longlist, 2011, for *Momentum.*

■ Writings

The Carbon Diaries 2015 (young adult novel), Hodder Children's Books (London, England), 2008, Holiday House (New York, NY), 2009.
The Carbon Diaries 2017 (young adult novel), Hodder Children's Books (London, England), 2009, Holiday House (New York, NY), 2010.
Momentum (young adult novel), Hodder Children's Books (London, England), 2011, Holiday House (New York, NY), 2012.

Also cowriter of the screenplay *Burst.*

■ Sidelights

Educator-turned-novelist Saci Lloyd tackles global warming, economic inequality, the rights of refugees, and other complex issues in her critically acclaimed dystopian novel *The Carbon Diaries 2015* and its sequel, *The Carbon Diaries 2017.* Her third title for young adult readers, *Momentum,* posits a frightening near-future London, England, as it dissolves into social chaos. For the politically minded Lloyd, a media studies teacher, addressing the grim realities of the modern world is an essential part of her nature. "I try to write the really big stories of the age and these big stories tend to come with an agenda," she remarked to London *Guardian* contributor Michelle Pauli. "It's hard to be 'hey, it's OK' about a huge chunk of glacier that's about to melt into the sea."

Born in Manchester, England, in 1967, Lloyd (whose first name is pronounced "Sach-ee") grew up in rural Anglesey, an island off the coast of North Wales, where her grandfather moved before opening a factory in nearby Llangoed. After taking several vacations in Anglesey, Lloyd's parents decided to settle there as well, working as smallholders. "My parents were doing the good life thing, but not in that middle class hippy way," she commented in a *British Broadcasting Corporation* interview. "They just liked doing a bit of farming." The offbeat lifestyle and rugged beauty of the countryside appealed to Lloyd, who enjoyed riding her scooter around the isle as a teenager. "I also used to spend lots of time fishing at Caim, to the left of Black Point," she recalled. "I'd sit with the loveliest gents you'd ever meet; unemployed steel workers from Shotton and Liverpool who'd share their ham and piccalilli sandwiches with me."

"I wanted to be part of a movement for change and I wanted to make people laugh. The characters aren't speaking some pre-ordained preachy dialogue, they are truly facing up to what I believe will be a near future reality."

—Saci Lloyd, discussing her motivation for writing her "Carbon Diaries" novels in an interview with Marya Jansen-Gruber.

Lloyd attended the University of Manchester to study linguistics and philosophy, but she dropped out after her first year, frustrated with an exam question about existentialism. Lloyd then entered a period marked by "insane jobs and weirdness," she told Pauli, finding work as a cartoonist, and, later, as a motorcycle courier, which lasted until she broke her leg. She also toured the United States in a

straightedge band, a clean-living subculture that emerged from hardcore punk music, before heading an interactive media team at an advertising agency. It was while working as a script editor for Beeban Kidron, a British film director, that Lloyd first entertained the idea of becoming a writer. "Being in film taught me to trust my instincts and realise that if it's not a big yes, it's a no," she told London *Evening Standard* contributor Viv Groskop.

After returning to college to study media, animation, and design, Lloyd landed a teaching position at the Newham Sixth Form College in London, where she instructs a diverse body of students, often from low-income families who hail from such nations as Ghana and Pakistan. "It's partly from working with those kinds of kids that I write the way I do," she confessed to Pauli. Believing that the curriculum does not adequately prepare her students for life after graduation, Lloyd often introduces political and social topics in her classroom. "If I am honest, I sit there in front of a group of 17- or 18-year-olds, about to go out into the world, who don't know what left-wing and right-wing means," she stated in a London *Observer* interview with Vanessa Thorpe. "When I was younger there was a viable political student movement, but that framework is not really there now. So I teach a lot about the news, facing reality and not dumbing down and hiding things." Lloyd's passions also inform her unconventional teaching methods, she remarked to Groskop: "In class I like to really engage people and have them all shouting, screaming and disagreeing. It is about teaching people how to think for themselves. That's how you get good results."

The Future Is Now

Lloyd's inspiration for her debut novel, *The Carbon Diaries 2015,* came her from interest in global warming, particularly in changes to the Gulf Stream, a powerful ocean current that originates in the Gulf of Mexico and flows into the Atlantic Ocean toward Europe. "When I read about the Gulf Stream [Anglesey is on its edge] shutting down, it was a real personal connection," she stated to Groskop. "I thought, 'That's my Gulf Stream. I can't believe we're about to bring a billion-year-old organic machine down due to our consumption.'"

As *The Carbon Diaries 2015* opens, readers learn that British government officials have instituted a mandatory carbon rationing system, intended to reduce energy usage by 60%, in response to the Great Storm that devastated the western coasts of Great Britain, France, and Spain. Effective January

8, 2015, the program allows each family a monthly allotment of Carbon Points to be spent on heat, food, and travel, forcing individuals, including the book's narrator, Lauren Brown, to limit (or even eliminate) car trips, television and computer time, showers, and other "essentials" of modern life. Lauren, a London design student who also plays bass for the dirty angels, her punk rock group, notices the effects on the city's residents after a blizzard hits Europe, causing widespread damage to the power grid in England. As she writes in her diary: "I'm starting to get scared. There was a line outside Tesco's supermarket for bread, like in the war. It's still bitter cold. I can't remember what it's like to be warm."

As the weeks pass, Lauren's friends and family members react to the energy crisis in vastly different ways. Her sister, Kim, who had planned to spend the year studying abroad, grows sullen and uncommunicative, and after she flagrantly breaches the rationing rules, the Brown family is visited by a member of the Carbon Offenders Recovery Program. Lauren's father, depressed over losing his job, starts a backyard garden and recklessly trades in the family car for a pig, which Lauren dubs "Larkin," after poet Philip Larkin. Lauren's mother, who gamely tries to maintain a brave face, leaves the house to join a women's group headed by Gwen Parry-Jones, one of Lauren's teachers. Meanwhile, Kieran, the Brown's next-door neighbor and Lauren's confidante, opens Carbon Dating, a matchmaking service, while Tracey Leader, the matriarch of a group of neighborhood ruffians, peddles carbon on the black market.

Lauren's personal life is also fraught with drama. Although the teen has eyes for Ravi Datta, a new classmate, she must compete for his affections with Thanzila Amar, the most beautiful girl in school. Lauren's grades suffer as she finds her assignments increasingly irrelevant in a world facing a new era of austerity. And when the dirty angels finally get their big break, a chance to tour England, Lauren must attend a retreat with her family; instead of canceling their performances, her bandmates—Adi, Claire, and Stacey—decide to replace her temporarily with another bassist.

Disaster in London, Drop-by-Drop

During the spring of 2015, a drought strikes Europe, leading to massive forest fires in France and Portugal and armed conflict between locals and immigrants in Southern Spain. The British government enacts emergency measures to ration water, leading

In *The Carbon Diaries 2017*, Lloyd explores global warming, human rights, and other complex subjects. (Cover art by Eric Brace. Copyright © Holiday House Inc. All rights reserved. Reproduced by permission.)

to a march on City Hall in which riot police kill five individuals. In Brussels, Belgium, a meeting of the European Parliament draws more than three million demonstrators, and when police attack a group of vandals, the protests turn violent; the army is called in to restore order, with thousands being placed under arrest. The political upheaval creates a climate of change across the continent, and citizens of Holland, Germany, and other nations vote to join England in rationing.

In autumn a steady rainfall begins, lasting for weeks and overwhelming London's sewer system, causing streets to flood in some areas and raising concerns about the effectiveness of the Thames Barrier, a wall protecting the city from the rising waters of the Thames River. A few days later, a massive storm hits England and heads toward London. With no hope of evacuating the city, Laura and her father join the neighbors in barricading the street with sandbags, then moving their provisions to the upper floor of their home. When the floodwaters arrive, Laura assists in the rescue of a stranded motorist, and, with Adi at her side, she saves Arthur, an elderly neighbor trapped in his home. In the aftermath of the storm, which killed thousands and left Kim seriously ill, the Browns reunite as a family, hoping to regain a sense of normalcy. On New Year's Eve, Laura writes in her diary: "I wish I had some big words to finish, but I've got nothing. I made it thru—but my family, the *angels*, college, the future . . . I don't know. Like Adi says, it's just one day at a time from now on."

The grand prize winner at the 2009 Green Book Festival Awards, *The Carbon Diaries 2015* garnered strong reviews. According to a critic in *Publishers Weekly*, Lloyd's novel "features a nicely developed sense of place, complex and believable characters and an all-too-plausible near-future scenario," and Ian Chipman, writing in *Booklist,* maintained that the work "is transformative without ever being didactic and teases out information with remarkable restraint that never feels like withholding." "The diary format contributes to readers' sense of the frenetic pace of Laura's collapsing world," a contributor stated in *Kirkus Reviews,* and Claire E. Gross similarly noted in *Horn Book* that the protagonist's "voice infuses accounts of blackouts and deprivations, riots and floods, with equal amounts immediacy and tart humor, placing readers squarely inside her world."

Water Wars

Set two years after the events of Lloyd's first title, *The Carbon Diaries 2017* takes place amidst a global water crisis. As 160 nations agree to carbon rationing to help lower greenhouse gas levels, the United States and Spain are experiencing severe civil unrest, China has forcibly relocated more than twelve million citizens, and the threat of a military conflict between Israel and Palestine haunts the Middle East. Now eighteen years old, Lauren Brown prepares to return to London after celebrating the holidays with her parents in rural Oxfordshire, where they own a small farm. When she arrives in the city, however, Laura finds herself kicked out of her apartment, and for help she turns to Claire, the lead singer of the dirty angels, who helps her find housing through Parry-Jones, now running an anarchist collective, and her assistant, Tano Adile.

Revolution is in the air. While preparing for the new school year—and an important gig with the dirty angels—Laura helps with Parry-Jones's efforts to establish a self-sufficient community along the London waterfront; hears disturbing news about the 2, a radical eco-terrorist group whose politics appeal to Laura's boyfriend, Adi; and protests a march by the United Front, a neo-Nazi group that has gained favor in some sections of London. When United Front members begin rioting, police clash with the demonstrators, and hundreds are injured and arrested; those who escaped, like Laura, still face punishment. As she writes in her diary: "Today the Home Secretary gave the police *sweeping emergency powers* to deal with all the protestors. He's even talking about freezing the carbon cards of any student proven to have been on the march. It's no good. I've got to get out of the Docks for a while. It's basically red hot here."

While staying with her parents in Abingdon, Laura discovers that Adi has decided to join the Red Cross, traveling to the Sudan to help victims of the African drought, and Tano will journey to Sicily, which is experiencing a refugee crisis as thousands of Africans attempt to flee to Europe. When the dirty angels are offered the opportunity to tour France with several other activist bands, Laura, Claire, and Stacey enlist their friend, Sam, to take Adi's place; during a stop in Nimes, however, police storm the festival grounds where they are staying, and the band members narrowly escape arrest. After receiving word that Adi has fallen gravely ill, Laura heads to Sicily, where she meets Tano and Parry-Jones, who, after having been imprisoned in England, plans to work with the Red Cross.

The High Cost of Revolution

As fighting breaks out on Israel's border, Great Britain seethes with rebellion in response to the harsh Citizen Tax, and Sicilian officials close down their ports. Laura and her friends decide to flee the island, using Tano's influence to secure a ferry that takes them to Italy. While traveling on foot through a small village, Laura and the others spot armed troops forcibly taking water from a well as locals attempt to mount a protest. She writes: "We looked at each other, nobody spoke—and then—without a word or a sign—we all walked forward and fell in line with the people. *There just wasn't anything else to do.*" After being arrested and spending more than a week in a squalid deportation camp, Laura returns to Abingdon, where she recuperates until she can travel to London.

With winter approaching, British officials grow increasingly worried over the massive protests against the Citizen Tax, which include bombings

Lloyd, here posing with copies of her popular dystopian novels, once stated, "I try to write the really big stories of the age and these big stories tend to come with an agenda." (Copyright © 2010 Newsquest Guardian Series. All rights reserved. Reproduced by permission.)

rumored to be the handiwork of the 2. A December strike outside of London's Parliament, which shuts down the central city, prompts the British Army to enter the city, and Laura again sides with the demonstrators, joining them in an assault on City Hall. Badly injured while trying to escape advancing troops, Laura is rescued by Sam and Adi, and while hospitalized she learns that the government has fallen. Energized by her involvement in the revolution, Laura makes a momentous decision about her future.

Like its predecessor, *The Carbon Diaries 2017* drew praise from the critics. A contributor in *Kirkus Reviews* observed that "despite the novel's grim dystopianism . . . Laura's story features unexpected moral complexity," and Chipman declared that "the friction of living life in times of radical upheaval remains potent, sobering, and awfully exciting." Lloyd's novel "has a deftness and authenticity it is difficult not to admire and celebrate," John Newman commented in *School Librarian*, and Gross stated that readers "looking for thought-provoking questions, challenging new themes, and a gripping tale of global peril will find much to appreciate."

Momentum, Lloyd's next work, depicts a London torn apart by class warfare after a worldwide fuel crisis. The work centers on the relationship between Hunter, a member of the ruling Citizens, and Uma, an Outsider who lives in the slum-like favelas that are controlled by the brutal, gun-wielding Kossaks. The novel, Lloyd told Pauli in the *Guardian,* is "an exacerbated version of now—longer working hours, more restrictions, more police powers, some of the way in which society is heading." In the words of London *Times* reviewer Amanda Craig, "*Momentum* is an edgy, stylish novel with a strong message about the dangers of nuclear power and the growing gulf between rich and poor that older teenagers will find entertaining."

Though Lloyd now teaches part-time so that she can spend more time writing, the bestselling author plans to stay active in the classroom. "I think it's strange if you get 'successful' and then give up what you love and just go and sit at home," she remarked to Groskop. Her mission, as always, "is to write big, rich stories about characters battling with reality." She hopes that her works inspire readers to become active in the political process. "In my experience

If you enjoy the works of Saci Lloyd, you may also want to check out the following books:

M.T. Anderson's *Feed* (2002), which projects a frightening future in which individuals are controlled via an electronic feed inserted into the brain.

Scott Westerfeld's *Uglies* (2005), which explores a world in which physical imperfection has been banished.

Ship Breaker (2010), Paolo Bacigalupi's dystopian novel that received the Michael L. Printz Award.

young people are extremely interested in issues, they are just not interested in a corrupt political system," Lloyd told Marya Jansen-Gruber of *Through the Looking Glass Children's Book Review*. "Yes, it's vital that they get involved."

■ Biographical and Critical Sources

BOOKS

Lloyd, Saci, *The Carbon Diaries 2015*, Hodder Children's Books (London, England), 2008, Holiday House (New York, NY), 2009.

Lloyd, Saci, *The Carbon Diaries 2017*, Hodder Children's Books (London, England), 2009, Holiday House (New York, NY), 2010.

PERIODICALS

Booklist, November 15, 2009, Ian Chipman, review of *The Carbon Diaries 2015*, p. 89; February 15, 2010, Ian Chipman, review of *The Carbon Diaries 2017*, p. 83.

Bulletin of the Center for Children's Books, June 1, 2009, Karen Coats, review of *The Carbon Diaries 2015*, p. 407; July-August, 2010, April Spisak, review of *The Carbon Diaries 2017*, p. 491.

Children's Bookwatch, September 1, 2009, review of *The Carbon Diaries 2015*.

Evening Standard (London, England), January, 26, 2010, Viv Groskop, "The Teacher Who Turned Down a Hollywood Fortune: *The Carbon Diaries'* Teenage View of an Environmentally Damaged

London Is the Talk of Tinseltown—but Teaching in a Plaistow College Is What Really Drives Its Author," p. 22.

Financial Times, October 11, 2008, James Lovegrove, review of *The Carbon Diaries 2015*, p. 18.

Guardian (London, England), June 4, 2011, Julia Eccleshare, "Guardian's Children's Fiction Prize: Schools and Scandals," review of *Momentum*, p. 14; July 15, 2011, Michelle Pauli, "Saci Lloyd: 'It's Not Squids in Outer Space.'"

Horn Book, May 1, 2009, Claire E. Gross, review of *The Carbon Diaries 2015*, p. 301; March-April, 2010, Claire E. Gross, review of *The Carbon Diaries 2017*, p. 63.

Kirkus Reviews, February 15, 2009, review of *The Carbon Diaries 2015*; January 15, 2010, review of *The Carbon Diaries 2017*.

Magpies, May, 2009, Fran Knight, review of *The Carbon Diaries 2015*, p. 42.

Observer (London, England), January 17, 2010, Vanessa Thorpe, "Forget Harry Potter: Saci Lloyd Thrills Teenagers with a Heroine Who Battles Climate Change and Extremism," p. 9.

Publishers Weekly, April 6, 2009, review of *The Carbon Diaries 2015*, p. 48.

School Librarian, summer, 2010, John Newman, review of *The Carbon Diaries 2017*, p. 116.

School Library Journal, May 1, 2009, Eric Norton, review of *The Carbon Diaries 2015*, p. 112; April, 2010, Jane Henriksen, review of *The Carbon Diaries 2017*, p. 163.

Times (London, England), August 6, 2011, Amanda Craig, "Only Six Days to Save the Planet," review of *Momentum*, p. 45.

Voice of Youth Advocates, June, 2010, Donna Miller, review of *The Carbon Diaries 2017*, p. 167.

ONLINE

British Broadcasting Corporation Web site, http://www.bbc.co.uk/ (March 18, 2010), "Anglesey Childhood Inspires Saci Lloyd's *Carbon Diaries*."

David Higham Associates Web site, http://www.davidhigham.co.uk/ (November 5, 2009), "Saci Lloyd."

Hodder Children's Books Web site, http://www.hodderchildrens.co.uk/ (October 1, 2011), "Saci Lloyd."

Saci Lloyd Home Page, http://www.sacilloyd.com (October 1, 2011).

Through the Looking Glass Children's Book Review Blog, http://lookingglassreview.blogspot.com/ (April 27, 2010), Marya Jansen-Gruber, "An Interview with Saci Lloyd, the Author of the Carbon Diary books."*

Melina Marchetta

■ Personal

Full name is Carmelina Marchetta; born March 25, 1965, in Sydney, New South Wales, Australia; daughter of Antonino and Adelina Marchetta. *Education:* Graduate of Australian Catholic University.

■ Addresses

Home—Sydney, New South Wales, Australia. *E-mail*—finnikin@gmail.com.

■ Career

St. Mary's Cathedral College, Sydney, New South Wales, Australia, teacher, 1996-2006. Former commercial consultant to a travel company.

■ Awards, Honors

Children's Book Council Book of the Year Award for older readers, Multicultural Book of the Year Award, Kids Own Australian Literature Award (KOALA), Variety Club Young People's category, 3M Talking Book of the Year Award, and Highly Commended designation, New South Wales Family Therapy Awards, all 1993, shortlist, German prize for literature, 1996, and Fairlight Talking Book Awards, 2000, all for *Looking for Alibrandi*; Australian Film Institute Award for Best Adapted Screenplay, and New South Wales Premier's Literary Award for best screenplay, both 2000, both for film *Looking for Alibrandi*; Children's Book Council Book of the Year Award, 2004, for *Saving Francesca*; Michael L. Printz Award, Young Adults Library Services Association, and Australian Book Industry Award, both 2009, both for *Jellicoe Road*; Aurealis Fantasy Award, 2009, for *Finnikin of the Rock.*

■ Writings

YOUNG-ADULT NOVELS

Looking for Alibrandi, Puffin Books (Ringwood, Victoria, Australia), 1992, Orchard Books (New York, NY), 1999.

Saving Francesca, Penguin Books (Camberwell, Victoria, Australia), 2003, Alfred A. Knopf (New York, NY), 2004.

On the Jellicoe Road, Penguin Books (Camberwell, Victoria, Australia), 2006, published as *Jellicoe Road,* HarperTeen (New York, NY), 2008.

The Piper's Son, Viking Australia (Camberwell, Victoria, Australia), 2010, Candlewick Press (Somerville, MA), 2011.

"CHRONICLES OF LUMATERE" SERIES; YOUNG-ADULT NOVELS

Finnikin of the Rock, Viking Australia (Camberwell, Victoria, Australia), 2008, Candlewick Press (Somerville, MA), 2010.

Froi Of the Exiles, Viking Australia (Camberwell, Victoria, Australia), 2011, Candlewick Press (Somerville, MA), 2012.

OTHER

Looking for Alibrandi (screenplay; based on the author's novel), Currency Press (Sydney, New South Wales, Australia), 2000.

The Gorgon in the Gully (children's book), Puffin Books (Camberwell, Victoria, Australia), 2010.

Contributor of short stories to anthologies, including *Family,* Reed Books, 1994, and *Nothing Interesting about Cross Street,* HarperCollins, 1996. Contributor to periodicals, including the *Sydney Morning Herald,* the *Australian,* and the *Australian Literary Review.*

■ **Adaptations**

Looking for Alibrandi was adapted as a motion picture, 2000. Marchetta's novels have been translated into seventeen languages.

■ **Sidelights**

A common thread throughout Melina Marchetta's novels is the search for identity, including where people belong (in a family or culture) and what defines them—such as the work they choose to do, the friendships and romantic relationships they have, and how they respond to the adversity and grief in their lives. Although Marchetta has forged an international reputation as an Australian author of award-winning young adult books, she has also wrestled with similar questions. In an interview with Noël De Vries on the Novel Rocket Web Site, the author commented, "Identity and displacement are very prominent themes in my writing because when you live in a country that has a 40,000 year history but only has 230 years of western occupancy and you're the daughter of a migrant whose family has only been in the country for sixty of those years, you are constantly trying to work out your place and where you belong."

A Sydneysider

Born in Sydney, Australia, in 1965, Marchetta is part of a large family of Italian descent. She grew up in the working-class district of Concord, lived in the Italian district of Leichardt for many years, and continues to reside in the city. Unlike some children, her educational experience had its ups and downs due to learning difficulties, and as a first grader, Marchetta was delayed in reading. With the help of her mother, who had wanted to become a teacher, Marchetta overcame her learning difficulties, although the experience left a residual shyness and lack of self-confidence.

Because she did not believe she would do well in the upper grades, at age fifteen Marchetta left school to work full time. A course at a business school taught her useful office skills, including typing, and she found work in banks and then at a travel agency. In an interview with *Australian Catholics,* Marchetta explained, "Although I was in the workforce, I was totally confused when I was seventeen. My friends were still at school. I had no idea if I was an adult or a child. I think that's why I will always concentrate on that age group in my writing. Because that's when I was most confused about where I belonged and what my identity was."

Her encounters with teenagers who visited the agency to plan travels abroad after their high-school graduation inspired Marchetta: "I used to look forward to them coming in," she noted in her *Australian Catholics* interview. "It made me realize I really liked being involved with young people." As a result, she decided to return to school and get her teaching credential. Meanwhile, Marchetta was also at work on her first novel, *Looking for Alibrandi,* which she began writing at age twenty-one. Over a six-year period, the book was rejected by six publishers and the manuscript was revised several times. When it was finally published in 1992, Marchetta was already in her second year of college.

Multicultural Hits

The protagonist of *Looking for Alibrandi* is a second-generation Italian-Australian schoolgirl named Josephine Alibrandi. The novel covers Jose's last two years at St. Martin's School, where she is a scholarship student. Although one of the top performers in her class, Jose feels like an outcast because of familial and cultural issues. The financial aid she receives distinguishes from her well-to-do classmates, who are overwhelmingly Australians of Anglo-Saxon descent. Jose thinks to herself that "no matter how smart I am or how much I achieve, I am always going to be a little ethnic from Glebe as far as these people are concerned." Jose doesn't fit in much better in Glebe, though. Her mother had her as an unwed teenager, and Jose's illegitimacy is the subject of both gossip and mild ostracism in the Italian enclave where they live. Jose's overbearing grandma, or Nonna, emigrated from Sicily as a young woman and still observes old-fashioned social mores, lamenting the fact that her daughter and granddaughter don't do the same.

"Believe me, I could write a book about problems. Yet my mother says that as long as we have a roof over our head we have nothing to worry about. Her naïveté really scares me."

—Protagonist Jose Alibrandi in *Looking for Alibrandi.*

Jose has dreams of becoming a rich and influential lawyer and she pines for John Barton, the captain of St. Anthony's school, who is the son of a well-known politician. But she keeps running into—and eventually starts dating—Jacob Coote, who is also the elected leader of his school, albeit one in a working-class neighborhood. Jose has a tempestuous relationship with Jacob, in large part because of her constant grappling with how she fits in and what she wants out of life. Her confused feelings only intensify when she learns that her biological father will be living in Sydney for a year. Although initially dead set against meeting him, she changes her mind when she gets into trouble at school and impulsively calls on him—both to have an advocate and to parade him in front of her classmates. She gradually develops a relationship with her father, and, at the same time, becomes more cognizant of both her grandmother and mother's sacrifices for her. By novel's end, she has grown up a bit, endured some harsh lessons about love and loss, and is better prepared for an unknown future.

In a *Booklist* assessment of *Looking for Alibrandi*, Anne O'Malley commented that "what emerges from this delightful first-person narrative is a strong, fresh, adolescent female voice." O'Malley also commended Marchetta for her "lively, well-drawn characters and realistic teen concerns." A *Publishers Weekly* contributor wrote, "The casting or plot may sound . . . [clichéd] but the characterizations are

unusually insightful and persuasive." Writing in *Horn Book* magazine, a reviewer called the novel "a quintessential girl book, and adolescent readers will relish the friendships, rivalries, and romance—as well as the thrilling bits of rebellion." *Looking for Alibrandi* won numerous awards and became immensely popular in Australia. Eventually it was made into a film, with Marchetta writing the screenplay, and it was released in 2000. The author revealed to De Vries that *Looking for Alibrandi* "was one of the few novels, at the time, that reflected multi-cultural Australia and despite having absolutely no idea what I was doing, its publication has been one of the definitive moments of my life."

After her debut, it would be eleven years before Marchetta published another novel. Her days were kept busy by her job as a teacher at St. Mary's Cathedral College, an all boys' school in Sydney. But she still managed to make progress on other works, as she explained on The Blurb Web site: "I write most of my first drafts . . . during extended holidays and then I spend the year re-working and editing after school." On Penguin's Between the Lines blog, the author remarked that in her next book, *Saving Francesca*, she used elements from St. Mary's—including teacher-student interaction and the physical layout—for the fictional St. Sebastian's setting. Her teaching experience informed her works in other ways, too. She told De Vries, "When I wrote *Francesca* and *Jellicoe*, I . . . had [the male students'] voices in my head all day long. I'm a very strong observer of my world and I believe it's a good talent to have when you're writing." Marchetta began writing *Saving Francesca* a month after the terrorist attacks of 9-11, a time during which she thought "many people were in some state of depression," she noted on the Penguin Web site. She added, "*Francesca* is the most personal of my novels. It was also the novel that proved to me that I wasn't a one hit wonder (yes, I did hear those words often)."

Saving Francesca revolves around sixteen-year-old Francesca Spinelli, who is facing the start of a new school year as part of the first group of female students to attend St. Sebastian's. Francesca is not a trailblazer by choice, but, instead, was forced by her mother, Mia, who thought her daughter would have more academic options there—and perhaps regain the spirit and individuality she showed as a preteen, before she toned down her personality to be accepted by the popular crowd. At St. Sebastian's there are only three other girls from her former school, and Francesca finds something to criticize and dislike about all of them—Tara (social/feminist fanatic), Justine (loser), and Siobhan (slut). Yet because of limited options, the quartet bands together in tentative friendship. They need each

An isolated teen struggles at her male-dominated private school while her mother battles depression in Marchetta's *Saving Francesca*. (Copyright © 2003 by Alfred A. Knopf, an imprint of Random House Children's Books, a division of Random House, Inc. Reproduced by permission.)

others' support as they face a school full of boys, whose responses to them range from indifference, to juvenile and crude behavior, to outright hostility.

Along with the stress of a new school environment and social group, Francesca's home life abruptly changes: her vibrant, energetic, and bossy mother doesn't get out of bed one day—and then another and another. Francesca's biggest critic, supporter, and most trusted confidant is suddenly not available. The diagnosis is depression. Initially, Francesca, her younger brother, Luca, and their father, Robert, attempt to run the household, but they aren't up to the task. Without Mia, they are rudderless. Francesca laments, "If my mom can't get out of bed in the morning, we all feel the same. Her silence has become ours, and it's eating us alive." The siblings are farmed out to different relatives while their mother recovers at home, cared for

by Robert. The separation is hard on both Francesca and Luca, who have an atypically close relationship.

Ironically, the school that seemed such a hardship to attend becomes a saving grace for Francesca. Between classes and her increasingly frequent time in detention, Francesca slowly gets to know some of the boys, including Tom Mackee (slob), Jimmy Hailler (bully), and Will Trombal (arrogant jerk), who become, respectively, buddies and a potential boyfriend. Along with her trio of girlfriends, they provide Francesca with friendship, support, advice, and a reprieve from her family's situation. Francesca begins to gain confidence socially, and her repressed personality makes a comeback. She also becomes more assertive at home, which is an unwelcome change, as far as her father is concerned. The two frequently clash, and her father suspects that Francesca partially blames him for her mother's condition. Yet it is Francesca's stubborn insistence on knowing the truth and even her disrespectful behavior that jolts the family and forces its tentative steps toward healing.

Writing in the *Bulletin of the Center for Children's Books*, Deborah Stevenson observed that in *Saving Francesca* "Marchetta . . . takes what could be a predictable problem novel and turns it into a rich exploration of maturation, identity, family, and friendship." A contributor to *Kirkus Reviews* noted that "Marchetta juggles her many characters deftly, infusing the teens and adults with depth and individuality." In her assessment for *Kliatt*, Claire Rosser suggested that "what makes the novel so much fun and so poignant at the same time is the terrific dialog—witty, cutting, intelligent, outrageous, sometimes affectionate." *School Library Journal*'s Roxanne Burg called *Saving Francesca* "a complex, deliberately paced, coming-of-age story" and praised the "terrific relationship between Francesca and her younger brother." *Booklist* writer Ilene Cooper stated, "Marchetta has a winning way with both teen and adult characters, individualizing them and showing their evolution." A *Publishers Weekly* reviewer singled out "Francesca's compelling voice" as noteworthy and added that the author "beautifully depicts the pain experienced by Francesca's whole family." And *Horn Book* contributor Lauren Adams concluded, "Marchetta proves her craft in this fresh, funny, and heartfelt portrait."

Some Day Your Printz Will Come

In 2006, Marchetta published *Jellicoe Road*, her most structurally complex work. The novel features alternating plot lines—one in the present day and one set two decades in the past. In addition, the author provides flashbacks to events of her protagonist's life that happened from three to more than ten years ago. The present-day story revolves around seventeen-year-old Taylor Markham, whose life has been one of emotional trauma. Her mother, who had her when she was still a teenager, succumbed to prostitution and drugs after her boyfriend disappeared, and abandoned Taylor in the town of Jellicoe when she was eleven. When Taylor was fourteen, a local man, known as the Hermit, committed suicide in front of her. Taylor has no family ties and is ostensibly a ward of the state; as such, she attends the residential Jellicoe School. Her deepest wish is to belong somewhere, but that manifests itself in her distancing herself from—and being reluctant to trust—others. She yearns for more attention from Hannah, her unofficial house mother, who is both involved in Taylor's life and yet frustratingly distant.

Hannah is writing a book, and Taylor has secretly read much of the manuscript. It is Hannah's story, set approximately twenty years earlier, that makes *Jellicoe Road*'s second plot line. It begins with a horrific accident on the Jellicoe Road involving cars carrying two families. A local boy, Fitz, arrives on scene and helps extract the three survivors: brother and sister Webb and Narnie, as well as a girl named Tate. Fitz also removes the five bodies before the cars explode. The orphaned teenagers are subsequently placed at the Jellicoe School. Along with Fitz, they became friends with a visiting teenager named Jude. The five are the founders of the territory wars, a yearly competition between the boarding school kids, the local students (known as Townies), and the cadets, a group of boys (of which Jude is a part) from a military school, whose curriculum includes a six-week stint camping near the Jellicoe Road.

Back in the present day, Taylor is in her last year at the Jellicoe School. She has been chosen as head of Lachlan house, and the departing seniors elect her as the leader of the entire school for the territory wars. Taylor is an unpopular choice, both because of her dismissive attitude toward most of the other students and due to her history with the leader of the cadets, Jonah Griggs. Three years ago, Jonah had briefly aided—and then foiled—Taylor's attempt to run away from school and find her mother. Her sense of betrayal adds an extra layer of hostility to the territory wars. Relationships between members of the other factions aren't much better. The Townies are headed by Chaz Santangelo, who has unresolved relationship issues with Taylor's best friend, Raffaela.

When Hannah suddenly leaves without any explanation or good-byes, it threatens Taylor's emotional stability. She is overwhelmed by her recurring

> *"Griggs is my second reminder to never ever trust another human being. My mother was the first . . . ."*
>
> —Taylor Markham in *Jellicoe Road*.

dream of a boy in a tree, who speaks to her; her fear of the visiting Brigadier, the leader of the cadets who seems to know Hannah; her uncertainty about how to lead a houseful of girls, especially the clingy younger ones; her conflicting feelings about Jonah Griggs; and her need to find her mother and Hannah. The territory wars provide, at first, a distraction and then become genuinely fun. Along the way, awkward friendships and romances develop. As the son of the local police chief, Chaz has access to information about Taylor's past. He shares it, and as Taylor tentatively opens up to this new group, she makes discoveries about her family background. Bolstered by the caring attitude of her friends—old and new—and her housemates, Taylor takes tentative steps toward trust, which brings a newfound sense of belonging. As the two plot lines wrap up, Taylor finds the answers she has so long sought about questions of family identity.

Many reviewers were impressed with the novel, often praising *Jellicoe Road*'s well-developed characters and plot. A reviewer for the *Bookshelves of Doom* Web site noted that the "writing is top-notch," adding that Marchetta's "characters are believable, so real that less than twenty pages in, I forgot I was reading a novel." "This book is full of gorgeous, fluid language, and complicated, well-drawn characters, and intricate, perfectly done plots," asserted a reviewer for the *Chicklish* Web site. *Booklist* reviewer Daniel Kraus was also impressed with *Jellicoe Road*, remarking that Marchetta "has a knack for nuanced characterizations and punchy dialogue." "Elegiac passages and a complex structure create a somewhat dense, melancholic narrative with elements of romance, mystery, and realistic fiction," asserted Suzanne Gordon in a *School Library Journal* review. And *Horn Book* contributor Lauren Adams concluded, "Suspenseful plotting, slowly unraveling mysteries, and generations of romance shape the absorbing novel."

In an interview with *Booklist*, the author discussed the origins of *Jellicoe Road*: "It was the boarding school setting that inspired me to write *Jellicoe*. I always loved stories and films about boarding school, especially the Enid Blyton novels. Some of my closest friends were boarders, so their view is

Jellicoe Road, **Marchetta's Printz Award-winning novel, intertwines two stories about loss, love, and redemption.**
(Cover photograph by Image 100 Photography/Veer. Copyright © HarperCollins. All rights reserved. Reproduced by permission.)

less romantic. The story's territory wars came from observing human behavior. I noticed how territorial people were when I was a teacher at a boys' school, and most of the kids had to share the courtyard. The older boys had their spot, and if the younger ones dared to come near them, there was instant conflict."

Jellicoe Road earned its most prestigious accolade, however, when it won the 2009 Michael L. Printz Award for excellence in young adult literature. Marchetta divulged to Kirsten Hubbard on the YA Highway Web Site that the award "was 100 percent surprise. . . . I love that it happened for *Jellicoe.* It's a hard novel to sell to the world and I remember being so proud when I finished writing it." In her Printz Award acceptance speech, the author offered additional comments about her work: "I've always experienced such a polarised reaction to this novel. People either love it with intensity, or don't get beyond the first thirty pages." She added, "For me, *Jellicoe Road* is a story of love between people, regardless of gender and age. It's about the mistakes

adults make for all the right reasons. It's about redemption being possible in the most tragic of circumstances. . . . It's about staying individual and still belonging to a community. It's about pointing out the beauty of wonder in the midst of ugliness."

Taking on Fantasy

For her next work, Marchetta left behind a contemporary setting to produce the high fantasy *Finnikin of the Rock.* The story begins in Lumatere, a kingdom within the land of Skuldenore. Lumatere is a peaceful and prosperous country, with its people divided into regions of the flatlands, river, mountains, forest, and the rock. Finnikin (of the Rock) is the son of Trevanion, the captain of the King's guard, and counts amount his playmates the royal heirs and their cousins. While still children, Finnikin, the crown prince Balthazar, and Lucian of the Monts make a blood pledge to serve, protect, and preserve the kingdom. Shortly thereafter, Lumatere is invaded and its royal family murdered or missing. In the mayhem that follows—what becomes known as "the five days of the unspeakable"—some of Lumatere's citizens take vengeance on a neighboring people who worship a different goddess. As the leader of these Forest Dwellers is burned at the stake, she utters a curse/prophecy, which produces a dark mist that hangs over the kingdom. Many of the citizens flee their country in fear, and then find that the spell makes them unable to return.

Like most others, Finnikin's family is torn apart: his stepmother remains inside Lumatere while his father, Trevanion, refuses to serve the imposter King and is therefore exiled and imprisoned. Finnikin is left in the care of Sir Topher, previously the King's first man, who takes on the youngster as his apprentice. For ten years, Sir Topher and Finnikin have traveled and labored to improve the living conditions of the Lumaterean refugees. Finnikin is working on *The Book of Lumatere,* a history of his country and people. Unfortunately, most of his additions are in the form of recording the names of the dead. In addition to being beset by natural disasters such as floods and plagues, some citizens become victims of ethnic cleansing in neighboring territories. Still, a tiny hope remains that one day the survivors can return home. When a secret message is relayed to Finnikin, he and Sir Topher travel to the remote headquarters of a religious order and meet the novice Evanjalin, who is gifted with the ability to "walk through the sleep" of her countrymen. She claims that Balthazar, the male heir to the Lumaterean throne, is still alive.

This news about the crown prince is a clarion call for Finnikin, whose focus shifts from helping secure a new homeland to the determination to return to Lumatere. Because many of the beleagureed citizens have succumbed to hopelessness, Finnikin, Evanjalin, and Sir Topher must try to rally them. They think that if they gain support in the form of religious, military, and political representatives from the pre-conflict era, they can convince the exiles to make the journey home. Even with numbers, they must contend with the curse on the kingdom, the impostor king's troops, and the difficulty of reconciliation between divided and emotionally tormented people. For some, the doubts increase the closer they come to their destination, and questions arise about whether Evanjalin is telling the truth about her visions, her motivations, and her identity. Finnikin must decide whether to have faith, despite his misgivings, and accept what he views as an undeserved role as a leader of his people.

Marchetta's change of genres did not dampen the enthusiasm of critics. A contributor to *Kirkus Reviews* declared that "readers will enjoy the rousing and complex plot, filled with political intrigue and frequent red herrings," while Lauren Adams credited the author for her "fully realized medieval world of bloody battles and dark mysticism" in a *Horn Book* assessment. A writer for *Publishers Weekly* noted that "magic, romance, intrigue, and adventure all play their parts as this dense, intricate epic unfolds." Writing in *School Library Journal*, Amy V. Pickett pronounced, "Melina Marchetta has crafted a world that is both fanciful and frighteningly real, with parallels to today's civil wars and refugee camps." And *Booklist*'s Lynn Rutan praised the author's "skillful world building" and "achingly real characters," concluding, "this standout fantasy quickly reveals that its real magic lies in its accomplished writing."

"I think my YA readership is aged between 13 and 80 something."

—Melina Marchetta, in a *YA Highway* interview.

Marchetta explained her switch of genres in an interview on the Books From Bleh to Basically Amazing Web site: "When Finnikin the character came to me, I knew I couldn't set it in the here and now. It would have been too political, so I decided to set it in a world that looked like the year 1000. But I didn't want to deal with the Crusades so the fantasy novel was born." The genre held other attractions, too: the author admitted on Lorraine Marwood's blog, "I love how epic a fantasy novel is allowed to be. Everything is so heightened, more romantic, more tragic, more cursed. There is no such thing as blasé. It's a bit biblical, in that way. . . . It's all those big themes of faith and questioning a higher power and redemption." Describing the skills needed for this type of work, Marchetta revealed to Hubbard, "I think the biggest challenge in writing fantasy is creating a world that doesn't exist. I had a taste of that with *Jellicoe* because most of that setting was fictitious except for the Sydney scenes. When I write fantasy I have to study a landscape that fascinates me and go with it. I wrote some of *Finnikin* in the Dordogne area of France and in Umbria Italy." Speaking with a contributor to the YA Bibliofile Web Site, Marchetta remarked, "I certainly find writing fantasy harder than writing realism. My strengths are dialogue, characterisation and relationships. Fantasy requires world building and descriptive language. But I decided long ago that in writing fantasy I'm going to stick [with] what I'm good at and improve what I'm not good at."

Characters Redux

In 2010, Marchetta presented *The Piper's Son*, which serves as a companion novel to *Saving Francesca*. While not a sequel, it picks up the story of supporting character Tom Mackee five years after the events of the first novel. *The Piper's Son* differs somewhat from Marchetta's earlier novels in that she gives equal billing to the stories of Tom and his aunt Georgie. Commenting on the Not Enough Bookshelves Web Site, Marchetta revealed, "Georgie is of my generation and in every one of my novels the adults have had their story told through the point of view of the teenager telling the story . . . .This time I wanted the adults to have a voice. Georgie and Tom are on the same journey. They're stuffing up relationships, they're grieving and they're both trying to hold the family together."

As *The Piper's Son* opens, Tom Mackees's family is in bad shape. His Uncle Joe died two years ago in a terrorist bombing of the London Underground. It is the second loss of this type that the Mackees have had to endure. Forty years ago, Tom's grandfather was killed in action during the Vietnam War, and his fellow soldiers were unable to retrieve his body. Added to that lingering grief, Joe's death is a crushing blow. Tom thinks to himself, "The Mackees can't be put back together again. There are too many pieces of them missing." Tom's father, Dominic, resorts to alcohol to numb his emotions. After enduring the behavior for a year, Tom's mother, Jacinta, separates from Dominic and moves with Tom's younger sister, Anabel, to Brisbane. Tom refuses to go with them, even though he has nothing else to do: he has dropped out of college and spends his time drinking, smoking weed, playing music, and not caring about anything or anyone else. In his misery, Tom also alienates his friends—Jimmy, Francesca, Tara, and Justine—who had been constant companions for three years, since they met in year eleven at St. Sebastian's. Tara had just become his girlfriend at the time of Joe's death, but he dropped her, along with everyone else.

The travails of Tom's aunt Georgie make up the other half of *The Piper's Son*. Unlike her mother (who remarried decades ago) or her twin brother, Dominic, Georgie did not have her own family to turn to after Joe's funeral; she's single and lives alone with her grief. The one person she turned to for help and comfort was Sam, her former boyfriend. The two had been in a relationship, but seven years ago, when they were taking a break, Sam got another woman pregnant and now shares custody of their son. Georgie felt betrayed, but after Joe's death, the former couple tentatively and half-heartedly rekindles their romance. Now Georgie finds herself in an embarrassing predicament: she is approaching middle age and becomes pregnant by Sam. Worse yet, she imagines her family and friends will negatively judge her for tacitly forgiving Sam and accepting him back into her life.

Meanwhile, Tom is spiraling downward: he has an alcohol-fueled accident and ends up at the hospital, and, shortly thereafter, his roommates kick him out of their flat. He asks Georgie if he can move in with her, and she consents—with the conditions of him not doing drugs and getting a job. He takes two part-time jobs, including one at the Union Pub, where Francesca and Justine work. He is not welcomed back. Francesca admonishes him by saying, "I know you're sad, Tom. But sometimes you're so mean that I wonder why any of us bother." Slowly, through his improved behavior and reliability, his coworkers begin to warm up to him. Tom even tries to make amends with Tara, who is in East Timor doing work related to her college degree. Regaining Tara's trust and affection will be a monumental challenge, but, because he still has feelings for her, it's one Tom accepts. In the midst of this, Tom's family receives news that the government has located and identified his grandfather's remains. This information jolts the Mackees, and as

If you enjoy the work of Melina Marchetta, you may also want to check out the following novels:

Meg Rosoff's *How I Live Now* (2004).
John Green's *Looking for Alaska* (2005).
Kristin Cashore's *Graceling* (2008).

the family members plan for the sad homecoming, they manage—with some prompting—to take steps toward reconciliation.

Voice of Youth Advocates' Dotsy Harland judged that in *The Piper's Son*, "Marchetta creates a poignant psychological portrayal of a close-knit family deeply affected by trauma." A *Publishers Weekly* contributor deemed the story "powerful and tragic," adding "Marchetta masterfully demonstrates the depth of emotion—and love—the characters feel." Reviewing *The Piper's Son* for *School Library Journal*, Patricia N. McClune declared, "It's a joy to watch Tom reconnect with his friends, his music, his family, and Tara. . . ." And Cheryl Preisendorfer, writing in *School Library Journal*, concluded, "Marchetta spins a stunning tale about the consequences and joys of belonging to a family"

Coming into Her Own

During her career, Marchetta has grappled with issues of identity, both her characters' and her own—in terms of her Italian heritage, with the description of herself as a writer, and with the labels that are attached to her work. In her Printz Award acceptance speech, Marchetta divulged, "my first novel received a strong response because it explored the life of a young Australian-Italian girl juggling two cultures. At times, like many other writers of semi-semi-autobiographical novels, I still feel quite defined by it." Later in her Printz speech, she commented, "I get asked over and over again, what the Printz actually means in the long run. . . . what it means to me, in all honestly, is that more people will read my work and ultimately, I think it's what most writers want—for their stories to be read and to be shared and to be discussed."

As for the tag of young-adult author, the author explained on the Books4yourkids Web site, "It's not that I don't consider myself a writer for young people, I do. But I think I write about young people, and not necessarily for young people. It never surprises me that someone my age would enjoy my novels. I am my audience." In a 2010 feature article in *The Australian,* journalist Sharon Verghi assessed, "Marchetta . . . seems to have emerged into a more confident, assured, perhaps even happier place in her mid-40s. The young woman who once cringed at the thought of describing herself as a writer has found her place in the writing world." Later, the author told Verghi, "At that time of *Alibrandi,* I didn't feel that [I deserved] the title of a writer, I couldn't say the word, I mumbled it. . . . I've overcome that now. I'm a writer. And I do think this will be probably the peak of my career, coming after 17 years. I think I'm doing my best writing at the moment."

■ Biographical and Critical Sources

BOOKS

Marchetta, Melina, *Finnikin of the Rock,* Candlewick Press (Somerville, MA), 2010.

Marchetta, Melina, *Jellicoe Road,* HarperTeen (New York, NY), 2008.

Marchetta, Melina, *Looking for Alibrandi,* Orchard Books (New York, NY), 1999.

Marchetta, Melina, *The Piper's Son,* Candlewick Press (Somerville, MA), 2011.

Marchetta, Melina, *Saving Francesca,* Alfred A. Knopf (New York, NY), 2004.

PERIODICALS

Age (Melbourne, Victoria, Australia), March 28, 2003, "Looking beyond Alibrandi."

Booklist, February 15, 1999, Anne O'Malley, review of *Looking for Alibrandi,* p. 1063; September 15, 1999, review of *Looking for Alibrandi,* p. 249; January 1, 2000, review of *Looking for Alibrandi,* p. 820; October 1, 2004, Ilene Cooper, review of *Saving Francesca,* p. 323; November 1, 2008, Daniel Kraus, review of *Jellicoe Road,* p. 34; March 1, 2009, "The Booklist Printz Interview: Melina Marchetta," p. 42; March 1, 2010, Lynn Rutan, review of *Finnikin of the Rock,* p. 73; February 15, 2011, Gillian Engberg, review of *The Piper's Son,* p. 72.

Bulletin of the Center for Children's Books, April, 1999, review of *Looking for Alibrandi,* p. 287; October, 2004, Deborah Stevenson, review of *Saving Francesca,* p. 88.

Horn Book, May, 1999, review of *Looking for Alibrandi,* p. 334; September-October, 2004, Lauren Adams, review of *Saving Francesca,* p. 591.; November-

December, 2008, Lauren Adams, review of *Jellicoe Road;* March 1, 2009, "Michael L. Printz Award"; May-June, 2010, Lauren Adams, review of *Finnikin of the Rock.*

Journal of Adolescent & Adult Literacy, November, 2001, Carol Reinhard, review of *Looking for Alibrandi,* p. 195.

Kirkus Reviews, September 1, 2004, review of *Saving Francesca;* August 1, 2008, review of *Jellicoe Road;* January 15, 2010, review of *Finnikin of the Rock.*

Kliatt, September, 2004, Claire Rosser, review of *Saving Francesca,* p. 14; November, 2004, Janet Julian, review of *Saving Francesca* (audiobook), p. 40; July 1, 2008, Claire Rosser, review of *Jellicoe Road,* p. 18.

Publishers Weekly, March 8, 1999, review of *Looking for Alibrandi,* p. 69; September 6, 2004, review of *Saving Francesca,* p. 64; January 11, 2010, review of *Finnikin of the Rock,* p. 50; January 31, 2011, review of *The Piper's Son,* p. 51.

School Library Journal, July, 1999, Miriam Lang Budin, review of *Looking for Alibrandi,* p. 97; September, 2000, Barbara Wysocki, review of *Looking for Alibrandi,* p.84; May, 2002, review of *Looking for Alibrandi,* p. 52; July, 2004, Francisca Goldsmith, review of *Saving Francesca,* p. 61; September, 2004, Roxanne Burg, review of *Saving Francesca,* p. 212; April, 2005, review of *Saving Francesca* (audiobook), p. S72; December 1, 2008, Suzanne Gordon, review of *Jellicoe Road,* p. 132; February, 2011, Amy V. Pickett, review of *Finnikin of the Rock,* p. 61; March, 2011; Patricia N. McClune, review of *The Piper's Son,* p. 166; August, 2011, Cheryl Preisendorfer, review of *The Piper's Son* (audiobook), p. 56.

Voice of Youth Advocates, June, 1999, review of *Looking for Alibrandi,* p. 115; October, 2004, Betsy Fraser, review of *Saving Francesca,* p.304; December, 2004, review of *Saving Francesca* (audiobook), p. 371; April, 2011, Dotsy Harland, review of *The Piper's Son,* p. 63.

ONLINE

The Australian, http://www.theaustralian.com.au/ (March 6, 2010), Sharon Verghi, "The Coming of Age."

AustralianCatholics.com, http://www.australiancatholics.com/ (winter, 2003), Michael McGirr, "The Best Days, The Worst Days"; (October 16, 2005), "A Class of Her Own," inteview with Melina Marchetta.

Between the Lines, http://penguinbtl.blogspot.com/ (September 14, 2011), "Melina Marchetta Talks *Looking for Alibrandi*"; (September 15, 2011), "Melina Marchetta on *Saving Francesca*"; (September 16, 2011), "Melina Marchetta Talks *On the Jel-*

licoe Road"; (September 17, 2011), "Melina Marchetta on *Finnikin of the Rock*"; (September 18, 2011), "Melina Marchetta on *The Piper's Son*."

The Blurb, http://penguinbtl.blogspot.com/ (January 15, 2012), "On the Road Again."

Books4yourkids.com, http://www.books4yourkids.com/ (March 3, 2011), "Melina Marchetta Interview."

BookDivas.com, http://www.bookdivas.com/ (October 16, 2005), "Melina Marchetta."

Books From Bleh to Basically Amazing, http://www.basicallyamazingashley.com/ (November 25, 2011), "Just Contemporary Interview—Melina Marchetta."

Chicklish, http://chicklish.co.uk/ (April 18, 2008), "Review: *On the Jellicoe* by Melina Marchetta."

In Film Australia Web site, http://www.infilm.com.au/ (October 16, 2005), Luke Buckmaster, review of *Looking for Alibrandi* (film).

Internet Movie Database, http://www.imdb.com/ (October 16, 2005), "Melina Marchetta."

Lateral Learning Speakers' Agency Web Site, http://www.laterallearning.com/ (October 16, 2005), "Melina Marchetta."

Lorrain Marwood Blog, http://lorrainemarwood wordsintowriting.blogspot.com/ (December 13, 2011), "Guest Author Interview—the Fabulous Melina Marchetta."

Not Enough Bookshelves, http://www.notenough bookshelves.com/ (March 3, 2011), "Interview with Melina Marchetta."

Novel Rocket, http://www.novelrocket.com/ (November 17, 2008), Noël De Vries, "YA Author Interview: Melina Marchetta."

Persnickety Snark, http://www.persnicketysnark.com/ (March 2, 2010), "Interview—Melina Marchetta (*The Piper's Son*)."

Puffin at Penguin Books Australia Web site, http://www.penguiin.com.au/ (October 16, 2005), "Melina Marchetta."

St. Mary's Cathedral College Web site, http://www.smccsydney.catholic.edu.au// (October 16, 2005).

Scan Online, http://www.lakemac.infohunt.nsw.gov.au/ (October, 1993), "Marchetta on Alibrandi."

The Siren Story, http://www.thestorysiren.com/ (June 23, 2010), "Author Interview & Giveaway: Melina Marchetta."

Triple J Film Reviews Online, http://www.abc.net.au/triplej/review/ (October 16, 2005) review of *Looking for Alibrandi* (film).

YA Bibliofile, http://www.yabibliophile.com/ (March 7, 2011), "Author Interview: Melina Marchetta."

YA Highway, http://www.yahighway.com/ (October 11, 2009), Kirsten Hubbard, "Interview with Melina Marchetta, Printz-Winning Author of *Jellicoe Road*."

YALSA, http://www.ala.org/yalsa/ (January 7, 2012), "Melina Marchetta: 2009 Michael L. Printz Award Acceptance Speech."

YA Reads, http://www.yareads.com/ (March 9, 2010), "Special Guest Author Interview: Melina Marchetta."*

Melissa Marr

■ Personal

Born July 25, 1972; married; children: two. *Education:* North Carolina State University, B.A., M.A. *Hobbies and other interests:* Tattoo art, visiting museums, travel, folklore, time with family.

■ Addresses

Home—Washington, DC. *Agent*—Rachel Vater, Folio Literary Management, 505 8th Ave., Ste. 603, New York, NY 10018. *E-mail*—melissa@melissa-marr.com.

■ Career

Writer and educator. Former teacher of literature; formerly worked as a bartender and waitress.

■ Member

Society of Children's Book Writers and Illustrators, Romance Writers of America, Science Fiction and Fantasy Writers of America.

■ Awards, Honors

Rita Award for Best Young Adult Book, Romance Writers of America, 2007, Books for the Teen Age selection, New York Public Library, 2008, and Notable Children's Book designation, International Reading Association, 2008, all for *Wicked Lovely.*

■ Writings

"WICKED LOVELY" SERIES

Wicked Lovely, HarperTeen (New York, NY), 2007.
Ink Exchange, HarperTeen (New York, NY), 2008.
Fragile Eternity, Bowen Press (New York, NY), 2009.
Radiant Shadows, HarperCollins (New York, NY), 2010.
Darkest Mercy, HarperCollins (New York, NY), 2011.

Also author of *"Stopping Time"* (e-book), HarperCollins (New York, NY), 2010, and *Old Habits* (e-book) HarperCollins (New York, NY), 2011.

"WICKED LOVELY: DESERT TALES" SERIES

Sanctuary (graphic novel), illustrated by Xian Nu Studio, Tokyopop (Los Angeles, CA), 2009.
Challenge (graphic novel), illustrated by Xian Nu Studio, Tokyopop (Los Angeles, CA), 2010.
Resolve (graphic novel), illustrated by Xian Nu Studio, Tokyopop (Los Angeles, CA), 2011.

OTHER

(With others) *Love Is Hell,* HarperTeen (New York, NY), 2008.
(With Kim Harrison, Jeaniene Frost, Vicki Pettersson, and Jocelynn Drake) *Unbound,* Eos (New York, NY), 2009.

Graveminder, Morrow (New York, NY), 2011.

(Editor, with Kelley Armstrong) *Enthralled: Paranormal Diversions,* HarperCollins (New York, NY), 2011.

Contributor of short fiction to anthologies, including *Love Struck,* HarperTeen (New York, NY), 2008, and *Naked City: Tales of Urban Fantasy,* edited by Ellen Datlow, St. Martin's Press (New York, NY), 2011.

■ Adaptations

Wicked Lovely is being adapted for a feature film, Wild West Picture Show Productions; "Wicked Lovely" series has been adapted for audiobook, by Recorded Books.

■ Sidelights

Voted "most likely to end up in jail" by her high school classmates, Melissa Marr did not seem destined for a career as a bestselling author. "They say, 'Write what you know,'" Marr told *Publishers Weekly* contributor Karen Springen. "What I know isn't cheerleader; it has a little bit of teeth to it." Those "teeth" could be felt in Marr's debut novel, *Wicked Lovely,* in which a teenage girl has the power to see and hear faeries. These are not the cute, pixy-like fairies of Victorian tales, but instead the more bothersome and evil denizens of the world of faerie that delight in teasing and tormenting humans. When the teenager is in turn noticed by a king of the faeries, the real trouble starts in this "assured debut," as Charles de Lint noted in the *Magazine of Fantasy and Science Fiction.*

Marr wrote five novels in the "Wicked Lovely" series, aimed at young adults, wrapping up her saga with the 2011 finale, *Darkest Mercy.* Her first adult title, *Graveminder,* also appeared in 2011. Additionally, the author supplied the story for a three-volume manga adaptation of the world of the "Wicked Lovely" books. In an interview with a contributor for the online *Red Room,* Marr noted of her obsession with faeries, vampires, demons, and ghosts: "I blame my mother and my grandmother for a lot of it. They fed me a solid diet of fairy tales and faery lore."

From Troubled Teen to Professor

Born in 1972, Marr was an avid reader from an early age. Speaking with Dee Gentle of the *Paranormal Romance Groups* Web site, Marr remarked of her childhood: "I grew up with traditional folklore, and as an adult, I read it for fun. I read vampire, shapeshifter, zombie, and demon lore too. I think that's a big part of *why* I write supernatural fiction: it's something I've always been interested in, believed in, and read." Her mother and grandmother were both very important in her youth, introducing her not only to the world of both fairy and faerie tales, but also to that of classic literature. Marr became an avid reader of books by Jack Zipes and Maria Tatar and of folklore in general. By the time she was twelve, she had determined to become a writer.

"I was the girl in the black leather jacket with the black fingernails, picked up after school by guys with loud cars and motorcycles. I carried straight-A grades, but I had a little trouble with rules. I tended to have a bit of an authority problem."

—Melissa Marr, in a *Publishers Weekly* interview.

"In high school, my closest friends were the leather jacket/black tee shirt crowd," Marr told the contributor for *Red Room.* "There were 'metalheads' and skaters and artists and punks and musicians and (eventually) bikers. They were the unusual, vibrant people." In a conversation with *Publishers Weekly* contributor James Bickers, Marr further noted of her high school years: "I was the girl in the black leather jacket with the black fingernails, picked up after school by guys with loud cars and motorcycles. . . . I carried straight-A grades, but I had a little trouble with rules. I tended to have a bit of an authority problem." After graduating from high school, Marr put herself through undergraduate and graduate work in English literature by bartending at a biker bar. Thereafter she taught literature at the college level for a decade, work she very much enjoyed. She also became the mother of two children. In her spare time, she began to pursue her old dream of becoming a writer. She experimented with stories, one of which she transformed into her first novel in the span of four months. Two months later, she was a breakthrough debut novelist with a three-book contract in hand. Marr remarked on this overnight success in a *Cynsations* interview with Cynthia Leitich Smith: "For me, it's been surreal. I never thought much about the 'being an author' part. I wrote a book. I've dreamed of seeing it in readers' hands."

The Realm of Faerie

In her first novel, *Wicked Lovely*, Marr posits a world in which the realm of faerie is very real. Seventeen-year-old Aislinn is a mortal who has the power to see the faeries. Aislinn has always lived in fear of the faeries, for they brutalize one another and torment humans. The teen seeks refuge in a converted train car where her best friend, Seth, lives, and which serves a safe zone because its iron walls are poison to faeries. Now, however, she notices that two faeries seem to be trailing her. One of these is handsome Keenan, the Summer King, who is in search of a queen who will be able to aid him in his revolt against his evil mother, Beira, the Winter Queen. Aislinn at first wants nothing to do with this power game, but the stakes are high: if she does not become the Summer Queen, the earth will freeze. She enlists Seth's help in this struggle.

The first installment of Marr's "Wicked Lovely" series introduces Aislinn, a teen who inherits the ability to see faeries and finds herself at the center of an otherworldly power struggle. (Copyright © HarperCollins Children's Books. All rights reserved. Reproduced by permission.)

Meanwhile, Beria has made a deal with Donia, Keenan's previous choice for queen: if Donia can prevent the match between Kennan and Aislinn, the Winter Queen will lift the spell she has cast on the younger woman.

A *Publishers Weekly* reviewer had high praise for this debut, noting: "Marr offers readers a fully imagined faery world that runs alongside an everyday world, which even non-fantasy (or faerie) lovers will want to delve into." Also writing in *Publishers Weekly*, Joanne R. Fritz thought this novel is "expertly crafted, alternating effortlessly among four different characters." Similarly, June H. Keuhn, reviewing the novel in *School Library Journal*, felt that it is "the unusual combination of past legends and modern-day life that gives a unique twist to this 'fairy' tale." A more mixed assessment was offered by a *Kirkus Reviews* contributor who noted: "Overlong wish-fulfillment, but enjoyably sultry." *Kliatt* reviewer Amanda MacGregor, however, had no such reservations about the work, concluding: "As the full extent of Aislinn's circumstances is revealed, readers will be hooked by her tale and surely pick up the next book,"

That next book, *Ink Exchange*, once again blends the fantasy realm of faerie and the gritty realism of the contemporary world. This novel focuses on Leslie, who appeared in *Wicked Lovely* as a friend of Aislinn. A high school senior, Leslie has had her world turned upside down. Sexually molested by friends of her drug-addict brother, she has been virtually abandoned by her family. Aislinn provides some help, but Leslie thinks that by getting a tattoo she can reclaim some kind of control over her life. Unfortunately for Leslie, the tattoo artist is actually a member of the faerie realm in service to Iriel, the Dark King. The tattoo Leslie gets connects her to Iriel, who wants to control her for his own evil ends. At the same time, Leslie is drawn to Aislinn's bodyguard, Niall, a former dark faerie. Janis Flint-Ferguson, writing in *Kliatt*, described *Ink Exchange* as a "violent tale of fairies in the gritty city and the havoc they wreak on the mortals who live there," while for a *Publishers Weekly* reviewer called it a "highly addictive read." Further praise came from *Booklist* contributor Krista Hutley, who felt that "this dark fantasy about survival and transformation is as mesmerizing as its urban faery subjects." Similarly, *School Library Journal* writer Lisa Prolman found the novel "impossible to put down."

Lust and Romance in the Faerie World

The action returns to Aislinn in the third series installment, *Fragile Eternity*. Now the Summer Queen, Aislinn attempts to keep her love for Seth even though she is beginning to feel more attracted to her consort, Keenan. Seth, for his part, does not want to be separated from Aislinn, and in desperation he attempts to become a faerie himself so that they can be together forever. A *Kirkus Reviews* contributor complained of "overwrought, repetitive writing," but Maggie Knapp, writing in *School Library Journal*, thought that "fans of the fey world will devour this." *Booklist* reviewer Lynn Rutan, had a mixed evaluation of the novel, noting that despite a "slim" plot, the book would be "popular with fans of the series."

The "Wicked Lovely" series continues with the 2010 installment, *Radiant Shadows*. Here, Marr once again focuses on a pair of unlikely lovers. A wild child, half-mortal and half-faerie, Ani meets Devlin, the brother of Sorcha, the High Queen of Faerie, and the two are instantly attracted. As it turns out, Devlin has been protecting Ani since her birth, and now he is pitted against Bananach, an evil faery who has been trying to kill her. Meanwhile, Sorcha longs for Seth, who now spends half the year in the mortal world and half in the world of faerie. *School Library Journal* writer Kristin Anderson dubbed this novel a "worthy addition to a fine series." On the other hand, Hutley, writing in *Booklist* found *Radiant Shadows* to be "utterly dependent on the rest of the series."

Marr brings her series to a conclusion with *Darkest Mercy*, in which the world of faerie moves toward war between the Summer and Winter courts. Keenan still feels conflicted in his emotions about his queen, Aislinn, and the one he truly loves, Donia, who has become the new Winter Queen. Aislinn feels a similar tug of emotions between Keenan and Seth. In the end, as the rival courts go to war, this strange love quadrangle is finally resolved. *Voice of Youth Advocates* reviewer Geri Diorio noted of this work: "Readers may mourn the end of the series, but they will be pleased with how Marr, a proper romance writer, gives everyone their hearts' desire." Marr remarked to Springen on the conclusion of this bestselling series: "It's tempting to write more in these characters' lives, and my publisher is certainly supportive of that, but at the end of the day, the integrity of the story outranks my emotions."

Graphic Novels and Adult Fiction

Marr is also the author of three graphic novels set in the same realm of faerie that she created for her "Wicked Lovely" series. The "Wicked Lovely: Desert Tales" books center on Rika, formerly a member of the Winter Court, who happily lives a solitary life in the desert, away from court intrigue. In the first book of the trilogy, *Sanctuary*, Rika is attracted to a human, Jayce, who comes to the desert to paint. But things become complicated with the arrival of Keenan, the Summer King, who seeks alliances with the Solitary Fey of the desert. His presence brings Rika to the attention of other desert faeries, and now she must make herself visible to Jayce in order to protect him, an action that initiates their relationship. Reviewing *Sanctuary,* a contributor for *Book Smugglers* Web site noted: "For such a short story there is quite a lot going on here but it could not be different with a writer such as Melissa Marr—there is both what is said and shown and is left unsaid."

Challenge picks up the action in the desert as the faeries fight among each other, partly because of Rika's attachment to the human, Jayce, yet also because she refuses to be pulled into the dark world of faerie politics. Keenan also makes another appearance, offering to keep order in the wake of an incapacitating injury to Sionnach, a friend of Rika's who has thus far kept order among the desert fey. But Keenan demands the fealty of all, including Rika, who must now make some hard decisions. The series concludes with *Resolve.*

With the 2011 work, *Graveminder,* Marr's penchant for dark fantasy is still in evidence. On the face of it, Claysville is a pleasant enough town, but it hides an eerie secret. Death has made a compact with the town: if a graveminder feeds the dead, then the inhabitants of Claysville will not die before the age of eighty. Furthermore, anyone born in Claysville must be buried there, or else they become one of the Hungry Dead. Now Rebekkah Barrow, returned to town for her grandmother's funeral, discovers that she is to be the next graveminder. Rebekkah also learns that her grandmother was killed by Daisha, one of the Hungry Dead. Rebekkah joins forces with Byron Montgomery, the local undertaker, to find Daisha before she creates more havoc. A *Publishers Weekly* reviewer dubbed this a "quirky dark fantasy fashioned around the themes of fate, free will—and zombies." *Voice of Youth Advocates* contributor Jonatha Basye also commended this work, writing: "Marr, a widely popular young adult author, has produced an adult novel that is worthy of praise." *Library Journal* reviewer Jennifer Anderson called the work "haunting, captivating, brilliant." Likewise, a *Kirkus Reviews* writer commented: "Fantasy-horror fans will demand more."

The Faeries Leak Through

Discussing the inspirations for her works in a *YA Reads* interview, Marr stated: "With folklore, there are so many interesting beings. I grew up believing in them—the beansidhe [banshees] in the woods, the ghost in the music box, the vampire who likes to walk in the old cemetery on the hill. . . . Add a steady diet of folklore, fairy tales, critical studies on the same, and a decade teaching literature, a few years teaching lit/gender studies . . . It all swirls together. So it's what leaks through when I write. Right now, the faeries leaked through first." Marr also noted in an interview with a contributor for the *Wondrous Reads* Web site that her work is driven by the truths her characters reveal: "I don't write for an audience; I write for my characters. The publishers and agents decide on the audience. I write the story I have to tell. That's the only way to do it. If I think about readers or editors when I write, I'm paying attention to the wrong voices, and I think that would hurt the story."

If you enjoy the works of Melissa Marr, you may also want to check out the following books:

Holly Black's *Valiant* (2005), an urban fantasy in which a runaway discovers a mysterious and dangerous faerie world.

Lament, a 2008 work by Maggie Stiefvater that centers on the relationship between a gifted teenage musician and a faerie assassin.

The Iron King (2010), Julie Kagawa's fantasy novel that borrows characters from Shakespearean literature.

Asked if she had advice for young writers by a contributor for *Yapping about YA*, Marr admitted, "No one answer fits all people." The author added: "The path, the process, the advice—it's all guesses. What worked for me hasn't worked for writers I've since met. For me, the most important thing was reading. I read voraciously in all sorts of genres, & then I analyze why a book did or didn't work for me. Getting a degree in lit (& teaching university lit) was how I became a writer. I didn't take creative writing courses or how-to. I don't do the BiC ('butt in chair') thing. . . . It's all so very individual."

■ **Biographical and Critical Sources**

PERIODICALS

Booklist, June 1, 2008, Krista Hutley, review of *Ink Exchange*, p. 66; April 1, 2009, Lynn Rutan, review of *Fragile Eternity*, p. 32; February 17, 2010, Krista Hutley, review of *Radiant Shadows*; March 15, 2011, Debbie Carton, review of *Teeth*, p. 57.

Bulletin of the Center for Children's Books, July-August, 2007, Cindy Welch, review of *Wicked Lovely*, p. 476.

Kirkus Reviews, May 15, 2007, review of *Wicked Lovely*; April 15, 2008, review of *Ink Exchange*; May 1, 2009, review of *Fragile Eternity*; January 15, 2011, review of *Darkest Mercy*; March 1, 2011, review of *Graveminder*; August 1, 2011, review of *Enthralled*.

Kliatt, May, 2008, Janis Flint-Ferguson, review of *Ink Exchange*, p. 13; September, 2008, Amanda MacGregor, review of *Wicked Lovely*, p. 30.

Library Journal, April 1, 2011, Jennifer Anderson, review of *Graveminder*, p. 84.

Magazine of Fantasy and Science Fiction, July, 2007, Charles de Lint, review of *Wicked Lovely*, p. 29.

Publishers Weekly, April 30, 2007, review of *Wicked Lovely*, p. 161; May 14, 2007, Joanne R. Fritz, review of *Wicked Lovely*, p. 8; June 25, 2007, James Bickers, "Flying Starts," pp. 26-28; February 18, 2008, review of *Ink Exchange*; April 28, 2008, review of *Ink Exchange*, p. 140; November 17, 2008, review of *Love Is Hell*, p. 59; August 2, 2010, Karen Springen, "Melissa Marr Is on a Wicked, Lovely Role," p. 25; April 4, 2011, review of *Graveminder*, p. 30.

School Library Journal, July, 2007, June H. Keuhn, review of *Wicked Lovely*, p. 106; June, 2008, Lisa Prolman, review of *Ink Exchange*, p. 146; February, 2009, Sharon Rawlins, review of *Love Is Hell*, p. 104; June, 2009, Maggie Knapp, review of *Fragile Eternity*, p. 131; July, 2009, Barbara M. Moon, review of *Sanctuary*, p. 104; September, 2010, Kristin Anderson, review of *Radiant Shadows*, p. 158, and Andrea Lipinski, review of *Challenge*, p. 179.

Teacher Librarian, October, 2010, Julie Prince, "Enter the Realm of Faeries: An Interview with Melissa Marr," p. 56.

Voice of Youth Advocates, June, 2007, Lynne Farrell Stover, review of *Wicked Lovely*, p. 164; August, 2010, Lynne Farrell Stover, review of *Radiant Shadows*, p. 268; April, 2011, Geri Diorio, review of *Darkest Mercy*, p. 84; June, 2011, Jonatha Basye, review of *Graveminder*, p. 188.

Washington Post Book World, June 24, 2007, Annette Curtis Klause, review of *Wicked Lovely*, p. 7.

ONLINE

Bitten by Books Web site, http://www.bittenbybooks.com/ (March 31, 2010), "Melissa Mar Interview."

Book Smugglers Web site, http://thebooksmugglers.com/ (July 21, 2009), review of *Sanctuary*.

Class of 2k7 Web site, http://classof2k7.com/ (August 24, 2010), "Melissa Marr."

Cynsations Blog, http://cynthialeitichsmith.blogspot. com/ (October 16, 2007), Cynthia Leitich Smith, "Author Interview: Melissa Marr on *Wicked Lovely.*"

HarperTeen Web site, http://www.harperteen.com/ (September 14, 2011), "Author Interview: Melissa Marr on *Wicked Lovely.*"

Melissa Marr Blog, http://melissa-writing. livejournal.com/ (September 14, 2011).

Melissa Marr Home Page, http://www.melissa-marr. com (September 14, 2011).

Omnivoracious Web site, http://www.omnivoracious. com/ (April 21, 2009), "Faeries, Our 'Good Neighbors': An Interview with Melissa Marr."

Paranormal Romance Groups Web site, http:// paranormalromance.org/ (July 1, 2008), Dee Gentle, interview with Melissa Marr.

Red Room Web site, http://redroom.com/ (September 5, 2008), "Interview with Melissa Marr."

Sugarscape Web site, http://www.sugarscape.com/ (March 28, 2011), "Exclusive: Melissa Marr Interview."

Wondrous Reads Web site, http://www.wondrous reads.com/ (March 31, 2011), "Author Interview: Melissa Marr."

Yapping about YA Blog, http://yappingaboutyoung adult.blogspot.com/ (January 15, 2008), "Interview with the Fabulous Melissa Marr."

YA Reads Web site, http://www.yareads.com/ (February 25, 2009), "Author Interview with Melissa Marr."

Ya Ya Yas Blog, http://theyayayas.wordpress.com/ (August 5, 2008), interview with Melissa Marr.*

Bear McCreary

■ Personal

Born February 17, 1979, in Fort Lauderdale, FL; son of Jay and Laura (Kalpakian) McCreary; married Raya Yarbrough, 2010. *Education:* University of Southern California, Thornton School of Music, degrees in composition and recording arts.

■ Addresses

Home—Los Angeles, CA.

■ Career

Musician and composer.

■ Awards, Honors

Emmy Award nomination, 2010, for title theme to *Human Target*.

■ Writings

COMPOSER; TELEVISION SOUNDTRACKS

Battlestar Galactica: Season One, La-La Land Records, 2005.

Battlestar Galactica: Season Two, La-La Land Records, 2006.

Battlestar Galactica: Season Three, La-La Land Records, 2007.

Terminator: The Sarah Connor Chronicles, La-La Land Records, 2008.

Eureka, La-La Land Records, 2008.

Caprica, La-La Land Records, 2009.

Battlestar Galactica: Season Four, La-La Land Records, 2009.

The Cape, La-La Land Records, 2009.

Human Target: Season 1, La-La Land Records, 2010.

Battlestar Galactica: The Plan and Razor, La-La Land Records, 2010.

Also composer for *Trauma*, NBC, 2009-10, and *The Walking Dead*, AMC, 2010—.

COMPOSER; MOVIE SOUNDTRACKS

Rest Stop: Dead Ahead, Element 1/Plan R Sountracks, 2006.

Wrong Turn 2: Dead End, La-La Land Records, 2007.

Rest Stop: Don't Look Back, La-La Land Records, 2008.

Also composer for *Step Up 3D*, Touchstone Pictures, 2010, and *Knights of Badassdom*, 2012.

OTHER

(Composer) *Dark Void* (videogame), Sumthing Else Music Works, 2010.
(Composer) *SOCOM 4: U.S. Navy Seals* (videogame), La-La Land Records, 2011.
Battlestar Galactica Songbook for Piano Solo, Hal Leonard Corporation (Milwaukee, WI), 2011.

Composed music to commemorate the final space shuttle flight, 2011.

■ **Sidelights**

Before the age of thirty, Bear McCreary found success as a composer of acclaimed musical scores for television series such as *Battlestar Galactica* and *Terminator: The Sarah Connor Chronicles*, earning the status as "one of the freshest talents in the scoring business," according to *Film Music Weekly*'s Daniel Schweiger. McCreary is best known for his TV work, but he also has movie and video game soundtracks to his credit. While success seemed to come soon for the composer, he had already put in years of study and preparation before he began working professionally. McCreary began playing the piano at age 5, starting studying film soundtracks and writing music on his own during middle school, and played in rock bands and wrote a screenplay and accompanying musical score before he graduated from high school. Legendary film score composer Elmer Bernstein took him on as a protégée, and McCreary earned degrees in composition and recording arts from the Thornton School of Music at the University of Southern California.

Mix Magazine's Bryan Reesman deemed McCreary "an indefatigable composer who juggles multiple film and television projects and seemingly thrives on creative pandemonium." He is also unique in the amount of interaction he has with his listeners. In an interview for the *Los Angeles Times*, McCreary told Jevon Phillips, that he spends "spends most of [his] waking hours in the studio," yet he connects with his followers via his blog, taking the time to explain and share his work in a way accessible to a layman. He has also reached out to fans by performing his soundtrack music live in concert. According to a writer for *International Musician*, McCreary "has the potential to become a true composer rock-star, complete with screaming fans and sold-out concerts in addition to a top-notch talent."

Nature or Nurture?

McCreary was born February 17, 1979, in Fort Lauderdale, Florida, but grew up in Bellingham, Washington. His first name, Bear, is his legal name, not a nickname. He told an interviewer for a Czech *Battlestar Galactica* Web site, "What can I say? My parents were hippies." His affinity for music may have a genetic element: his family tree includes musicians, and his paternal grandparents were music teachers. His younger brother, Brendan, also chose a career in music—the two often collaborate—although McCreary pointed out to Teresa Jusino in a Tor.com interview, "if you look at the DNA, the genetic pool of my family, my brother got the rock n' roll gene." Genre considerations aside, McCreary credits his parents for being "very nurturing of musicians and musical passion when we were growing up. We really grew up in this environment where if you wanted to . . . write orchestral music or be a rock star, nobody ever told us that that was a risky thing to do. Nobody ever told us to get a day job, or plan ahead for a rainy day," he explained to Jusino. McCreary's parents also introduced him to film by taking him to the movie theater when he was very young. "I was so small that I couldn't hold down the theater seat!" he divulged to Schweiger in *Film Music Magazine*.

McCreary began taking piano lessons as a five year old. He told *GameSpot* contributor Sophia Tong, "I studied piano about 11 or 12 years . . . . I was always good. But I never really liked to practice." Movies, however, remained a fascination for the youngster and helped lead him to his calling. He revealed to Schweiger that "somewhere when I was eight or nine, my interest in music and movies collided, and I started really listening critically to film music. Whenever I saw a movie with my friends growing up, I'd be excited about the score and they wouldn't even notice there was music in the movie." To pursue his interest, McCreary created his own screenplay and wrote a 75-minute score for it during his senior year of high school. His determination and talent got noticed, and McCreary was introduced to legendary film composer Elmer Bernstein. He told Tong that Bernstein "kind of took me under his wing, and I was his final protégée for several years."

McCreary then headed to the University of Southern California to attend music school. The program he was in did not include film scoring until its fourth year, so, in the meantime, he explored other options. In his interview with Tong, McCreary recalled, "When I was 19, I got an accordion . . . and started to actually practice that and over the course of a couple of years got pretty good . . . ." He also took classes in classical composition, a discipline in which he was originally reluctant to take part. The decision paid off nicely, however. In an article for the *Daily Trojan*, Kathleen Bishop reported that "McCreary's temporary change of heart put him in the USC history books. He is the only undergraduate ever to have two pieces, 'The Collapse of St. Francis' and 'Sparks and Shadows,' performed by the USC Symphony." His work ethic also caught the attention of his teachers, as Bishop noted: James Hopkins described his former student as "'very self-motivated, which is one of the most important aspects for someone who is going into the arts rather independently.'"

During his freshman year at USC, McCreary met Steve Kaplan, who would become an integral part of his career as his engineer and producer. In a *Mix Magazine* interview with Bryan Reesman, McCreary commented, "In college, Steve and I were . . .

workaholics. . . . it was helpful that he and I can handle all the abuse that comes with working on a schedule like this. We ended up working together a lot." McCreary stayed at USC for a fifth year to focus on the recording arts, even though he had already begun scoring student and independent films. He mentioned in *International Musician*, "I was writing for whoever I could get to play, and I got a lot of experience orchestrating and conducting, and collaborating with filmmakers." He added, "It was a tremendous learning experience, and I learned how to get a good sound out of a small ensemble." The work provided another lesson. McCreary pointed out to Randall Larson on the Cinefantastique Web site that working on student films "really prepared me for the ego bruising that you get in the collaborative process, which is not something they can really prepare you for in class."

A groundbreaking composer, McCreary is perhaps best known for his work on the acclaimed television series *Battlestar Galactica.*

Despite his overwhelming schedule, McCreary kept up his apprenticeship with Bernstein. He told Tong that "even during my time at USC, I was studying with and working for [Bernstein] and really learning the tools of the trade in the film music business." McCreary recognizes his good fortune in having Bernstein as a mentor. In an article for *International Musician,* he admitted that Benstein's "music would have been an influence on me even if I'd never met him. However, he was really there for me, both musically and personally, and had a tremendous impact on my life."

Overnight Success, A Decade in the Making

Considering McCreary's impressive track record, it was not surprising that he was ready when a professional opportunity presented itself. In 2003 the SyFy channel decided to produce a miniseries based upon the late-1970s science fiction television series *Battlestar Galactica.* Later, executives expanded it into a series. As Thomas Rogers summarized in an article for Salon.com, "the show follows a fleet of human survivors from the Twelve Colonies of Kobol—a group of planets decimated by a surprise attack from the Cylons. The Cylons are a race of partially humanoid robots created by humans who then turned on their makers. Protecting the tiny fleet of survivors is a large aircraft-carrier-like spaceship called the Battlestar *Galactica,* whose crew is the main focus of the show. In each episode, the humans must evade the Cylons as they slowly make their way to salvation on the mythical planet Earth."

Veteran composer Richard Gibbs was tapped to create the score but, because of the aggressive production time frame, asked McCreary to help him. In an interview with Schweiger, McCreary said, "The two of us worked with director Michael Rymer very closely in creating this signature *Battlestar Galactica* sound. When the series got picked up, Richard was brought back in but decided to return to feature films. I was the ideal choice to pick up the reins." Within a year of graduating from college, McCreary had his first composing job. In an *International Musician* feature article, McCreary didn't dismiss the notion of fortuitous timing, but he clarified, "I had done a tremendous amount of work trying to find a way to get my music out there. There's a certain amount of luck involved, and I did everything I could to make every opportunity I could."

The show's producers insisted that *Battlestar Galactica*'s score not be orchestral, wanting to differentiate it from the stereotypical science-fiction film soundtrack. A contributor to *International Musician*

observed that McCreary "started out minimally, with two ethnic instruments, the duduk and bansuri, with percussion accompaniment. He later added gamelan, an Indonesian traditional percussion orchestra, and uilleann pipes." In an interview on National Public Radio's *Weekend All Things Considered,* McCreary explained to Guy Raz that "my philosophy was that it would be music from as many different cultures around the world as possible. So, while there is a lot of Japanese and Chinese influence, there's also a lot of Middle Eastern influence, there's South American and African sounds. There's [also] a lot of purely Western sounds." The music for the initial episodes featured only a few performers, but McCreary acknowledged to Raz, "at the end of the series, we scored the final episode with about a 60-piece orchestra and 10 or 15 soloists. So, you're talking about 75, 80 musicians. So, it obviously evolved and grew."

The quality of the show's music drew appreciative listeners and critics, and five CDs with music from the series were released commercially. Schweiger asserted in *Film Music Weekly* that "McCreary has used *Battlestar Galactica* to reveal himself as one of the most innovative and intriguing composers on TV." The *Wall Street Journal*'s Greg Sandow praised McCreary's "sharp and sensitive score," while Kelly West, writing for CinemaBlend.com, judged that McCreary's "music adds an extra layer of excellence to the scifi series." In an article for *Cinefantastique,* Schweiger added, "McCreary has helped the show achieve its goal of making you take what was once *Star Wars*-inspired camp with absolute and profound seriousness. No more so than with its music's meditative, religioso tone." And *New Jersey Star Ledger* contributor Alan Sepinwall declared that with his work for in the medium of television, McCreary has "been able to do transcendent work in an area that's too often underappreciated."

The composer himself recognized that something unique had taken place with *Battlestar Galactica.* In an *International Musician* feature article published less than a year before the last episode aired, McCreary summed up his feelings about working on the series: "I just want to soak up every moment, every cue, and every solo, every time we record. I don't think there will ever be a show like this again."

Beyond BSG

McCreary's work on *Battlestar Galactica* drew the attention of other production executives, including those planning to create a television show based on the *Terminator* movie franchise. Three films had been released before the TV version, *Terminator: The Sarah Connor Chronicles,* aired. The television version picks up chronologically after *Terminator 2: Judgment Day,* focusing on the high-school years of John Connor, the future leader of the human resistance against the machines. Because his existence is crucial for the survival of humanity, killer robots disguised as ordinary people have been sent back in time to kill him. *Terminator: The Sarah Connor Chronicles* focuses on John and his mother, Sarah, as they try to evade the present-day authorities, keep ahead of the Terminators, and try to find a way to halt development of Skynet, the computer system whose development of self-awareness is the impetus for Judgment Day's worldwide nuclear attack.

With his score, McCreary told Larson, "I wanted to acknowledge the first two films and really make this show feel like it's connected to *Terminator 2* . . . . Obviously that's what they're trying to do with the series itself. . . . [and] the music is probably the most important thing you can do to tie it in with that franchise." McCreary's score incorporates the movies' well-known theme into the soundtrack, with an ominous, mechanical-sounding staccato representing the deadly machine. Yet he also creates leitmotifs for the humans, particularly the melancholy melodies representing Sarah, a mother with the foreknowledge of civilization's collapse. Larson judged that *Terminator: The Sarah Connor Chronicles* "exhibits some of McCreary's most persuasive melodic writing, emphasizing the drama of the story as it affects Sarah and her son John . . . ." In the same article, McCreary admitted, "That was the one place where I wanted to really deviate from the tone of the first two films, because the emotional side of those films was very cold and very distant, and it worked very well, but that's not gonna fly for . . . [the TV series]."

"I like to use every project I work on as a chance to be a better writer."

—McCreary, in an interview with David Raiklen for *Film Music Magazine.*

Like with *Battlestar Galactica,* McCreary's music for *Terminator: The Sarah Connor Chronicles* was released on CD. In a review of the soundtrack for *Film Score Monthly,* Steven A. Kennedy described the latest

Terminator soundtrack as having a "richly satisfying set of tracks," and pointed out, "there is a beautiful lyricism to 'Sarah Connor's Theme.'" Writing for the *Blogger News Network,* Zach Freeman judged that "McCreary establishes a sense of fast-moving action and intrigue early on and sticks with it throughout the album," adding that the composer "demonstrates his untouchable talent in every track."

Although *Terminator: The Sarah Connor Chronicles* was canceled after its second season, McCreary quickly found other television work, including stints with *Eureka, The Cape,* and *Caprica,* the latter of which was a prequel to *Battlestar Galactica.* The show lasted only one season, but McCreary's scoring was again the subject of praise. On the Blogcritics Web Site, Chris Beaumont judged that McCreary's "work for *Caprica* is just another example of the magic he works over the notes. His music is compelling, exciting, mournful, and definitely original." "[T]here's a seamless balance between epic and intimate, and the composer's knack for rhythms and dense percussion textures is evident throughout *Caprica,*" noted KQEK's Mark R. Hasan. And in an assessment for the Review Fix Web site, Ron Hatcher decreed, "McCreary has delivered a touching, ominous, thrilling musical journey," concluding "for fans of *Battlestar Galactica,* this spin-off album is an exhilarating listening experience."

In 2010, McCreary worked on *Human Target,* a television series based on a comic book of the same title. *Human Target* follows the exploits of a bodyguard who poses as his clients in order to protect them. McCreary, who served as the composer for the show's first season, told Jusino, "The score that I was able to write for the show was nothing like contemporary scoring at all. It feels like Alan Silvestri, John Williams, Jerry Goldsmith, Elmer Bernstein, or any of the guys I grew up listening to." Critics, such as IGN Music's Eric Goldman, noticed the difference: "McCreary's score for *Human Target* allowed him to delve into the trappings of a bigger than life hero for the first time, complete with the fanfare we expect from such a character." On the Blogcritics Web Site, Brian Fitzpatrick remarked, "I felt like McCreary's music gave this television show the feel of a movie each week—truly capturing the pulse of the action on screen." After describing the score as "a bundle of rich, sophisticated, and catchy music" and noting "The enthusiasm that's behind the music is infectious and the spirited, adventurous tone is tangible," a reviewer for the Score Notes Web site concluded, ". . . it's hard to fathom that this great music hails from a modern television series and not some Spielberg blockbuster. That's how good it is." For his part, McCreary revealed to Cyriaque Lamar on the IO9 Web site that "The first season of *Human Target* . . . pushed me to become a much more sophisticated orchestral writer. It was a dream come true—this was the kind of music I grew up on, this was the kind of music that made me want to become a composer in the first place."

McCreary's next musical opportunity came in the form of videogames, and he composed soundtracks for *Dark Void* and *SOCOM 4: U.S. Navy Seals*. Although it was a new medium for the composer, his creative approach did not change, as he explained to Lamar: "Ultimately, TV and games are very similar—I'm thinking about character themes, I'm thinking about the big picture narratively, I'm thinking about how I want the audience to feel. . . . Once I get writing, it's not very different at all." The production quality of games caught McCreary's attention, however. Speaking with Tong, McCreary observed that "games are becoming more cinematic, and the narrative experience is becoming more and more important. . . ." He continued by telling Tong, "the analogy I always make is that you want it to feel like there's a conductor inside your . . . [gaming console] watching you and conducting this orchestra, and when you start making changes, he cues his orchestra, and they change what they're doing. A conductor is a human being, and music is an emotional experience, so it's a combination of technology and emotional art that is coming together in video game music."

Bringing Music to the People

In 2006, during his tenure with *Battlestar Galactica*, McCreary held the first concerts featuring his music from the show. He told Raz that what started as a whim took off: "I was astonished that fans would want to come out and see soundtrack music for a cable TV show performed live. It's really—it's still dawning on me how many people out there are passionate about this music and appreciate it outside of the show." After another performance in 2008, reviewer Eric Goldman observed on the IGN Music Web site, "It's normal to hear cheers when a favorite song is played in concert, and that's what occurred here. It's just that the 'songs' were musical cues from a TV series." Goldman added, "while the music is incredibly effective as accompaniment to the series, it was very impressive how well it worked on its own." The popularity of these events seemed to perplex McCreary. He explained to Phillips, "I didn't become a TV and film composer because I wanted to play sold-out rock concerts, but that's what's ended up happening. And it's fun. I'm grateful for the opportunity to play the music that means so much to those people, and to me, live in a concert setting with all of the musicians that I work with in the studio."

If you enjoy the music of Bear McCreary, you may also want to check out the following soundtracks:

Peter Gabriel's *Passion: Music For The Last Temptation Of Christ* (1989).
Brian Tyler's score for *Frank Herbert's Children of Dune* (2003).
Ramin Djawadi's score for *Game of Thrones* (2011).

Shortly after his first live concerts, McCreary came up with another way to reach out to his audience. He started a blog on his Web site, describing the music for the season three episodes of *Battlestar Galactica*. McCreary admitted to Jusino, "I really didn't think that there would be an audience out there for something so detail-oriented in terms of scoring." He was wrong; it was a hit. While McCreary told Jusino that "it's fun to find a way to share what I do with people who love soundtrack music," others were more effusive. *Hollywood Reporter* contributor Ann Donahue credited McCreary's blog for providing "a fascinating look at the process of making music for film and television." McCreary's posts have expanded to include photos as well as audio and video clips. He told Sepinwall, "My blog has become increasingly detailed, but increasingly personal, it was something that I briefly hesitated to write up, because writing is a very intensely personal and miserable process for everyone. People that don't write, whatever it is, they just assume you sit down and it magically pours out like Amadeus, and it's definitely humbling to know that it doesn't necessarily happen that way."

By balancing talent with determination and an intense work ethic, McCreary has created a lengthy credit list for a relatively young composer. Yet it is the quality of those scores that captures the attention of listeners and critics alike. West argued that McCreary's "ability to create interesting sounds and music that enhance the mood of some of the more emotional scenes he's scored is part of what makes him stand out in his field." The composer earned an even higher accolade in 2009, when the IO9 Web site included McCreary on its list of the ten best science fiction composers. In an video interview during 2011's 7 International Film Music Festival, McCreary provided his take on the ranking: "It's very humbling for me to be on a list with John Williams and Jerry Goldsmith and Bernard Herrmann—these are the composers I grew up admiring. I hope that one day I will be able to be on that list; I don't know if I should be yet—but I'm working at it. I'm going to just keep working and keep writing and hope that I get to do what those guys . . . have done: which is to work their whole life and always be making music. That's my ultimate goal."

■ Biographical and Critical Sources

PERIODICALS

Bellingham Herald, January 12, 2005, Kie Relyea, "Score for the Stars: Bellingham High Grad Now Composes for *Battlestar Galactica.*"

Daily Trojan, December 2, 2003, Kathleen Bishop, "USC Thornton School of Music Alumnus Continues Scoring Films."

Hollywood Reporter, April 17, 2008, Ann Donahue, "McCreary Carries the Tune for the *Battlestar* Minions."

Wall Street Journal, June 7, 2007, Greg Sandow, "What *Battlestar Galactica* Taught Me about Verdi."

ONLINE

AmericanMusicPreservation.com, http://www. americanmusicpreservation.com/ (June 20, 2006), Steven A. Kennedy, "*Battlestar Galactica*—Season Two."

Battlestar Galactica, http://www.bsg.cz/ (November 1, 2011), "Exclusive Interview for BSG.cz with Bear McCreary."

Bear McCreary Official Site, http://www.bear mccreary.com/ (January 14, 2012).

Blogcritics, http://www.blogcritics.org/ (June 12, 2009), Chris Beaumont, "Music Review: *Caprica*— Music Composed by Bear McCreary"; (October 25, 2010), Brian Fitzpatrick, "Music Review: Bear McCreary—*Human Target* Soundtrack."

Blogger News Network, http://www.bloggernews. net/ (January 6, 2009), Zach Freeman, "Music Review: *Terminator: The Sarah Connor Chronicles* Original Television Soundtrack."

Cinefantastique, http://www.cinefantastiqueonline. com/ (February, 2006), Daniel Schweiger, "A Different Trek: Bear McCreary Redefines the Sound of Space Scoring Aboard the *Galactica*"; (March 9, 2008), Randall Larson, "The Score: Bear McCreary—From *Battlestar Galactica* to *Terminator.*"

Film Music Magazine, http://www.filmmusicmag. com/ (January, 2007), Daniel Schweiger, "Bear McCreary: Scoring *Battlestar Galactica's* Brave New World"; (August 10, 2009), "CD Review: *Battlestar Galactica*: Season 4"; (March 14, 2011), David Raiklen, "Scoring Session with Composer Bear McCreary."

Film Music Media, http://www.filmmusicmedia. com/ (May 23, 2011), Kaya Savas, "*SOCOM 4:* U.S. Navy SEALs by Bear McCreary (Review)."

Film Music Weekly, November 9, 2007, Daniel Schweiger, "Bear McCreary's Space Opera Continues Its Innovative Course to Earth."

Film Score Monthly, http://www.filmscoremonthly. com/ (November 4, 2011), Steven A. Kennedy, "*Terminator: The Sarah Connor Chronicles.*"

G4, http://www.g4tv.com/ (February 6, 2010), Rick Damigella, "Don't Pass This One By—the *Dark Void* Soundtrack Review"; (April 10, 2010), Rick Damigella, "8-Bit Bear—the *Dark Void* Zero Soundtrack Review."

Gamespot, http://www.gamespot.com/ (August 30, 2011), Sophia Tong, "Sound Byte: Meet the Composer—Bear McCreary."

Hardwareheaven.com, http://www.hardwareheaven. com/ (January 11, 2010), "Bear McCreary—*Dark Void* Composer—Interview."

IGN Music, http://www.music.ign.com/ (April 14, 2008), Eric Goldman, "*Battlestar Galactica* Rocks Live"; (June 22, 2009), Finn White, "*Caprica* Soundtrack Review"; (December 2, 2010), Eric Goldman, "*Human Target*: Season 1 Soundtrack Review."

International Musician, http://www.afm.org/im/ (July, 2008), "Bear McCreary among the Stars."

IO9, http://io9.com/ (June 11, 2009), "The 10 Best Science Fiction Composers"; (June 7, 2010), "Composer Bear McCreary Jumps from *Battlestar Galactica* to Videogames."

KQEK, http://www.kqek.com/ (June 16, 2009), Mark R. Hasan, "CD: *Caprica.*"

Los Angeles Times, http://www.latimes.com/ (October 5, 2006), Litty Mathew, "It's Enough to Make You Cry"; (June 7, 2009), David Ng, "Bear McCreary's Symphonic Sounds for *Battlestar Galactica*"; (January 15, 2020), Jevon Phillips, "*Caprica* Countdown: The Music of the Master, Bear McCreary."

Mix, http://www.mixonline.com/ (August 1, 2008), Bryan Reesman, "Composer Spotlight: Bear McCreary."

Music On Film, http://www.musiconfilm.net/ (June 8, 2005), Jonathan Shearon, "*Battlestar Galactica*: Season One."

New Jersey Star Ledger, http://www.nj.com/ (June 22, 2008), Alan Sepinwall, "Sepinwall on TV: Michael Giacchino and Bear McCreary, Score Keepers."

Original Sound Version, http://www.originalsound version.com/ (February 12, 2010), Jayson Napolitano, "*Dark Void* Soundtrack: Condemned to the Void?"

Pop Matters, http://www.popmatters.com/ (November 23, 2010), Teresa Jusino, "The New Champion: An Interview with Bear McCreary of *Human Target.*"

Review Fix, http://www.reviewfix.com/ (July 23, 2009), Ron Hatcher, "Bear's Music before the Show Doesn't Disappoint."

Salon, http://www.salon.com/ (April 2, 2008), Thomas Rogers, "Everything You Were Afraid to Ask about *Battlestar Galactica.*"

Score Notes, http://www.scorenotes.com/ (fall, 2008), "review of *Eureka*"; (January, 2009), "review of *Sarah Connor Chronicles*"; (summer, 2009), "review of *Caprica*"; (December, 2010), "review of *Human Target.*"

Seattle Post-Intelligencer, http://www.seattlepi.com/ (April 26, 2011), "Music Review: Bear McCreary—*Human Target* Soundtrack."

Soundtrack.net, http://www.soundtrack.net/ (July 29, 2009), Mike Brennan, "*Battlestar Galactica*: Season Four Soundtrack."

Television Blend, http://www.cinemablend.com/ television/ (December 16, 2010), Kelly West, "The *Cape* Creator Says Bear McCreary's Theme Music Rocks."

Tor.com, http://www.tor.com/ (November 12, 2010), Teresa Jusino, "An Interview with Bear McCreary: TV's Most Popular Music Geek."

TV.com, http://www.tv.com/ (December 15, 2007), "An Exclusive Interview with Bear McCreary."

Walking Dead Blog, http://blogs.amctv.com/the-walking-dead/ (November 19, 2010), Clayton Neuman, "Q&A—Bear McCreary (Composer)."

Zombie Zone News, http://www.zombiezonenews. com/ (October 12, 2011), "Picking Brains with Wednesday Lee Friday: Bear McCreary."

OTHER

Weekend All Things Considered, NPR, June 21, 2009, "*Battlestar Galactica*: Beyond Background Music," McCreary interview with Guy Raz.*

Robin McKinley

■ Personal

Born November 16, 1952, in Warren, OH; daughter of William (in the U.S. Navy and Merchant Marines) and Jeanne Carolyn (a teacher) McKinley; married Peter Dickinson (an author), January 3, 1992. *Education:* Attended Dickinson College, 1970-72; Bowdoin College, B.A. (summa cum laude), 1975. *Hobbies and other interests:* Gardening, horses, walking, travel, many kinds of music, and life as an expatriate and the English-American culture chasm.

■ Addresses

Home—Hampshire, England. *E-mail*—nuraddin @robinmckinley.com.

■ Career

Writer, 1975—. Ward & Paul (stenographic reporting firm), Washington, DC, editor and transcriber, 1972-73; Research Associates, Brunswick, ME, research assistant, 1976-77; bookstore clerk in Maine, 1978; teacher and counselor at private secondary school in Natick, MA, 1978-79; Little, Brown, Inc., Boston, MA, editorial assistant, 1979-81; barn manager on a horse farm, Holliston, MA, 1981-82; Books of Wonder, New York, NY, clerk, 1983; freelance reader, copy and line editor, "general all-purpose publishing dogsbody," 1983-91.

■ Awards, Honors

Horn Book Honor Book designation, 1978, for *Beauty,* 1985, for *The Hero and the Crown,* 1988, for *The Outlaws of Sherwood,* and 1995, for *Knot in the Grain;* Best Books for the Teen Age citation, New York Public Library, 1980, 1981, and 1982, all for *Beauty;* Best Young-Adult Books citation, American Library Association (ALA), 1982, and Newbery Honor Book designation, ALA, 1983, both for *The Blue Sword;* Newbery Medal, and Notable Book designation, ALA, both 1985, both for *The Hero and the Crown;* World Fantasy Award for best anthology, 1986, for *Imaginary Lands;* Best Books for the Teen Age citation and Best Adult Book for the Teen Age, ALA, both 1994, both for *Deerskin;* Mythopoeic Award for Adult Literature, 2003, for *Sunshine.* D.H.L., Bowdoin College, 1986, Wilson College, 1996.

■ Writings

FICTION

Beauty: A Retelling of the Story of Beauty and the Beast, Harper (New York, NY), 1978.

The Door in the Hedge (short stories), Greenwillow (New York, NY), 1981.

The Blue Sword, Greenwillow (New York, NY), 1982, reprinted, Ace Books (New York, NY), 2007.

The Hero and the Crown, Greenwillow (New York, NY), 1984, reprinted, Ace Books (New York, NY), 2007.

(Editor and contributor) *Imaginary Lands* (short stories; includes "The Stone Fey"), Greenwillow (New York, NY), 1985.

The Outlaws of Sherwood, Greenwillow (New York, NY), 1988, reprinted, Firebird (New York, NY), 2002.

My Father Is in the Navy (picture book), illustrated by Martine Gourbault, Greenwillow (New York, NY), 1992.

Rowan (picture book), illustrated by Donna Ruff, Greenwillow (New York, NY), 1992.

Deerskin (adult fantasy), Putnam (New York, NY), 1993.

A Knot in the Grain and Other Stories, Greenwillow (New York, NY), 1994.

Rose Daughter, Greenwillow (New York, NY), 1997.

The Stone Fey, illustrated by John Clapp, Harcourt (San Diego, CA), 1998.

Spindle's End, Putnam (New York, NY), 2000.

(With husband, Peter Dickinson) *Water: Tales of Elemental Spirits*, Putnam (New York, NY), 2002.

Sunshine (adult novel), Berkeley Books (New York, NY), 2003.

Dragonhaven, Putnam (New York, NY), 2007.

Chalice, Putnam (New York, NY), 2008.

(With husband, Peter Dickinson) *Fire: Tales of Elemental Spirits*, Putnam (New York, NY), 2009.

Pegasus, Putnam (New York, NY), 2010.

Contributor to anthologies, including *Elsewhere II*, edited by Terri Windling and Mark Arnold, Ace Books, 1982; *Elsewhere III*, edited by Terri Windling and Mark Arnold, Ace Books, 1984; and *Faery*, edited by Terri Windling, Ace Books, 1985. Also contributor of book reviews to numerous periodicals. Author of column, "In the Country," for *New England Monthly*, 1987-88.

ADAPTER

Rudyard Kipling, *Tales from the Jungle Book*, Random House (New York, NY), 1985.

Anna Sewell, *Black Beauty*, illustrated by Susan Jeffers, Random House (New York, NY), 1986.

George MacDonald, *The Light Princess*, illustrated by Katie Thamer Treherne, Harcourt (San Diego, CA), 1988.

■ **Adaptations**

Random House recorded *The Blue Sword* (1994) and *The Hero and the Crown* (1986) on cassette.

■ **Sidelights**

Author Robin McKinley is known for her "down-to-earth truths and emotional resonance," according to Anita L. Burkam in *Horn Book*. Winner of the prestigious Newbery Medal, McKinley has been celebrated for her fantasy novels and for her retellings of fairy tales. Though often dubbed a young adult novelist, McKinley pens tales for readers of all ages. McKinley commented to *Publishers Weekly Online* contributor Michael Levy: "I don't differentiate in the way that the genre creators want differentiation to be made. I feel that I have never written children's or YA stories particularly. What I write, if you have to label it, is crossover, and I think that much of the stuff that is called children's or YA is in fact crossover and is equally valid for anyone who likes to read fantasy." In an interview with John Morgan, posted on McKinley's home page, the author further addressed this issue: "I write my books for the people who want to read them," adding, "Good books are good books, whether they're told from a child's or teenager's point of view, or are accessible and comprehensible to children as well as to adults."

McKinley's fantasy novels and renditions of classic fairy tales have a feminist twist; no weak-kneed damsels in distress, McKinley's protagonists are females who do things rather than "waiting limply to be rescued by the hero," as the author explained on her home page. Indeed, Lesley S.J. Farmer remarked in *Kliatt*, "McKinley's tales tend to favor a feminist perspective and independence." Similarly, Marilyn H. Karrenbrock writing in *Dictionary of Literary Biography* noted: "McKinley's females do not simper; they do not betray their own nature to win a man's approval. But neither do they take love lightly or put their own desires before anything else. In McKinley's books, the romance, like the adventure, is based upon ideals of faithfulness, duty, and honor." In novels such as *The Blue Sword*, *The Hero and the Crown*, *Chalice*, and *Pegasus*, she fills her fantasy realms with realistic detail and powerful characters, attracting readers both young and old. McKinley has also collaborated with her husband, writer Peter Dickinson, on the story collections *Water: Tales of Elemental Spirits* and *Fire: Tales of Elemental Spirits*.

The Power of the Word

McKinley "grew up a military brat and an only child [who] decided early on that books were much more reliable friends than people," as she wrote on her home page. She was born in her mother's hometown of Warren, Ohio, while her naval officer father was serving abroad. Once reunited, the family moved every two years, from California to Japan to New York, and she found comfort in fictional worlds. "Writing has always been the other side of reading for me," the author further commented. "It never occurred to me not to make up stories." However, as a young girl, she also had identity issues. "I despised myself for being a girl," she once commented, "and ipso facto being someone who stayed at home and was boring, and started trying to tell myself stories about girls who did things and had adventures."

McKinley also grew up loving horses. In Japan, she took riding lessons. She would ride on a bus two hours every Saturday as a nine year old to the stables where she took these lessons, learning to ride on an old gelding named Playboy. "It is not surprising that McKinley's peripatetic childhood, constant reading, and desire for adventure should lead to the creation of a world where real and unreal meet," noted Karrenbrock. "Most of her favorite fantasies extolled exploits almost exclusively male, but the stories she told herself were concerned with girls who stumbled and bumbled their way to triumphant conclusions."

"Once I got old enough to realize that authorship existed as a thing one might aspire to, I knew it was for me," McKinley recalled on her home page. "I even majored in English literature in college, a good indication of my fine bold disdain for anything so trivial as earning a living." She saw herself as a writer in the J.R.R. Tolkien or H. Rider Haggard vein, but unlike those authors, she was "going to tell breathtaking stories about *girls* who had adventures."

Like her youth as a military brat, McKinley's education was also somewhat peripatetic. She attended a preparatory school in Maine and then to Pennsylvania for her first two years of college. In 1972, she took some time off from college to work as a translator and transcriber in Washington, DC, then finished up her college education back in Maine, where she graduated summa cum laude from Bowdoin College. McKinley stayed on in Maine for several more years, working in a bookshop and experimenting with writing. Her first publication, written only a few years after graduating from Bowdoin, was inspired by viewing an adaptation of "Beauty and the Beast" on television. She was so disappointed with what she saw that she began to write a version of the classic fairy tale herself.

Taking on a Classic

The result was *Beauty: A Retelling of Beauty and the Beast*, "an excellent example of a relatively rare but

by no means unknown genre, the expanded and personalized version of an old fairy tale," as Karrenbrock noted. Often with such retellings, authors will attempt to make the tales more contemporary or more realistic, Karrenbrock further observed. "McKinley does not do either of these. She retains the magic; indeed she adds to it in the description of the enchanted castle."

Beauty—or Honour, as she is named in McKinley's version—is an awkward child, not a beauty, and her "evil sisters" are caring and kind. "Many truths can be found in these pages," Daniel P. Woolsey commented in *Children's Literature in Education.* "Beauty shows us that the underdog can prevail, for we see a plain, unsociable, and overly intellectual girl rise to the challenge put before her and grow into maturity in the process. As we watch the dynamic and uneven growth of the relationship between Beauty and Beast, we recognize anew that some people may elicit our love and our fear at the same time."

Beauty won praise from readers and critics alike, many of whom applauded McKinley's handling of fantasy in the medieval setting. "The aura of magic around the Beast and his household comes surprisingly to life," commented a *Choice* critic. The winner of several literary awards, *Beauty* instantly established McKinley as a powerful new voice in young-adult literature, and it has remained one of McKinley's most popular novels.

Years after publishing *Beauty,* McKinley returned to the story it was based on: *Rose Daughter.* Far from being a sequel to *Beauty,* however, *Rose Daughter* has "a more mystical, darker edge," according to Sally Estes in *Booklist.* In the novel, readers learn about the early family life and personalities of the three sisters: the acerbic Jeweltongue; Lionheart, a physically daring girl; and the title character Beauty. Unlike the original tale of "Beauty and the Beast," the relationship between the three sisters is loving rather than hostile. Although they have been raised in the city by their wealthy and widowed father, when he loses his business the family relocates to a rural cottage where new hardships bring the family closer together.

One central element of *Rose Daughter* is the flower of the title: in the sisters' new home roses are extremely difficult to cultivate, but Beauty discovers while working in her country garden that she possesses a skill for raising the beautiful flower. She also finds herself plagued by disturbing dreams of a dark corridor, a memory of her mother, and the scent of roses. The Beast is a legendary local figure, a tragic hero who is only half-man, and when Beauty journeys to his castle and begins tending the magic roses in his garden, other flora and fauna return to the Beast's former wasteland. A romance develops between the two, and Beauty's tenderness toward the Beast eventually unlocks the curse that has beset him. "As before, McKinley takes the essentials of the traditional tale and embellishes them with vivid and quirky particulars," declared a contributor for *Publishers Weekly*. Jennifer Fakolt, reviewing *Rose Daughter* for *Voice of Youth Advocates*, asserted that the author "has captured the timelessness of the traditional tale and breathed into it passion and new life appropriate to the story's own 'universal themes' of love and regeneration," while the *Publishers Weekly* reviewer wrote that McKinley's "heady mix of fairy tale, magic and romance has the power to exhilarate."

The World of Damar

Prior to writing *Beauty*, McKinley had begun work on several stories set in a fictional world she called Damar. As she once explained, "I had begun . . . to realize that there was more than one story to tell about Damar, that in fact it seemed to be a whole history, volumes and volumes of the stuff, and this terrified me. I had plots and characters multiplying like mice and running in all directions." The first "Damar" book to appear was the story collection *The Door in the Hedge,* which was published in 1981. *The Blue Sword*, McKinley's second novel, was published one year later. The hero in this second "Damar" book is Harry Crewe, a young woman who must forge her identity and battle an evil force at the same time. After Harry is kidnapped, she learns from her kidnappers how to ride a horse and battle as a true warrior. While she struggles in the tradition of the legendary female hero of Damar, Aerin, the teen becomes a hero in her own right.

Although *The Blue Sword* is set in a fantasy world— Damar was characterized as "pseudo-Victorian" by Darrell Schweitzer in *Science Fiction Review*—critics

have found Harry to be a heroine contemporary readers may well understand. Like *Beauty*, *The Blue Sword* earned McKinley both recognition and praise, including a Newbery Honor Book designation. In *Booklist* Sally Estes described the novel as "a zesty, romantic heroic fantasy with . . . a grounding in reality that enhances the tale's verve as a fantasy."

In *The Hero and the Crown*, the next "Damar" novel, readers are taken back in time to learn about Aerin, the legendary warrior woman Harry so reveres. McKinley once explained: "I recognized that there were specific connections between Harry and Aerin, and I deliberately wrote their stories in reverse chronological order because one of the things I'm fooling around with is the idea of heroes: real heroes as opposed to the legends that are told of them afterwards. Aerin is one of her country's greatest heroes, and by the time Harry comes along, Harry is expected—or Harry thinks she is—to live up to her. When you go back and find out about Aerin in *The Hero and the Crown*, you discover that she wasn't this mighty invincible figure. . . . She had a very hard and solitary time of her early fate."

When readers first meet Aerin in *The Hero and the Crown*, she is graceless and clumsy; it takes her a long time to turn herself into a true warrior, and she suffers many traumas. Yet she is clever and courageous, bravely battling and killing the dragons that are threatening Damar. Merri Rosenberg asserted in the *New York Times Book Review* that McKinley "created an utterly engrossing fantasy, replete with a fairly mature romantic subplot as well as adventure." To *Horn Book* contributor Mary M. Burns, *The Hero and the Crown* is "as richly detailed and elegant as a medieval tapestry. . . . Vibrant, witty, compelling, the story is the stuff of which true dreams are made." Writing in the *New Statesman*, Gillian Wilce cited the novel's "completeness, [and] its engaging imagination," while *Wilson Library Bulletin* contributor Frances Bradburn called the novel a "marvelous tale of excitement and female ingenuity."

Upon winning the coveted Newbery Medal in 1985 for *The Hero and the Crown*, McKinley shared her feelings: "The Newbery award is supposed to be the peak of your career as a writer for children or young adults. I was rather young to receive it; and it is a little disconcerting to feel—okay, you've done it; that's it, you should retire now." Far from retiring, however, McKinley has continued to write retellings of traditional favorites as well as original novels and stories. She has returned on occasion to Damar, as she does in *A Knot in the Grain and Other Stories*. The tales in this collection, according to *Bulletin of the Center for Children's Books* critic Betsy

Hearne, bear "McKinley's signature blend of the magical and the mundane in the shape of heroines" who triumph and find love despite the obstacles they face. They also demonstrate McKinley's "remarkable ability to evoke wonder and belief," asserted *Horn Book* contributor Ann A. Flowers. A reviewer for *Publishers Weekly* called *A Knot in the Grain* a "thrilling, satisfying and thought-provoking collection."

Also set in the world of Damar, McKinley's story "The Stone Fey" first appeared in *Imaginary Lands* and was republished as an illustrated book, with artwork by John Clapp. The tale centers on Maddy, a shepherdess, who falls in love with a Stone Fey, a fairy with skin the color of stone. Entranced by her new love, Maddy drifts away from the people and things she loves until she realizes that the Fey can-

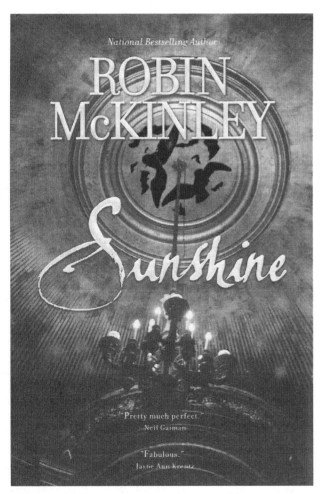

Winner of the Mythopoeic Fantasy Award for Adult Literature, *Sunshine* **concerns the unlikely relationship between a young woman and a vampire in a post-apocalyptic world.** (Copyright © Penguin Putnam Inc. All rights reserved. Reproduced by permission.)

not return her affections. A contributor for *Publishers Weekly* noted that, "while staying true to her penchant for presenting strong female protagonists, . . . McKinley strikes a softer note with this deeply romantic yet ultimately clear-eyed love story." In *Booklist* Carolyn Phelan deemed *The Stone Fey* a "haunting story," and Virginia Golodetz, writing in *School Library Journal,* described McKinley's writing as "passionate."

Offering a New Perspective

The Outlaws of Sherwood exhibits McKinley's talent for revising and reviving traditional tales. Instead of concentrating on Robin Hood—or glorifying him—the novel focuses on other members in his band of outlaws and provides carefully wrought details about their daily lives: how they get dirty and sick, and how they manage their outlaw affairs. Robin is not portrayed as the bold, handsome marksman and sword handler readers may remember from traditional versions of the "Robin Hood" story. Instead, he is nervous, a poor shot, and even reluctant to form his band of merry men. Not surprisingly, McKinley's merry men include merry *women* among their number. "The young women are allowed to be angry, frankly sexual, self willed—and even to outshoot the men, who don't seem to mind," observed *Washington Post Book World* reviewer Michele Landsberg in discussing the author's alteration of the well-known story. In another characteristic revisioning by McKinley, Maid Marian stands out as a brilliant, beautiful leader and an amazingly talented archer. *The Outlaws of Sherwood* is "romantic and absorbing . . . [and] the perfect adolescent daydream where happiness is found in being young and among friends," concluded Shirley Wilton in her review for *Voice of Youth Advocates*.

The adult novel *Deerskin* also demonstrates McKinley's talent for creating new tales out of the foundations of old ones. As Hearne noted, *Deerskin* presents a "darker side of fairy tales." Based on Perrault's "Donkeyskin," a story in which a king assaults his own daughter after his queen dies, the novel focuses on mature themes: it relates how a beautiful princess is raped by her father after the death of her mother. This "is also a dog story," Hearne reminded readers: Princess Lissar survives the brutal attack and heals emotionally because of her relationship with her dog, Ash. "Written with deep passion and power, *Deerskin* is an almost unbearably intense portrait of a severely damaged young woman. . . . There is also romance, humor, and sheer delight," commented Christy Tyson in *Voice of Youth Advocates*. In *School Library Journal*, Cathy Chauvette deemed the book "a riveting and relentless fairy tale, told in ravishing prose."

With *Spindle's End*, McKinley once again revamps a fairy tale for modern readers. Using "Sleeping Beauty" as a template, she creates a "novel of complex imagery and characters," according to a critic for *Family Life*. In this tale the infant princess Briar Rose is cursed on her name day by the evil fairy, Pernicia, and then—as in the original—taken away to a remote and magical land to be raised, her real identity concealed, in an attempt to escape the wrath of Pernicia. In McKinley's take, the good fairy Katriona takes the young princess away to her village of Foggy Bottom, renames her Rosie, and raises her while awaiting her twenty-first birthday—when she will supposedly prick her finger on a spinning-wheel spindle and fall into an eternal sleep. In order to confound Pernicia, Rosie and her friend Peony exchange places at her birthday. Rosie's kiss awakens the sleeping Peony, who in turn marries the prince, leaving Rosie free to continue the simple life she loves and to marry the village blacksmith.

Writing in *School Library Journal*, Connie Tyrrell Burns felt that in *Spindle's End* "McKinley once again lends a fresh perspective to a classic fairy tale, developing the story of 'Sleeping Beauty' into a richly imagined, vividly depicted novel." In *Booklist* Estes noted that McKinley's reinterpretation of the old fairy tale "takes readers into a credibly developed world." "Full of humor and romance as well as magic and adventure, and with an ending that has a decided twist," Estes concluded, "this spellbinding novel is bound to attract McKinley's fans and those who relish the genre." A critic for *Publishers Weekly* called *Spindle's End* a "luscious, lengthy novel" that is "dense with magical detail and all-too-human feeling."

Fantasies with a Different Twist

"Elegant prose and lyrical descriptions capture reader interest while an increasingly tense plot maintains it," wrote a *Kirkus Reviews* contributor in a review of McKinley's novel *Chalice*. In this original fantasy, the author spins a story that focuses on a young woman named Mirasol. Serving the Master of Willowlands as a Chalice, or servant, Mirasol is also a beekeeper. However, her task now is a pressing one: to mend her damaged world by finding a way to bind her Master, a Prince of Fire who causes everything he touches to burn, to the fragile land that is now wracked by earthquakes and other destruction. Noting that Mirasol is a characteristic McKinley heroine "who discovers her impressive powers as she finds her way," *Booklist* critic Lynn Rutan praised the novel's evocative narration as "a sensory delight." In *Publishers Weekly* an equally impressed reviewer characterized *Chalice* as a "high

fantasy as perfectly shaped and eloquently told" as McKinley's best-known novels, the critic concluding that the romantic tale will be greeted as "a lavish and lasting treat" by the author's many fans. "Teens who long for beautiful phrases and descriptive writing will find themselves drinking in this rich fairy tale as if it were honey," predicted Heather M. Campbell in her review of *Chalice* for *School Library Journal*.

Booklist contributor Jennifer Mattson characterized McKinley's novel *Dragonhaven* as something of "a curveball" for the author's fans due to its modern-day setting. However, readers soon discover what Mattson dubbed "a distinctly fantastical aspect" to the Wyoming nature preserve where fifteen-year-old protagonist Jake lives with his naturalist father. Jake is studying Draca Australiensis, the last remaining species of dragon on Earth. When he secretly raises a young dragon whose mother has been killed by poachers, Jake challenges prevailing theories about how humans and dragons have coevolved and also gains an intimate knowledge of the gigantic fire-breathing creatures. In *Dragonhaven* "McKinley renders her imagined universe . . . potently," wrote a *Publishers Weekly* reviewer, the critic adding that the "tightly wound and solitary Jake" is a protagonist who is "classic McKinley." According to a *Kirkus Reviews* writer, the novel treats readers to a "sharply incisive, wildly intelligent dragon fantasy involving profound layers of science and society, love and loss and nature and nurture." In *Kliatt* Paula Rohrlick wrote that McKinley's "engrossing fantasy is suspenseful and highly detailed," and Jake's "self-deprecating sense of humor helps make [*Dragonhaven*] . . . a truly wonderful read."

In addition to novel-length fiction, McKinley has also written original picture books for children. *Rowan* is a story about a girl selecting and loving a pet dog, while *My Father Is in the Navy* portrays a young girl whose father has been away for some time: as he is about to return, she tries to remember what her father looks like. Reviewing *Rowan*, a contributor for *Publishers Weekly* called it an "affable tale of a girl and her pet," while in *School Library Journal* JoAnn Rees called *My Father Is in the Navy* a "warm, loving look at a family group." Other books by McKinley that are geared for younger readers include short retellings of classics like Anna Sewell's *Black Beauty*, George MacDonald's *The Light Princess*, and Rudyard Kipling's *The Jungle Book*.

Powerful Storytelling

A novel inspired, in part, by McKinley's appreciation of the *Buffy the Vampire* television series, *Sunshine* was awarded the Mythopoeic Fantasy Award for

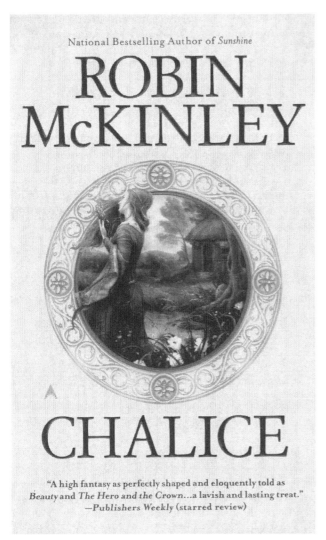

National Bestselling Author of *Sunshine*

ROBIN McKINLEY

CHALICE

"A high fantasy as perfectly shaped and eloquently told as *Beauty* and *The Hero and the Crown*...a lavish and lasting treat."
—*Publishers Weekly* (starred review)

In *Chalice*, a young woman must bind her new master, a Prince of Fire who causes everything he touches to burn, to their fragile land, which is on the verge of annihilation. (Cover illustration by Cory Ench and Catska Ench. Ace Books, 2009. Reproduced by permission of The Berkley Publishing Group, a division of Penguin Group (U.S.A.) Inc.)

Adult Literature in 2003. Sunshine is the nickname of twenty-something Rae Seddon, a talented baker who works at her stepfather's restaurant—along with her mom, her boyfriend, Mel, and the rest of the close-knit staff. Charlie's Coffeehouse is in a not-so-trendy part of town, but it's relatively safe. In the aftermath of the Voodoo Wars between humans and supernatural creatures, that is always a consideration. The most dangerous of the Others are vampires; humans don't survive encounters with them. One night, when Sunshine is at her family's old lake house, she is captured by vampires. They imprison her in an old mansion, chaining her to the wall next to Constantine, a rogue vampire. Desperate to escape, Sunshine draws on hidden powers that her grandmother had once cultivated in her: she magically changes her pocket knife into a key and frees herself and her vampire co-prisoner, and then manages to protect him from the rising sun with more magical powers. Such an extraordinary event puts both the human Special Other Forces and the vampire gangs on alert, and Sunshine knows that she must ultimately help Constantine battle the vampires that are surely pursuing them.

This prize-winning tale earned high praise from reviewers. *Booklist* contributor Kristine Huntley, for example, called it a "luminous, entrancing novel with an enthralling pair of characters at its heart." Similarly, a *Publishers Weekly* reviewer felt that the "charm of this . . . [tale] derives from McKinley's keen ear and sensitive atmospherics, deft characterizations and clever juxtapositions of reality and the supernatural." For a *Kirkus Reviews* writer, the novel is an "intriguing mix of Buffy the Vampire Slayer and Harry Potter-ish characterization."

McKinley's *Pegasus* is a fantasy in which "descriptions of the culture of a society of winged horses, or pegasi, take central place," according to *Horn Book* reviewer Deirdre F. Baker. In this tale, royal humans and pegasi have long been allied in Basinland, but it is not until the advent of Princess Sylvi that humans have been able to communicate with the flying horses. It is the bond between Sylvi and her personal pegasus, Ebon, that allows the princess to communicate in the silent speech of the pegasi, but such an ability also causes difficulties, as it is a threat to the position of the magician-interpreters of the human realm. Some of these royal magicians attempt to do whatever it takes to keep Sylvi and Ebon apart.

School Library Journal reviewer Misti Tidman felt that McKinley's "story is strong and fresh, and the characters are nuanced and believable." A *Kirkus Reviews* contributor similarly commended the "lush, dense prose and the careful unfolding of a nuanced tale" in this work, further calling it "magnificent and magical." For *Booklist* writer Daniel Kraus, "McKinley's storytelling is to be savored," and a *Publishers Weekly* reviewer found it "an enchanting fantasy that the author's many fans will love."

McKinley spins further tales of fantasy with Dickinson in the two story collections, *Water* and *Fire*. John Peters explained in *School Library Journal* that the former collection is comprised of six "masterfully written stories" that, with their "distinct, richly detailed casts and settings," will "excite, enthrall, and move even the pickiest readers." The stories in the collection are not true collaborations, in that the authors do now write stories together; instead, they alternate tales in the collection. In *Water*, McKinley contributes three fantasy tales with plucky heroines; one of the stories harkens back to the magic land of Damar, the setting of her *The Hero and the Crown*. This collection "explores aspects of water both benign and malignant," noted a *Kirkus Reviews* contributor. A *Publishers weekly* reviewer similarly termed *Water* a "a collection of enchanting tales linked by an aquatic theme."

McKinley continue their elements-themed story collections with *Fire*. Here McKinley contributes the short story "Hellhound," in which young Miri takes in a strange dog whose eyes seem to burn red. Her novella, "First Flight," deals with a shy young boy who has a talent for healing that proves valuable in helping a crippled dragon learn to fly. A *Publishers Weekly* reviewer dubbed "First Flight" the "standout contribution" of the collection, while *Booklist* critic Krista Hutley called all five tales in this collection "masterful in character, setting, and plot." Likewise, Tidman, again writing in *School Library Journal*, commented: "This collection of beautifully crafted tales will find a warm welcome from fans of either author, as well as from fantasy readers in general." *Journal of Adolescent & Adult Literacy* reviewer Shelly Shaffer noted: "McKinley and Dickinson have created a collection of stories that readers of any age will love."

The Writing Life

In 1992, McKinley married Dickinson and moved from her homes in New York and Maine to England, where she still lives. The couple first lived in Hampshire in an "enormous old ramshackle house in the country," as McKinley told Levy in *Publishers Weekly Online*. However, after a time this house proved to be too remote for their liking, and the couple moved into a nearby town, occupying two small houses on one property. McKinley has an office in her cottage.

In "Twenty Hundred Words," an interview posted on her home page, McKinley discussed where she gets the ideas for her fiction: "I have an imagination that gets sparked off by things, and produces stories. Everything that interests me feeds my imagination, and so I am in the extremely pleasant position of *needing* to follow my interests so I can do what I do, which is write stories." She remarked to Morgan, "Good fantasy talks about our deepest inner selves, about the dreams and longings and hopes and fears and strivings that make us human. The great thing about fantasy is that you can drag dreams and longings and hopes and fears and strivings out of your subconscious and call them 'magic' or 'dragons' or 'fairies' and get to know them better."

In an interview with *Publishers Weekly* contributor Mitzi Brunsdale, the author commented on her penchant for using fairy tale motifs in her writing: "I tend to believe that every writer has one, single, archetypal source story. You inform it and it informs you. If you're a writer, depending on how clever you are, and how big a net your particular story casts, the stories you write are more or less recognizable reworkings of your one story. My story happens to be Beauty and the Beast."

"If you're a storyteller, your own life streams through you, onto the page, mixed up with the life the story itself brings; you cannot, in any useful or genuine way, separate the two."

—Robin McKinley, in the author's note to *Rose Daughter.*

"As a compulsive reader myself, I believe that you are what you read," McKinley once commented. "My books are also about hope—I hope. Much of modern literature has given up hope and deals with anti-heroes and despair. It seems to me that human beings by their very natures need heroes, real heroes, and are happier with them. I see no point in talking about how life is over and it never mattered anyway. I don't believe it."

■ Biographical and Critical Sources

BOOKS

Children's Literature Review, Gale (Detroit, MI), Volume 10, 1986, Volume 127, 2007.
Dictionary of Literary Biography, Volume 52: *American Writers for Children since 1960: Fiction*, Gale (Detroit, MI), 1986.
Novels for Students, Volume 33, Gale (Detroit, MI), 2010.
St. James Guide to Fantasy Writers, St. James Press (Detroit, MI), 1996.

St. James Guide to Young Adult Writers, 2nd edition, St. James Press (Detroit, MI), 1999.

PERIODICALS

Booklist, October 1, 1982, Sally Estes, review of *The Blue Sword,* p. 198; August, 1994, Frances Bradburn, review of *A Knot in the Grain and Other Stories,* p. 2039; August, 1997, Sally Estes, review of *Rose Daughter,* p. 1898; November 1, 1998, Carolyn Phelan, review of *The Stone Fey,* p. 484; April, 15, 2000, Sally Estes, review of *Spindle's End,* p. 1543; April 15, 2002, Sally Estes, review of *Water: Tales of Elemental Spirits,* p. 1416; October 15, 2003, Kristine Huntley, review of *Sunshine,* p. 399; October 1, 2007, Jennifer Mattson, review of *Dragonhaven,* p. 44; September 1, 2008, Lynn Rutan, review of *Chalice,* p. 89; September 1, 2009, Krista Hutley, review of *Fire: Tales of Elemental Spirits,* p. 81; October 1, 2010, Daniel Kraus, review of *Pegasus,* p. 88.

Bulletin of the Center for Children's Books, September, 1993, Betsy Hearne, review of *Deerskin,* p. 16; June, 1994, Betsy Hearne, review of *A Knot in the Grain and Other Stories,* p. 327; November, 2009, Kate Quealy-Gainer, review of *Fire,* p. 118; December, 2010, April Spisak, review of *Pegasus,* p. 197.

Children's Literature in Education, June, 1991, Daniel P. Woolsey, review of *Beauty: A Retelling of the Story of Beauty and the Beast,* p9. 129-135.

Choice, July and August, 1979, review of *Beauty,* p. 668.

Family Life, December 1, 2000, review of *Spindle's End,* p. 127.

Horn Book, January-February, 1985, Mary M. Burns, review of *The Hero and the Crown,* pp. 59-60; July-August, 1985, Robin McKinley, "Newbery Medal Acceptance," pp. 395-405; July-August, 1985, Terri Windling and Mark Alan Arnold, "Robin McKinley," pp. 406-409; July-August, 1994, Ann A. Flowers, review of *A Knot in the Grain and Other Stories,* pp. 458-459; September-October, 1997, Lauren Adams, review of *Rose Daughter,* pp. 574-575; May-June, 2000, Anita L. Burkam, review of *Spindle's End,* p. 317; July-August, 2002, Anita L. Burkam, review of *Water,* p. 466; September-October, 2007, Deirdre F. Baker, review of *Dragonhaven,* p. 581; November-December, 2009, Anita L. Burkam, review of *Fire,* p. 681; November-December, 2010, Deirdre F. Baker, review of *Pegasus,* p. 96.

Journal of Adolescent & Adult Literacy, September, 2010, Shelly Shaffer, review of *Fire,* p. 72.

Kirkus Reviews, December 1, 1978, review of *Beauty,* p. 1307; June 1, 2002, review of *Water,* p. 808; August 15, 2003, review of *Sunshine,* p. 1039; August 1, 2007, review of *Dragonhaven;* August 15, 2008, review of *Chalice;* October 1, 2009, review of *Fire;* October 1, 2010, review of *Pegasus.*

Kliatt, July, 2003, Lesley S.J. Farmer, review of *Water,* p. 33; May, 2005, Donna Scanlon, review of *Sunshine,* p. 34; September, 2007, Paula Rohrlick, review of *Dragonhaven,* p. 15.

New Statesman, November 8, 1985, Gillian Wilce, review of *The Hero and the Crown,* p. 28.

New York Times Book Review, January 27, 1985, Merri Rosenberg, review of *The Hero and the Crown,* p. 29; November 13, 1988, Michael Malone, review of *The Outlaws of Sherwood,* p. 54; January 18, 1998, Kathryn Harrison, review of *Rose Daughter,* p. 18; May 14, 2000, Elizabeth Devereaux, review of *Spindle's End,* p. 27.

Publishers Weekly, August 31, 1992, review of *Rowan,* p. 78; April 25, 1994, review of *A Knot in the Grain and Other Stories,* p. 80; June 16, 1997, review of *Rose Daughter,* p. 60; August 31, 1998, review of *The Stone Fey,* p. 77; March 27, 2000, review of *Spindle's End,* p. 82; September 2, 2002, review of *Water,* p. 77; September 29, 2003, review of *Sunshine,* p. 47, and Mitzi Brunsdale, interview with McKinley, p. 48; August 20, 2007, review of *Dragonhaven,* p. 69; July 21, 2008, review of *Chalice;* October 11, 2010, review of *Pegasus,* p. 45.

School Library Journal, January, 1983, Karen Stang Hanley, review of *The Blue Sword,* p. 86; May, 1992, JoAnn Rees, review of *My Father Is in the Navy,* p. 91; September, 1993, Cathy Chauvette, review of *Deerskin,* p. 261; September, 1997, Julie Cummins, review of *Rose Daughter,* pp. 219-220; January, 1999, Virginia Golodetz, review of *The Stone Fey,* p. 130; June, 2000, Connie Tyrrell Burns, review of *Spindle's End,* p. 150; June, 2002, John Peters, review of *Water,* p. 142; December, 2004, Beth Wright, "Once upon a Time: A Librarian Looks at Recent Young-Adult Novels Based on Fairy Tales," p. 40; September, 2007, Beth Wright, review of *Dragonhaven,* p. 203; October, 2008, Heather M. Campbell, review of *Chalice,* p. 154; September, 2009, Misti Tidman, review of *Fire,* p. 166; December, 2010, Misti Tidman, review of *Pegasus,* p. 119.

Science Fiction Review, August, 1983, Darrell Schweitzer, review of *The Blue Sword,* p. 46.

Voice of Youth Advocates, April, 1989, Shirley Wilton, review of *The Outlaws of Sherwood,* p. 44; August, 1993, Christy Tyson, review of *Deerskin,* p. 168; December, 2009, Jonatha Bayse, review of *Fire,* p. 422; February, 2011, Jennifer Crispin, review of *Pegasus,* p. 574.

Washington Post Book World, November 6, 1988, Michele Landsberg, review of *The Outlaws of Sherwood,* p. 15.

Wilson Library Bulletin, January, 1987, Frances Bradburn, review of *The Hero and the Crown*, p. 60.

ONLINE

Interviews in Sherwood Web site, http://www.boldoutlaw.com/ (September 5, 2011), Allen W. Wright, interview with Robin McKinley.

HarperTeen Web site, http://www.harperteen.com/ (November 1, 2011), "Robin McKinley."

Penguin.com, http://us.penguingroup.com/ (November 1, 2011), "An Interview with Robin McKinley."

Publishers Weekly Online, http://www.publishersweekly.com/ (November 11, 2010), Michael Levy, "Q&A with Robin McKinley."

Robin McKinley Home Page, http://www.robinmckinley.com (November 1, 2011).

Speculative Book Review Blog, http://speculativebookreview.blogspot.com/ (November 5, 2010), "Interview: Robin McKinley."*

Laura McNeal

■ Personal

Born in Tempe, AZ; married Tom McNeal (a writer and contractor), 1993; children: Sam, Hank. *Education:* Brigham Young University, B.A.; Syracuse University, M.A. (fiction writing).

■ Addresses

Home—Fallbrook, CA.

■ Career

Author and journalist. Taught middle-school and high-school English in Salt Lake City, UT.

■ Awards, Honors

(With husband, Tom McNeal) California Book Award for juvenile literature, 1999, Best Book for Young Adults designation, American Library Association, and Books for the Teen Age selection, New York Public Library (NYPL), all for *Crooked*; (with Tom McNeal) Children's Literature award, PEN Center USA, 2003, and Books for the Teen Age selection, NYPL, both for *Zipped*; Books for the Teen Age selection, NYPL, for *The Decoding of Lana Morris*; National Book Award finalist in young people's literature, 2010, for *Dark Water*.

■ Writings

Dark Water (young adult novel), Knopf (New York, NY), 2010.

Short stories included in anthology *The Bigger the Better, the Tighter the Sweater.* Contributor to periodicals, including *San Diego Reader.*

WITH HUSBAND, TOM MCNEAL

The Dog Who Lost His Bob (juvenile fiction), illustrated by John Sandford, Albert Whitman (Morton Grove, IL), 1996.
Crooked (young adult novel), Knopf (New York, NY), 1999.
Zipped (young adult novel), Knopf (New York, NY), 2003.
Crushed (young adult novel), Knopf (New York, NY), 2006.
The Decoding of Lana Morris (young adult novel), Knopf (New York, NY), 2007.

■ Sidelights

Laura McNeal earned a National Book Award nomination for the 2010 release *Dark Water*, her first solo effort as a young adult writer. But success was nothing new to McNeal, who was already an accomplished novelist, having previously completed four highly regarded works with her husband, Tom, including the award-winning titles *Crooked* and *Zipped*. The hallmarks of the McNeal's stories, critics note, are their fully-formed characters, perceptive and realistic dialogue, and suspenseful plotlines. "A lot of our research was done as actual teenagers," the authors noted in an interview published in *Zipped*. "We had to live through adolescence, and it's kind of nice to have something to show for it."

Born in Tempe, Arizona, Laura McNeal enjoyed a vagabond childhood, growing up near U.S. Air Force bases in Iceland, New Mexico, and South Carolina. Her family settled in West Point, Utah, when McNeal was thirteen years old, and she attended Clearfield High School. After graduating from Brigham Young University, McNeal taught middle-school and high-school English at a private school in Salt Lake City. She later earned a master's degree in fiction writing from Syracuse University. In 1993, she married Tom McNeal, a writer and building contractor, and the couple moved to Fallbrook, California, a town known as the "Avocado Capital of the World."

Two Heads Are Better Than One

The McNeal's first collaboration, a picture book titled *The Dog Who Lost His Bob*, was published in 1996. *Crooked* their debut work for teen readers, appeared three years later. Set in the small town of Jemison, New York, *Crooked*, focuses on the unlikely relationship between Clara Wilson, a sensitive and intelligent high school freshman, and Amos MacKenzie, a quiet schoolmate whose popularity soars after he is attacked and injured by the thuggish Tripp brothers. In their interview in *Zipped*, the McNeals stated that the writing process for *Crooked* "was like an unplanned car trip. Laura got behind the wheel and drove for one chapter and then slept in the backseat while Tom drove. We switched off after each chapter, so there was the more or less weekly thrill of finding yourself in a new place."

"Each of the books we wrote together was, for us, an unexpected form of courtship."

—Laura McNeal, discussing her working relationship with her husband, Tom McNeal.

As the school year progresses, Clara senses that change is in the offing. Her best friend, Gerri, grows increasingly distant, criticizing Clara's plans to attend a horse camp as well as her reluctance to get cosmetic surgery to fix her crooked nose. Meanwhile, Clara's father, who is often away on business, and her mother, an underemployed store clerk, appear to be drifting away from each other. With money tight at home, Clara decides to supplement the income from her paper route by offering to run errands for her elderly neighbors, and she prepares a special flyer advertising her services, one of which she sends to Amos, who lives along her route and whose seriously ill father delivers milk to the Wilson's home. With a push from Amos's best friend, Bruce Crook, Clara and Amos begin dating.

While walking home one evening, Amos stumbles upon Charles and Eddie Tripp, the town bullies, vandalizing a neighbor's yard, and Charles bludgeons Amos with an aluminum bat, sending him to the hospital with a concussion. Though Amos is too frightened to identify his attackers, Eddie confronts him at school, threatening more harm if Amos ever talks to the police. Still, Amos's battle scars earn the approval of his classmates, who elevate him to hero status, and he begins running with the popular crowd, many of whom look down upon Clara. Confused and angered by Amos's seeming betrayal and the dissolution of her parent's marriage, Clara accepts a ride one afternoon from Eddie, drawn to his rugged good looks even though she distrusts him. When he takes her to an isolated spot in the woods, however, she grows frightened and forces him to take her home.

After Amos's father dies of cancer, Eddie and Charles grow bolder and more menacing, delivering a dead snake to the MacKenzie's home and killing one of Amos's prized homing pigeons. Determined to stop them, Amos spies on the Tripps one evening, learning of their plans to break into Clara's house when she is home alone one night, and he arrives to find Clara trapped in her attic with Eddie and Charles closing in, "a terrifying climax that reveals everyone's true nature," according to *Horn Book* critic Lauren Adams. Despite the novel's serious subject matter, Adams noted that "the tangible yearning and imperfect goodness of both protagonists prevents the novel itself from succumbing to darkness," and a *Publishers Weekly* contributor observed that the book's "strength lies in the interactions between Clara and Amos and their relationships with their respective families."

Love and Other Deceptions

Zipped, the McNeal's second novel, also takes place in Jemison. The work centers on Mick Nichols, a

A former English teacher, McNeal poses with her husband and frequent coauthor, Tom, at the Fourteenth Annual Pen USA Literary Awards Festival. (Copyright © Lee Celano/Getty Images. All rights reserved. Reproduced by permission.)

fifteen year old who, after accidentally opening an e-mail, discovers that his stepmother, Nora, is having an affair. The revelation stuns Mick, who had grown close to Nora, a caring individual who teaches at the local junior high and with whom Mick had shared his feelings about Lisa Doyle, a cute classmate. Though he withholds the information about the affair from his father, Mick decides to investigate further, downloading the e-mails and vowing to keep tabs on Nora's computer while attempting to track down her lover, a man named Alexander Selkirk.

At Nora's suggestion, Mick applies for a weekend job at the Village Greens, a residential community for the elderly, where he is put to work maintaining the grounds under the direction of Maurice Gritz, his controlling and insulting team leader. To his surprise, Mick finds himself working alongside Lisa, and the two strike up a relaxed friendship, based in

part on their mutual distrust of Gritz. Though she enjoys Mick's company, Lisa, a Mormon, develops an interest in Joe Keesler, a young missionary who has just transferred to Jemison, and her attraction to Keesler draws snickers from her best friend, Janice Bledsoe.

One day, while trying to avoid Nora, Mick meets his friend, Winston Reece, in the park, and he accepts Winston's dare to approach a pair of attractive college girls, one of whom, Myra Vidal, asks for his e-mail address. Myra later contacts Mick, and as they spend time together she becomes his confidante, offering sage advice after hearing his concerns about Lisa and Nora. Mick's continued efforts to locate Selkirk prove fruitless, however, until an offhand comment by Winston leads to the man's true identity: Mr. Cruso, one of Nora's fellow teachers. Enraged, Mick damages Cruso's expensive car then lies about his actions to Lisa.

As Mick struggles with his conscience, Lisa battles problems of her own. She falls in love with Keesler only to learn that he has a girlfriend, and she becomes worried when Janice enters a relationship with Gritz, who is sexually harassing one of Lisa and Mick's coworkers and is engaged in some suspicious activity at the complex, which has seen a rise in burglaries. As Lisa summons the courage to tell the police about Gritz, Mick confesses his secrets to Myra, who helps the teen come to terms with his anger about Nora's betrayal. In the process, "Mick learns that the adults whom he has idolized have their own problems, and that relationships are far more complex than he ever imagined," Miranda Doyle wrote in *School Library Journal*. "Themes of good and evil and the gray zone in between, of betrayal, of forgiveness, of love, of tolerance, abound," Claire Rosser noted in *Kliatt*, and a *Kirkus Reviews* contributor remarked that the McNeals "spin a wonderfully rich story."

Finding It Hard to Fit In

The McNeals set their third collaborative novel, *Crushed*, in a familiar locale: Jemison. By this time, the authors had refined their writing methods; as Laura McNeal explained in an interview that was published in *Crushed*: "Now we write outlines and talk about what we think is going to happen in the end. We still take turns, but we write longer segments, sixty or eighty pages. When one person is absolutely sick of the characters and disheartened about the plot, it's time to trade. Taking a month or two away from the story and then coming back to it, finding it transformed and improved by the other person, is extremely rejuvenating."

In *Crushed,* Audrey Reed enters Jemison High as a junior, having transferred from a small private school with her best friends, C.C. Mudd and Lea Woolcott, and C.C.'s younger brother, Brian. Ignored, ridiculed, or harassed by her classmates, Audrey is immediately smitten with Wickham Hill, a handsome, smooth-talking newcomer from South Carolina, and she accepts his invitation to study together, during which he spends more time talking than cracking the books. Audrey then reluctantly allows Wickham to cheat off her test in physics class.

Audrey also draws the attention of Theo Driggs, a hulking miscreant whose mere presence frightens other students, and Clyde Mumsford, a shy youth who helps care for his cancer-stricken mother. Jealous of Audrey's relationship with Wickham, Clyde uses software from his father's company to find disturbing information about Wickham's past, which he shares with Audrey. Outraged at the inva-

McNeal explores the plight of undocumented workers in *Dark Water,* a tragic yet lyrical young adult novel.
(Copyright © 2010. Used by permission of Alfred A. Knopf, an imprint of Random House Children's Books, a division of Random House, Inc.)

sion of privacy, Audrey believes Clyde to be the author of Jemison High's scandalous *Yellow Paper,* a tabloid that reveals unflattering secrets about the school's teachers and students. She shares her opinion with Theo, who was the target of a recent article, and he turns his anger on Clyde.

Audrey's life becomes even more complicated after Mrs. Leacock accuses her of cheating, noting the similarities between her report and one of Wickham's, which he convinced Audrey to write. When her father's business venture fails, their roomy home is repossessed, and they are forced to move to a cramped apartment. Adding insult to injury, Wickham refuses to return her calls, and he begins dating Lea behind Audrey's back. While examining a copy of the *Yellow Paper,* which contains a shameful rumor about Leacock, Audrey realizes Clyde couldn't have written the articles, and when Audrey is accosted by Theo in the school parking lot, Clyde comes to her rescue, leading to a fragile and tender friendship. "Readers will sympathize with these individuals, some of whom mature, and some of whom do not," Karen Hoth maintained in *School Library Journal,* and a *Publishers Weekly* reviewer commented that in *Crushed,* the McNeals "carefully construct a compelling story about youthful mistakes—and how to make amends."

Of Snicks and Sketches

A work of magical realism by the McNeals, *The Decoding of Lana Morris* was described as a "subtle yet complex, slightly surreal story about the power of wishing" by a critic in *Kirkus Reviews.* The protagonist, sixteen-year-old Lana Morris, lives in Two Rivers, a small Nebraska town, with her heartless foster mother, Veronica Winters, and her husband, Whit, who seems all too interested in his teenage ward. With school out for the summer, Lana helps care for the "Snicks," as Veronica derisively refers to her home's other residents: four children—Garth, Tilly, Carlito, Alfred—all of whom have special needs.

During an outing to nearby Hereford with her next-door neighbor, Chet, and his scurrilous friends, Lana enters an antique shop run by a curious elderly woman, Julia Hekkity. Upon discovering an old leather drawing kit containing exquisite papers, the artistic-minded Lana feels compelled to purchase the item, and when she sketches a portrait of Chet, omitting the tell-tale mole growing by his nose, it disappears from his face. More chillingly, Veronica loses her arm in a car accident after Lana erases that appendage from a picture she drew of her nemesis.

When an inspector from Protective Services arrives at the home, finding it in disarray, Lana realizes that Garth, Tilly, Carlito, and Albert could be separated from one another. Alerted by a friendly caseworker that state officials are headed to the Winters' home, Lana and Chet gather the four youngsters and race to Hereford, where Lana hopes to find inspiration for one last drawing that will save her unconventional but close-knit "family." *The Decoding of Lana Morris* drew praise from *Booklist* critic Jennifer Hubert, who stated that the McNeals "offer up yet another complex and richly characterized story," and a reviewer in *Publishers Weekly* noted that the tale "brims with affecting characters and an eerie plotline, colored by elements of the supernatural."

The Fires That Burn

Laura McNeal's *Dark Water,* a stirring romance, is set against the backdrop of the 2007 California wildfires that destroyed more than 1,500 homes and

McNeal received a National Book Award nomination for *Dark Water,* a novel inspired in part by her experiences as a journalist covering undocumented workers.

killed at least 9 people. Based in part on the author's own experiences during that devastating event, *Dark Water* concerns Pearl DeWitt, a fifteen year old living with her mother on her Uncle Hoyt's avocado ranch in Fallbrook. While heading to school one day, Pearl notices Amiel de la Cruz Guerrero, one of the undocumented workers who gather in an empty lot, desperately hoping to earn a day's pay, and she is intrigued by his unusual and playful antics. After convincing Hoyt to hire the youth, who rarely speaks, Pearl attempts to communicate with Ariel, writing him a note in Spanish.

Talked into skipping school by her best friend, Greenie Coombs, Pearl decides to explore Agua Prieta Creek (known as Dark Water Creek to the locals), and comes upon Amiel riding his bike. Later, with her cousin Robby, Pearl returns to the area, discovering a makeshift shelter containing several of Amiel's belongings, and during another visit, at night, she surprises the boy, who escorts her back to the road. As Pearl recounts: "He turned away and I heard, for a second or two, his light footsteps on the path. Whether he waited for me to unlock my bike and ride away, watching over me still, or whether he ran immediately back to his house in the woods I couldn't tell. He was too familiar with a life in hiding to let me know his position in the darkness."

When Amiel injures himself trying to juggle machetes for the amusement of the other migrant workers, Pearl brings water and bandages to his camp, finally earning his trust, and they share a kiss. "It wasn't wrong in theory," Pearl thinks to herself. "It wasn't forbidden. But I understood that it was very strange and different, someone like him and someone like me. The people who have nothing aren't allowed to touch the people with cars and houses. They can work here. That's all." As the summer passes, the pair grow closer: Amiel teaches Pearl how to catch crayfish, his favorite meal, and he finally reveals the horrible truth about the injury that damaged his vocal cords.

That fall, wildfires spread across the region, forcing a mandatory evacuation of Fallbrook. Concerned that Amiel will not leave the woods, Pearl tells her mother and uncle that she has found safety with Greenie's family, then heads to the river. Pearl and Amiel plan to wait out the fire by submerging themselves under the water, but Pearl's cell phone dies before she is able to contact Hoyt, who, after uncovering her plan, has driven into the fire to rescue her. Pearl survives, but in the hospital, where she recuperates from shock and hypothermia, she learns that her actions have had tragic consequences.

"Six months from this day, a fire would leap from east to west, from Rainbow to Fallbrook. Eight lanes is a lot of concrete for a fire to cross, and I would have told you there was no way it could ever happen."

—Pearl DeWitt in *Dark Water.*

Dark Water garnered solid reviews. Katie Bircher, critiquing the novel in *Horn Book,* observed that "McNeal captures the desperation of both love and survival with wrenching authenticity," and in *School Library Journal* Allison Tran stated that readers "will . . . be rewarded with much thought-provoking substance in this novel's complex characters and hauntingly ambiguous ending." "Notable for well-drawn characters, an engaging plot and, especially, hauntingly beautiful language, this is an outstanding book," remarked a contributor in *Kirkus Reviews.*

Raising her readers' awareness of the immigrant experience was one of the reasons behind McNeal's decision to write *Dark Water.* "In my experience, undocumented workers prefer to be invisible," she stated in an interview with Eisa Ulen on the *National Book Award* Web site. McNeal added, "When things get bad economically, though, it's a sad fact that people look around for someone to blame. It's easier to fear, dislike, and blame groups of people who are unfamiliar or unknown. That's why writing about Amiel, trying to make him particular and comprehensible and, I hope, sympathetic, was so important to me."

■ Biographical and Critical Sources

BOOKS

McNeal, Laura, and Tom McNeal, *Zipped,* Knopf (New York, NY), 2003.

McNeal, Laura, and Tom McNeal, *Crushed,* Knopf (New York, NY), 2006.

McNeal, Laura, *Dark Water,* Knopf (New York, NY), 2010.

PERIODICALS

Booklist, September 1, 1996, Stephanie Zvirin, review of *The Dog Who Lost His Bob,* p. 144; October 15, 1999, Debbie Carton, review of *Crooked,* p. 429; January 1, 2006, Jennifer Mattson, review of *Crushed,* p. 84; April 1, 2007, Jennifer Hubert, review of *The Decoding of Lana Morris,* p. 41.

Bulletin of the Center for Children's Books, February, 2006, Deborah Stevenson, review of *Crushed,* p. 275; July-August, 2007, Deborah Stevenson, review of *The Decoding of Lana Morris,* p. 478.

Horn Book, November, 1999, Lauren Adams, review of *Crooked,* p. 743; January 1, 2006, Jennifer Mattson, review of *Crushed,* p. 84; January-February, 2011, Katie Bircher, review of *Dark Water,* p. 96.

Kirkus Reviews, February 15, 2003, review of *Zipped,* p. 312; December 15, 2005, review of *Crushed,* p. 1325; April 15, 2007, review of *The Decoding of Lana Morris;* August 1, 2010, review of *Dark Water.*

Kliatt, January, 2005, Claire Rosser, review of *Zipped,* p. 15; January, 2006, Claire Rosser, review of *Crushed,* p. 10; May, 2007, Myrna Marler, review of *The Decoding of Lana Morris,* p. 16.

Publishers Weekly, January 17, 2000, review of *Crooked,* p. 57; February 10, 2003, review of *Zipped,* p. 188; February 6, 2006, review of *Crushed,* p. 71; May 7, 2007, review of *The Decoding of Lana Morris,* p. 61.

Sacramento Bee (Sacramento, CA), November 15, 2010, Kathy Morrison, "*Dark Water* Shows Fire Season from a Southern California Teen's Perspective."

School Library Journal, February, 2003, Miranda Doyle, review of *Zipped,* p. 142; January, 2006, Karen Hoth, review of *Crushed,* p. 138; June, 2007, Geri Diorio, review of *The Decoding of Lana Morris,* p. 154; October, 2010, Allison Tran, review of *Dark Water,* p. 121.

Standard-Examiner (Ogden, UT), October 18, 2010, Jesus Lopez, Jr., "Clearfield High Grad Nominated for Author Award for *Dark Water.*"

Voice of Youth Advocates, February, 2006, Lois Parker-Hennion, review of *Crushed,* p. 488; August, 2007, Marla K. Unruh, review of *The Decoding of Lana Morris,* p. 260; December, 2010, Susan Allen, review of *Dark Water,* p. 457.

ONLINE

Carrie Keyes Web site, http://www.carriekeyes.com/ (November 2, 2010), "A Conversation with Laura McNeal, National Book Award Finalist for *Dark Water.*"

National Book Award Web site, http://www.national book.org/ (October 1, 2011), Eisa Ulen, interview with Laura McNeal.

Tom and Laura McNeal Home Page, http://mcneal books.com (October 1, 2011).

San Diego Reader, http://www.sdreader.com/ (January 26, 2006), Laura McNeal, "A Conversation with the Author."*

Patrick Ness

■ Personal

Born 1971, in Fort Belvoir, VA; immigrated to England, 1999; became naturalized British citizen, 2005; son of a U.S. Army sergeant; married, 2006; husband's name, Marc. *Education:* University of Southern California, B.A. (English literature), 1993.

■ Addresses

Home—London, England. *Agent*—Michelle Kass, Michelle Kass Associates; officemichellekass.co.uk.

■ Career

Writer. Former corporate writer in Los Angeles, CA; freelance writer, beginning c. 1997. Oxford University, Oxford, England, instructor in creative writing; Booktrust writer-in-residence, 2009.

■ Awards, Honors

Guardian Children's Fiction Prize and Booktrust Teenage Prize, both 2008, Branford Boase Award shortlist and Carnegie Medal shortlist, both 2009, and Best Book for Young Adults designation, American Library Association (ALA), all for *The Knife of Never Letting Go;* Costa Children's Award, 2009, Carnegie Medal shortlist, 2010, Booktrust Teenage Prize shortlist, and Best Book for Young Adults designation, ALA, all for *The Ask and the Answer;* Arthur C. Clarke Award shortlist, and Carnegie Medal, 2011, both for *Monsters of Men;* Galaxy National Book Award, 2011, for *A Monster Calls.*

■ Writings

"CHAOS WALKING" TRILOGY; FOR YOUNG ADULTS

The Knife of Never Letting Go, Walker Books (London, England), 2008, Candlewick Press (Cambridge, MA), 2009.

The Ask and the Answer, Candlewick Press (Somerville, MA), 2009.

Monsters of Men, Candlewick Press (Somerville, MA), 2010.

OTHER

The Crash of Hennington (adult novel), Flamingo (London, England), 2003.

Topics about Which I Know Nothing (short fiction), Flamingo (London, England), 2004.

A Monster Calls (young adult novel; based on an idea by Siobhan Dowd), illustrated by Jim Kay, Candlewick Press (Somerville, MA), 2011.

Contributor to periodicals, including *Genre,* the London *Daily Telegraph,* and the London *Guardian.*

■ Sidelights

"There ain't nothing but Noise in this world, nothing but the constant thoughts of men and things coming at you and at you and at you, ever since the spacks released the Noise germ during the war, the germ that killed half the men and every single woman, my ma not excepted, the germ that drove the rest of the men mad, the germ that spelled the end for all Spackle once men's madness picked up a gun."

The thoughts of Todd Hewitt, the protagonist of Patrick Ness's award-winning novel *The Knife of Never Letting Go,* introduce readers to the alien world of the "Chaos Walking" trilogy, a set of dystopian thrillers aimed at a young adult audience. As Todd's story progresses, however, he discovers that virtually everything he has been taught about his past is a lie, and after fleeing his isolated hometown, Todd finds himself at the heart of a civil war that threatens the future of his planet. The works in Ness's trilogy, which also includes *The Ask and the Answer* and *Monsters of Men,* "make readers question our own society—political power, the twin threats of despotism and terrorism, mass communications, torture—but above all they're gripping, thrilling, hurtling stories in which the brilliant ideas serve a great plot and strong characters, rather than the other way around," in the words of a London *Independent on Sunday* contributor.

Though the works in the "Chaos Walking" trilogy are considered science fiction, Ness admits that he didn't make a conscious decision to write in that genre. Discussing reader reaction to *The Knife of Never Letting Go* in a *Just Imagine Story Centre* interview, the author stated, "It had a great response from sci-fi readers, which I warmly welcome. So, while this is a colony on another planet, and there's an alien species, it's also a Western—set in a frontier town with cowboys and horses and so on. It's also a chase narrative." He continued, "I demand the right to use absolutely anything that I can. I'm the one setting the limits."

The son of a U.S. Army drill sergeant, Ness was born in Fort Belvoir, Virginia, in 1971, but lived there only a few months before moving to Hawaii. When Ness was six, his family moved again to Washington state, and Ness later attended the University of Southern California, earning a bach-

> "*. . . the swamp is the only place anywhere near Prentisstown where you can have half a break from all the Noise that men spill outta theirselves, all their clamor and clatter that never lets up, even when they sleep, men and the thoughts they don't know they think even when everyone can hear.*"
>
> —Protagonist Todd Hewitt in *The Knife of Never Letting Go.*

elor's degree in English literature in 1993. He spent a number of years working as a corporate writer in Los Angeles, California ("If you're American and hated your cable company, I probably wrote you a letter of apology," he jokingly remarked on his home page), before publishing his first short story in *Genre* magazine in 1997. Two years later, Ness moved to London, England, after falling in love with an Englishman he met while on vacation in Great Britain, and he became a naturalized British citizen in 2005. Ness married his partner, Marc, in 2006.

The Impossibility of Silence

After completing two books for adults, *The Crash of Hennington,* a novel, and *Topics about Which I Know Nothing* a collection of short fiction, Ness began writing *The Knife of Never Letting Go.* Inspired in part by the inventive language of the characters in Russell Hoban's celebrated novel *Riddley Walker,* which imagines a civilization decades after a nuclear holocaust, the work also addresses the topic of information overload. "Teenagers' lives," Ness told *Booklist* contributor Michael Cart, "are all online; everyone's connected, and there are no secrets. Teenagers today have less privacy than anybody in the whole history of the Western world. The next logical step is contained in a question: What if you had no choice? If you had to hear and everybody could hear you and you couldn't get away?"

That is the issue facing Todd and the men of Prentisstown, a rural settlement on New World, the planet where, some two decades earlier, a group of space colonists that included Todd's parents landed, seeking a place to exercise their religious freedoms. The males quickly fell victim to the "Noise," which makes one's thoughts audible to others. (As Todd reflects: "The Noise is a man unfiltered, and without a filter, a man is just chaos walking.") Strangely, the women of New World were unaffected by the Noise, yet they are all dead, killed by the Spackle, an indigenous species. The Spackle were later annihilated during a war with the colonists, who were led by David Prentiss, now the mayor of Todd's village, the only settlement to survive the conflict.

As he nears his thirteenth birthday, when he will be considered an adult, Todd senses a void in the Noise while working in the swamp with his dog, Manchee (the Noise also allows men to communicate with the animals of New World). His discovery, which he broadcasts through his Noise, frightens and angers the men of Prentisstown, and they march on Todd's home, where he lives with Ben and Cillian, who cared for him after his parents died. Realizing the danger, Ben implores Todd to flee through the swamp, hinting that other villages still exist while equipping him with a map, a journal, and a hunting knife.

As Todd reaches the swamp, he encounters, to his astonishment, a girl, the first he has ever seen. After surviving an attack by the town's maniacal preacher, Aaron, the pair ventures on, stopping for supplies at the twisted wreckage of the girl's spaceship, which crashed on the planet, killing her parents. Frustrated by his inability to communicate with the girl, whose thoughts he cannot read, Todd nonetheless offers to help her escape from Mayor Prentiss and his posse, who are giving chase. The girl soon earns Todd's trust by destroying a bridge, thus stalling the Mayor, and by disclosing her name, Viola Eade. Todd receives another jolt when he and Viola are met by the bridge's elderly guardian, Hildy, who arranges for them to stay in Farbranch, a farming community, before journeying to Haven, where it is hoped that Viola, whose parents were on a scouting mission, can make contact with a spaceship carrying thousands of settlers who are due to arrive in New World later that year.

Prentiss's forces, now grown into an army, eventually reach Farbranch, forcing Todd, Viola, and Manchee to flee once again as the townspeople are slaughtered. Convinced that Prentiss wants Todd, an innocent who seems incapable of harming anyone, to join his army, they set off for Haven. During their odyssey, they learn about the sad history of Prentisstown (once called New Elizabeth) through the journal, which was written by Todd's mother; come face-to-face with a Spackle, whom Todd kills with his knife, a fearful deed that haunts the youth; and fend off attacks from Davy Prentiss, the mayor's son, and the preacher, who trails them relentlessly and eventually kills Manchee. When they cross paths with Ben, who miraculously escaped from Prentisstown, he reveals several horrifying truths about New World: Todd learns that the war with the Spackle, who were unjustly blamed for causing the Noise, a natural phenomenon, was started by the settlers, and that the women of New Elizabeth, including Todd's mother, were massacred by Prentiss, who mistrusted their ability to hear his thoughts.

After Ben sacrifices himself to stop Davy Prentiss from locating Todd and Viola, and Davy shoots Viola, Todd carries her nearly lifeless body into Haven, where he finds the town square empty, save for a single man on horseback: Prentiss, who has appointed himself the ruler of New World. "The cliffhanger ending is as effective as a shot to the gut," Ian Chipman commented in *Booklist*. Winner of the prestigious *Guardian* Children's Fiction Prize as well as the Booktrust Teenage Prize, *The Knife of Never Letting Go* garnered strong reviews. "Having a runaway hero whose pursuers can not only see and track him, but can hear his thoughts too, makes for a tense read," Frank Cottrell Boyce remarked in the London *Guardian,* and Claire E. Gross, writing

Ness received the 2009 Costa Children's Award for *The Ask and the Answer,* the second installment in his acclaimed "Chaos Walking" trilogy. (Copyright © Marco Secchi/Getty Images. All rights reserved. Reproduced by permission.)

in *Horn Book,* observed that "the psychological and sociological impact of being unable to shut out others' thoughts—or hide your own—is creatively explored." According to *School Library Journal* critic Megan Honig, "Todd, who narrates in a vulnerable and stylized voice, is a sympathetic character who nevertheless makes a few wrenching mistakes."

Of Leaders and Tyrants

Todd and Viola's story continues in *The Ask and the Answer,* the second installment of Ness's "Chaos Walking" trilogy. Imprisoned in a bell tower, Todd finds himself at the mercy of now-President Prentiss, who puts him to work in a Spackle prison camp, alongside Davy. Prentiss, who has found an antidote for the Noise, rendering his thoughts inaudible to any other person, begins exerting his control over the people of Haven (renamed New Prentisstown) by dividing their families, confining all of the females to buildings that serve as houses of healing. In one of the houses, unbeknownst to Todd, Viola recuperates from her gunshot wound under the care of Mistress Coyle, a gifted healer who raises questions about Prentiss's actions.

As Todd falls under the sway of President Prentiss, who gives the teen increasing responsibilities while gradually relaxing his restrictions on the town's inhabitants, Viola learns that Coyle once fronted a covert resistance group, known as the "Answer," during the war with the Spackle. Certain that Prentiss intends to harm the women of Haven, as he did in Prentisstown, Mistress Coyle resurrects the Answer, moving her forces to an abandoned mining camp outside of town. In response to a series of bombings carried out by Coyle and her allies, Prentiss forms the "Ask," a heavily armed military unit, and the conflict escalates when Prentiss compels the women to wear identification bands, used to brand sheep.

Events at the Spackle camp are equally troubling. After Todd and Davy are ordered to place the same identification bands on the Spackle, they riot, and Prentiss's guards open fire, killing hundreds. Later, the Spackle camp comes under fire during an attack on New Prentisstown by the Answer, and only one Spackle, known as 1017, survives, with Todd's help. Though the teen at first blames Coyle for the bloodbath, Prentiss, who has been manipulating and controlling Todd through his Noise, admits that he is responsible for the carnage. Viola, too, comes to the realization that Coyle's motives are as dangerous as Prentiss's, and that the leader of the Answer has been using her to further her own agenda.

When a huge Spackle army advances on the town, seeking vengeance, Prentiss rallies his troops, which have been preparing for battle with the Answer, just as another scout ship prepares to land on New World.

Ness altered his storytelling approach in *The Ask and the Answer,* using the alternating voices of Todd and Viola to narrate the tale. As he related in his *Just Imagine Story Centre* interview, "Viola is so vital in *The Knife,* and she needs to also tell the story—it's a bigger story and they have very different experiences in it and the difference is what's important. They find themselves on opposite sides, or what seems like opposite sides—it's a complicated process they go through. I wanted to do both sides of the story to explore the shades of grey."

Like *The Knife of Never Letting Go, The Ask and the Answer* received a host of honors, including the 2009 Costa Children's Award. A *Publishers Weekly* critic described the novel as "a provocative examination of the nature of evil and humanity," and Gross stated that Todd's "struggle to reconcile his supposed innocence . . . with his unforgivable actions will provoke as much thought as the depictions of slavery, genocide, terrorism, and torture." In the words of *School Library Journal* reviewer Vicki Reutter, "Science fiction lovers will be looking for the next installment in this fast-paced and imaginative series."

The Battle for Peace

Warfare erupts on New World in *Monsters of Men,* the conclusion to the "Chaos Walking" trilogy. As the initial Spackle attack decimates Prentiss's army, Viola makes contact with the pilots of the scout ship, Bradley and Simone, who must decide if they should use their powerful weapons against the Spackle. Such an action would save both the Ask and the Answer but would also leave power in the hands of Prentiss, who controls an entire army through his Noise, as well as endanger the lives of the new colonists, who are fast approaching the planet. When Viola impulsively fires a missile into the Spackle troops, hoping to save Todd's life during a heated battle, it creates a stalemate between the warring parties.

As Todd, Viola, and Bradley attempt to broker a peace with the Sky, the leader of the Spackle, they face continued resistance from Prentiss, whose powers continue to grow, and Coyle, who finds a willing accomplice in Simone. Meanwhile, the other healers attempt to help the women of New Prentis-

The Thrilling Conclusion to the Award-Winning Series

CHAOS WALKING
BOOK THREE

MONSTERS OF MEN

PATRICK NESS

Human colonists battle an alien race for control of a planet where living creatures thrive on shared communication in *Monsters of Men*, the thrilling conclusion to Ness's "Chaos Walking" trilogy. (Cover photograph by Harald Sund/The Image Bank/Getty Images. Copyright © 2010 by Patrick Ness. Reproduced by permission of Candlewick Press on behalf of Walker Books, London.)

stown battle a deadly infection caused by the identification bands, including Viola, whose health begins to deteriorate.

Into this mix Ness introduces a third narrator, that of 1017, known to his people as the Return, who poignantly recounts the enslavement of the Spackle. Like Todd, his former captor, the Return cannot abide killing, and he reunites Todd with Ben, who was mortally wounded by Davy Prentiss and healed by the Spackle, a process that taught him the secret of New World, a planet where all living creatures are entwined through the sharing of information. Just when peace seems attainable, Prentiss hijacks the spaceship and sets the forests ablaze, killing the

Sky. The Return, now filled with hate, prepares the Spackle for battle, leading to a final, violent confrontation with Prentiss, Viola, and Todd.

Describing Ness's "Chaos Walking" trilogy as "remarkable," London *Times* contributor Amanda Craig deemed *Monsters of Men* "an intensely moral, thoughtful work," and Jonathan Hunt, writing in *Horn Book*, called the novel a "timely examination of human nature, human society, and the terrible costs of violence." A *Publishers Weekly* reviewer also praised the "grueling but triumphant tale," and Chipman maintained that "it's the characters that ultimately stand out in this final act—the connections that bind them and change them and ruin them and redeem them." In his *Booklist* interview with Cart, Ness stated, "I really believe that a major theme of the trilogy is redemption; you have to believe anybody can be redeemed; otherwise, there's no hope for us." Another key element of the works, Ness believes, is the concept of "difference." As he told the *Independent on Sunday* reporter, "I think our biggest failing as a species is the inability to see difference as difference—it's either better, so we have to pull it down, or it's worse, so we can exploit it. Difference is rarely ever just difference."

A Most Unusual Collaboration

Ness's fourth young adult title, the highly regarded *A Monster Calls*, had its origins as a story idea by Siobhan Dowd, the celebrated British author who died in 2007. Denise Johnstone-Burt, an editor at Walker Books who had commissioned a story from Dowd before her passing, took possession of the 1,500-word manuscript and, seeing its promise, offered the work to Ness. "It was a cracking start with a story laid out with great efficiency which I envy," Ness told *Publishers Weekly* interviewer Julia Eccleshare, adding, "I felt, 'This is a writer who's got a story to tell, a great story to tell regardless of impact, regardless of its legacy.' It was just that she could feel the story coming together. It was all about to fall into place and she was about to begin. That's why I took it on. It's a thrilling feeling for any writer."

A Monster Calls, described as "heart-wrenching and thought-provoking" by *Horn Book* contributor Cynthia K. Ritter, focuses on Conor O'Malley, a sensitive and lonely thirteen year old who is bullied at school, tortured by a recurring nightmare, and terrified at the prospect of losing his mother, who has cancer. At night Conor is visited by a monster, in the form of a giant yew tree, that tells him three folkloric tales, then demands a fourth story from Conor—the truth behind the teen's nightmare.

Discussing the theme of the work on the *Booktrust* Web site, Ness related, "I think the novel is about loss, . . ., but also about the fear of loss, which is universal, I think. Everyone knows what it's like to lie in bed late at night worrying about if the worst ever happened. Loss, I think, we can handle better than the worry that leads up to it, which can kill us. That's what I was really interested in exploring."

Reviewing *A Monster Calls* in *Booklist*, Chipman remarked that "Ness twists out a resolution that is revelatory in its obviousness, beautiful in its execution, and fearless in its honesty," and a *Publishers Weekly* critic stated that the work "tackles the toughest of subjects by refusing to flinch, meeting the ugly truth about life head-on with compassion, bravery, and insight." A highlight of the work, observed a contributor in *Kirkus Reviews,* is the black-and-white artwork of Jim Kay, "which surrounds the text, softly caressing it in quiet moments and in others rushing toward the viewer with a nightmarish intensity."

A number of reviewers complimented Ness's ability to communicate Dowd's original vision. Craig declared that "Ness has captured Dowd's unique imagination while writing the story in a voice that is entirely his own," and Boyce commented in the *Guardian* that "perhaps the most impressive thing about [*A Monster Calls*] is that it's nothing like Ness's other books and nothing like Dowd's. Like the monster, it has a life of its own." Boyce concluded that Ness has "produced something deeply comforting and glowing with—to use a Siobhan Dowd word—solace." Discussing the singular nature of the collaboration, Ness told Eccleshare, "I feel it's my book in a particular way. It felt like it is something private between me and Siobhan. Something that no one can touch."

Personal growth is a hallmark of Ness's work. "What is important [to] me in the Chaos Walking books and is the whole point of *A Monster Calls* is the complexity of a person," he told a reporter in the London *Independent.* "That you are at one time many contradictory things. That a terrible thought doesn't make you a terrible person. That a mistake is natural and human even though everybody blames you for it. You are going to mess up but that is not the point; the point is how you react to it, how you fix it, how you grow from it."

Ness enjoys writing for a young adult audience, finding it a challenge to keep his readers entertained and engaged. "Your reader is interested in a guileless, fresh, first-time-we-talked-about-it way," he stated in the *Independent.* "What a great liberation that is. And teenagers, if you respect them, will follow you a lot further than adults will, without fear of being a genre that they may not like or have been told not to like. They just want a story."

> *"What is important me in the Chaos Walking books and is the whole point of* A Monster Calls *is the complexity of a person. That you are at one time many contradictory things. That a terrible thought doesn't make you a terrible person. That a mistake is natural and human even though everybody blames you for it. You are going to mess up but that is not the point; the point is how you react to it, how you fix it, how you grow from it."*
>
> —Patrick Ness, in the London *Independent.*

■ Biographical and Critical Sources

BOOKS

Ness, Patrick, *The Knife of Never Letting Go,* Walker Books (London, England), 2008, Candlewick Press (Cambridge, MA), 2009.

PERIODICALS

Booklist, September 1, 2008, Ian Chipman, review of *The Knife of Never Letting Go,* p. 97; August 1, 2009, Ian Chipman, review of *The Ask and the Answer,* p. 66; July 1, 2010, Ian Chipman, review of *Monsters of Men,* p. 62; November 15, 2010, Michael Cart, "Making Noise about Chaos," p. 42; July 1, 2011, Ian Chipman, review of *A Monster Calls,* p. 52.

Bookseller, March 4, 2011, Caroline Horn, "A Monster Calling: Patrick Ness Follows His Prize-winning Chaos Walking Trilogy by Completing a Novel Begun by the Late Siobhan Dowd," p. 23.

Daily Mail (London, England), May 6, 2011, Sally Morris, review of *A Monster Calls,* p. 58.

Financial Times, April 26, 2008, James Lovegrove, review of *The Knife of Never Letting Go,* p. 19.

Guardian (London, England), June 14, 2008, Frank Cottrell Boyce, "The Silent Bark: Don't Let the 'Young Adult' Tag Put You Off This Deftly Told Tale of a Boy's Flight," review of *The Knife of Never Letting Go,* p. 14; September 25, 2008, Alison Flood, "Sharp Take on Power of Knives Wins *Guardian* Book Prize," p. 17; September 27, 2008, Julia Eccleshare, "And the Winner Is . . . Julia

Eccleshare Celebrates *The Knife of Never Letting Go,* by Patrick Ness," p. 14; May 7, 2011, Frank Cottrell Boyce, "A Good Death," review of *A Monster Calls,* p. 14.

Horn Book, November-December, 2008, Claire E. Gross, review of *The Knife of Never Letting Go,* p. 712; September-October, 2008, Claire E. Gross, review of *The Ask and the Answer,* p. 570; November-December, 2010, Jonathan Hunt, review of *Monsters of Men,* p. 99; September-October, 2011, Cynthia K. Ritter, review of *A Monster Calls,* p. 93.

Independent (London, England), May 10, 2011, "Nightmarish Tale Goes like a Dream," review of *A Monster Calls,* p. 18; June 24, 2011, "The Whole Truth for Teenagers," interview with Ness, p. 22.

Independent on Sunday (London, England), May 2, 2010, "Hold on to That Handrail," profile of Ness, p. 38.

Kirkus Reviews, August 15, 2008, review of *The Knife of Never Letting Go;* August 15, 2009, review of *The Ask and the Answer;* August 1, 2010, review of *Monsters of Men;* July 15, 2011, review of *A Monster Calls.*

Kliatt, September, 2008, Paula Rohrlick, review of *The Knife of Never Letting Go,* p. 18.

Publishers Weekly, August 31, 2009, review of *The Ask and the Answer,* p. 59; August 2, 2010, review of *Monsters of Men,* p. 46; June 20, 2011, review of *A Monster Calls,* p. 54.

School Library Journal, November, 2008, Megan Honig, review of *The Knife of Never Letting Go,* p. 133; January, 2010, Vicki Reutter, review of *The Ask and the Answer,* p. 110; September, 2010, Eric Norton, review of *Monsters of Men,* p. 159; September, 2011, Krista Welz, review of *A Monster Calls,* p. 164.

Sunday Telegraph (London, England), April 10, 2005, Patrick Ness, "It's Great to Be British . . . at Last," p. 5.

Sunday Times (London, England), May 22, 2011, Nicolette Jones, review of *A Monster Calls,* p. 42.

Times (London, England), November 22, 2008, Amanda Craig, "A Winning Walk through Chaos," review of *The Knife of Never Letting Go,* p. 15; May 22, 2010, Amanda Craig, "Fast Forward to Hope," review of *Monsters of Men,* p. 8; May 14, 2011, Amanda Craig, "Monsters to Torment Their Minds," review of *A Monster Calls,* p. 25.

ONLINE

Booktrust Web site, http://www.booktrust.org.uk/ (October 1, 2011), Madelyn Travis, interview with Ness; (October 1, 2011), "Patrick Ness and Jim Kay Answer Our Questions about Their Latest Novel *A Monster Calls.*"

Just Imagine Story Centre Web site, http://www.justimaginestorycentre.co.uk/ (October 1, 2011), "An Interview with Patrick Ness."

Patrick Ness Home Page, http://www.patrickness.com (October 1, 2011).

Publishers Weekly Online, http://www.publishersweekly.com/ (June 23, 2011), Julia Eccleshare, "Q & A with Patrick Ness and Denise Johnstone-Burt."

Readings Web site, http://www.readings.com.au/ (February 15, 2010), Andrew McDonald, interview with Ness.

Walker Books Web site, http://www.walker.co.uk/ (October 1, 2011), "Patrick Ness Q&A."*

■ Personal

Born June 15, 1968, in Chicago, IL; son of Douglas (a systems analyst) and Mary Lee (a prison nurse) Rapp. *Education:* Clark College, Dubuque, B.A., 1991.

■ Addresses

Home—New York, NY. *Office*—Edge Theater Company, 880 Third Ave., 16th Fl., New York, NY 10022.

■ Career

Playwright and novelist. Vassar College and Dartmouth College, artist-in-residence; Juilliard School of Music, New York, NY, playwright-in-residence, 2000—. Director, *Winter Passing,* feature film, 2005. Member of Less the Band (rock group). Worked in book publishing for five years; worked as furniture mover.

■ Awards, Honors

Best Books for Young Adults and Best Books for Reluctant Readers citations, American Library Association, both 1995, both for *Missing the Piano;* Her-

Adam Rapp

bert & Patricia Brodkin scholarship, National Playwright's Conference, and Camargo Foundation fellowship to France, both 1997, both for *Trueblinka;* Princess Grace fellowship for playwriting, 1999 and 2006; Roger L. Stevens Award from the Kennedy Center Fund for New American Plays, 2000; Suite Residency with Mabou Mines, 2000; Lincoln Center LeComte du Nouy Award (two-time recipient); Elliott Norton Award for Best New Script, Best New Play selection, Independent Reviewers of New England, and selected as one of the Burns Mantle Ten Best Plays of 2000-01, *Chronicle* of U.S. theater, all for *Nocturne;* Helen Merrill Award for Emerging Playwrights, 2001; *Los Angeles Times* Book Award nomination, 2004, for *Under the Wolf, under the Dog;* Juilliard fellowship, 1999-2001, and 2004-06; Pulitzer Prize in drama finalist, 2006, and Jefferson Award for best new work, both for *Red Light Winter;* Schneider Family Book Award, 2006, for *Under the Wolf, under the Dog;* Michael L. Printz Honor Book, 2010, for *Punkzilla.*

■ Writings

YOUNG ADULT NOVELS

Missing the Piano, Viking (New York, NY), 1994.
The Buffalo Tree, Front Street (Asheville, NC), 1997.
Little Chicago, Handprint Books (Brooklyn, NY), 1998.
The Copper Elephant, Front Street (Asheville, NC), 1999.

Little Chicago, Front Street (Ashville, NC), 2002.

Thirty-three Snowfish, illustrated by Timothy Basil Ering, Candlewick Press (Cambridge, MA), 2003.

Under the Wolf, under the Dog, Candlewick Press (Cambridge, MA), 2004.

The Year of Endless Sorrows, Farrar (New York, NY), 2007.

Punkzilla, Candlewick Press (Somerville, MA), 2009.

Ball Peen Hammer (graphic novel), illustrated by George O'Connor, First Second (New York, NY), 2009.

The Children and the Wolves, Candlewick Press (Somerville, MA), 2012.

PLAYS

Netherbones, produced at Steppenwolf Theatre, Chicago, IL, 1995.

Ghosts in the Cottonwoods, produced at New York Shakespeare Festival, 1996.

Trueblinka, produced at New York Shakespeare Festival, 1997.

Blackfrost, produced at New York Shakespeare Festival, 1997.

Night of the Whitefish, produced at New York Shakespeare Festival, 1998.

Finer Noble Gases (also see below), produced at Ojai Playwrights Conference, 2000.

Nocturne (produced by American Repertory Theater, Cambridge, MA, 2000), Faber & Faber (New York, NY), 2002.

Faster (also see below), produced in New York, 2000.

Dreams of the Salthorse, produced at Juilliard School of Music, New York, NY, 2000.

Animals and Plants, (produced by American Repertory Theater, Cambridge, MA, 2001), Broadway Play Publishing (New York, NY), 2009.

Blackbird (also see below), produced at Bush Theater, London, England, 2001.

Stone Cold Dead Serious (also see below), produced by American Repertory Theater, Cambridge, MA, 2002.

Finer Noble Gases, produced at Actors Theater, Louisville, KY, 2002.

Gompers (produced by Eugene O'Neill Theater Center, Waterford, CT, 2003), Broadway Play Publishing (New York, NY), 2005.

Stone Cold Dead Serious and Other Plays (contains *Finer Noble Gases, Faster,* and *Stone Cold Dead Serious*), Faber & Faber (New York, NY), 2004.

Red Light Winter (first produced at the Steppenwolf Theater, Chicago, IL, 2005), Faber & Faber (New York, NY), 2006.

(With others) *CouchWorks,* produced at The Tank, New York, NY, 2005, performed under new title, *Members Only,* produced at The Tank, New York, NY, 2005.

Jack on Film (produced at American Airlines Theatre, New York, NY, 2006), published in *Twenty-four by Twenty-four: The Twenty-four Hour Plays Anthology,* edited by Mark Armstrong and Sarah Bisman, Playscripts (New York, NY), 2009.

Essential Self-Defense, (produced at Playwrights Horizons, New York, NY, 2007), Faber & Faber (New York, NY), 2007.

American Sligo, (produced at Rattlestick Theatre, New York, NY, 2007), Broadway Play Publishing (New York, NY), 2008.

Bingo with the Indians, (produced at Flea Theater, New York, NY, 2007), Broadway Play Publishing (New York, NY), 2009.

Kindness, (produced at Peter Jay Sharp Theatre, New York, NY, 2008), Samuel French (New York, NY), 2010.

The Metal Children, (produced at Vineyard Theater, New York, NY, 2008), Faber & Faber (New York, NY), 2010.

Classic Kitchen Timer, produced at Flea Theater, New York, NY, 2009.

Rose (part of the "Hallway Trilogy"), produced at Rattlestick Theatre, New York, NY, 2011.

Paraffin (part of the "Hallway Trilogy"), produced at Rattlestick Theatre, New York, NY, 2011.

Nursing (part of the "Hallway Trilogy"), produced at Rattlestick Theatre, New York, NY, 2011.

TELEPLAYS AND SCREENPLAYS

The Jury (one episode), Fox, 2004.

(And director) *Winter Passing,* Focus Features, 2005.

The L Word (one episode), Showtime, 2006.

Blackbird, Blackbird Project, 2007.

In Treatment (seven episodes), HBO, 2010.

■ Sidelights

"Adam Rapp is a creator of all trades," noted John Hogan in the *Graphic Novel Reporter.* An award-winning author of hard-hitting, gritty novels for teens, Rapp is also a polished playwright with more than a dozen plays to his credit; a screenwriter and writer for HBO and Showtime television series; and a musician who has played in several bands. Additionally, Rapp is a director of film and theater productions and has penned a graphic novel.

Rapp's critically acclaimed novels for young adults address tough issues of peer abuse and dysfunctional families. Reviewers of Rapp's *Missing the Piano, The Buffalo Tree, The Copper Elephant Thirty-three Snowfish, Under the Wolf, under the Dog,* and *Punkzilla* have commended the author for his ability to create believable characters whose triumphs over adversity are not easily won. "Rapp writes about naively innocent adolescents caught in violent and emotionally isolated places," explained Ann Angel in the *ALAN Review.* Rapp is pleased that his novels seem to have struck a chord with young readers. "I think kids are incredibly resilient and much smarter than we think they are," he told Angel in an interview for the *ALAN Review.* "I hate the idea of sheltering kids from challenging books. It's just another form of conservative fear that promotes ignorance more than anything else."

Rapp further commented on his role as young adult author to Alexandra Ares in a *Manhattan Chronicles* interview: "I love writing about teenagers because there's just so much ripe possibility in their lives. It's a cauldron of sex and drugs and the pressure to achieve and SAT scores and what am I and who do I want to be. It's all about questioning authority and finding your voice as a human being. Conflict is everywhere. And there's puberty too. It's an endless canvass."

A Difficult Childhood

Rapp's own difficult childhood has served as the basis for much of his work. As he explained in an interview with a contributor for the *Vineyard Theater* Web site: "I find that I have a lot to say about adolescence, particularly the early teen years. Being raised by a single mother, I dealt with a lot of uncertainty. For part of fifth grade I struggled through reform school and then spent four years of high school at a military academy. There's so much chaos during those years, with the pressures of puberty, sexual identity, standardized tests, and our high-stakes achievement culture. I am haunted by those years in the Midwest and they have proven to be incredibly fertile for storytelling."

Rapp grew up in Joliet, Illinois, and his family included an older sister and younger brother. Their mother supported them by working as a prison nurse, and his brother Anthony was a talented stage prodigy. At one point, Anthony was cast in a Broadway production of *The Little Prince and the Aviator,* so the family moved to New York City. "I was an eighth grader, and my mom literally came into the half time of a basketball game to tell us we

"I love writing about teenagers because there's just so much ripe possibility in their lives. It's a cauldron of sex and drugs and the pressure to achieve and SAT scores and what am I and who do I want to be. It's all about questioning authority and finding your voice as a human being. Conflict is everywhere."

—Adam Rapp, in a *Manhattan Chronicles* interview.

were moving to New York the next day," Rapp told Tim Sanford in an interview for *Playwrights Horizons.* Rapp's brother was to play opposite Michael York in a musical that was publicly financed. "So [my brother] suddenly was thrust into the spotlight, and my sister and I were pulled out of our lives in Joliet," Rapp told Sanford. "And I was the starting point guard on the eighth grade basketball team. I had a girlfriend. I was looking forward to track season. It was really hard on me. I was really angry."

The family first settled in an apartment in Manhattan that was much too small for them, then took their per diem rent payments and rented one unfurnished floor of an old mansion in the borough of Staten Island. This rental did not even have a refrigerator, so the family kept their food on the windowsill for cooling. "It was like Dickens, it was ridiculous," Rapp remarked to Sanford. The stage project was abandoned by its producers and investors, however, when it was discovered that York could not sing. The family found themselves stranded in New York and it took two months for Rapp's mother to save enough money to get the family back to Illinois. This inaugurated what became a peripatetic lifestyle for Rapp and his siblings, who lived in hotel rooms around the country as Anthony performed in musicals such as *Evita, Oliver!,* and *The King and I.*

Later, Rapp's mother arranged for Rapp to live with his father and stepmother while she accompanied Anthony on tour. The situation was unpleasant for Rapp, and he became involved in so much delinquent activity that he landed in a reform school; he was later sent to a military academy in Wisconsin. Ultimately he earned a scholarship at the school, playing three sports and keeping a 3.0 grade point average. "I was a troubled youth," Rapp admitted in an interview with *American Theatre* writer Karen Fricker. "There were a lot of problems." Despite the worries, Anthony's success was a bright spot in all their lives. "We had nothing," Rapp told Fricker, noting that even for his mother, living in hotel rooms on the road with her son was a unique experience. "There was nothing to look forward to. Joliet is a dismal, sad little town. Every time I go back there, there is this sense that I am never going to leave." This upbringing also put a strain in the relations between Rapp and his mother, and throughout his fiction and plays Rapp deals details troubled relationships with mothers.

Reading became Rapp's salvation, he admitted to Angel. As a teen, he discovered the writings of J.D. Salinger, in particular Salinger's *Catcher in the Rye*, the classic novel of disenchanted youth, narrated by the character Holden Caulfield. "I started making all of these great friends that I would have otherwise never met," he recalled of his favorite books. "I feel like I know Holden Caulfield better than many of the guys I played basketball with in college." For Rapp, sports became a ticket out of Joliet. He earned a scholarship to play for Clarke College in Dubuque, Iowa, where he took his first writing class and found his calling. "I knew right then that was what I wanted to do," he told Fricker. His early literary output also forged a more mature relationship with Anthony, who was still living at home. The two had fallen out, but Rapp began sharing his short stories with his little brother. "When I told him that I had started writing," Rapp recounted to the *American Theatre* interviewer, "he sent me some of his own stories—and that's how we started hanging out again."

Dialogue Is Key

At Clarke College, Rapp captained the basketball team and graduated with a degree in fiction writing. He then moved to New York City, where he could divide his time between his two passions: playing street basketball and writing. Anthony eventually moved there, too, finding early success on Broadway and in some feature-film roles. Between parts, he began directing off-Broadway plays, and Rapp began assisting him, which led to an attempt at writing for the stage. His play *Ghosts in the Cottonwoods* was selected for the New Work Now! series of the prestigious New York Shakespeare Festival in 1996. Set in rural Appalachia, the play revolves around a tremendously dysfunctional family whose members are based in part on the family of one of Rapp's college friends. "They had beautiful music in their voices," Rapp recalled to Fricker in *American Theatre*. "I became obsessed by the way they said things and made up words—it was a strange form of poetry for me."

Living in New York, Rapp became an avid eavesdropper, which gave his imagination unlimited fodder, and much of his work has evolved from this habit. "It always starts with the voice," he told Angel. "I have never successfully written in the third person. If there's a rhythm or a musicality that interests me, I become obsessed with the character and just have this need to spend time with him or her. Sometimes I'll be in the park playing ball and I'll hear a kid say something that I've never heard before. Sometimes one word can set me off."

Rapp's next play, *Trueblinka*, won its creator two awards—a scholarship from the National Playwright's Conference and a Camargo Foundation grant to Cassis, France. The success also helped *Ghosts in the Cottonwoods*, which went on to premier at Chicago's Victory Gardens and be produced in Los Angeles. Rapp has continued to pen works for the stage, including *Netherbones*, *Blackfrost*, and *Finer Noble Gases*, all of which have enjoyed successful productions.

However, the work that firmly launched his career as a writer was Rapp's first novel for young adults, *Missing the Piano*. Published in 1994, *Missing the Piano* was named a Best Book for Young Adults and Best Book for Reluctant Readers by the American Library Association.

Missing the Piano is the story of Mike Tegroff, a talented basketball player whose life is disrupted when his younger sister is cast in *Les Misérables*. Since their mother must accompany her daughter on the road, Mike is sent to live with his father and stepmother, whom he detests. Once his mother and sister have departed, the stepmother refuses to shelter him, so his father takes him to a military academy. Mike finds the place more than just a harsh change from his normal teenage routine; it is a brutal, insulated world whose code of honor seems farcical. The older students beat and taunt the younger cadets, and racial prejudice is rampant. Mike's African American roommate is the victim of cruel slurs, and after he is beaten by other students and expelled, Mike feels guilty for not coming to his rescue.

A *Publishers Weekly* contributor called *Missing the Piano* a "promising but not entirely successful debut novel," noting that "the main characters' voices are authentic and generally engaging." *Booklist* reviewer Stephanie Zvirin admitted that some passages are disturbing but felt that "the novel's harsh language fits the intensity of the story, which Rapp successfully moderates with some flashes of irreverent humor and the actions of a caring teacher."

Tough-minded Teen Protagonists

Rapp's second novel for young adults, *The Buffalo Tree*, was published in 1997. Like *Missing the Piano*, it draws upon the author's experiences in a reform

An Oregon runaway tries to reconnect with his dying brother in *Punkzilla*, **Rapp's gritty, award-winning young adult novel.** (Cover photograph by Jamie VanBuskirk/iStockphoto. Copyright © 2009 by Adam Rapp. Jacket illustration © 2009 by Timothy Basil Ering. Reproduced by permission of Candlewick Press, Somerville, MA.)

school, introducing readers to the Hamstock Boys Center, where twelve-year-old Sura has been sent for stealing hood ornaments from automobiles. As Rapp remarked to Angel: "One of the things that concerns me is the lack of adult supervision, and more specifically, caring adult supervision at various reform schools and juvenile detention centers. I think there's a kind of Darwinian brutality that can run rampant when kids are given power, and if you're on the wrong end of the pecking order things can be very scary."

In *The Buffalo Tree*, Sura finds himself the only detainee at Hamstock who is not African American or Hispanic, and he recounts the brutal atmosphere that works to criminalize the boys further. Even with strict rules and regulations, abuse from other

teens makes life at Hamstock a daily nightmare. Guards at the detention facility ignore potentially harmful situations or even become involved in them. Sura is tough enough to survive, but he witnesses more timid boys, like his roommate, Coly Jo, become targets of the worst bullies. Coly Jo has been sent to Hamstock for breaking and entering people's homes, where he watched them sleep. Picked on by the others, Coly Jo dies after being forced to climb a dead tree in one of the center's sadistic rituals. Sura's next roommate escapes with the intention of murdering his father. Sura himself finds salvation in running. "Although the brutality is unremitting, the book is hard to put down," wrote *Horn Book* contributor Nancy Vasilakis, adding that Sura's "tone of bravado relieves the harshness without resorting to sentimentality." *Booklist* reviewer Susan Dove Lempke called Rapp's prose "challenging, demanding that readers become immersed in the richly realized, dark look at an American subculture," while a *Publishers Weekly* reviewer of *The Buffalo Tree* asserted that the author's "graphic images and use of first-person, present-tense narrative makes Sura's hellish story all the more real and immediate."

Rapp's first two novels found an appreciative audience among teens and educators alike, and in 1999, he was invited to spend a week as an author-in-residence at a suburban Chicago high school. As he told *ALAN Review* interviewer Penny Blubaugh, it "was one of the most surprisingly important events of my career as an author." He met with the student staff of Ridgewood High's literary magazine and school newspaper, and he spoke to groups of students who came to visit from other high schools. He recalled being shocked when he visited an English class one day and saw eighty students all holding a copy of *The Buffalo Tree*, ready to talk about it with him. "With novels, there's this built-in disappearing act," he told Blubaugh. "I can write the story, but there is no immediate public culpability. The book is a thing on its own. At Norridge, this romantic idea I had of novelist-as-escape-artist was instantly proven false, and for all the right reasons." This particular ninth-grade class was designed to improve the English skills of those for whom English was as a second language, or who had encountered other difficulties. The teacher had students illustrate a book cover with favorite scenes from *The Buffalo Tree* to show Rapp. "Somehow, this almost moved me to tears," he told Blubaugh. "I'm still not sure why. I guess it's because they actually took the time."

Rapp's third novel for young adults, *The Copper Elephant*, appeared in 1999. It is set in a nightmarish, post-apocalyptic world, where the environment has been decimated by acid rain. Children are housed in brutal orphanages or taken as slave labor to work in lime pits. The novel's protagonist is eleven-year-old Whensday Bluenose, whose best friend dies in the dangerous underground mines. An elderly man saves Whensday from a similar fate, but not before she is sexually assaulted by an authority figure from the omnipotent Syndicate. Her rescuer then lands in trouble with the Syndicate and is falsely accused of murder, but Whensday knows who the true culprit is: a developmentally disabled teenager. In the end, a pregnant Whensday comes across a renegade group of women determined to reproduce in an effort to save their world.

A *Horn Book* reviewer found the novel "compelling despite the unrelenting cruelty; Whensday's gripping narration describes the hellish landscape so skillfully that readers will find themselves gasping for air." *Booklist* contributor Debbie Carton asserted that "this raw-voiced story is both distinctive and unique, with Rapp's grim vision brilliantly executed."

Kids on the Run

The plot of Rapp's next novel for young adults, *Little Chicago,* continues in the same dark vein of his earlier fiction, concentrating on the effects of child abuse. Blacky Brown is an eleven-year-old boy who has been molested by his mother's boyfriend. He finds he has no one but himself to rely on after his mother, siblings, friends, and social services fail to support or shield him. The only friendship he finds is from a girl who has also been rejected by the others at school, another "freak." The book's choppy first-person narrative reflects Blacky's inability to cope with his life, a horrifying existence filled with pain, neglect, poverty, filth, and fear. In his desperation, Blacky gets a gun. In the end, after throwing the gun away, the boy departs into the woods, looking to escape.

According to *School Library Journal* writer Connie Tyrrell Burns, it was the "bleakest yet" of Rapp's novels. She commented: "The sense of hopelessness in this disturbing novel is almost physically painful." The book prompted other warnings. A *Publishers Weekly* contributor said that it "contains metaphors and vocabulary that, more sophisticated than the messenger, reveal the hand of the author at work." Writing for *Booklist,* Gillian Engberg advised that "some of the scenes' repellent details verge on the gratuitous and occasionally the sensational." However, Lauren Adams remarked in *Horn Book* that "Rapp's portrayal of the abused child is sensitive, sympathetic, and honest."

Four runaway children with backgrounds even more gruesome than Blacky's populate *Thirty-three Snowfish.* In this novel, Rapp explores the desperation of young teens who were introduced to sex, drugs, and violence very early in their lives. Boobie is on the run with his infant brother after killing his parents. Curl is fifteen, a drug addict and prostitute. Custis has escaped from the control of a man who produces child pornography and snuff films. Together they flee in a stolen car into rural Illinois, where two of the teens die. Custis and the baby are rescued by an elderly black man named Seldom, who takes them into his home. Despite the boy's racist attitude, it is the first healthy relationship with an adult that he has known.

The story both shocked and stimulated reviewers. A *Publishers Weekly* reviewer responded that "readers may have trouble stomaching the language . . . as well as the horrors so flatly depicted and, in the end, so handily overcome." In *School Library Journal,* Joel Shoemaker judged that "spare descriptions and stellar characterization reel readers into the dark and violent world" and concluded that the book "invites both an emotional and intellectual response and begs to be discussed." And a *Kirkus Reviews* contributor found that "with his customary ear for the language of the marginalized teen, Rapp . . . allows his characters to present themselves in total unselfconsciousness, frankly and powerfully laying out the squalor of their existence."

Desperate yet Hopeful

In *Under the Wolf, under the Dog,* troubled sixteen-year-old protagonist Steve Nugent has been committed to Burnstone Grove, a residential treatment facility for teenagers with drug addictions or suicidal tendencies. Writing in the autobiography that his therapist urged him to create, titled "A Pretty Depressing Time in My Life," Steve recounts his harrowing younger life and the tragedies that led to his emotional problems and stay in the facility. He describes in tragic detail his mother's wrenching death from cancer, his older brother's suicide, his father's deep depression and emotional instability, and his own increasingly bizarre and destructive behavior, propelled by substance abuse. As difficult as his life has been so far, Steve finds reasons to hope as he interacts with fellow patients and gets treatment for his severe depression, unresolved grief, and other problems.

Horn Book critic Anita L. Burkam found "no anger in Steve's voice, and hardly any grief, just bemusement at his own unpredictable actions, which readers will recognize as cries for help." Reflecting Rapp's early dedication to the works of J.D. Salinger, *Booklist* reviewer Cindy Dobrez observed,

"Steve Nugent is a character as distinctive and disturbing as Salinger's Holden Caulfield was fifty years ago." *Kliatt* reviewer Paula Rohrlick called the book a "gritty, wrenching, and convincing tale about a teen in crisis." Rapp's novel is a "disturbing but memorable read for mature teens," Rohrlick concluded. *School Library Journal* contributor Francisca Goldsmith stated: "Rapp offers teens well-constructed peepholes into harsh circumstances, with a bit of hope tinting the view."

The Year of Endless Sorrows follows the turbulent early adult life of its unnamed narrator as he tries to advance from Midwestern doldrums to the spark and glamour of life in New York City. Moving to the big city and rechristening himself Homon (short for "Homonculus"), the young man struggles with the new and dramatically different atmosphere. His attempts to ignite a literary career are consistently stymied. The aspiring writer takes a low-level, low-paying job in a publishing house—delighted to do so because it is so quintessentially a New York type of job—and acquires a shabby apartment with three slobs for roommates. As he tries to overcome his poor fashion choices and the Midwestern earnestness he cannot seem to shed, he ponders the unattainable women around him before courting lovely Polish immigrant Basha.

"Homon is, then, a particular kind of Everyman. What distinguishes his story from others like it is his creator's gift for language and sense of humor," remarked a *Kirkus Reviews* contributor. "This sweet, stagy bildungsroman never departs familiar territory, but it has lots of winning set pieces," commented a *Publishers Weekly* critic. The *Kirkus Reviews* critic named it "a familiar story originally rendered."

Rapp's 2009 young-adult novel, *Punkzilla*, a Michael L. Printz Honor Book, once again charts the story of a troubled teen. Here, fourteen-year-old Jamie, called "Punkzilla," sets off on a desperate road trip from Oregon to Memphis to see his older brother Peter, who is dying of cancer. Jamie, who suffers from ADD, has been AWOL from his military school, living on the urban streets, scoring drugs, stealing iPods, and selling sexual favors. Living in a halfway house in Portland, Oregon, Jamie gets word of his brother's illness and heads east to reach Peter before it is too late. His subsequent road trip, during which he hitchhikes and rides aboard a Greyhound bus, is told in a series of unsent letters to his gay playwright brother, written en route. Along the way, Jamie meets a broad spectrum of people, and he has his first loving sexual experience. The teen ultimately finds a haven with his brother's gay lover, who gives him lodging and helps Jamie unlock his own creative impulses.

Rapp's novel earned high praise from reviewers. "Exquisitely true in its raw but vulnerable voice, this story is a compulsive read," lauded Carolyn Le-

hman in *School Library Journal*. Similarly, *Booklist* contributor Daniel Kraus observed: "This is devastating stuff, but breathtaking, too." A *Kirkus Reviews* writer felt that "Rapp mines his Midwestern roots for another well-realized tale of raw teenage woe." *Horn Book* contributor Jonathan Hunt focused on the author's prose, praising "Rapp's quirky idiomatic expressions, striking word choices, and stream-of-consciousness prose style." A *Publishers Weekly* critic remarked that "the teenager's singular voice and observations make for an immersive reading experience."

The multitalented Rapp turns to the graphic novel format for another work from 2009, *Ball Peen Hammer*. The gritty and often brutal environment of his young-adult novels is present in this tale about four people living in a postapocalyptic world degraded environmentally and socially. A young and idealistic novelist, Aaron, has found refuge in a basement with Welton, a young man dying of a disease similar to AIDS. Unknown to them at first, there are two others living on a different floor of this building. The actress Exley once had a connection to Welton, who still considers Exley his true love. Exley has taken up with a youth named Horlick. All four of them are involved in a macabre government program.

This graphic novel, illustrated by George O'Connor, manages "to hit home with the taut force of a good short story," according to *School Library Journal* reviewer Mark Flowers. A *Publishers Weekly* reviewer offered a mixed assessment of the same work, noting that Rapp's "story can be thought provoking, although at times his plotting and metaphors—and the unrelenting grimness of the story—feel heavy-handed." Writing for *Booklist*, Francisca Goldsmith observed that Rapp's *Ball Peen Hammer* "attests his flair for dramatic staging and well-developed characters and plotting."

The Play's the Thing

Alongside his career as a successful novelist, Rapp has also continued to write and direct plays. "Rapp's plays blurt rude truths, embrace the obscene and refuse to play nice," noted David Ng in *American Theatre*. "They aren't afraid to let it all hang out." Ng also noted the "uncompromising . . . bleak worldview" Rapp's stage plays present.

In the late 1990s, Rapp was living in New York City's East Village with his brother Anthony, who had attained fame in the hit Broadway musical *Rent*. A third roommate served to inspire Rapp's play

A talented and versatile artist, Rapp stands behind the camera on the set of his 2005 film, *Winter Passing,* **which he wrote and directed.** (Copyright © Focus Features/Album/Newscom. All rights reserved. Reproduced by permission.)

Nocturne, which debuted in October 2000 as part of the American Repertory Theatre's New Stages Series. *Nocturne*'s story is a family tale that the unnamed narrator, once a piano prodigy, recounts in a first-act monologue. He reveals that fifteen years earlier, he was a seventeen-year-old in Joliet driving a car whose brakes suddenly failed and struck his young sister, beheading her. The play's second act follows the aftermath of the tragedy: their parents' marriage dissolves, and the narrator's father spends time in a psychiatric facility and even threatens to kill his son at one point. The narrator recounts his move to New York City, where he gives up music entirely and instead becomes obsessed with books and literature. He returns to Joliet at the request of his estranged father, who has been diagnosed with cancer. *Variety* contributor Markland Taylor called *Nocturne* "an unremittingly dark play" and noted that "the playwright edits himself much more ruthlessly in act two, cutting much closer to the blood and bone of his central character." Taylor concluded that Rapp was "a playwright . . . to watch with keen interest." Theatergoers had several more op-

portunities to see Rapp's work that year; in 2000, he premiered three other plays: *Faster, Dreams of the Salthorse,* and *Finer Noble Gases.*

Still more plays were to come. In 2001, Rapp's *Animals and Plants* was produced in Cambridge under the auspices of the American Repertory Theatre. The two-act work revolves around two drug couriers from North Carolina who are waylaid by a snowstorm. As they sit the storm out in a motel room, tensions mount. Taylor, writing in *Variety,* called *Animals and Plants* "a lurid comedic phantasmagoria of life on the underside of Middle America," finding its dialogue "rough-spoken, raunchy, and sometimes guffawingly funny. . . . Rapp relishes language." The playwright also had a two-act drama premiere in London. *Blackbird* visits an ailing and abusive Gulf War Veteran and his girlfriend, a former stripper with a heroin addiction, on Christmas Eve. According to Matt Wolf in a *Variety* review, Rapp strayed from the "grave austere beauty" of *Nocturne* with a play that, despite its subject matter, "suffers from a dismaying case of the cutes."

The next year, *Stone Cold Dead Serious* was produced by the American Repertory Theatre. Taylor, writing for *Variety,* said the play "mixes blackly comic moments with sentimental ones" and missed the "individual voice" Rapp showcased in previous plays. Rapp's 2006 play, *Red Light Winter,* was a finalist for the Pulitzer Prize in drama. The story of two college friends—now in their twenties—who take a trip to Amsterdam and have relations with the same prostitute, the play "mines the shadows of human connectedness," according to *San Francisco Chronicle* reviewer Jessica Werner Zack. Rapp's drama creates a "bizarre, emotionally charged love triangle," according to Zack. Something of a departure for Rapp, this play explores not battered lives but "unrequited love," Zack explained.

One of Rapp's trademark dysfunctional families is at the heart of his 2007 play *American Sligo,* about wrestling legend Art 'Crazy Train' Sligo, who is about to retire. Family, friends, and fans gather for a final supper before his last match, with less than wholesome results. "Fathers who play hero to their sons get it in the neck here, with this cruelly funny treatment of a professional wrestler whose festive dinner before his final match turns ugly under the scornful eye of his son," noted *Daily Variety* reviewer Marilyn Stasio of this play. Reviewing the drama in the *New York Times,* Caryn James felt that it "bolsters [Rapp's] reputation as a writer and especially as a director." Another play from 2007, *Bingo With the Indians,* concerns three members of a small theater group from New York who are so desperate to get money to produce their new play that they travel to a small New Hampshire town to rob a Bingo game at a local church. Their scheme is compromised, however, when one of the three, the theater director who hails from this town, is recognized by a local youth with theatrical ambitions. *Daily Variety* contributor Sam Thielman was not impressed with this production, writing: "As always, Rapp sows the seeds of razor-sharp, incisive drama, but for a guy so widely acclaimed, he sure spends a lot of time exploring co-prophilia, pedophilia and twee metatheatricality." A similar mixed review was offered by *New York Times* writer James, who noted: "A dark comedy that starts with a sitcom premise and finally invokes questions about the meaning of life, the play spins out of control, but that forgivable chaos comes from a writer who hasn't reined in his overabundance of ideas."

In the 2008 play, *Kindness,* Rapp delves into his own relationship with his mother, telling the story of a woman who travels to New York with her sixteen-year-old son to see a Broadway musical. The son, Dennis, and his mother, ill with cancer, do not get on; indeed, the woman ends up attending the musical with a cab driver while Dennis is enchanted back at the hotel by a strange young woman. "On the whole," wrote *Daily Variety* reviewer Stasio, "Adam Rapp is a lot more fun when he's being crude and rude." Stasio further noted: "*Kindness,* however, finds the scribe in a mellower mood, sympathetically observing a Midwestern mother and her son on a sentimental visit to New York." Writing in *New York,* Scott Brown felt that this play "never quite fills out its baggy dimensions, and feels stranded between Rapp's usual wintry squalor and his riskier epic instincts." Similarly, *New York Times* reviewer Charles Isherwood felt that while Rapp "can write dense, tense, funny dialogue infused with threat and unspoken hostilities, . . . the exchanges in *Kindness* feel mostly arid and devoid of emotional authenticity, resulting in a play that shares the same qualities."

The Metal Children, from 2010, fuses Rapp's career as a young adult novelist to that as a playwright. Here he has a young adult novelist traveling to middle America to defend a writer's moral obligation to speak the truth, no matter how uncomfortable. The play was inspired by the fact that Rapp's novel, *The Buffalo Tree,* was banned by a small Pennsylvania town for its graphic language and sexual content. Rapp went to the town to debate the censorship issue, but came away wondering if, indeed, his novel was appropriate for young readers. In his play, Rapp reproduces this incident when young adult author Tobin Falmouth is invited to speak at a school board hearing in the American heartland about the banning of his novel, *The Metal Children.* "Veering uneasily between satirical humor about the culture wars and a serious depiction of the central character's lapse into near-catatonic depression, the play doesn't succeed on either count," wrote Frank Scheck in the *Hollywood Reporter. New Yorker* reviewer John Lahr, however, found more to like in the play, terming it a "rueful, compelling fantasy, which dramatizes the paradoxical gap between the artist and his artifact." Isherwood, writing again in the *New York Times,* also praised this "provocative if improbable comedy-drama."

Rapp fuses three plays into one with his *Hallway Trilogy,* set in a dilapidated Lower East Side tenement building. *Rose,* the first work, takes place in 1953, the day after the death of playwright Eugene O'Neill. It deals with the psychological problems of an actress, Rose, who believes that the superintendant of the building, whose name also happens to be Eugene O'Neill, is actually the famous playwright. *Paraffin,* the second play in the trilogy, tells of a Gulf War veteran who falls in love with his brother's wife on the night of the New York City blackout of 2003. *Nursing* is set in the year 2053, when all diseases have been eliminated. The apartment building has now been turned into a museum of nursing, and the hallway is covered in Plexiglass, turning it into a theater where volunteers are injected with disease for the enjoyment of spectators. Isherwood, writing in the *New York Times,* felt that this trilogy "contains some of Mr. Rapp's most sensitive and mature writing." Writing in the *Daily Variety,* Stasio felt this trilogy is "the kind of flashy project that resident theater companies love to play with." Stasio further explained: "The constant element here is the hallway setting of a grubby tenement on Manhattan's Lower East Side. Variables include the shifting time frame and changing cast of characters. But the unifying theme? Aye, there's the rub." Lahr, on the other hand, called the cycle of plays "ambitious" in his *New Yorker* review, and felt that of the three plays, *Nursing* is the "boldest and the most unsettling."

Rapp confesses that he is drawn to writing for the stage because of the camaraderie inherent in a production. He told *Boston Phoenix* writer Carolyn Clay: "When you have a play in rehearsal, you have a family. The novelist part of me has always felt solitary and secluded. I'm not very good at parties. . . . Theater became a great excuse to talk to people." Novels, he noted, seem to take him much longer to write. "But the playwriting is this fever thing," he explained to Clay. "The plays kind of burst out of me, and I don't know why. The stuff I write about in plays tends to be the stuff that keeps me up at night, and the stuff I write about in novels tends to be the things I think about during the day." Rapp has also directed many of his plays, and he commented on this part of the artistic process to *Metro Online* contributor T. Michelle Murphy: "I feel like the script is something that's kind of a template or blueprint. And then as a director I want to get into the rehearsal room and have as much fun as possible and play and see what the actors bring." Rapp added: "As I've gotten older—and a little more experienced and a little less concerned with being great or something—I've had a lot more fun. And I think the worlds that I've been involved in within my plays have gotten a lot more interesting to me. The process has been a lot richer because of it."

An Obsessive Writer of Unvarnished Truth

Speaking with *Bomb* Web site contributor Marsha Norman on his prolific output of both plays and novels, Rapp explained his writing technique: "When I start something I don't stop until I am finished. But I don't start until it's grabbing me by my throat. When I'm in that mode it's all I do. I'll basically sleep with my laptop. Not because I feel pressure to finish but because I know that there's a

kinetic thing that takes over and if I lose that feeling of freefall then I have lost a piece in some way." Rapp also noted to Ares in his *Manhattan Chronicles* interview that he thinks about his writing—whether it be young adult novels or plays—for a long time before he actually begins a work. He takes notes and jots down the occasional bit of dialogue or plot reference. "But I only start writing when it has to happen," he told Ares. Then the writing comes rapidly, and he will spend the next several months or even a year cleaning up this first-draft material. Rapp further elaborated on the process to Ng in an *American Theatre* interview: "I'm pretty obsessive-compulsive and I'm very fast. I tend to not write for a long period of time until I can't not write, and then I write first drafts in gallops. I won't eat right. I forget to do my laundry. . . . When I write, that takes over and I can't do anything else. There's something exciting about that free fall, but then my life gets really screwed up. I've lost lots of relationships because of my having to ignore everything."

If you enjoy the works of Adam Rapp, you may also want to check out the following books:

Matt de la Peña's *We Were Here* (2009), a gritty road-trip novel about three juvenile delinquents who escape from a detention center.
Hold Still, a 2009 work by Nina LaCour that concerns a teenage girl's reaction to her best friend's suicide.
Jon Barnes's *Tales of the Madman Underground* (2009), about a troubled high school senior and the members of his school-mandated therapy group.

Rapp discussed the portrayal of brutality in his works with *ALAN Review* interviewer Angel, asserting: "I am not interested in romanticizing or sensationalizing violence. I am interested in honoring what I know to be true. I've seen and lived through certain things that no one should be exposed to. . . . I think violence can become gratuitous when it's not serving the story. I try to steer clear of this as much as possible. In general I feel that my responsibility as an artist is to tell the truth, and it's as simple as that." In an interview with Brian Bartels for the *Fiction Writers Review,* Rapp further considered his obligation to recount unvarnished truths as an author of young adult fiction: "When I write 'YA' stuff I don't consider the age of the audience at all. I find that 'writing down' to kids is condescending. They deserve the toughest, purist truths and it's my job as a storyteller to provide that for them. The things kids see on the street don't get dumbed down for them, so why should books do that? I never even consider the YA genre when I'm writing. I try and keep that completely out of my mind."

■ **Biographical and Critical Sources**

PERIODICALS

ALAN Review, fall, 2000, Ann Angel, "The Bad Boys of YA," p. 7, Ann Angel, "E-view with Adam Rapp," p. 10, and Penny Blubaugh, "An Author in Residence?," p. 14.

American Drama, winter, 2005, "Profile: Adam Rapp," p. 110.

American Theatre, January, 1997, Karen Fricker, "Adam and Anthony Rapp: Genuine Bohemia," p. 50; January, 2004, review of *Stone Cold Dead Serious,* p. 126; October, 2007, David Ng, "Cutting Loose with Adam Rapp," p. 38; March, 2011, Rande Gener, "Rapp Sheet," review of *Hallway Trilogy,* p. 20.

Back Stage, May 20, 2010, David Sheward, review of *The Metal Children,* p. 40; March 3, 2011, David Sheward, review of *Hallway Trilogy,* p. 56.

Back Stage East, October 12, 2006, "Adam Rapp Wins Princess Grace Award," p. 2.

Bomb, spring, 2006, "Adam Rapp."

Booklist, June 1, 1994, Stephanie Zvirin, review of *Missing the Piano,* p. 1804; September 1, 1997, Susan Dove Lempke, review of *The Buffalo Tree,* p. 107; November 15, 1999, Debbie Carton, review of *The Copper Elephant,* p. 615; August, 2002, Gillian Engberg, review of *Little Chicago,* p. 1947; November 15, 2004, Cindy Dobrez, review of *Under the Wolf, under the Dog,* p. 585; November 15, 2006, Jerry Eberle, review of *The Year of Endless Sorrows,* p. 33; March 1, 2009, Francisca Goldsmith, review of *Ball Peen Hammer,* p. 33; April 15, 2009, Daniel Kraus, review of *Punkzilla,* p. 43.

Books, April 15, 2007, review of *The Year of Endless Sorrows,* p. 11.

Boston Herald, October 18, 2000, Terry Byrne, review of *Nocturne.*

Boston Phoenix, October 12, 2000, Carolyn Clay, "Night Music," interview with Adam Rapp.

Bulletin of the Center for Children's Books, December 1, 2004, Deborah Stevenson, review of *Under the Wolf, under the Dog,* p. 182.

Daily Variety, May 23, 2006, Gordon Cox, "Playwrights Takes Rapp," p. 5; October 6, 2006, Gordon Cox, "Rapp to Say Grace Again," p. 4; September 25, 2007, Marilyn Stasio, review of *American Sligo,* p. 10; November 13, 2007, Sam Thielman, review of *Bingo with the Indians,* p. 6; October 14, 2008, Marilyn Stasio, review of *Kindness,* p. 2; May 21, 2010, Marilyn Stasio, review of *The Metal Children,* p. 6; March 1, 2011, Marilyn Stasio, review of *Hallway Trilogy,* p. 4.

Hollywood Reporter, May 28, 2010, Frank Scheck, review of *The Metal Children,* p. 21.

Horn Book, July-August, 1997, Nancy Vasilakis, review of *The Buffalo Tree,* p. 461; January, 2000, review of *The Copper Elephant,* p. 83; September-October, 2002, Lauren Adams, review of *Little Chicago,* p. 580; January-February, 2005, Anita L. Burkam, review of *Under the Wolf, under the Dog,* p. 98; March-April, 2006, "Schneider Family Book Award," p. 236; May 1, 2009, Jonathan Hunt, review of *Punkzilla.*

Kirkus Reviews, February 1, 2003, review of *Thirty-three Snowfish,* p. 237; September 15, 2004, review of *Under the Wolf, under the Dog,* p. 918; October 15, 2006, review of *The Year of Endless Sorrows,* p. 1041; April 1, 2009, review of *Punkzilla.*

Kliatt, September 1, 2004, Paula Rohrlick, review of *Under the Wolf, under the Dog,* p. 15.

Library Journal, November 15, 2006, Stephen Morrow, review of *The Year of Endless Sorrows,* p. 59.

Library Media Connection, March 1, 2005, review of *Under the Wolf, under the Dog,* p. 69.

New York, October 27, 2008, Scott Brown, review of *Kindness,* p. 67.

New Yorker, May 31, 2010, John Lahr, "Reality Checks," review of *The Metal Children,* p. 80; March 7, 2011, John Lahr, review of *Hallway Trilogy,* p. 86.

New York Times, May 14, 2003, Jesse McKinley, "Adam Rapp Parlays the Angst of His Childhood into Plays and Novels," p. E1; March 29, 2007, Charles Isherwood, "Under Ominous Cloud Formations, Ominous Anomie," review of *Essential Self-Defense;* September 26, 2007, Caryn James, "Odd Crew Gathers Round at the Twilight of a Wrestler," review of *American Sligo;* November 10, 2007, Caryn James, "In Search of Sex, Money, and the Meaning of Life," review of *Bingo with the Indians;* October 14, 2008, Charles Isherwood, "Welcome to New York; Now Go Find a Friend," review of *Kindness;* May 10, 2010, Charles Isherwood, "Warning: Reading Can Be Hazardous to Your Health," review of *The Metal Children;* February 25, 2011, Charles Isherwood, "Love Thy Neighbor? Yeah, Right," review of *Hallway Trilogy,* p. C1.

Publishers Weekly, May 23, 1994, review of *Missing the Piano,* p. 90; April 7, 1997, review of *The Buf-*

falo Tree, p. 93; March 11, 2002, review of *Little Chicago,* p. 73; January 13, 2003, review of *Thirty-three Snowfish,*p. 61; October 23, 2006, review of *The Year of Endless Sorrows,* p. 30; May 25, 2009, review of *Punkzilla,* p. 59; August 10, 2009, review of *Ball Peen Hammer,* p. 42.

School Library Journal, April, 2002, Connie Tyrrell Burns, review of *Little Chicago,* p. 196; April, 2003, Joel Shoemaker, review of *Thirty-three Snowfish,* p. 166; October, 2004, Francisca Goldsmith, review of *Under the Wolf, under the Dog,* p. 176; July 1, 2009, Carolyn Lehman, review of *Punkzilla,* p. 90; November 1, 2009, Mark Flowers, review of *Ball Peen Hammer,* p. 143.

Variety, November 6, 2000, Markland Taylor, review of *Nocturne,* p. 29; April 16, 2001, Markland Taylor, review of *Animals and Plants,* p. 38; June 18, 2001, Matt Wolf, review of *Blackbird,* p. 26; February 18, 2002, Markland Taylor, review of *Stone Cold Dead Serious,* p. 43; November 19, 2007, Sam Thielman, review of *Bingo with the Indians,* p. 48.

Voice of Youth Advocates, December 1, 2004, Adam Rapp, review of *Under the Wolf, under the Dog,* p. 394.

ONLINE

Adam Szymkowicz Blog, http://aszym.blogspot.com/ (October 27, 2010), Adam Szymkowicz, "I Interview Playwrights Part 273: Adam Rapp."

American Theatre Wing, http://www.american theatrewing.org/ (April 11, 2010), biography of Adam Rapp.

Bomb, http:// bombsite.com/ (spring, 2006), Marsha Norman, "Adam Rapp."

Edge Theater Company Web site, http://www. edgetheater.org/ (April 11, 2010), "Adam Rapp."

Fiction Writers Review, http://fictionwritersreview. com/ (May 18, 2009), Brian Bartels, "Shadow Sounds: Music as Character [An Interview with Adam Rapp, *Punkzilla*]."

Front Street Books Web Site, http://www.front streetbooks.com/ (August 10, 2007), biography of Adam Rapp.

Graphic Novel Reporter, http://www.graphicnovel reporter.com/ (September 30, 2009), John Hogan, "Apocalypse Now," interview with Adam Rapp.

KGBBarLit, http:// www.kgbbar.com/ (August 10, 2007), Graceanne Bellow, review of *The Year of Endless Sorrows.*

Manhattan Chronicles, http://www.manhattan chronicles.com/ (September 6, 2011), Alexandra Ares, "Adam Rapp: Don't Wait for Anyone to Anoint You."

Metro Online, http://www.metro.us/ (August 25, 2011), T. Michelle Murphy, "Savage and Magical: Interview with Adam Rapp."

Playwrights Horizons, http://www.playwrights horizons.org/ (September 6, 2011), Tim Sanford, "Artist Interview: Adam Rapp Discusses *Kindness* with Artistic Director Tim Sanford."

San Francisco Chronicle Online, http://articles.sfgate. com/ (February 4, 2010), Jessica Werner Zack, "Adam Rapp Tackles Love in *Red Light Winter.*"

*Time Out New York,*http://newyork.timeout.com/ (April 11, 2010), Helen Shaw, "40th Anniversary."

Vineyard Theater Web site, http://www.vineyard theatre.org/ (September 6, 2011), interview with Adam Rapp.*

Philip Reeve

■ Personal

Born 1966, in Brighton, England; married; children: one son. *Education:* Attended Cambridgeshire College of Arts and Technology (now Anglia Ruskin University) and Brighton Polytechnic (now University of Brighton). *Hobbies and other interests:* Walking, drawing, writing, reading.

■ Addresses

Home—Devon, England.

■ Career

Illustrator, author, and bookseller. Children's book illustrator, 1994—. Producer and director of stage plays.

■ Awards, Honors

Whitbread Children's Book Award shortlist, and Gold Award, Nestlé Smarties Book Prize, both 2002, and Best Book of the Year designation, *Washington Post,* Best Book for Young Adults designation, American Library Association (ALA), and Blue Peter Book of the Year Award, all 2003, all for *Mortal Engines;* Best Book for Young Adults designation, ALA, and W.H. Smith People's Choice Award shortlist, 2004, both for *Predator's Gold;* London *Guardian* Children's Fiction Prize, 2006, and *Los Angeles Times* Book Prize for young adult fiction, 2007, both for *A Darkling Plain;* Carnegie Medal, 2008, for *Here Lies Arthur;* Carnegie Medal shortlist, 2010, for *Fever Crumb.*

■ Writings

"HUNGRY CITY CHRONICLES" SERIES; YOUNG-ADULT SCIENCE FICTION

Mortal Engines, Scholastic (London, England), 2001, HarperCollins (New York, NY), 2003.
Predator's Gold, Scholastic (London, England), 2003, Eos (New York, NY), 2004.
Infernal Devices, Eos (New York, NY), 2006.
A Darkling Plain, Eos (New York, NY), 2006.
(With Chris Priestley) *The Teacher's Tales of Terror/ Traction City: A World Day Flip Book,* Scholastic (London, England), 2011.

"LARKLIGHT" TRILOGY; YOUNG-ADULT FANTASY

Larklight: A Rousing Tale of Dauntless Pluck in the Farthest Reaches of Space, illustrated by David Wyatt, Bloomsbury (New York, NY), 2006.

Starcross; or, The Coming of the Moobs!; or, Our Adventures in the Fourth Dimension!: A Stirring Tale of British Vim upon the Seas of Space and Time, illustrated by David Wyatt, Bloomsbury (London, England), 2007, published as *Starcross: A Stirring Adventure of Spies, Time Travel, and Curious Hats,* Bloomsbury (New York, NY), 2007.

Mothstorm; or, The Horror from beyond Georgium Sidus!; or, A Tale of Two Shapers: A Rattling Yarn of Danger, Dastardy and Derring-do upon the Far Frontiers of British Space!, illustrated by David Wyatt, Bloomsbury (London, England), 2007, published as *Mothstorm: The Horror from beyond Georgium Sidus!,* Bloomsbury (New York, NY), 2008.

"FEVER CRUMB" SERIES; YOUNG-ADULT SCIENCE FICTION

Fever Crumb, Scholastic (London, England), 2009, Scholastic (New York, NY), 2010.

A Web of Air, Scholastic (London, England), 2010, Scholastic (New York, NY), 2011.

Scrivener's Moon, Scholastic (London, England), 2011.

JUVENILE FICTION

(Self-illustrated) *Horatio Nelson and His Victory* ("Dead Famous" series), Hippo (London, England), 2003, published as *Horatio Nelson and His Victory* ("Horribly Famous" series), Scholastic (London, England), 2011.

Here Lies Arthur, Scholastic (London, England), 2007, Scholastic (New York, NY), 2008.

No Such Thing as Dragons, Scholastic (New York, NY), 2010.

Coauthor, with Brian P. Mitchell, of musical *The Ministry of Biscuits.*

"BUSTER BAYLISS" SERIES; FOR CHILDREN

Night of the Living Veg, illustrated by Graham Philpot, Scholastic Children's Books (London, England), 2002, new edition, illustrated by Steve May, 2006.

The Big Freeze, illustrated by Graham Philpot, Scholastic Children's Books (London, England), 2002, new edition, illustrated by Steve May, 2006.

Day of the Hamster, illustrated by Graham Philpot, Scholastic Children's Books (London, England), 2002.

Custardfinger, illustrated by Graham Philpot, Scholastic Children's Books (London, England), 2003.

ILLUSTRATOR

Terry Deary, *Wicked Words* ("Horrible Histories" series), Andre Deutsch (London, England), 1996.

Terry Deary, *Dark Knights and Dingy Castles* ("Horrible Histories" series), Andre Deutsch (London, England), 1997.

Terry Deary, *The Angry Aztecs* ("Horrible Histories" series), Andre Deutsch (London, England), 1997, published with *The Incredible Incas* (also see below), 2001.

Chris D'Lacey, *Henry Spaloosh!,* Hippo (London, England), 1997.

Michael Cox, *Awful Art* ("The Knowledge" series), Hippo (London, England), 1997.

Michael Cox, *Mind-blowing Music* ("The Knowledge" series), Hippo (London, England), 1997.

Peter Corey, *Coping with Love,* Hippo (London, England), 1997.

Michael Cox, *Smashin' Fashion* ("The Knowledge" series), Hippo (London, England), 1998.

Kjartan Poskitt, *More Murderous Maths,* Hippo (London, England), 1998, published as *Desperate Measures,* Scholastic (London, England), 2008.

Chris D'Lacey, *Snail Patrol,* Hippo (London, England), 1998.

Terry Deary and Barbara Allen, *Space Race* ("Spark Files" series), Faber (London, England), 1998.

Terry Deary and Barbara Allen, *Shock Tactics* ("Spark Files" series), Faber (London, England), 1998.

Terry Deary and Barbara Allen, *Chop and Change* ("Spark Files" series), Faber (London, England), 1998.

Terry Deary and Barbara Allen, *Bat and Bell* ("Spark Files" series), Faber (London, England), 1998.

Kjartan Poskitt, *Isaac Newton and His Apple* ("Dead Famous" series), Hippo (London, England), 1999.

Hayden Middleton, *Come and Have a Go If You Think You're Cool Enough!,* Hippo (London, England), 1999.

Hayden Middleton, *Come and Have a Go If You Think You're Mad Enough!,* Hippo (London, England), 1999.

Alan MacDonald, *Henry VIII and His Chopping Block,* Scholastic (London, England), 1999.

Alan MacDonald, *Al Capone and His Gang,* Scholastic (London, England), 1999.

Terry Deary, *Rowdy Revolutions* ("Horrible Histories" series), Scholastic (London, England), 1999.

Terry Deary and Barbara Allen, *Magical Magnets* ("Spark Files" series), Faber (London, England), 1999.

Terry Deary, *The Incredible Incas,* Hippo (London, England), 2000.

Margaret Simpson, *Cleopatra and Her Asp,* Hippo (London, England), 2000.

Alan MacDonald, *Oliver Cromwell and His Warts* ("Dead Famous" series), Hippo (London, England), 2000.

Terry Deary and Barbara Allen, *The Secrets of Science* ("Spark Files" series), Faber (London, England), 2000.

Margaret Simpson, *Elizabeth I and Her Conquests,* Hippo (London, England), 2001.

Margaret Simpson, *Mary, Queen of Scots and Her Hopeless Husbands,* Hippo (London, England), 2001.

Kjartan Poskitt, *Do You Feel Lucky? The Secrets of Probability* ("Murderous Maths" series), Hippo (London, England), 2001.

Mike Goldsmith, *Albert Einstein and His Inflatable Universe* ("Dead Famous" series), Hippo (London, England), 2001.

Michael Cox, *Elvis and His Pelvis,* Hippo (London, England), 2001.

Phil Robins, *Joan of Arc and Her Marching Orders* ("Dead Famous" series), Scholastic (London, England), 2002.

Kjartan Poskitt, *Vicious Circles and Other Savage Shapes* ("Murderous Maths" series), Hippo (London, England), 2002.

Kjartan Poskitt, *Professor Fiendish's Book of Diabolical Brainbenders* ("Murderous Maths" series), Hippo (London, England), 2002.

Kjartan Poskitt, *Numbers: The Key to the Universe* ("Murderous Maths" series), Hippo (London, England), 2002.

Kjartan Poskitt, *The Phantom X* ("Murderous Maths" series), Hippo (London, England), 2003.

Kjartan Poskitt, *The Fiendish Angletron* ("Murderous Maths" series), Hippo (London, England), 2004.

Kjartan Poskitt, *The Magic of Pants: A Conjuror's Compendium of Underpants Tricks to Delight All Ages (and Sizes),* Scholastic (London, England), 2004, published as *Pantsacadabra! A Conjuror's Compendium of Underpants Tricks to Delight All Ages,* 2007.

Kjartan Poskitt, *A Brief History of Pants, or, the Rudiments of Pantology,* Scholastic (London, England), 2005, published as *Pantology: A Brief History of Pants,* 2008.

Kjartan Poskitt, *Urgum the Axeman,* Scholastic (London, England), 2006.

Kjartan Poskitt, *The Perfect Sausage,* Hippo (London, England), 2007.

Kjartan Poskitt, *Urgum and the Seat of Flames,* Scholastic (London, England), 2007.

Kjartan Poskitt, *Urgum and the Goo Goo Bah!,* Scholastic (London, England), 2008.

■ Adaptations

The "Buster Bayliss" novels were adapted as audiobooks by Chivers Children's Audio Books, 2003.

■ Sidelights

Carnegie Medal-winner Philip Reeve is the author of more than a dozen rich, fascinating, and original young adult novels. His works offer readers a dark vision of a far-future Earth where mobile cities devour other metropolises; a journey to the stars and back with a humorous twist; and an exploration of the world of dragons. "Reeve's inventive style and skillfully crafted stories enable him to stand alone as a highly original writer in his own right, and one of the best contemporary writers of fantasy and science-fiction," noted Elizabeth O'Reilly on the *British Council* Web site. "[His] fiction is highly visual and cinematic, and the alternative worlds he creates are vivid, energetic and abundant with detail and action." In works such as his highly-acclaimed "Hungry City Chronicles," his stand-alone historical novel, *Here Lies Arthur,* and his lighthearted space trilogy, "Larklight," Reeve has created fully-formed and nuanced alternate worlds peopled by casts of characters straight out of the pages of Charles Dickens, one of Reeve's favorite writers.

In many of Reeve's books, technology and its negative effects are major motifs. His character Fever, from his 2009 novel, *Fever Crumb,* complains at one point: "It is irrational to build machines whose principles you do not understand and whose actions you cannot predict." Speaking with Sarah Wood in *Teenreads.com,* Reeve explained his own position on the role of technology: "Actually I believe technology can be an enormous force for good; I think it has improved our lives immeasurably, and most of the problems it throws up can probably be solved by the further application of technology. On the other hand, sci-fi stories are generally more interesting if the technology goes a bit mad and eats the cat or something."

From Illustrator to Author

Born in Brighton, England, in 1966, Reeve wrote his first story when he was just a youngster. In an interview with a contributor for *Hortorian.com,* Reeve commented on the origins of his literary ambitions: "I think I've been making up stories for as long as I can remember. Certainly, from the age of about 7, I was always 'writing a book', which was usually a ropey knock-off of whatever I happened to be reading at the time—*Narnia,* or *Swallows and Amazons,* or Alan Garner. I used to illustrate them too." Along with Garner, Reeve's favorite authors included J.R.R. Tolkien, Rosemary Sutcliff, Ray Bradbury, Robert Heinlein, and J.G. Ballard. In

"I keep thinking of these strange ideas and images, and a story is a machine for getting them out of my head and into other people's heads."

—Philip Reeve, in a *Thirst for Fiction* interview.

addition to reading and writing, Reeve also enjoyed acting and drawing. By his teenage years he was also making films with a Super-8mm camera. Reeve studied art and illustration at college and then returned to Brighton, working in an independent bookstore while writing and directing low-budget films. Eventually he turned his art talents to cartooning and then, by the 1990s, to working as a freelance illustrator.

The scores of books he has illustrated include series such as Terry Deary's "Horrible Histories," Kjartan Poskitt's "Murderous Maths," and the "Dead Famous" series, for which Reeve also wrote a title, *Horatio Nelson and His Victory.* All the while, however, his early fascination with writing had never left him. In an interview with a contributor for the *Hero Press Blog,* Reeve noted that he got into professional writing "more by accident than design." He added: "I've enjoyed writing stories ever since I was a child, but it never really occurred to me that I'd be able to get published or make a living at it. In my twenties I wrote a lot of comedy and theatre stuff and some no-budget films; things that I could produce myself rather than having to show to publishers or commissioning editors." However, the author further explained, once he began to illustrate books regularly in the 1990s, he was always working against a deadline and no longer had time for such experiments. Thus he went back to writing prose and ultimately came up with the far-future world that would inform his first novel, *Mortal Engines.*

The World of Mortal Engines

In 2001 Reeve introduced *Mortal Engines,* the first of a quartet of novels that make for a "a highly original and dynamic adventure tale," according to O'Reilly. Reeve sets his series thousands of years in the future, long after the legendary Sixty-Minute War destroyed civilization in the twenty-first century. Now the world is controlled by the philosophy of Municipal Darwinism, in which huge moveable cities move around the Great Hunting Ground of what was formerly Europe on wheels or caterpillar tracks,

capturing other cities which they then cannabalize for their raw materials, and taking their citizens as slaves. Big cities thus prey on smaller ones, and the smaller ones, in turn, prey on villages and settlements that are still fixed on the ground. Much the same was happening to rural England during the years Reeve was imagining this future world: cities were expanding, incorporating smaller towns into their metropolitan regions. "It's a rusty retro-future," Reeve told the interviewer for *Hero Press,* "and also a perfect setting for good old-fashioned adventure stories, which is what the books [in the series] really are."

Reeve further explained the origins of this future world to a contributor for the *Thirst for Fiction* Web site: "I was working on a different story—a sort of alternate Victorian *Mad Max* kind of thing—when the idea of a moving city (which isn't particularly original) occurred to me, and then the idea of moving cities that chase and eat each other (which is, as far as I know). I immediately scrapped the story I'd been writing and got to work on *Mortal Engines,* although writing was just a hobby at the time so it was many, many years before it reached its final form." In an interview with Madelyn Travis on the *Booktrust Children's Book* Web site, Reeve commented on another inspiration: "Although *Mortal Engines* is nominally set in the future, I always wanted it to feel like a historical novel, and all the influences on it are historical. There is quite a lot of the Napolenoic era and Victorian times and even classical societies." This aspect of the work was, in turn, inspired by the films of former Monty Python member Terry Gilliam. "*Brazil* [a Gilliam feature film] is probably the genesis of *Mortal Engines,*" Reeve told Rick Margolis in a *School Library Journal* interview. "The film's sort of retro-future world, full of strange machinery, had a huge influence on me when I first saw it in 1985."

A decade in the planning and writing, Reeve's immensely popular *Mortal Engines* led to three sequels in what became known as the "Hungry City Chronicles," including the novels *Predator's Gold, Infernal Devices,* and *A Darkling Plain.* Writing in the London *Guardian* on the occasion of Reeve winning that newspaper's Children's Fiction Prize for 2006, Julia Eccleshare described the resulting four-book series: "The ride is a fast one and full of the unexpected. Reeve seems effortlessly able to whisk up entirely credible cities with ladders and walkways, unfurling sails and dangling ropes, as well as complicated dramas with cascading subplots. Saving it all from the weightiness that this might imply is Reeve's humour." Another factor setting these books apart from other fantasies is Reeve's refusal to portray his huge cast of characters as simply black-or-white terms. "Reeve's characters have an uncertain status and may behave villainously or virtuously on different occasions," noted Eccleshare. Primary among those characters are Tom Natsworthy, a teenager with an optimistic and sometimes naïve way of viewing the world, and Hester Shaw, an edgy and disfigured young woman who joins Tom on his adventures.

In *Mortal Engines*, London, a Traction City built in tiers like a massive layer cake, possesses an ancient and deadly weapon, thanks to Thaddeus Valentine, the ultimate scavenger. With such a weapon (essentially an enhanced nuclear bomb), London will be able to take over the stationary settlements that now checkerboard what was at one time Asia. The earth-bound inhabitants of those towns are looked upon as heretics by those in mobile cities. Tom Natsworthy, who works as a Third Class Apprentice Historian, sees Valentine, an elder historian, as a heroic figure; he also has a sweet spot for Valentine's beautiful daughter, Katherine. Hester Shaw, on the other hand, despises the elder historian, for Valentine murdered her parents in order to secure the weapon. When she attempts to stab Valentine, Tom stops her. Instead of showing his appreciation, Valentine simply throws both the teens overboard to the wastelands below. Now the duo attempts to find Valentine once again and stop him before he unleashes the nuclear bomb. Meantime, in London, Katherine and an apprentice of the Guild of Engineers also attempt to divert nuclear carnage.

This first series installment earned high praise from many quarters. *School Library Journal* reviewer Sharon Rawlins termed it an "exciting and visually descriptive novel," and *Horn Book* contributor Anita L. Burkam wrote: "The book's tone of high adventure and danger; the grimy yet fantastical postapocalyptic setting; the narrow escapes, deepening loyalties, and not-infrequent bitter losses—all keep readers' attention riveted." Likewise, *Booklist* writer Sally Estes dubbed *Mortal Engines* a "page-turner . . . [that] will have readers eagerly suspending disbelief to follow the twists and turns of the imaginative plot." Paula Rohrlick, writing in *Kliatt*, also felt that this "wildly imaginative British tale is full of marvelous details . . ., humor, and grand adventures." Further praise came from a *Publishers Weekly* reviewer who noted that, "like the moving cities it depicts, Reeve's debut novel is a staggering feat of engineering, a brilliant construction that offers new wonders at every turn," and from a *Kirkus reviews* contributor who thought that "readers who enjoy violent, titanic clashes between good and evil will he absorbed from beginning to end."

The second series installment, *Predator's Gold,* is set two years later. Tom and Hester now are traders on their own airship and are being pursued by the radi-

In *Mortal Engines*, the first work in the "Hungry City Chronicles," Reeve projects a distant future world in which large, mobile cities prey on smaller towns, consuming their resources. (Copyright © Philip Reeve, 2001. Cover illustration by David Frankland. Reproduced with the permission of Scholastic Ltd. All Rights Reserved.)

cal environmental group, Green Storm, whose mission it is to destroy all of the Traction Cities. The pair takes refuge in the mobile city of Anchorage, ruled by the beautiful young Freya. It is Freya's desire to take her Traction City back to its original location across the frozen wastes to the Dead Continent, formerly America. Complicating this journey is the deadly predator city, Arkangel, trailing Anchorage, and the Lost Boys gang, whose mission is to burgle cities. When Hester sees Tom kissing Freya, she takes off in a fit of jealousy in their airship to sell the location of Anchorage to Arkangel for a bit of "predator's gold," or payment for divulging a secret. "Reeve ratchets up the action and the violence in the sequel," noted Estes in a

Booklist review. Similarly, a *Publishers Weekly* contributor felt that "fans of the first book will not be disappointed." Rohrlick also found this an "exciting sequel" in her *Kliatt* review.

It is sixteen years later when the action begins in *Infernal Devices.* Tom and Hester live a quiet existence in the town of Anchorage-in-Vineland with their fifteen-year-old daughter, Wren. Her parents may enjoy this quiet life, but Wren is bored, and she is easily duped by the Lost Boys, who trick her into stealing a legendary artifact before kidnapping her. After Wren is sold as a slave to an old enemy, the blustery Pennyroyal on the pleasure raft-city of Brighton, Tom and Hester set off to the rescue, just as other enemies from the past resurface, including the Green Storm and Anna Fang—now in the guise of the evil robot Stalker Fang. "The pace and the violence escalate to a thrilling climax and hint of more battles to come," noted *Booklist* reviewer Estes. Tim Wadham, writing in *School Library Journal,* found the climax to this adventure "breathtaking," and *Kliatt* reviewer Rohrlick felt that readers will be "enthralled once again by Reeve's wonderfully imaginative world."

The series closes with the award-winning *A Darkling Plain,* set just over a year after the conclusion of *Infernal Devices.* The Green Storm is still attempting to re-establish settlements on the surface of the planet and create farmland out of the wastelands, but the Traction Cities, including London, continue in their mission of Municipal Darwinism. After a truce between the factions falls apart, the Stalker Fang unveils a plan to destroy all life on the planet, and Tom, Hester, and Wren "are drawn into the resulting mayhem," according to *School Library Journal* contributor Beth Wright. A *Publishers Weekly* reviewer felt that this fourth novel brings the series to a "fine conclusion," further noting: "Complex, intelligent and rewarding, Reeve's world is truly one to get lost in." A *Kirkus Reviews* contributor declared: "All stops are pulled out in this pyrotechnic conclusion." Martha V. Parravano in *Horn Book* found the concluding volume and the series as a whole "brilliant . . . and exhilarating." Parravano further observed that the series is "inventive to the max, epic yet always human-centered; and . . . it remained so up to the very last page."

Victorian Houses in Space

From mobile cities, Reeve turned to Victorian houses that float in space with his *Larklight: A Rousing Tale of Dauntless Pluck in the Farthest Reaches of Space,* the first work in a trilogy. With this novel,

"Reeve brilliantly creates a world where the environs of space are governed by credibly 19th-century assumptions," according to a *Kirkus Reviews* contributor. The year is 1851; Britain has colonized the solar system. Art Mumby and his sister, Myrtle, happily reside in this enlarged British Empire in their rambling old house, Larklight, traveling through space. Adventures start with the arrival of giant white spiders, the First Ones, who want to recapture their empire from the British. Art and Myrtle escape their besieged house, believing their father has been killed. They are saved by the space pirate, Jack Havock, and after numerous adventures manage to reunite with their family. *School Library Journal* contributor Connie Tyrrell Burns called this a "wildly imaginative sci-fi pirate adventure [that] has tongue-in-cheek humor and social commentary on accepting those who are different." Similar praise came from *Horn Book* reviewer Claire E. Gross, who called *Larklight* a "deliciously imaginative romp," as well as a "genre-defying work that melds deadpan comedy, anticolonial political satire, sci-fi epic, and pirate caper with aplomb." A *Publishers Weekly* reviewer focused on the comedy element in the novel, noting that "Reeve's humor is oh-so-British and utterly entertaining."

Reeve reprises the Mumby family in *Starcross: A Stirring Adventure of Spies, Time Travel and Curious Hats,* in which Art and Myrtle travel with their mother—who is also an ancient entity—across space to Starcross. This resort is supposed to be the best the solar system has to offer, but the Mumbys surely do not find the relaxing vacation they were hoping for in this "rambunctious, fast-moving tale," as a *Publishers Weekly* reviewer dubbed it. The same reviewer also felt that Reeve spoofs colonial attitudes as well as genres such as the spy thriller and the science-fiction space opera in this "dashing and outrageous sequel." Similarly, a *Kirkus Reviews* contributor felt that this novel "lives up to the standard set by *Larklight,*" while Burns, writing again in *School Library Journal,* found the work "tongue-in-cheek, hilarious, and wildly imaginative."

Reeve concludes his trilogy with *Mothstorm: The Horror from beyond Georgium Sidus!,* in which the Mumbys once again thwart a desperate challenge to the solar system. It is Christmas when the family receives a message that there is a great danger lurking, and they set off for the planet Georgium Sidus, or Uranus, to uncover the danger, which comes in the form of an evil creator of solar systems, Mothmaker. This Shaper is intent on conquering the solar system and turning all its human inhabitants into slaves, and Art and Myrtle are determined not to let this happen. Jennifer D. Montgomery, writing in *School Library Journal,* noted of this novel: "One

"I think the 'stuff' was better in the past—the trains, the clothes, the machines—everything had more character then. Modern technology doesn't appeal to me but a great big steam engine does."

—Philip Reeve, speaking to London *Guardian* contributor Julia Eccleshare.

might describe it as a cross between science fiction, action movie, soap opera, and situation comedy. In sum, it's simply a jolly good read." A similar assessment was offered by a *Kirkus Reviews* contributor who concluded: "This tale will satisfy fans in inimitably jolly fashion."

From Dark Age Britain to Dragon Lore

Reeve has also written stand-alone novels, including his 2007 Carnegie Medal-winning work, *Here Lies Arthur,* his idiosyncratic take on the King Arthur legend. Speaking with the contributor for *Thirst for Fiction,* Reeve noted that his turn to the Arthurian legend was inspired by the obsession he had with the legend when he was a teen. The film *Excalibur* inspired him to read the works of Sir Thomas Malory and Alfred Tennyson and also drew him to the work of the Pre-Raphaelites. However, those versions of the Arthurian legend are more fantastical and magical, so, as Reeve explained, "I decided mine would have to take the opposite approach and be as gritty and down-to-earth as possible." Reeve also remarked to a contributor for the online *Teen Ink* that the numerous retellings of Arthur forced him to think outside the box and wonder: "If there had been a real King Arthur, might he not have been just a small-time warlord who somehow ended up getting all these wonderful tales spun about him? And then I thought, Well, who's spinning these stories? And that was where Gwyna came from, and she was my way into the book."

In Reeve's version, Arthur is a not-so-successful warlord. The only reason that his name comes down to posterity is that he had a very good publicity agent and spin doctor known as Merlin. Thus, on one level, Reeve's novel is a metaphor for the manner in which stories and legends are cultivated. Travis noted of Reeve's *Here Lies Arthur:* "In stark contrast to the chivalrous hero of medieval romance, Reeve's Arthur is an uncouth, brutal warlord. Merlin—here Myrddin, in keeping with the story's Welsh provenance—is a bard rather than a magi-

cian, orchestrating events and spinning tales in order to transform the decidedly earthbound leader into the stuff of legend." Gwyna, the book's narrator, is a servant girl whom Myrddin takes under his wing.

In the novel, Gwyna passes as a boy, serving first as a soldier in Arthur's band of warriors before she finally takes on a new role as a maid for Guinevere. The reader experiences some of the most familiar of Arthur's adventures, from his magical extracting of the sword from the stone to the day of his death; however, in Gwyna's telling, neither the events nor the characters are nearly so regal as in legend. Supernatural elements are also shown to be mere magical tricks by the bard, Myrddin.

"Arthurian lore has inspired many novels for young people, but few as arresting as this one," wrote *Booklist* reviewer Carolyn Phelan of *Here Lies Arthur.* Other reviewers also had praise for this retelling. A *Publishers Weekly* contributor, for example, felt that "Reeve, like Myrddin, turns hallowed myth and supple prose to political purposes" in this work that spoofs the art of political spin. Similarly, *Horn Book* writer Gross noted: "Reeve's brilliant, brutal re-creation of Arthurian myth is a study in balance and contradiction: it is bleak yet tender; impeccably historical, yet distinctly timely in its driving sense of disillusionment." Further praise came from *School Library Journal* reviewer Burns who termed the novel "a multilayered tour de force for mature young readers," and from a *Kirkus Reviews* contributor who dubbed it "absorbing, thought-provoking and unexpectedly timely." And Rohrlick was prescient in her assessment, concluding in her *Kliatt* review: "It's a marvelous read, unsentimental yet deeply moving, and it's sure to garner well-deserved awards."

Reeve creates a "somber but rewarding tale," according to a *Publishers Weekly* reviewer, in another stand-alone title, *No Such Thing as Dragons.* The tale features a young boy named Ansel who is mute. His parents sell him to a dragon slayer, Brock, as a servant. However, it turns out that Brock is simply a con artist. He sells his skills to gullible and superstitious villagers and country folk and presents them with the skull of a crocodile to demonstrate his success. He wants Ansel as his servant, for he believes that the youth will not be able to warn gullible villagers about this scam. One day, though, the pair confronts a real dragon and must defeat it to save a young girl whom villagers have left as a sacrifice. In the process, Ansel "is able to find his voice, both literally and figuratively," wrote Wadham in *School Library Journal.* The *Publishers Weekly* contributor further termed this a "beauti-

Reeve notes that his "Hungry City Chronicles," and "Larklight" trilogy were influenced by his favorite childhood authors, once stating, "I often feel that I'm trying to recapture the feeling I got from reading [J.R.R.] Tolkien, Rosemary Sutcliff and Alan Garner as a boy."

fully written, understated story." For *Booklist* reviewer Ian Chipman, *No Such Thing as Dragons* bore a similarity to *Here Lies Arthur* in that both examine "the cracks between life and lore." Chipman went on to term this a "short but not simplistic novel." A *Kirkus Reviews* contributor had higher praise for *No Such Thing as Dragons,* declaring it a "gem, much like those rumored to rest in a dragon's hoard." Similarly, *Horn Book* reviewer Burkam felt that this novel is "taut with tension and flowing with Reeve's commanding language."

Before the Transformation

Reeve provides a prequel to his "Hungry City Chronicles" with the 2009 novel, *Fever Crumb.* Set a century or more before the heyday of Traction Cities, this tale takes place in London when it is still stationary. It features the young eponymous heroine, an orphan raised by the Order of Engineers to be logical and rational in a world that is neither.

Housed in the head of an unfinished statue of the despised former ruler of London, the mutant Scriven named Auric Godshawk, Fever is hardly ready for her first adventure outside of this sheltered atmosphere. But she is assigned to work with Kit Solent, an archaeologist who has found a cache of items from Godshawk. Fever is confronted directly with the clambering scene of this post-apocalyptic London, a sort of "medieval backwater," as Chipman described it in *Booklist,* still strewn with technological detritus that does not decay. She also faces a larger challenge when Solent informs Fever that she has been implanted with Godshawk's memories. Now, with a Traction City approaching, she is accused of being a dreaded Scrivener, a mutant strain of humanity. Fever must avoid capture by vigilantes while she desperately tries to uncover the secret of her origins, a secret that has world-shaking implications.

A *Publishers Weekly* reviewer dubbed this an "exciting steampunk adventure . . . guaranteed to please Reeve's fans—and very likely broaden their ranks."

Similarly, a *Kirkus Reviews* contributor found this "an essential read for fans and a great entry point for newcomers to the world." *School Library Journal* reviewer Wadham also praised the novel and its author, noting: "Reeve is not just an excellent writer, but a creator with a wildly imaginative mind." Likewise, Chipman remarked: "Reeve's captivating flights of imagination play as vital a role in the story as his endearing heroine." And writing for the London *Guardian*, Frank Cottrell Boyce termed *Fever Crumb* a "terrific read, a sci-fi Dickens, full of orphans, villains, chases and mysteries."

Reeve returns to the world of *Fever Crumb* in his 2010 sequel, *A Web of Air*, which takes place two years after the events in the first novel. Fever, after discovering secrets about her real parentage, is working with an itinerant acting troupe, touring throughout the ruins of Europe. Theatrics and her rational background are not a perfect fit, however. In one of the small towns the troupe visits, Fever encounters a reclusive young inventor, Arlo Thursday, who is attempting to rediscover human flight, and helps him with his efforts. A *Kirkus Reviews* contributor called this novel "imaginative, inventive and exciting." Misti Tidman, writing in *School Library Journal*, also had praise for this novel, noting: "Reeve's intricately imagined world, combined with a fast-paced plot, offers a rich, rewarding reading experience."

The action continues in the 2011 series installment, *Scrivener's Moon*, which finds Fever on yet another quest, this time to the far north in the company of her Scriven mother. Meanwhile, a rebuilt London prepares for its first journey as a Traction City, but not all citizens are overjoyed about this. There is the beginning of an uprising intended to return the city to its stationary form. A reviewer for the online *Thirst for Fiction* felt that while *A Web of Air* reads like a "light frolick," this installment "takes the series back to its darker, grander origins, back to the grimy cities that are beginning to traction-ise, back to the loud noises, smells and gargantuan scales of the great moving vehicles that can carry entire cities upon their backs."

Though his works have garnered praise for their elaborate and imaginative settings and action-packed narratives, Reeve also takes care to present fully realized characters. "I think that if you're creating an imaginary world," he told Wood, "it ought to be at least as interesting as the real world, and one of the things that makes the real world interesting is that very few people are wholly good or evil. Having bad people do good things and good people do bad things makes it much more fun to write, and, hopefully, to read."

Describing his writing process in the *Hortorian.com* interview, Reeve observed: "I don't plan anything. I usually start out with an opening image and a closing image and a few vague notions for things that might happen in between, and I start writing at the beginning and try to find my way through. . . . If I planned it advance, I'd just get bored and never bother to finish it." Asked if he had any advice for aspirign authors, Reeve stated in his *Teen Ink* interview: "Read a lot, and write a lot. You probably do this anyway if you seriously want to be an author, but it really is important." He also expressed that the idea that young writers must be diligent about their craft: "It's like sport, or drawing, or playing a musical instrument; practice, practice, practice; it's the only way to be any good."

■ Biographical and Critical Sources

BOOKS

Reeve, Philip, *Fever Crumb*, Scholastic (London, England), 2009.

PERIODICALS

Booklist, November 1, 2003, Sally Estes, review of *Mortal Engines*, p. 491; August, 2004, Sally Estes, review of *Predator's Gold*, p. 1920; May 15, 2006, Sally Estes, review of *Infernal Devices*, p. 61; October 1, 2006, Diana Herald, review of *Larklight: A Rousing Tale of Dauntless Pluck in the Farthest Reaches of Space*, p. 52; July 1, 2007, Sally Estes, review of *A Darkling Plain*, p. 58; November 1, 2007, Todd Morning, review of *Starcross: A Stirring Adventure of Spies, Time Travel and Curious Hats*, p. 48; August 1, 2008, Carolyn Phelan, review of *Here Lies Arthur*, p. 69; January 1, 2010, Ian Chipman, review of *Fever Crumb*, p. 80; August 1, 2010, Ian Chipman, review of *No Such Thing as Dragons*, p. 51.

Bookseller, August 10, 2001, Tara Stephenson, review of *Mortal Engines*, p. 33; June 27, 2008, Caroline Horn, "I Feel Like a Proper Writer at Last," interview with Reeve, p. 10.

Bulletin of the Center for Children's Books, March, 2004, Janice M. Del Negro, review of *Mortal Engines*, p. 294; November, 2004, Timnah Card, review of *Predator's Gold*, p. 141.

Chronicle, January, 2004, Don D'Ammassa, review of *Mortal Engines*, p. 31.

Guardian (London, England), April 8, 2006, Josh Lacey, review of *A Darkling Plain*; September 29, 2006, Julia Eccleshare, "Back to the Beginning," p. 20; June 26, 2009, Frank Cottrell Boyce, review of *Fever Crumb*, p. 14.

Horn Book, November-December, 2003, Anita L. Burkam, review of *Mortal Engines,* p. 755; September-October, 2004, Anita L. Burkam, review of *Predator's Gold,* p. 596; July-August, 2006, Martha V. Parravano, review of *Infernal Devices,* p. 450; November-December, 2006, Claire E. Gross, review of *Larklight,* p. 724; September-October, 2007, Martha V. Parravano, review of *A Darkling Plain,* p. 587; January-February, 2008, Claire E. Gross, review of *Starcross,* p. 93; November-December, 2008, Claire E. Gross, review of *Here Lies Arthur,* p. 713; January-February, 2009, Claire E. Gross, review of *Mothstorm: The Horror from beyond Georgium Sidus!,* p. 101; March-April, 2010, Claire E. Gross, review of *Fever Crumb,* p. 68; September-October, 2010, Anita Burkam, review of *No Such Thing as Dragons,* p. 92.

Kirkus Reviews, October 15, 2003, review of *Mortal Engines,* p. 1275; August 15, 2004, review of *Predator's Gold,* p. 216; May 1, 2006, review of *Infernal Devices;* September 15, 2006, review of *Larklight,* p. 965; April 15, 2007, review of *A Darkling Plain;* October 1, 2007, review of *Starcross;* October 15, 2008, review of *Here Lies Arthur* and *Mothstorm;* March 1, 2010, review of *Fever Crumb;* August 15, 2010, review of *No Such Thing as Dragons;* September 1, 2011, review of *A Web of Air.*

Kliatt, November, 2003, Paula Rohrlick, review of *Mortal Engines,* p. 10; September, 2004, Paula Rohrlick, review of *Predator's Gold,* p. 16; May, 2006, Paula Rohrlick, review of *Infernal Devices,* p. 13; May, 2007, Paula Rohrlick, review of *A Darkling Plain,* p. 18; November 2008, Paula Rohrlick, review of *Here Lies Arthur,* p. 17.

Magpies, May, 2002, review of *Mortal Engines,* p. 38; March, 2004, Rayma Turton, review of *Predator's Gold,* p. 43.

Publishers Weekly, October 27, 2003, review of *Mortal Engines,* p. 70; August 16, 2004, review of *Predator's Gold,* p. 64; August 28, 2006, review of *Larklight,* p. 54; May 28, 2007, review of *A Darkling Plain,* p. 64; November 5, 2007, review of *Starcross,* p. 64; October 6, 2008, review of *Here Lies Arthur,* p. 55; February 15, 2010, review of *Fever Crumb,* p. 133; July 19, 2010, review of *No Such Thing as Dragons,* p. 130.

School Librarian, winter, 2001, review of *Mortal Engines,* p. 214; winter, 2002, review of *Night of the Living Veg,* p. 202; spring, 2004, Michael Holloway, review of *Predator's Gold,* p. 34; winter 2010, Karen King, review of *A Web of Air,* p. 247.

School Library Journal, December, 2003, Sharon Rawlins, review of *Mortal Engines,* p. 864; September, 2004, Sharon Rawlins, review of *Predator's Gold,* p. 216; June, 2006, Tim Wadham, review of *Infernal Devices,* p. 164; November, 2006, Rick Margolis, interview with Reeve, p. 33, and Connie Tyrrell Burns, review of *Larklight,* p. 148; June, 2007, Beth Wright, review of *A Darkling Plain,* p. 158; December, 2007, Connie Tyrrell Burns, review of *Starcross,* p. 142; December, 2008, Connie Tyrrell Burns, review of *Here Lies Arthur,* and Jennifer D. Montgomery, review of *Mothstorm,* p. 136; April, 2010, Tim Wadham, review of *Fever Crumb,* p. 166; September, 2010, Tim Wadham, review of *No Such Thing as Dragons,* p. 163; August, 2011, Philip Reeve, "The Worst Is Yet to Come," p. 34; September, 2011, Misti Tidman, review of *A Web of Air,* p. 168.

Tribune Books (Chicago, IL), November 23, 2003, review of *Mortal Engines,* p. 4.

Voice of Youth Advocates, October, 2004, Sarah Flowers, review of *Predator's Gold,* p. 318.

ONLINE

Booktrust Children's Books Web site, http://www.booktrustchildrensbooks.org.uk/ (September 15, 2011), Madelyn Travis, "From the Future to the Past," interview with Reeve.

British Broadcasting Corporation Web site, http://www.bbc.co.uk/ (September 29, 2004), interview with Reeve.

British Council Literature Web site, http://literature.britishcouncil.org/ (September 16, 2011), Elizabeth O'Reilly, "Philip Reeve: Critical Perspective."

Financial Times Online, http://www.ft.com/ (June 28, 2008), Anna Metcalfe, "Small Talk—Philip Reeve."

Hero Press Blog, http://www.heropress.net/ (May 2, 2010), "Six of the Best with Philip Reeve."

Hortorian.com, http://hortorian.com/ (September 27, 2010), interview with Reeve.

Philip Reeve Home Page, http://www.philip-reeve.com (September 15, 2011).

Teen Ink Web site, http://www.teenink.com/ (September 15, 2011), interview with Reeve.

Teen Reading Club Web site, http://www.teenrc.ca (August 19, 2011), "Fabulous Friday Interview Series 7: Philip Reeve."

Teenreads.com, http://www.teenreads.com/ (April 1, 2010) Sarah Wood, interview with Reeve.

Thirst for Fiction Web site, http://www.thirstforfiction.com/ (September 15, 2011), interview with Reeve; (September 17, 2011), review of *Scrivener's Moon.**

Dana Reinhardt

■ Personal

Born March 11, 1971, in Los Angeles, CA; married Daniel Sokatch; children: Noa, Zoe. *Education:* Vassar College, earned degree; attended New York University School of Law.

■ Addresses

Home—Los Angeles, CA. *E-mail*—info@dana reinhardt.net.

■ Career

Novelist. Worked as a waitress, fact checker for a film magazine, reader for a publishing company, and associate producer for the television series *Frontline.*

■ Awards, Honors

Sydney Taylor Honor Award, Association of Jewish Librarians, for *A Brief Chapter in My Impossible Life;* Sydney Taylor Book Award, Association of Jewish Librarians, California Book Award, and Top Ten Best Fiction for Teens designation, American Library Association, all for *The Things a Brother Knows.*

■ Writings

YOUNG ADULT NOVELS

A Brief Chapter in My Impossible Life, Wendy Lamb Books (New York, NY), 2006.
Harmless, Wendy Lamb Books (New York, NY), 2007.
How to Build a House, Wendy Lamb Books (New York, NY), 2008.
The Things a Brother Knows, Wendy Lamb Books (New York, NY), 2010.
The Summer I Learned to Fly, Wendy Lamb Books (New York, NY), 2011.

■ Adaptations

Reinhardt's novels have been adapted as audiobooks by Listening Library.

■ Sidelights

Critics often remark on the strong, realistic characters that award-winning author Dana Reinhardt creates for her stories, whether she's writing about an adopted girl meeting her birth mother or a boy whose older brother has just returned from war. Reinhardt is the author of five novels for young adults, including her critically-acclaimed debut *A Brief Chapter in My Impossible Life* and *The Summer I Learned to Fly.* Her stories often deal with themes of family and healing. Reinhardt notes that when she writes, she is most concerned about creating a compelling coming-of-age story. "I want nothing more than for someone to think, That was a good story. I really enjoyed that book," she said in an online interview with *Teen Ink.*

Taking a Risk

Reinhardt was born in Los Angeles, California, in 1971, and grew up in that area. She spent time on the East Coast as well, attending boarding school in Connecticut before earning a degree from Vassar College. She also studied for a time at New York University School of Law. Though Reinhardt enjoyed writing throughout her school years, she didn't seriously think of pursuing a career in the field. "In my fantasy, writing was what I wanted to do," she recalled to the *Teen Ink* contributor. "But when I was about to graduate and the world stretched out in front of me, I thought, I can't just write, you know, I need a job. I had this wave of practicality wash over me. I thought, Writing isn't something I can just do—I have to find a job and get paid and have a career. So I went off and did all sorts of other things until I had the time and the courage to try my hand at writing again."

Indeed, Reinhardt held several jobs before she tried to write her first novel, telling *Cynsations* interviewer Cynthia Leitich Smith, "I've been a waitress, a social worker, an answerer of telephones on a crisis hot line, a fact checker for a movie magazine, a reader for a now defunct young adult label at a mass-market publishing house, a law student, and a producer for documentary TV." But when she was finally ready to enter the world of literature, she found the process of writing came rather naturally to her, and she completed her first novel in just two and a half months. "It was the most fun time I've had writing so far. And I think a lot of that was just jumping into something that felt so undoable," she commented to Dan Brodnitz on the *About Creativity* Web site.

Reinhardt's first work, *A Brief Chapter in My Impossible Life,* tells the story of Simone Turner-Bloom, an adopted teen who, in the book's opening pages, confesses that she has no interest in getting to know her biological mother: "I've never wanted to learn

anything about my real family tree. In my mind I've cut down those branches and left a bare, solitary trunk. I know no details. Except for one. Her name: Rivka."

When Rivka reaches out to Simone, however, the liberal, atheist high schooler agrees to meet her birth mother, and she is shocked to discover that Rivka, a Hasidic Jew, is dying of cancer. The revelations about Rivka's religious background and failing health force Simone to reconsider her views on love, faith, death, and other complex subjects. Reinhardt explained to Rick Margolis of *School Library Journal* that she wanted to write a young adult novel that explored Jewish identity without focusing on the Holocaust or anti-Semitism: "I tried to think of a situation where a kid—right around the age of 16, when we think we know everything about the world—could find out something new about herself." The author continued, "I really wanted to spring this on her out of nowhere."

A Brief Chapter in My Impossible Life earned a Sydney Taylor Honor Award and received winning reviews. "This is an outstanding first novel by an enormously talented writer," Claire Rosser declared in *Kliatt,* and Janet Hilbun, writing in *School Library Journal,* observed that the book "deals with big issues without being preachy or sappy." A contributor in *Kirkus Reviews* noted that "Simone's first-person voice is funny and unforgettable," and Rosser maintained that "each character is a fully realized human being because of Reinhardt's skill."

Speaking in Different Voices

Reinhardt's follow-up book, *Harmless,* centers on three freshmen at a private school who tell a lie that spins out of control. When lifelong friends Emma and Anna are introduced to Mariah, an adventurous sort with a wild side, they begin hanging with an older crowd and lying to their parents to cover their tracks. Caught in a lie about their whereabouts one evening, the girls make up a story that that one of them was attacked by a stranger, and an innocent homeless man is arrested for the crime. Considering her misdeed, Anna asks: "How could three girls with our backgrounds, girls who had never been in trouble, how could girls like that do something so terrible?"

It's a "something" that Reinhardt has often pondered, she told Smith. "There's a certain kind of news story that always grabs my attention," the author remarked. "It has a headline that looks something like this: Local Kid Commits Bad or Horrible or Even Unspeakable Act." She continued, "I think the public tends to write off these kids as bad seeds. But I always look at these stories as stories about good kids who have made bad choices, and there's a difference there that I was interested in exploring with this book."

Like its predecessor, *Harmless* garnered solid reviews. "Unpredictability and suspense will keep readers turning the pages and questioning their own sensibilities," wrote *School Library Journal* contributor Kelly Czarnecki, and a *Publishers Weekly* reviewer describe the work as "a psychologically taut drama," adding that Reinhardt "convincingly creates three flawed heroines to whom teens can relate." Although Rosser noted that readers may find it "hard to like these girls," Frances Bradburn in *Booklist* commented that Reinhardt "offers a well-constructed object lesson in responsibility that will set teens thinking." According to a contributor in *Kirkus Reviews* the author "infuses the story with enough drama to avoid banality."

Reinhardt's next work, *How to Build a House*, takes readers to rural Tennessee. In her *Cynsations* interview, Reinhardt noted that the book focuses on Harper Evans, a girl who spends the summer "building a house for a family who lost theirs in a tornado, while sorting through her feelings about her own family's demise." Harper, a seventeen-year-old Californian, leaps at the chance to join Homes from the Heart, a volunteer program, after her stepmother walks out on Harper's unfaithful father, taking the teen's half-brother and stepsisters with her. As Harper remarks, "I know a thing or two about people whose homes have been destroyed. Their lives uprooted. Everything gone."

Once in Bailey, Tennessee, a town hit hard by a tornado months earlier, Harper and her fellow volunteers set about reconstructing a home belonging to a needy but proud family. As Harper learns to handle a circular saw and other power tools, she also forms new friendships and comes to a gradual understanding of life's complexities. The author weaves together flashbacks from Harper's life, including her on-again, off-again relationship with classmate Gabriel, with her summer story, focusing on the teen's growing independence as well as her budding romance with Teddy, the boy whose home she is helping to build.

The idea for *How to Build a House*, Reinhardt told *BookPage* contributor Heidi Henneman, came to her during a walk through her Los Angeles neighborhood: "A ton of new houses were going up in the area, and I was literally living with the sound of hammering all the time. . . . It started me thinking about the permanency and the impermanency of home."

In Reinhardt's *The Things a Brother Knows*, a teen joins his brother, a troubled combat veteran, on a cross-country trek. (Jacket Cover copyright © 2010 by Wendy Lamb Books, an imprint of Random House Children's Books, a division of Random House, Inc. Used by permission of Wendy Lamb Books, an imprint of Random House Children's Books, a division of Random House, Inc.)

A number of reviewers complimented Reinhardt on her relatable and resilient protagonist. Kathleen E. Gruver in *School Library Journal* described Harper as "a sympathetic, believable character whose narrative voice expresses wit and heartbreak," and Henneman remarked that the author's "smart, funny and poignant writing style strikes a chord of compassion and self-awareness. . . ." Critics also celebrated the author's clever literal and literary exploration of home. *Horn Book* contributor Jennifer M. Brabander reported that "the many parallels between the house-building and the home-wrecking (then rebuilding) are clearly drawn but subtle and believable," and a *Publishers Weekly* reviewer observed that the "meticulously crafted book illustrates how both homes and relationships can be resurrected through hard work, hope and teamwork."

Healing Journeys

Reinhardt told Norah Piehl in *Teenreads.com* that she began thinking about her next book, *What a Brother Knows,* after being struck by stories of American combat veterans "who came home different: changed, absent some essential piece of their former selves." This story is told from the perspective of Levi Katznelson, a teenager whose older brother, Boaz, has just returned from an unnamed war in the Middle East, withdrawn and showing signs of Post-traumatic stress disorder. At night, the protagonist, Levi, hears Boaz screaming: "I can't make out the words but there they are. Word after word after word. Deep in the phantom hours, when the rest of the world is sleeping, Boaz is lost someplace where he's forgotten he doesn't talk much anymore."

The award-winning book deals with sensitive and even disturbing subject matter, including war's toll on soldiers and families, yet ultimately it is a coming-of-age story about Levi, who ends up taking a walking journey with his brother, trekking from Boston, Massachusetts to Washington, DC. As the siblings make their way to the nation's capital, "Levi's growing comprehension of Boaz's internal turmoil is gracefully and powerfully evoked," according to a *Publishers Weekly* reviewer. "In the end, I think, part of Levi's growth is coming to the understanding that his brother, and people in general, are nuanced and complex, and you have to dig deep and ask questions and know that there are certain things you may never totally understand about somebody else," Reinhardt said in her interview with Piehl.

Called "timely" by a number of critics, *What a Brother Knows* also garnered praise for its ability to evoke powerful emotions. Bradburn noted that "Re-

inhardt sensitively explores universal traumas that usurp the lives of many soldiers and their loved ones," and Amy Cheney, writing in *School Library Journal,* remarked that the novel's "characters don't seem like characters but feel bigger and more complex, and they live on after readers have turned the page." In 2011, *What a Brother Knows* received the Sydney Taylor Book Award for Teen Readers.

"There are too many things to run away from. There's what happened to Dad and Jane and how what happened to them happened to everybody in our family. There's Gabriel and how everything between us seems to add up to nothing. There Tess and who she is and isn't to me anymore. There's the way I feel when I wake up in the morning in my empty house."

—Protagonist Harper Evans in *How to Build a House.*

More recently, Reinhardt completed *The Summer I Learned to Fly,* in which she again explores themes of familial disharmony and fellowship. Set in the mid-1980s, the novel centers on Drew, a lonely, fatherless thirteen year old who befriends Emmett Crane, the runaway she discovers outside her mother's gourmet cheese shop. As the weeks pass, the pair become close companions, and when Emmett confesses that he is going to head north in search of a legendary healing spring, hoping its magic will restore his broken family, cautious Drew makes a surprising decision.

Jennifer M. Brabander, writing in *Horn Book,* described *The Summer I Learned to Fly* as a "quietly compelling coming-of-age novel," and a *Publishers Weekly* contributor remarked that "this quiet novel invites readers to share in its heroine's deepest yearnings, changing moods, and difficult realizations." According to a critic in *Kirkus Reviews,* "Drew's journey into self-knowledge unfolds in a lucid voice that is thoughtful and entertaining without being showy." In the words of *School Library Journal* critic Suanne Roush, "Reinhardt has written another book that will resonate with any readers learning to spread their wings and fly."

Taking Writing—and Readers—Seriously

Describing her writing process to Brodnitz, Reinhardt admitted that although she does not work with outlines, she usually knows what direction she wants to take her narrative, as well as the book's ending. "But in general, for me," she stated, "the fun about writing is finding out what happens between the beginning and the end of the story." That said, Reinhardt approaches her writing in a disciplined manner. "I try to write Monday through Friday as if I had a real job," she told Brodnitz. "My goal for each day can change but in general, my rule is that my workday's not done until I have three pages, which is roughly 1,000 words. . . ."

Reinhardt also spends a lot of time making sure that her writing will feel genuine to her readers. She reads aloud her words, especially the dialogue, and even asked a sixteen-year-old friend to help her translate a conversation into realistic text messages for *Harmless*. As she told Brodnitz, "Kids, as readers, have no tolerance for inauthenticity, and they can smell [inauthentic] moments a mile away. So if you write about a piece of technology or music and you get it wrong, it's going to ruin the book for them. Those things I definitely have vetted with kids I know who will pick up details. You know, 'Kids don't wear Doc Martens anymore' or, 'That kind of guy wouldn't listen to that kind of music.'"

Reinhardt plans to continue writing for a teen audience. As she stated on her home page, "I was a young adult when I fell in love with reading and I can remember how books made me feel back then. How they provided both comfort and escape. That might make me sound like a shut-in, but I wasn't. I was just open to the experience books offered, probably more open than I am now as an adult. And I like writing for that sort of audience."

■ Biographical and Critical Sources

PERIODICALS

Reinhardt, Dana, *A Brief Chapter in My Impossible Life*, Wendy Lamb Books (New York, NY), 2006.
Reinhardt, Dana, *Harmless*, Wendy Lamb Books (New York, NY), 2007.
Reinhardt, Dana, *How to Build a House*, Wendy Lamb Books (New York, NY), 2008.
Reinhardt, Dana, *What a Brother Knows*, Wendy Lamb Books (New York, NY), 2010.

PERIODICALS

Booklist, January 1, 2006, Holly Koelling, review of *A Brief Chapter in My Impossible Life*, p. 85; December 1, 2006, Frances Bradburn, review of *Harmless*, p. 39; April 15, 2008, Gillian Engberg, review of *How to Build a House*, p. 40; October 1, 2010, Frances Bradburn, review of *The Things a Brother Knows*, p. 81; June 1, 2011, Frances Bradburn, review of *The Summer I Learned to Fly*, p. 89.

Bulletin of the Center for Children's Books, February, 2006, Deborah Stevenson, review of *A Brief Chapter in My Impossible Life*, p. 283.

Horn Book, July 1, 2008, Jennifer M. Brabander, review of *How to Build a House*, p. 456; November-December, 2010, Jonathan Hunt, review of *The Things a Brother Knows*, p. 102; July-August, 2011, Jennifer M. Brabander, review of *The Summer I Learned to Fly*, p. 158.

Kirkus Reviews, January 15, 2006, review of *A Brief Chapter in My Impossible Life*, p. 88; February 1, 2007, review of *Harmless*, p. 128; April 15, 2008, review of *How to Build a House*; June 1, 2011, review of *The Summer I Learned to Fly*.

Kliatt, January, 2006, Claire Rosser, review of *A Brief Chapter in My Impossible Life*, p. 10; January, 2007, Claire Rosser, review of *Harmless*, p. 18; May, 2008, Claire Rosser, review of *How to Build a House*, p. 16.

Los Angeles Times, July 27, 2008, Susan Carpenter, review of *How to Build a House*.

Publishers Weekly, January 2, 2006, review of *A Brief Chapter in My Impossible Life*, p. 63; January 15, 2007, review of *Harmless*, p. 53; April 7, 2008, review of *How to Build a House*, p. 61; August 30, 2010, review of *The Things a Brother Knows*, p. 55; May 23, 2011, review of *The Summer I Learned to Fly*, p. 46.

School Library Journal, February, 2006, Rick Margolis, "Meet the Parent: In Dana Reinhardt's First Novel, a Teen Is (Reluctantly) Reunited with Her Birth Mother," p. 39; March, 2006, Janet Hilbun, review of *A Brief Chapter in My Impossible Life*, p. 228; March, 2007, Kelly Czarnecki, review of *Harmless*, p. 218; June 1, 2008, Kathleen E. Gruver, review of *How to Build a House*, p. 148; December, 2010, Amy Cheney, review of *The Things a Brother Knows*, p. 125; June, 2011, Suanne Roush, review of *The Summer I Learned to Fly*, p. 131.

Voice of Youth Advocates, April, 2006, Sarah Cofer, review of *A Brief Chapter in My Impossible Life*, p. 51; October, 2010, Cheryl Clark, review of *The Things a Brother Knows*, p. 356; June, 2011, Timothy Capehart, review of *The Summer I Learned to Fly*, p. 172.

ONLINE

About Creativity Web site, http://about-creativity.com/ (December 15, 2008), Dan Brodnitz, "An Interviewer with Dana Reinhardt."

A Chair, a Fireplace & a Tea Cozy Blog, http://blog. schoollibraryjournal.com/teacozy/ (February 9, 2011), Liz Burns, "Interview: Dana Reinhardt."

Bildungsroman Blog, http://slayground.livejournal. com/ (June 22, 2007), "Interview: Dana Reinhardt."

BookPage Web site, http://www.bookpage.com/ (August 25, 2009), Heidi Henneman, "Dana Reinhardt: Redefining the Place Called Home," and Renee Kirchner, review of *Harmless.*

Cynsations Blog, http://cynthialeitichsmith.blogspot. com/ (June 26, 2008), Cynthia Leitich Smith, "Author Interview: Dana Reinhardt on *Harmless.*"

Dana Reinhardt Home Page, http://www.dana reinhardt.net (August 1, 2011).

Random House Web site, http://www.randomhouse. com/ (November 29, 2006), biographical essay by Reinhardt.

Teen Ink Web site, http://www.teenink.com/ (August 1, 2011), interview with Reinhardt.

Teenreads.com, http://www.teenreads.com/ (August 25, 2009), Belinda Williams, review of *Harmless;* Norah Piehl, review of *How to Build a House;* (September, 2010), Norah Piehl, interview with Reinhardt.*

Marcus Sedgwick

■ Personal

Born 1968, in Kent, England; married; children: Alice. *Education:* Bath University, earned degree in politics.

■ Addresses

Home—Sussex, England.

■ Career

Author and editor. Worked as a bookseller for Heffers (children's bookshop), Cambridge, England; as a sales manager for Ragged Bears (children's book publisher), Somerset, England; and as an editor for Templar Publishing, Dorking, England; writer, 1994—; Walker Books, London, England, sales manager, until 2009. Stone carver and wood engraver; performer with International Band of Mystery ("Austin Powers" tribute band and acting troupe), as drummer Basil Exposition. Writer in Residence at Bath Spa University, 2009—.

■ Awards, Honors

Branford Boase Award, 2000, for *Floodland;* Edgar Allan Poe Award nomination, Mystery Writers of America (MWA), Independent Reading Association award nomination, and Portsmouth Book Award nomination, all 2001, all for *Witch Hill;* Carnegie Medal shortlist, *Guardian* Children's Fiction Prize shortlist, and Blue Peter Book Award shortlist, all 2002, all for *The Dark Horse;* Sheffield Book Award shortlist, *Guardian* Book Award nomination, and Edgar Allan Poe Award shortlist, MWA, all for *The Book of Dead Days;* Booktrust Teenage Prize shortlist, Salford Book Award shortlist, Angus Book Award shortlist, Best Book for Young Adults designation, American Library Association (ALA), Portsmouth Book Award, North East Teenage Book Award, and Notable Tradebooks for Young People selection, National Council for the Social Studies/Children's Book Council, all 2007, all for *The Foreshadowing;* Booktrust Teenage Book Prize, for *My Swordhand Is Singing;* Costa Children's Book Award shortlist, for *Blood Red, Snow White;* Carnegie Medal shortlist, 2010, and Michael L. Printz Award Honor Book, ALA, 2011, for *Revolver;* London *Guardian* Fiction Prize shortlist, 2010, and Carnegie Medal shortlist, 2011, both for *White Crow;* Blue Peter Most Fun Story with Pictures Prize, 2011, for *Lunatics and Luck.*

■ Writings

Floodland, Orion (London, England), 2000, Delacorte (New York, NY), 2001.

Witch Hill, Delacorte (New York, NY), 2001.

The Dark Horse, Orion (London, England), 2002, Wendy Lamb (New York, NY), 2003.

(Editor) Helen Ward, *The Dragon Machine,* illustrated by Wayne Anderson, Templar (Dorking, England), 2003.

Cowards, Orion (London, England), 2003.

The Book of Dead Days (also see below), Orion (London, England), 2003, Wendy Lamb (New York, NY), 2004.

A Winter's Tale (picture book), illustrated by Simon Bartram, Templar (London, England), 2003, published as *A Christmas Wish,* Dutton (New York, NY), 2003.

(Reteller) *The Emperor's New Clothes* (picture book), illustrated by Alison Jay, Chronicle Books (San Francisco, CA), 2004.

The Dark Flight Down(sequel to *The Book of Dead Days*), Orion (London, England), 2004, Wendy Lamb Books (New York, NY), 2005.

The Foreshadowing, Orion (London, England), 2005, Wendy Lamb Books (New York, NY), 2006.

My Swordhand Is Singing, Wendy Lamb Books (New York, NY), 2006.

Blood Red, Snow White, Orion (London, England), 2007.

The Kiss of Death, Orion (London, England), 2008.

Flood and Fang ("Raven Mysteries" series), illustrated by Pete Williamson, Orion (London, England), 2009.

Ghosts and Gadgets ("Raven Mysteries" series), illustrated by Pete Williamson, Orion (London, England), 2009.

Revolver, Orion (London, England), 2009.

Lunatics and Luck ("Raven Mysteries" series), illustrated by Pete Williamson, Orion (London, England), 2010.

Vampires and Volts ("Raven Mysteries" series), illustrated by Pete Williamson, Orion (London, England), 2010.

White Crow, Orion (London, England), 2010, Roaring Brook Press (New York, NY), 2011.

Magic and Mayhem ("Raven Mysteries" series), illustrated by Pete Williamson, Orion (London, England), 2011.

Midwinterblood, Orion (London, England), 2011.

Contributor to *The Restless Dead: Ten Original Stories of the Supernatural,* edited by Deborah Noyes, Candlewick Press (Cambridge, MA), 2007. Contributor of book reviews to the London *Guardian.*

ILLUSTRATOR

Nick Riddle, editor, *Outremer: Jaufre Rudel and the Countess of Tripoli: A Legend of the Crusades,* Fisher King, 1994.

June Counsel, *Once upon Our Time,* Glyndley Books, 2000.

■ Sidelights

Since the publication of his debut young adult title, *Floodland,* British author Marcus Sedgwick has released a score of critically-acclaimed novels and children's books, has been shortlisted for England's prestigious Carnegie Medal, and has secured a loyal and large fan base. *Hack Writers* contributor Callum Graham noted of Sedgwick: "A dominant force in the teenage fiction, his books are a mysterious blend of gothic and adventure which have earned him a place on the bookshelves of children not just in the UK but across the world."

"It's a strange thing if you stop to think about it, to decide to assemble the random dreamings in your mind and put them in some kind of order so that other people might derive emotion from them," Sedgwick noted in his Michael L. Printz Award Honor Book speech, reprinted on the *American Library Association* Web site, "But that's what we do, and we do it because there's an itch in our minds telling us to; a feeling that we want to convey to others." That "itch" in Sedgwick's mind often produces novels with a dark twist to them: realistic tales of environmental disaster, fires, Norse raiders, revolution, and war; and fantasies involving dark magic, zombies, and vampires. A contributor for the *Achuka* Web site noted the "darkly gothic seriousness" that runs through many of Sedgwick's novels. Similarly, *British Council* contributor James Procter observed that much of Sedgwick's work draws on folk narratives, fairy tales, Greek myths, and Norse legends, to tell tales of "the eternal struggle between good and evil." Procter added: "Like the storytelling traditions upon which he draws, there is a dark side to much of Sedgwick's fiction which deals unflinchingly with sensitive subjects such as death and violence."

In his *Achuka* interview, Sedgwick explained: "For some reason I've always loved the gothic. I don't know why. Maybe it's got something to do with the fact that my earliest memory is being pushed in the pram down the lane to the twelfth century churchyard in the little village I grew up in. Maybe not. But although I love all this dark stuff, I do so with a sense of humour." Speaking with Michelle Pauli in the London *Guardian,* Sedgwick further explained: "Over the years I've got this reputation for writing slightly dark things, but I'm a firm believer that it's not what you do but how you do it, every time.

There is almost nothing you can't tackle in a teenage novel, it's just how you do it. That to me is the important thing."

Born in Kent, England, in 1968, Sedgwick was heavily influenced by his father, who loved reading. "We were taught to treat books with reverence," Sedgwick told Pauli. "You would never put a book on the floor, you'd never break its spine, you'd never write in a book. Dad would always give us a book every birthday and Christmas and it was almost symbolic—you must have a book, it's an important thing." The love for books turned into a love of writing, as well. Sedgwick published his first piece in a fanzine when he was just sixteen; tellingly, it was a horror story. Speaking with Graham, Sedgwick explained that he has always had a proclivity for the darker side of things: "At school I was a first generation goth."

"There is almost nothing you can't tackle in a teenage novel, it's just how you do it. That to me is the important thing."

—Marcus Sedgwick, speaking to Michelle Pauli in the London *Guardian.*

Sedgwick took a degree in politics at Bath University, and then followed a series of jobs, including employment as a teacher and a bookseller. The bookselling job happened to be in the children's department, and Sedgwick soon came to love his inventory. Since that time, all of Sedgwick's day jobs have been in children's publishing. The author stayed in children's publishing as a book representative and then sales manager for Walker Books, until 2009. By that time, however, he had already become a popular writer for young adults. His writing career began in 1994, as he started work on what would become his first novel, *Floodland.* Initially, because he did not want to have special treatment as a result of his role in the publishing field, he submitted his work under a pseudonym. Soon enough, however, he realized that his work met all the standards of quality he had come to expect of the titles he represented to booksellers.

Tales of Disaster and Dislocation

Sedgwick hit the ground running with his debut title, *Floodland,* winning the Branford Boase Award. This environmental tale centers on Zoe, a young

girl who has been separated from her parents when global warming raises the sea levels and floods lowlands around the globe. In search of her parents, Zoe comes to the Island of Eels, which is embroiled in tribal wrangling over diminishing supplies. There she meets the youth, Munchkin, who aids her in her quest.

A *Publishers Weekly* reviewer was not enthusiastic about this tale, noting that "despite some page-turning chapters, Zoe and her story lack the credibility to sustain readers." More positive in her assessment was *School Library Journal* contributor Ellen Fader, who felt that "most readers will enjoy this survival story for its heart-pounding plot and dystopic setting, and will appreciate the warm, happy ending." Similarly, Joanna Rudge Long, writing in *Horn Book,* thought that "this first novel is sufficiently taut, accessible, and swift moving to make it an effective cautionary tale."

Nightmares lead to a hidden history of witchcraft in Sedgwick's second novel, *Witch Hill.* Here, young Jamie's baby sister is killed when their home burns down. Traumatized, the youth is sent to his aunt's home in Crownhill to recover. However, nightmares of an old witch plague his sleep. Soon it becomes apparent that this little village was the site of a witch burning centuries earlier, during the Civil War in England. Meanwhile, the reader learns that perhaps Jamie's sister did not die after all. The twin strands of the novel come together in a "fiery . . . climax," according to *Booklist* contributor John Peters, who cautioned readers against indulging in "this suspenseful tale at bedtime." Janet Hilburn, writing in *School Library Journal,* felt that "Jamie's story is forced and too slowly revealed," but also noted that this is "basically a readable suspense novel with likable characters."

With his third novel, *The Dark Horse,* Sedgwick turns to historical fiction, or in this case prehistorical fiction, in a tale of belonging and betrayal. The Dark Horse of the title is a band of marauders that threaten the Storn, a tribe living in a setting that Long described in *Horn Book* as "mythic, resembling Scotland's Hebrides." Sigurd is a boy of the Storn, and his adopted sister Mouse was raised by wolves. She has the ability to communicate with animals as a result. As the Dark Horse approach, Sigurd and Mouse react in very different ways to the threat. Reviewing this novel in *School Library Journal,* Coop Renner noted: "Making no concessions to moralizing or romanticizing, Sedgwick's tale is rich, involving, and vivifying." Long similarly remarked that "the bleak setting is fully realized, the alternating point of view is effective, and the events are gripping: they'll hold readers to the end of this grim adventure." A *Kirkus Reviews* writer offered a more mixed assessment, noting that the author "crafts an effective tale that, despite the unconvincing transformation of Mouse, will draw readers in and keep them entranced." Higher praise came from a *Publishers Weekly* reviewer who termed it a "tale of dark enchantment [that] depicts a primitive tribe in a north country, reminiscent of Norse sagas," and from *Booklist* contributor Debbie Carton, who lauded the "fast pace, hint of magic, and satisfyingly enigmatic conclusion."

Talking with the Dead

Sedgwick turns to magic and history in a pair of novels featuring a young servant, Boy, and his magician master, Valerian. *The Book of Dead Days* is set in a crumbling European city during the eighteenth century. Boy is surprised and dismayed to find his master in desperate straits, and he then learns that Valerian has made a dangerous pact with a demon.

Together with an orphaned girl named Willow, they search for a way in which to break the promise. A *Kirkus Reviews* contributor found this a "fascinatingly brooding tale," further praising Sedgwick's evocation of the city they inhabit as a "wonderfully gloomy character with twisting alleys, forgotten catacombs, and underground canals." Similarly, a *Publishers Weekly* writer termed this a "gothic chiller" with a "well rendered" atmosphere. "Unexpected twists keep the action moving, and the suspense never flags," wrote Bruce Anne Shook in *School Library Journal,* and Ilene Cooper, reviewing the work in *Booklist,* concluded: "This is a haunting novel, and the possibility of more is definitely enticing."

More of Boy and Willow's adventures are served up in the sequel, *The Dark Flight Down.* Here, Valerian is dead and Boy is the prisoner of Emperor Frederick, whose one goal is to never die. Frederick and Boy both think that the secret to eternal life might be found in a volume of Valerian's works on magic; the question is, who will find it first? Cooper, writ-

A former bookseller and editor, British author Sedgwick has earned a host of honors for his young adult novels, including the Branford Boase Award and a number of Carnegie Medal nominations. (Photographer Kate Christer, and Orion Children's Books, an imprint of the Orion Publishing Group, London. Copyright © Kate Christer. All rights reserved. Reproduced by permission.)

ing again in *Booklist,* felt that "Sedgwick's writing is gloriously textured, and the plot is intricate, even heart-stopping," while *Horn Book* reviewer Long found this sequel "as satisfyingly atmospheric as the first volume."

Sedgwick deals in somewhat more contemporary history with his 2006 novel, *The Foreshadowing,* set during World War I. In this tale, Alexandra "Sasha" Fox is troubled with terrifying visions when her older brother is sent off to combat in France. She has seen the future before, having had a vision of the death of one of her friends as a youth. Now, at seventeen, she has dreams of seeing her brother killed. She has already lost one brother in the war, and she vows to save the other. Joining a nursing corps, Sasha heads to France, hoping to stop this death foretold. "Readers will be haunted by the unusually powerful, visceral view of war's horrors," thought Gillian Engberg in a *Booklist* review. Higher praise came from a *Kirkus Reviews* contributor who termed the novel "brilliant," and from *Kliatt* writer Claire Rosser, who noted: "Sedgwick keeps this story going relentlessly, with short chapters, haunting images, a courageous heroine, and questions about honor and patriotism that continue to resonate." Likewise, a *Publishers Weekly* reviewer dubbed this a "powerful and haunting WWI story [that] probes ideas of death and healing, fate and free will."

Sedgwick fashions a horror fantasy novel with *My Swordhand Is Singing,* set in the forests of eastern Europe in the seventeenth century. Tomas and his son, Peter, cut wood for a living near the village of Chust. With winter coming on, villages suddenly begin to die. Peter soon discovers the horrible truth: the undead are rising and killing the locals to add to their ranks. Now it is up to Peter and a Gypsy youth named Sofia to confront the undead with a magical sword from his father's past. *Kliatt* reviewer Paula Rohrlick found this offering "creepy and full of dark atmosphere." Similarly, a *Kirkus Reviews* writer termed it "effective gothic horror with a mystical touch," and a *Publishers Weekly* reviewer likewise observed that "Sedgwick knows his way around a gothic setting, and readers will likely devour this bone-chiller." *School Library Journal* contributor D. Maria LaRocco also had praise for this work, calling it "an outstanding tale of suspense and horror with detail enough to produce shivers."

More gothic chills are served up in *The Kiss of Death.* Set again in the seventeenth century, this novel features Marko, who must travel to Venice to find his missing father, a doctor. There he encounters young Sorrel, whose own father was a patient of Marko's father. Together they set out to find the missing man; Sorrel hopes that by so doing she will be able to get to the root of her father's madness. But their quest is made more difficult by the Shadow Queen and her vampire attendants. "Sedgwick is . . . tremendous at that worst form of horror, when a trusted person turns out to have gone over to the dark side," wrote Mary Hoffman in a *Guardian* review. Similar praise came from London *Times* contributor Amanda Craig, who found the novel "gripping," and added: "What makes Sedgwick such an interesting author is not just his imagination, which has a consistently unpredictable and original cast to it . . . but his voice."

Mystery and Horror across the Centuries

Sedgwick leaves horror behind for his 2007 novel, *Blood Red, Snow White,* about British author Arthur Ransome, who spent several years as a foreign correspondent during the Russian Revolution. Ransome, the author of such children's classics as *Swallows and Amazons,* and the first winner of the Carnegie Medal for children's literature, was also the author of *Old Peter's Russian Tales,* a book that captivated Sedgwick as a youngster, which partly explains his interest in writing this fictional biography. *Blood Red, Snow White* is based on Ransome's love affair with Evgenia Petrovna Shelepina, the secretary of Leon Trotsky and a woman Ransome later married. She was able to smuggle three million rubles worth of diamonds and pearls out of Russia with her. This deed, along with the fact that the British secret service actually suspected Ransome of being a Bolshevik spy, further inspired Sedgwick's novel.

Drawing on Ransome's diaries and autobiography, Sedgwick divides his novel into three parts. In the first, he recounts Russian history using stories out of Ransome's *Old Peter's Russian Tales;* the second section looks at Ransom's reaction to the revolution; and the third recounts his efforts to spirit his lover out of Russia and his reunion with his daughter in England. Danuta Kean, writing in the London *Independent on Sunday Online,* called *Blood Red, Snow White,* "a mesmerising retelling of Ransome's time in Russia during the Revolution, [that] should appeal to adults as well as Sedgwick's loyal band of teenage readers." *Sunday Times* contributor Nicolette Jones also commended this work, calling it a "sophisticated novel, making convincing use of Ransome's voice." A reviewer for the *Times Education Supplement Online* found it a "a thoughtful, ambitious novel, easily accessible," and *Books for Keeps* writer Jack Hope called it an "absorbing and stimulating tale that cements [Sedgwick's] position as one of the most powerful and innovative writers of contemporary fiction for this age."

Sedgwick's award-winning novel *Revolver* is set north of the Arctic Circle in 1910. The tale opens with young Sig Anderrson sitting with his father's frozen corpse in the family's remote cabin while his stepmother and sister go for help. Then a giant of a man, Gunther Wolff, shows up at the cabin demanding the gold that Sig's father, Einar, had supposedly stolen from him. Wolff is a psychopath and earlier killed Sig's mother. Now this man threatens Sig and his family once again, and the only means to survival may be the father's old Colt pistol, tucked away in the cabin. But can Sig go against his mother's pacifist teachings to use the weapon? Noting that *Revolver* is a short novel, *Guardian* reviewer Hoffman was quick to point out that it is "not slight: the issue of whether violence is ever unavoidable is both topical and difficult, and this deceptively simple story raises enormous questions." *Horn Book* reviewer Dean Schneider called this a "memorable tale, one that will appeal to fans of Gary Paulsen, Jack London, and even Cormac McCarthy." For *Booklist* contributor Ian Chipman, *Revolver* is a "carefully crafted story effectively rigidified by taut plotting and the crystalline atmospherics of its isolated setting," while a *Kirkus Reviews* contributor termed it a "chilling, atmospheric story that will haunt readers with its descriptions of a desolate terrain and Sig's difficult decisions." Similarly, a *Publishers Weekly* reviewer concluded: "Sedgwick lures his readers into deeper thinking while they savor this thrillingly told tale."

Sedgwick turns again to his trademark horror in *White Crow*, which explores the concept of life after death. The story, which spans two centuries, is told from three different points of view. In a contemporary tale, Rebecca moves with her father to the tiny seaside village of Winterfold, where she meets a Ferelith, an enigmatic goth girl who enjoys participating in rebellious and dangerous activities. Meanwhile, a second narrative develops through the journals of a priest who lived in the village in 1798, detailing his investigations, together with a local doctor, into the afterlife. Soon these plotlines converge in a novel that is, as *Booklist* reviewer Daniel Kraus noted, "genuinely scary." A *Publishers Weekly* reviewer also had praise for *White Crow*, noting that "Sedgwick keeps readers guessing to the very end." Likewise, a *Kirkus Reviews* contributor termed the novel "wickedly macabre and absolutely terrifying" while *School Librarian* reviewer Rachel Bowler found that this "modern gothic thriller is an engrossing read from start to finish."

Sedgwick has also produced lighter works for younger readers, including picture books and a humorous mystery series. He teamed with illustrator Pete Williamson on a number of volumes in the "Raven Mysteries" series of humorous gothic stories, targeted at readers eight and older. The tales are all narrated by the irascible raven, Edgar, guardian of the Otherhand family at their family seat of Castle Otherhand. At the heart of the series is the missing fortune of the family. Speaking with a contributor for the *Booktrust Children's Books* Web site, Sedgwick noted of his turn to writing for younger children in the *Raven Mysteries* series: "I love writing books for younger readers, and also writing books with (really bad) jokes in them—it's nice to have a bit of fun sometimes!" In an interview with Caroline Horn in the *Bookseller*, Sedgwick voiced a similar sentiment: "As much as I love writing for teenagers, I want to do more and different things. I'm famous for being a gloom merchant and for writing dark and serious books . . . but I do have a sense of humour and I thought it would be fun to explore it and go younger."

Notes on the Writing Life

Until he quit work as a sales manager for Walker Books, Sedgwick was restricted to writing on weekends. Now he has the luxury of spending entire days in his garden shed in Sussex that functions as his office. In a *Bookbag* interview, Sedgwick explained that it usually takes him about a year to produce a novel, "though most of that time is thinking/dreaming/planning and not writing." On his home page, Sedgwick commented on what motivates him as a writer: "I write because I love it. You can't be a writer if you don't—it's too hard otherwise."

"It's a strange thing if you stop to think about it, to decide to assemble the random dreamings in your mind and put them in some kind of order so that other people might derive emotion from them. But that's what we do, and we do it because there's an itch in our minds telling us to; a feeling that we want to convey to others."

—Marcus Sedgwick, in his Michael L. Printz Award speech.

After many years working in children's publishing, Sedgwick is savvy about marketing. He realizes that his young readers will soon outgrow out his novels for teens. Thus, he started his "Raven Mysteries" series for younger readers in part so as to capture an up-and-coming audience for his young adult titles. Responding to a question from Graham in the *Hack Writers* interview regarding why he chose to write for the young adult audience, Sedgwick responded: "You write what you want to write. I naturally felt happy writing for that age group." He also noted the sense of freedom one has in writing for younger readers. Whereas adult fiction is "obsessed with genre," as he further remarked to Graham, children's fiction is divided by age group rather than genre. "Teenagers are less judgmental about reading and don't expect a genre. You could write about . . . I don't know . . . robot dinosaurs." After a moment's reflection, he added to Graham: "Actually, maybe that wouldn't be a good idea. Not for me anyway."

■ Biographical and Critical Sources

PERIODICALS

Booklist, October 1, 2001, John Peters, review of *Witch Hill*, p. 320; February 1, 2003, Debbie Carton, review of *The Dark Horse*, p. 995; September 15, 2003, Karin Snelson, review of *A Christmas Wish*, p. 248; September 1, 2004, Ilene Cooper, review of *The Book of Dead Days*, p. 123; October 1, 2004, Carolyn Phelan, review of *The Emperor's New Clothes*, p. 338; June 1, 2005, Ilene Cooper, review of *The Dark Flight Down*, p. 1792; April 1, 2006, Gillian Engberg, review of *The Foreshadowing*, p. 43; November 15, 2007, Ian Chipman, review of *My Swordhand Is Singing*, p. 37; May 1, 2010, Ian Chipman, review of *Revolver*, p. 49; May, 2011, Daniel Kraus, review *White Crow*, p. 85.

Book Report, November-December, 2001, Barry Schwartz, review of *Floodland*, p. 66.

Bookseller, May 20, 2005, Mandy Spurr, review of *The Foreshadowing*, p. 13; November 21, 2008, Caroline Horn, "A Raven with Something to Crow About," p. 26.

Books for Keeps, July, 2007, Jack Hope, review of *Blood Red, Snow White*.

Guardian (London, England), October 11, 2008, Mary Hoffman, review of *The Kiss of Death*, p. 14; September 4, 2009, Mary Hoffman, review of *Revolver*, p.14.

Horn Book, March, 2001, Joanna Rudge Long, review of *Floodland*, p. 213; March-April, 2003, Joanna Rudge Long, review of *The Dark Horse*, p. 217; November-December, 2004, Joanna Rudge Long, review of *The Book of Dead Days*, p. 718; May-June,

2006, Claire E. Gross, review of *The Foreshadowing*, p. 330; November-December, 2008, Joanna Rudge Long, review of *The Dark Flight Down*, p. 725; March-April, 2010, Dean Schneider, review of *Revolver*, p. 73; July-August, 2011, Katie Bircher, review *White Crow*, p. 161.

Kirkus Reviews, December 1, 2002, review of *The Dark Horse*, p. 1773; November 1, 2003, review of *A Christmas Wish*, p. 1320; September 1, 2004, review of *The Emperor's New Clothes*, p. 874; October 1, 2004, review of *The Book of Dead Days*, p. 968; September 1, 2005, review of *The Dark Flight Down*, p. 982; April 15, 2006, review of *The Foreshadowing*, p. 415; September 15, 2007, review of *My Swordhand Is Singing*; March 15, 2010, review of *Revolver*; June 2011, review of *White Crow*.

Kliatt, May, 2006, Claire Rosser, review of *The Foreshadowing*, p. 14; September, 2005, Lesley Farmer, review of *The Dark Flight Down*, p. 14; September, 2007, Paula Rohrlick, review of *My Swordhand Is Singing*, p. 18.

Publishers Weekly, January 29, 2001, review of *Floodland*, p. 90; December 23, 2002, review of *The Dark Horse*, p. 72; September 22, 2003, review of *A Christmas Wish*, p. 71; September 6, 2004, review of *The Emperor's New Clothes*, p. 61; December 20, 2004, review of *The Book of Dead Days*, p. 60; July 10, 2006, review of *The Foreshadowing*, p. 83; November 12, 2007, review of *My Swordhand Is Singing*, p. 57; March 15, 2010, review of *Revolver*, p. 56; November 8, 2010, review of *Revolver*, p. 35; May 9, 2011, review of *White Crow*, p. 54.

Reading Today, June, 2001, Lynne T. Burke, review of *Floodland*, p. 32.

School Librarian, summer, 2010, D. Telford, review of *Lunatics and Luck*, p. 101; fall, 2010, Rachel Bowler, review *White Crow*, p. 182; summer, 2011, Kathryn Tyson, review of *Vampires and Volts*, p. 105.

School Library Journal, March, 2001, Ellen Fader, review of *Floodland*, p. 256; September, 2001, Janet Hilburn, review of *Witch Hill*, p. 232; November, 2001, Lori Craft, review of *Floodland*, p. 76; March, 2003, Coop Renner, review of *The Dark Horse*, p. 237; October, 2003, Susan Patron, review of *A Christmas Wish*, p. 67; October, 2004, Maria B. Salvadore, review of *The Emperor's New Clothes*, p. 129; November, 2004, Bruce Anne Shook, review of *The Book of Dead Days*, p. 154; February, 2006, Walter Minkel, review of *The Dark Flight Down*, p. 136; July, 2006, Dylan Thomarie, review of *The Foreshadowing*, p. 112; November, 2007, D. Maria LaRocco, review of *My Swordhand Is Singing*, p. 137; April, 2010, Vicki Reutter, review of *Revolver*, p. 168; August, 2011, Heather M. Campbell, review *White Crow*, p. 120.

Sunday Times, July 22, 2007, Nicolette Jones, review of *Blood Red, Snow White*.

Times (London, England), July 21, 2007, Nicolette Jones, review of *Blood Red, Snow White*, p. 49; August 23, 2008, Amanda Craig, review of *The Kiss of Death*, p. 15.

ONLINE

Achuka, http://www.achuka.co.uk/ (September 17, 2011), interview with Sedgwick.

Alternative Magazine Online, http://alternative magazineonline.co.uk/ (September 23, 2010), Marty Mulrooney, "Interview—In Conversation with Marcus Sedgwick (Author)."

American Library Association Web site, http://ala. org/ (September 17, 2011), Marcus Sedgwick, "2011 Printz Honor Speech."

Associated Content, http://www.associatedcontent. com/ (January 9, 2009), Keri Withington, review of *Blood Red, Snow White.*

Bookbag, http://www.thebookbag.co.uk/ (May 30, 2009), "The Interview: Bookbag Talks To Marcus Sedgwick"; (September 18, 2011), review of *Kiss of Death.*

Booktrust Children's Books, http://www.booktrust childrensbooks.org.uk/ (September 17, 2011), "The Winners of the Blue Peter Book Awards 2011."

British Council Web site, http://www.britishcouncil. org/ (September 17, 2011), James Procter, "Marcus Sedgwick: Critical Perspective."

Children's Literature Comprehensive Database, http:// www.childrenslit.com/ (February 1, 2009), "Q&A with Marcus Sedgwick."

Guardian Online, http://www.guardian.co.uk/ (July 16, 2010), Michelle Pauli, "Marcus Sedgwick: There Is Almost Nothing You Can't Tackle in a Teenage Novel."

Great Northern, http://allthingsransome.blogspot. com/ (July 31, 2008), review of *Blood Red, Snow White.*

Hack Writers, http://www.hackwriters.com/ (April 1, 2010), Callum Graham, interview with Sedgwick.

Independent on Sunday Online, http://www.indepen dent.co.uk/ (June 17, 2007), Danuta Kean, "What Drew Former Goth Marcus Sedgwick to the Author of Wholesome Family Adventures, Arthur Ransome?."

Marcus Sedgwick Home Page, http://www.marcus sedgwick.com (September 17, 2011).

Orion Books Web site, http://www.orionbooks.co. uk/ (February 1, 2009), Danuta Kean, "Marcus Sedgwick Explains Why Readers of All Ages Are Drawn into His Tales of Adventure and Imagination," and "Marcus Sedgwick Talks about the Real-life Mystery and Adventure behind His Novel *Blood Red, Snow White.*"

Random House Web site, http://www.randomhouse. com/ (February 1, 2009), "Marcus Sedgwick."

Times Education Supplement Online, http://www.tes. co.uk/ (May 27, 2008), review of *Blood Red, Snow White.**

N.H. Senzai

■ Personal

Born in Chicago, IL; daughter of a civil engineer father; married Farid Senzai (a professor of political science); children: Zakaria (son). *Education:* University of California, Berkeley, B.S., 1994; Columbia University, M.I.B., 2001.

■ Addresses

Home—Union City, CA. *Agent*—Michael Bourret, Dystel & Goderich Literary Management, One Union Square W., Ste. 904, New York, NY 10003. *E-mail*—nhsenzai@yahoo.com.

■ Career

Writer and intellectual property consultant. Across-World Communications, Santa Clara, CA, director of market development, 1998-2000; Intellectual Capital Management Group, Sonoma, CA, consultant, 2000-05; LECG Corporation, senior consultant, 2005-07; EnnovationZ (environmental services company), Mountain View, CA, cofounder, 2007-08; Foresight Valuation Group, Palo Alto, CA, director, 2009—.

■ Member

Society of Children's Book Writers and Illustrators.

■ Awards, Honors

Notable Social Studies Trade Books for Young People, National Council for the Social Studies/ Children's Book Council, Asian/Pacific American Award for Young Adult Literature, and Middle East Book Award for Youth Literature, all 2010, Bank Street Best Children's Book of the Year, Bank Street College of Education, and Teachers Choice Award, International Reading Association, both 2011, all for *Shooting Kabul.*

■ Writings

Shooting Kabul (novel), Simon & Schuster Books for Young Readers (New York, NY), 2010.

■ Sidelights

Shooting Kabul, N.H. Senzai's immigrant story geared toward the younger side of a young adult audience, almost didn't get written. As Senzai explained in the book's author note section, "I resisted it for many years. Why? Because it deals with many sensitive and personal issues—9-11, the war on terror, Islam, Afghan culture and politics, coupled with my husband's family history and escape from Kabul, Afghanistan." She added, "But no matter how hard I tried to ignore it, the story kept niggling the back of my mind. So finally, I was compelled to tell it."

To create her novel, Senzai borrowed and built upon the experiences of her husband, Farid Senzai. In 1979, Farid was ten years old, and his father worked as a professor of agriculture at Kabul University. Afghanistan, which was already experiencing armed political rebellion, was invaded by the Soviet Union. Under the guise of making a pilgrimage to Mecca, Farid's family hastily left the country. Senzai remarked on her home page, "They had an amazing journey that had them fleeing Soviet forces which were after my husband's father because he was an intellectual." The Senzai family eventually ended up in the United States, where Farid went through an adjustment period but then flourished.

In an interview with Mitali Perkins on her blog, *Mitali's Fire Escape*, Senzai reiterated the reasons for her cautionary approach toward adapting her husband's history for *Shooting Kabul*. She noted, "I'm not an Afghan, so I tread carefully and made sure I researched the right answers before folding it into the story." Accuracy was key for Senzai. She added that "there is tremendous complexity in explaining things like terrorism, Afghan culture, Islamic practices etc. and I wanted to do it in a nuanced, truthful way that could be understood by young and old alike." Senzai was, perhaps, uniquely qualified to tell the story. She has lived and traveled around the world, and by observing many cultures she has "learned firsthand that although people may look, speak or even act differently, their core values are the same," she pointed out in her conversation with Perkins.

World Traveler

Senzai was born Naheed Hasnat in Chicago, Illinois. She is of Indian and Pakistani heritage; her parents immigrated to the United States in the 1960s. Shortly after her birth, the family moved to San Francisco, California. They weren't there long. On her home page, Senzai wrote, "When I was four, my father, a civil engineer, was transferred to Jubail, Saudi Arabia, to help build an industrial city rising next to the Persian Gulf." Because of the severely hot climate and the general lack of entertainment, Senzai spent considerable time in the school library. In an interview with Cynthia Leitich Smith for the *Cynsations* blog, the author revealed that it was the Jubail Academy's "librarians Mrs. Hackworth and Mrs. Murray, who planted the seeds of my writing career."

"I grew up speaking two languages, balancing life lived on the edge of two cultures, and, happily, two cuisines—tandoori chicken and hot dogs, grilled side by side on the 4th of July."

—N.H. Senzai, in an essay on her home page.

Senzai then moved on to London, England, to attend an all-girls boarding school for high school. After that, it was another westward move to the University of California, Berkeley. When she decided on graduate school, it was a fortuitous decision to head to New York and Columbia University: it was there that she met her future husband, Farid. Her husband made another, not so tangible contribution to Senzai's writing career. After they were married, he attended Oxford University in England to pursue a doctoral degree. On her Web site, Senzai admitted that the setting itself was motivational: "Walking down the magical, historic streets of the Oxford, I often passed the Eagle and Child Pub where the Inklings met, a group of writers which included C.S. Lewis and J.R.R. Tolkien. Living in such a literary city, I got serious about finishing a novel."

Shooting Kabul opens in Afghanistan in 2001. Six months earlier, Habib Nurzai, the family patriarch, told his wife, Zafoona, and children, Noor, Fadi, and Mariam, that they would be leaving the country. While the Nurzais had lived abroad previously—they resided in Wisconsin, where Mariam was born, while Habib studied for his doctorate in agricultural studies—this departure is as disappointing as it is necessary. After earning his degree in 1996, Habib returned to Afghanistan in the hopes of using his expertise to help his fellow countrymen rebuild the county and achieve peace. As Habib recalled, "the Taliban asked me to help get rid of the country's vast poppy fields that were used to make drugs." The Taliban's good intentions soon gave way to less commendable goals. Habib explained to his children how the Taliban started as a group of young and idealistic religious students, but once in power they implemented a stringent version of Islam and expected all to comply. Beards for men and burkas for women became mandatory, and things such as photography, kite flying, music, books, and movies were banned. They also closed schools for girls. Later, the Taliban allied with Osama Bin Laden and al-Qaeda.

The Taliban wants Habib to become an ambassador, and he knows his refusal could have dire consequences. In addition, Zafoona is ill and needs better medical care than is available in Kabul. So Habib secretly arranges for his family to leave the country. He pays a taxi driver to take them to Jalalabad. There they will be picked up by an army truck that will transport them across the border to Pakistan. Before the Nurzais and other fleeing citizens can board the trucks, Taliban agents arrive. In the scramble, eleven-year-old Fadi loses his grip on his little sister's hand. The truck races off, and Mariam is left in the darkness. Although Habib begs the driver to go back, he won't. The family stays for a time in a refugee camp in Peshawar, Pakistan. They try to track down Mariam with no luck, but pay for agents to continue the search. Because Miriam is a U.S. citizen, she will be able to enter the United States when she is found. The rest of the family must get to America before their asylum papers expire.

The Nurzais, minus Mariam, make it to the San Francisco bay area of California where they initially stay with relatives—Uncle Amin and his family. The remainder of *Shooting Kabul* centers on Fadi and his concurrent battle with guilt as well as his adjustment to a new life as an American middle-school student. Things get worse when September 2011 arrives. In addition to grieving the victims of the Twin Towers, members of the local Afghan community are on edge because they're not sure how their fellow Americans will now react to them. Although Fadi experiences some bullying at school, he also finds a friend in Anh. Fadi likes photography and is thrilled to learn his school has a photography club—then quickly crushed to find out about the fifty-dollar fee to participate. His family barely has money for necessities; Habib's earnings as a taxi driver don't match what he could earn as a college teacher. Noor, who is balancing being a regular teenager with helping the family financially, gives Fadi the money from her earnings at McDonald's. Still searching for ways to rescue his sister, Fadi works with Anh and enters a photography contest, hoping to win the grand prize of a trip to India. He imagines he can reenter his homeland, find Mariam and bring her home, and restore the honor he believes he forfeited. By story's end, Fadi discovers that although things don't always work out the way he hopes or plans, there are good people who are willing to help total strangers out, just because it is the right thing to do.

Shooting Kabul earned solid reviews. "This is a sweet story of family unity," observed Kristin Anderson in *School Library Journal.* Steven Kral similarly noted in *Voice of Youth Advocates* that "Fadi's world is one of strong familial ties, Islam, and a vibrant, strong immigrant community." A contributor to *Kirkus Reviews* remarked that "Senzai crafts a wrenching tale . . . putting a human face on the war in Afghanistan." And Perkins deemed the work "a quick page-

An eleven-year-old boy attempts to return to war-torn Afghanistan to find his missing sister in *Shooting Kabul,* Senzai's debut work of fiction. (Copyright © Naheed Hasnat. Jacket illustration copyright © 2010 by Yan Nascimbene. Reproduced with permission Richard Solomon Artists Representative.)

If you enjoy the work of N.H. Senzai, you may also want to check out the following books:

The Breadwinner (2001), a novel by Deborah Ellis that examines life in Afghanistan under Taliban rule.

Leaving Glorytown: One Boy's Struggle Under Castro by Eduardo F. Calcines (2009).

Thanhha Lai's *Inside Out & Back Again* (2011), which follows a young girl's journey from war-torn Saigon to Alabama.

turner" that "beautifully illuminates life in war-torn Afghanistan and evokes empathy for those who flee to our country for sanctuary."

■ Biographical and Critical Sources

BOOKS

Senzai, N.H., *Shooting Kabul*, Simon & Schuster Books for Young Readers (New York, NY), 2010.

PERIODICALS

Booklist, June 1, 2010, Gillian Engberg, review of *Shooting Kabul*, p. 78.

Bulletin of the Center for Children's Books, July-August, 2010, Maggie Hommel, review of *Shooting Kabul*.

Kirkus Reviews, May 1, 2010, review of *Shooting Kabul*.

School Library Journal, June, 2010, Kristin Anderson, review of *Shooting Kabul*, p. 120.

Voice of Youth Advocates, August, 2010, Steven Kral, review of *Shooting Kabul*, p. 256.

ONLINE

Cynsations Web log, http://cynthialeitichsmith.blogspot.com/ (July 26, 2010), Cynthia Leitich Smith, interview with Senzai.

Mitali's Fire Escape, http://www.mitaliblog.com/ (June 30, 2010), Mitali Perkins, "A Chat with N.H. Senzai, Author of *Shooting Kabul*."

N.H. Senzai Home Page, http://www.nhsenzai.com/ (November 13, 2011).*

Ruta Sepetys

■ Personal

Name is pronounced "Roota Suh-pettys"; born November 19, 1967, in Detroit, MI; daughter of George (a design studio owner) and Phyllis Sepetys; married; husband's name, Michael (a photographer). *Education:* Hillsdale College, B.S. (international finance and French); ICN, Nancy, France, masters in international management; received diploma from Centre d'Etudes Europenes, Toulon, France.

■ Addresses

Home—Brentwood, TN. *Office*—Sepetys Entertainment Group, 5543 Edmondson Pike #8A, Nashville, TN 37211-5808.

■ Career

Writer and entertainment manager. C. Winston Simone Management/Deston Songs, West Coast manager; 1990-94; Sepetys Entertainment Group, Inc., president and founder, 1994—; Belmont University, Nashville, TN, adjunct professor. Serves on advisory board for the Mike Curb College of Entertainment and Music Business. Previously worked as a representative for Air France.

■ Member

Society of Children's Book Writers and Illustrators.

■ Awards, Honors

Work-in-progress grant, Society of Children's Book Writers and Illustrators; *Booklist* Top 10 Historical Fiction for Youth list, 2011, and William C. Morris YA Debut Award finalist, 2012, both for *Between Shades of Gray.*

■ Writings

Between Shades of Gray, Philomel Books (New York, NY), 2011.

■ Adaptations

Between Shades of Gray was adapted as an audiobook.

■ **Sidelights**

In her debut novel, the young adult title *Between Shades of Gray*, Ruta Sepetys details one of the crimes against humanity conceived by Josef Stalin, the supreme ruler of the Soviet Union, and largely carried out by his secret police: the attempted extermination of the Lithuanian people that started during World War II. In June of 1940, Stalin annexed the Baltic states of Lithuania, Latvia, and Estonia. Those countries were swallowed up by the behemoth Soviet Union, vanishing from maps. They would not reappear until the early 1990s. Estimates are that nearly a third of Lithuania's population of 1.2 million was executed, imprisoned, or deported. The generally agreed-upon number of deportation is 300,000, which took place between 1941 and 1953.

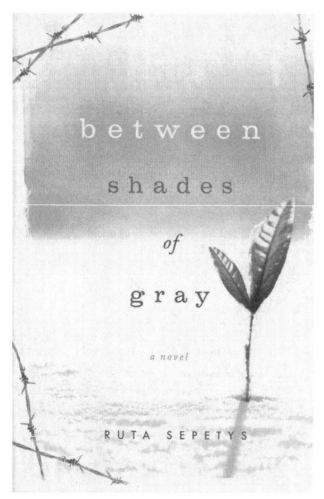

Set during World War II, *Between Shades of Gray* **concerns a Lithuanian family's harrowing experiences in a Soviet labor camp.** (Cover photograph by iStockphoto.com/Smitt. Used by permission of Philomel Books, A Division of Penguin Young Readers Group, A Member of Penguin Group (USA) Inc., 345 Hudson Street, New York, NY 10014. All rights reserved.)

Although there were survivors, their trauma did not end when they were finally able to return home, for those places no longer existed. Their houses, belongings, and sometimes even their names had been usurped by Soviets. They were told where to live, and their words and actions were monitored by the KGB, the Soviet Union's national security agency. In her author's note, Sepetys explained that "speaking about their experience meant immediate imprisonment or deportation back to Siberia. As a result, the horrors they endured went dormant, a hideous secret shared by millions of people."

In *Between Shades of Gray*, Sepetys focuses on a microcosm of this national nightmare—the experiences of the Vilkas family, beginning in June of 1941. While the characters are fictional (except for one, Dr. Samodurov), aspects of their personalities are patterned on actual people, and some of the events described in the novel are based on accounts from survivors. *Between Shades of Gray* is an extremely personal story for Sepetys: she is an American of Lithuanian heritage, and her paternal grandfather, whose given name was Jonas, was a high-ranking officer in the Lithuanian military. As such, he would have been executed by Stalin. He escaped the country with his wife and ten-year-old son, the author's father, and the family spent time in refugee camps in Austria and Germany before immigrating to the United States.

Sepetys traveled to Lithuania in 2005, fourteen years after the country had regained its independence, and visited cousins she had never known. She innocently asked if they had any pictures of her grandfather and, as she disclosed to Ingrid Roper of *Publishers Weekly*, "was stunned to learn that they had burned every picture of him, to expunge any connection and to avoid persecution. Then they told me more about what happened to those who didn't escape." In a discussion with Ann Giles on the *Bookwitch* Web site, Sepetys revealed, "I knew of course of the deportations, but not my family's involvement." While her extended family's experiences were a revelation to her, she told Giles that her grandfather undoubtedly knew about what had happened. She explained that "in hindsight he absolutely knew, and now that opens up so much about my grandfather. So much more makes sense now . . . why his shoulders would look like he was carrying this sense of guilt, which he did not tell my father. And when I came home and said 'Dad, do you know that when you fled they came for your cousins?' and he had no idea."

Sepetys decided she had to tell the story. The result was *Between Shades of Gray*, which has earned widespread acclaim. In a review of the novel for the

Chapter 16 Web site, Fernanda Moore cautioned that while it "is not a book for the faint of heart," it is "an invaluable testament to a ghastly chapter in twentieth-century history and should become required reading for students of World War II, who deserve to know the story of Stalin's victims as surely as they do those of Hitler."

The Accidental American

After the author's grandfather escaped Lithuania, his family—which eventually included a daughter—spent nine years in refugee camps. They hoped to immigrate to Australia. But, as Sepetys informed Giles, fate intervened: "they went to the boat to get to Australia. But they refused my family because my aunt Ruta had a cough. So the next day they went over to the boat to the United States and got on. . . . And that's how we ended up in the US." Sepetys was born on November 19, 1967, in Detroit, and was raised in Michigan with her parents, a brother, and a sister. In a video about *Between Shades of Gray* posted on YouTube, Sepetys remarked that "growing up in the States with a name like Ruta Sepetys . . . has always raised questions. People hear my name and they say, 'what are you?' And I answer, 'I'm Lithuanian.'"

Although Sepetys said she always dreamed of being a writer, she got her start in the performing arts. She told Ed Furniture of the *Ink 19* Web site, "At five, I was taking tap and ballet and theatre. I started taking piano lessons when I was eight years old, and began studying with an opera coach when I was 13. Although I didn't continue very long with the piano, I studied opera for over nine years." Sepetys earned a partial scholarship to study opera at Hillsdale College, but decided instead to pursue a finance degree.

After finishing college, Sepetys moved to Los Angeles. Her brother, John, had gone to music school in California and was interning with Desmond Child, a writer and producer of chart-topping songs. She told Furniture, "Desmond's management company was looking for an assistant for their West Coast associate Stacey Dutton, and my brother recommended me." Sepetys got the job, worked tirelessly, and even when Dutton relocated to New York, Desmond and his business partner, Winston Simon, kept her on, and she was soon promoted to management. In her interview with Furniture, she lauded the duo: "Desmond and Winston believed in me, and taught me almost everything I know. They are incredible businessmen and wonderful human beings." Sepetys added, "In 1994, Desmond moved from Los Angeles to Miami, and I decided to stay in LA and start my own management firm. Desmond and Winston actually gave me seed money to start my company. I was so fortunate."

Sepetys ran her artist-development business in Los Angeles for nine years, before relocating it to Tennessee in 2003. Despite her success in the business world, being an author remained an unfulfilled desire. It was her husband, Michael, who gave her the push she needed. In an interview on the *Elevensies* Web site, Sepetys admitted, "I'd drag my husband into every bookstore, inhaling the amazing scent of paper. One day he said, 'Enough. I want to see your first chapter before the end of the week.'" In the ensuing years, Sepetys joined a writing group, attended conferences, endured critiques, and even received a work-in-progress grant from the Society of Children's Book Writers and Illustrators. Her first completed work was a mystery for younger readers, but an agent at Writers House was more interested in a short sample she submitted, the seed of *Between Shades of Gray.*

Grayness Descends

The experiences of the Vilkas family are the foundation of *Between Shades of Gray.* The members are Lina, who is fifteen when the story opens; her younger brother, Jonas; her mother, Elena, who is both beautiful (with "honey-colored hair and . . . bright blue eyes") and educated (she speaks fluent Russian); and her father, Kostas, a university provost. The family enjoys an upper-middle-class lifestyle in Kaunas, Lithuania: Lina has a goose-down duvet on her bed and has had several dresses made for special occasions, and the family has posed for family portraits, enjoyed restaurant meals, attended soccer matches, and gone shopping for luxuries, not just necessities. Lina is also an aspiring artist who has been accepted into a prestigious summer art program, and one of her best friends is her cousin Joana, who wants to be a doctor.

The Vilkas's seem the epitome of a loving, upstanding family. But to Soviet dictator Josef Stalin, they are enemies. Stalin created lists of supposedly anti-Soviet Lithuanian citizens, including political activists, members of the police and military, teachers and librarians, and those considered to be intellectuals. In mid-June of 1941, when her father isn't home, the Soviet secret police, or NKVD, burst into the Vilkas's house and order them to leave in twenty minutes. They are forced onto a truck with other prisoners and taken to a train station.

At the station, chaos and confusion reign as people try to find or stay with family members, wonder what will happen to them, and wrestle with luggage that consists of a hodgepodge of clothing, supplies, and treasured belongings. Before long, the trains depart. Lina, her brother, and her mother are part of a procession to the Altai region of the Soviet Union, more than a third of the way across the massive country and north of China. Cramped together in an overfilled cattle car, the family becomes acquainted with others who will share their fate, including Miss Grybas, a teacher; a man who is a banker; Mrs. Rimas, a librarian; Mr. Stalas, who is pessimistic and complaining from the start; and another teenager, Andrius Arvydas, who is with his mother.

"There were only two possible outcomes in Siberia. Success meant survival. Failure meant death. I wanted life. I wanted to survive."

—Protagonist Lina in *Between Shades of Gray.*

The two-month train journey is beset with hunger, sickness, and death. The deceased are tossed aside like garbage, while the living are labeled as thieves and prostitutes. When they arrive at Altai, the group of prisoners of which Lina is a part is sent to work on a kolkhoz, or collective farm. Lina, her mother, and her brother live in a shack with a local woman who forces them to pay rent. The farm's crops are seized by the guards, and less-than-meager rations are given to workers. The guards tell them they have to sign documents saying they agree to work on the farm, pay an expensive war tax, and admit they are criminals. Doing so means a sentence of twenty-five years of hard labor; refusing brings the risk of harsher treatment and an uncertain fate.

At first, many of the prisoners refuse, but a portion of the group concedes, one by one. People are divided between those who steadfastly battle hopelessness and those who succumb to believing the degrading judgments of their captors. The spirited ones try to make the best of the situation. They are kind and supportive of one another. They hold onto their former lives by recounting details of meals, celebrations, and beloved relatives. They gather for Christmas and also help Lina celebrate her sixteenth birthday, during which she receives a treasured gift from Andrius. Lina has her own special way of clinging to hope: she finds solace in art. Whether it be tracking their forced travel by

crafting innocuous-looking maps or recording the people and actions that occur around her, she releases her emotions onto paper and bears witness.

After ten months at the camp, Lina and her family are part of a smaller group that is sent away from Altai. Their journey continues northward, on trucks and then a barge. The 300 members end up beyond the Arctic Circle, on the edge of the Laptev Sea, at the Trofimovsk labor camp, which they are required to help build. The conditions are so bad that Lina thinks longingly of Altai and the hut they shared there. Beyond the cold is the 180 days with little to no light, the inadequate clothing and shelter, and diseases such as scurvy, dysentery, and typhus. As their health deteriorates, the situation becomes desperate. But help comes from unlikely sources, including a brave doctor. And although it will be years before she returns home, Lina survives to tell her story.

Since its publication, *Between Shades of Gray* has garnered considerable critical acclaim. Suzi Feay of the *Financial Times* described the novel as being "filled with horror but lightened by hope and resilience. A classic in the making." In the *Wall Street Journal,* Alexandra Alter praised Sepetys's "stark, unsparing prose" and categorized the work as "a suspenseful, drama-packed survival story, a romance and an intricately researched work of historical fiction." Calling the story "a harrowing page-turner," a *Publishers Weekly* contributor pointed out that "the narrative skillfully conveys the deprivation and brutality of conditions" that the deportees faced. Minneapolis *Star Tribune* editor Laurie Hertzel said simply, "This book sings with truth."

Reviewers complimented Sepetys for publicizing a little-known chapter of history. Writing in *Booklist,* Michael Cart deemed *Between Shades of Gray* "beautifully written and deeply felt" and added that it is "an important book that deserves the widest possible readership." A contributor to *Kirkus Reviews* remarked that "Sepetys' flowing prose gently carries readers through the crushing tragedy of this tale that needs telling." In a review for *School Library Journal,* Renee Steinberg noted that "unrelenting sadness permeates this novel, but there are uplifting moments when the resilience of the human spirit and the capacity for compassion take over." And *School Librarian*'s Chris Brown concluded, "The really hopeful ending is that books such as this exist; books which tell stories powerful forces try to hide."

Lifting the (Iron) Curtain

Sepetys explained to Anneli Rufus in the *East Bay Express* that "there are millions of people whose lives were taken or affected during the Soviet occupation. Yet very few people knew the story. I wanted to write a novel to honor the people of the Baltics and also to illustrate the power of love and patriotism." The author's Lithuanian heritage is a source of pride, and yet that very identity was threatened by Stalin. In her video for *Between Shades of Gray*, Sepetys stated that those ordinary citizens who were added to Stalin's list of state enemies "were all arrested, the men separated from the women. . . . The men went to prison, and the women were sent to Siberia. And with no risk of pregnancies, Stalin's plan for genocide would be complete. However, he underestimated their will to live."

Because some of Sepetys's relatives persevered, she was able to meet them and discover the truth. To round out her story, the author also interviewed other survivors. Initially, though, people were reluctant to speak to her, their silence on the subject conditioned by more than fifty years of governmental repression. As relayed in Karen MacPherson's article for the *Seattle Times*, "Sepetys decided that she needed to write a novel, rather than a nonfiction volume, as a way of making people more willing to talk with her. With that decision, Sepetys gained people's trust, 'and I was sent from one person's house to the next person's house.'" The stories she heard were shocking and heartwrenching, but the revelation for Sepetys "was learning about the force of life and the power of love. The survivors told me countless, harrowing stories and described how they were able to bear the unbearable. They used hope instead of hate," she related on the *BermudaOnion* blog.

Sepetys conducted other types of research too. She told Maryann Yin of the *GalleyCat* Web site, "I spent time in an old Soviet cattle car that was used for the deportations. Sitting inside and knowing that the car had made repeated trips to and from the Baltics, ferrying people to their death, was overwhelming. It was so dark and small. I imagined the fear, the discomfort, and the children crying. I also took part in a simulation experience in a former Soviet prison. To say it was an unpleasant experience would be an understatement. It was filthy and terrifying."

When writing *Between Shades of Gray*, the author imbued some characters with personality traits of her actual family members. In an online interview with Madelyn Rosenberg, Sepetys disclosed, "My grandfather was a very kind and gentle person. I tried to imagine him as a little boy and came up with the character of Jonas." Speaking with *School Library Journal*'s Rick Margolis, Sepetys revealed, "Lina's mother, Elena, is essentially my mother. Some of the things she says are literally things that

If you enjoy the work of Ruta Sepetys, you may also want to check out the following books:

Esther Hautzig's memoir *The Endless Steppe: Growing Up in Siberia* (1968).
Peter Sís's *The Wall* (2007), his memoir, in picture book form, about what it was like to grow up in communist Czechoslovakia during the Cold War era.
Haya Leah Molnar's *Under a Red Sky* (2010), which recounts her childhood in communist Romania.

my mom has said. And Lina's father is very much like my father. He's an artist, and it felt natural to give Lina a talent for art." Lina's idol is Edvard Munch, a Norwegian best known for his 1893 painting *The Scream*. In a discussion on the *Stalking the Bookshelves* Web site, Sepetys explained the decision to make him part of the story: "Munch himself, and his art, represented to me all aspects of the deportees' experience—pain, confusion, death, anger, love, and the struggle and torture to simply stay alive."

In her video for *Between Shades of Gray*, Sepetys acknowledged, "I wrote the book, but really history wrote this story." She continued, "I am so grateful to Philomel . . . and the many publishers worldwide who have taken a chance on me and are helping bring this story out of the dark."

■ Biographical and Critical Sources

BOOKS

Sepetys, Ruta, *Between Shades of Gray*, Philomel Books (New York, NY), 2011.

PERIODICALS

Booklist, February 1, 2011, Michael Cart, review of *Between Shades of Gray*, p. 68.
Bookseller, January 28, 2011, Marilyn Brocklehurst, review of *Between Shades of Gray*, p. 34.
Financial Times, April 16, 2011, Suzi Feay, "Teen Fiction: Between Shades of Grey," p. 15.
Horn Book, May-June 2011, Dean Schneider, review of *Between Shades of Gray*, p. 103.

Kirkus Reviews, January 15, 2011, review of *Between Shades of Gray.*

Publishers Weekly, January 3, 2011, review of *Between Shades of Gray,* p. 51; February 28, 2011, Ingrid Roper, "YA Novel Unearths Lost Chapter in History," p. 20; April 11, 2011, Diane Roback, "Children's Fiction Bstsellers," p. 16; September 5, 2011, Rachel Deahl, "Philomel Nabs WWII Debut," p. 8.

School Librarian, Summer 2011, Chris Brown, review of *Between Shades of Gray,* p. 122.

School Library Journal, March, 2011, Rick Margolis, "Super Sad Love Story: Ruta Sepetys's 'Between Shades of Gray' Is a Heartbreaking Tale of Courage," p. 22, and Renee Steinberg, review of *Between Shades of Gray,* p. 170.

Voice of Youth Advocates, April 2011, Judy Brink-Drescher, review of *Between Shades of Gray,* p. 69.

ONLINE

BermudaOnion's Weblog, http://www.bermudaonion.net/ (March 22, 2011), "Author Interview: Ruta Sepetys."

Bookwitch, http://www.bookwitch.wordpress.com/ (November 23, 2011), Ann Giles, "Ruta Sepetys – 'I Pretty Much Killed Everyone'."

Chapter 16, http://www.chapter16.org/ (March 21, 2011), Fernanda Moore, "The Forgotten Holocaust."

Chicago Tribune, http://www.chicagotribune.com/ (September 21, 2011), William Hageman, "'Hope & Spirit' Exhibit: Exposing Cruelty, Hoping for Justice."

Easy Bay Express, http://www.eastbayexpress.com/ (April 6, 2011), Anneli Rufus, "Lamenting Lithuania with Ruta Sepetys."

Elevensies, http://www.2011debuts.livejournal.com/ (January 23, 2010), "Introducing: 2011 Debut Author Ruta Sepetys."

GalleyCat, http://www.mediabistro.com/galleycat/ (March 24, 2011), Maryann Yin, "Ruta Sepetys on Historical Fiction Research."

Graveyards.com, http://graveyards.com/ (November 23, 2011), Matt Hucke, "Lithuanian National Cemetery."

Ink 19, http://www.ink19.com/ (November 23, 2011), Ed Furniture, "Ruta Sepetys."

Los Angeles Times, http://www latimes.com/ (March 27, 2011), Susan Carpenter, "Not Just for Kids: *Between Shades of Gray* by Ruta Sepetys."

Madelyn Rosenberg, http://www.squealermusic.com/ (March 1, 2011), "Ruta Sepetys: *Between Shades of Gray.*"

Music Industry News Network, http://www.mi2n.com/ (November 11, 2003), "First Annual Indianapolis Music Conference Attracts Top Level Artist Management Companies."

New York Times, http://www.nytimes.com/ (April 8, 2011), Linda Sue Park, "A Teenager's View of the Gulag."

NorthStar Entertainment, http://www.northstar-ent.com/ (August 17, 2011), "Author Ruta Sepetys is Featured in Franklin (TN) Life."

Seattle Times, http://www.seattletimes.com/ (June 4, 2011), Karen MacPherson, "*Between Shades of Gray* Reveals Horror and Hope."

Stalking the Bookshelves, http://www.stalkingthebookshelves.blogspot.com/ (March 15, 2011), "Interview with author Ruta Sepetys."

StarTribune, http://www.startribune.com/ (March 19, 2011), Laurie Hertzel, "A Terrible Time, Punctuated with Hope."

Telegraph, http://www.telegraph.co.uk/ (April 1, 2001), Craig Nelson, "Stalin World Opens to Visitors."

Wall Street Journal, http://online.wsj.com/ (March 19, 2011), Meghan Cox Gurdon, "A Tale for Children of Braving Soviet Tyranny"; (March 25, 2011), Alexandra Alter, "An Unlikely Story for Teens."

YA Reads, http://www.yareads.com/ (April 16, 2011), "Interview with Ruta Sepetys."

YouTube, http://www.youtube.com/ (November 25, 2011), "*Between Shades of Gray,* Ruta Sepetys."*

Natalie Standiford

■ Personal

Born November 20, 1961, in Baltimore, MD; daughter of John Willard Eagleston (a pediatrician) and Natalie Elizabeth (a documentary videomaker) Standiford; married Robert Craig Tracy (a banker), April 29, 1989. *Education:* Brown University, B.A., 1983. *Hobbies and other interests:* "Travel, movies, going to the beach, all kinds of music, exploring junk shops, staying up late."

■ Addresses

Home—New York, NY. *Agent*—Sarah Burnes, c/o The Gernert Company, 136 East 57th St., New York, NY 10022; sburnesthegernertco.com. *E-mail*—natstand@aol.com.

■ Career

Writer, editor, musician, and novelist. Shakespeare & Co. Booksellers, New York, NY, clerk, 1983; Random House, New York, editorial assistant, 1984-85, assistant editor, Books for Young Readers division, 1985-87; freelance writer, New York, 1987—. Member of New York City Author Read-Aloud Program, 1992—. Bass player in the rock bands Ruffian and Tiger Beat.

■ Member

Society of Children's Book Writers and Illustrators, Authors Guild, Authors League of America.

■ Awards, Honors

Fifty Books of the Year citation, Federation of Children's Book Groups (United Kingdom), 1992, for *Space Dog the Hero;* Puffin Award, Alaska Association of School Librarians, 1992, for *The Bravest Dog Ever: The True Story of Balto;* Junior Library Guild selection, Best Children's Books of the Year, Bank Street College of Education, CYBILS Literary Awards finalist, 2009, Best Books for Young Adults, American Library Association (ALA), 2010, and Stuff for the Teen Age, New York Public Library, 2010, all for *How to Say Goodbye in Robot;* Best Fiction for Young Adults selection, ALA, 2011, for *Confessions of the Sullivan Sisters.*

■ Writings

The Best Little Monkeys in the World, illustrated by Hilary Knight, Random House (New York, NY), 1987.

Dollhouse Mouse (picture book), illustrated by Denise Fleming, Random House (New York, NY), 1989.

The Bravest Dog Ever: The True Story of Balto, illustrated by Donald Cook, Random House (New York, NY), 1989.

The Headless Horseman (adapted from Washington Irving's "The Legend of Sleepy Hollow"), illustrated by Donald Cook, Random House (New York, NY), 1992.

Brave Maddie Egg, Random House (New York, NY), 1995.

Astronauts Are Sleeping (picture book), illustrated by Allen Garns, Knopf (New York, NY), 1996.

The Stone Giant: A Hoax that Fooled America, illustrated by Bob Doucet, Golden Books (New York, NY), 2001.

How to Say Goodbye in Robot (young adult novel), Scholastic Press (New York, NY), 2009.

Confessions of the Sullivan Sisters (young adult novel), Scholastic Press (New York, NY), 2010.

UNDER PSEUDONYM JESSE HARRIS

Aidan's Fate, Knopf (New York, NY), 1992.

The Catacombs, Knopf (New York, NY), 1992.

The Fear Experiment, Knopf (New York, NY), 1992.

The Obsession, Knopf (New York, NY), 1992.

The Possession, Knopf (New York, NY), 1992.

UNDER PSEUDONYM EMILY JAMES

Santa's Surprise (picture book), Bantam (New York, NY), 1992.

Jafar's Curse (chapter book based on Disney movie *Aladdin*), Disney (New York, NY), 1993.

The Mixed-Up Witch (picture book), Bantam (New York, NY), 1993.

Fifteen: Hillside Live! (middle-grade novel based on the Nickelodeon television soap opera, *Fifteen*), Grosset & Dunlap (New York, NY), 1993.

Aladdin's Quest, Mega-Books, 1993.

"SPACE DOG" SERIES; ILLUSTRATED BY KELLY OECHSLI

Space Dog and Roy, Avon (New York, NY), 1990.

Space Dog and the Pet Show, Avon (New York, NY), 1990.

Space Dog in Trouble, Avon (New York, NY), 1991.

Space Dog the Hero, Avon (New York, NY), 1991.

"THE POWER" SERIES, YOUNG ADULT HORROR; UNDER PSEUDONYM JESSE HARRIS

The Power #2: The Witness, Knopf (New York, NY), 1992.

The Power #4: The Diary, Knopf (New York, NY), 1992.

The Power #7: Vampire's Kiss, Knopf (New York, NY), 1992.

"DATING GAME" SERIES: YOUNG ADULT NOVELS

The Dating Game, Little, Brown (New York, NY), 2005.

Breaking Up Is Really, Really Hard to Do, Little, Brown (New York, NY), 2005.

Can True Love Survive High School?, Little, Brown (New York, NY), 2005.

Ex-Rating, Little, Brown (New York, NY), 2006.

Speed Dating, Little, Brown (New York, NY), 2006.

Parallel Parking, Little, Brown (New York, NY), 2006.

"LEGALLY ELLE WOODS" SERIES: BASED ON THE CHARACTER CREATED BY AMANDA BROWN; YOUNG ADULT NOVELS

Blonde at Heart, Hyperion Paperbacks for Children (New York, NY), 2006.

Beach Blonde, Hyperion Paperbacks for Children (New York, NY), 2006.

Vote Blonde, Hyperion Paperbacks for Children (New York, NY), 2006.

Blonde Love, Hyperion Paperbacks for Children (New York, NY), 2006.

Author's works have been translated into Dutch.

■ **Adaptations**

The Bravest Dog Ever was adapted as an audiobook, Random House, 2006; *How to Say Goodbye in Robot*, was adapted as an audiobook, Brilliance Audio, 2010.

■ **Sidelights**

Natalie Standiford has earned praise for *How to Say Goodbye in Robot* and *Confessions of the Sullivan Sisters*, her award-winning young adult novels. Standiford's books are noted for their well-drawn characters, intricate plots, and witty dialogue. A former children's book editor, Standiford remarked to Naomi Canale in a *Dreams Can Be Reached* interview that "what motivates me most is that I love my work. I love that my job requires so much reading and writing, the things I enjoy most. And writing can sometimes feel like a form of problem-solving. When you find an answer, it's very satisfying."

Standiford was born in Baltimore, Maryland, in 1961. The daughter of a pediatrician father and a documentary videographer mother, Standiford demonstrated an interest in the literary arts at a young age. When she wasn't at ballet practice, violin lessons, or gymnastics classes, Standiford was writing her own stories or devouring books, including such classic tales as *Ramona and Beezus* and *Little Women*. In third grade, Standiford wrote her first novel, "The Hither-Heather Hiding Place," about seven siblings who construct a fort to hide from their mother. Her fifth grade teacher, whom Standiford remembers with fondness, helped her to recognize her own writing abilities.

While still in high school, Standiford interned at a newspaper, the *Baltimore Sun*. She was allowed to shadow a features reporter who interviewed celebrities when they visited the city. Standiford's love of languages spanned beyond her native tongue to include French, Russian, and Spanish. It is no surprise, then, that she majored in Russian language and literature at Brown University, which gave her the opportunity to spend a semester studying in the Soviet Union before the fall of Communism, in the city of Leningrad (since renamed St. Petersburg, Russia). "It was weird and interesting and fun and cold," Standiford shared in an essay on her home page.

Following Her Own Path

After graduating from college in the early 1980s, Standiford made her way to New York City with the intention of becoming a professional writer. Unsure of how to launch her career, however, she began working at Shakespeare & Co. Booksellers. After a year there, Standiford landed a job in the young readers division at Random House, eventually rising to the position of assistant editor. "I worked for Jane O'Connor, who writes the Fancy Nancy books and is also a brilliant editor," she commented in a *Hiding Spot* online interview. "I learned so much there. But all experiences are useful to a writer—that's one of the great things about being one."

Although Standiford enjoyed her work at Random House, she still wanted to pursue her own writing ambitions. Deciding to make a bold move, Standiford quit her job after three years and became a full-time freelance writer. Inspired by her publish-

ing career, Standiford began writing easy readers, picture books, and chapter books; her debut title, *The Best Little Monkeys in the World,* appeared in 1987. "Being an editor was a huge help, especially in the beginning of my career," she commented in an online interview with *Manga Maniac Café.* "I learned how publishing works, how an editor thinks, how to shape a story and what goes into the writing of children's books." Standiford added, "Working in publishing also helped desensitize me to criticism of my work."

Standiford took the greatest pleasure in writing for young adults. "I really like the energy of the teen readers—that passion. It's great to write for people who get so excited," Standiford told *Baltimore City Paper* interviewer Lee Gardner. Immersing herself in the genre of young adult fiction led Standiford to become friends with other YA authors, such as Libba Bray, Dan Ehrenhaft, and Barnabas Miller. Together, they formed a band, "Tiger Beat," and perform in New York City bookstores. Standiford plays bass guitar. She also plays in "Ruffian," a nearly all-female rock band.

Learning to Speak Robotese

Two of Standiford's best-known works are aimed at a teen audience. Released by Scholastic Press in 2009, *How to Say Goodbye in Robot* focuses on a complex and intense—though not romantic—relationship between two high school seniors, Beatrice Szabo and Jonah Tate. The story is told from the perspective of Beatrice, a sensitive teen who views herself as an permanent outsider, having changed homes and schools numerous times over the years due to her father's career in academia. To protect herself from the emotional impact of each departure, Beatrice adopts a detached, wooden demeanor; as a result, her mother accuses her of behaving like a robot.

When the family must make yet another move, this time to Baltimore, Beatrice is forced to adapt to a new school to complete her final year of high school. Beatrice makes friends with the class outcast, Jonah, known derisively as "Ghost Boy" because of his pale skin. The pair of insomniacs bond over "Night Lights," a local late-night radio talk show, while trying to solve a mystery involving Jonah's past. Standiford, a self-professed night owl, notes that her memories of listening to "Nightcaps," a national radio call-in show, influenced her narrative. "I've always wanted to find a way to use those radio callers—and the way the night brings out the strangeness in people—in a book," she related in her *Hid-*

An emotionally distant girl forms an intense friendship with the school outcast in Standiford's *How to Say Goodbye in Robot*. (Cover art by Phil Falco. Cover art Copyright © 2009 Scholastic Inc. Reprinted by permission of Scholastic Inc.)

As the novel unfolds, Bea narrates Jonah's discovery that his brain-damaged twin brother, Matthew, who he thought died years earlier in a car crash, is actually alive. When Jonah learns that his brother is in an institution, Jonah seeks Bea's help to draw his brother back into the family circle. Reviewer Terry Miller Shannon in *Teenreads.com* described *How to Say Goodbye in Robot* as "a moving page-turner. Bea is so finely drawn that one might expect her to walk off the page. In addition, her relationship with Ghost Boy is refreshingly difficult to categorize. Several mysteries thread through the story; the one regarding Jonah's family is particularly intriguing, with an emotional and unexpected resolution."

"I was the one who hated moving, until I finally got used to it. I learned not to get too attached to anything. I stopped thinking of the houses we lived in as my house, or the street we lived on as our street. Or my friends as my friends."

—Beatrice Szabo, the narrator of *How to Say Goodbye in Robot.*

Standiford's novel received honors from the American Library Association and the New York Public Library and garnered solid reviews. "A decidedly purposeful not-love story, this has all the makings of a cult hit," stated a contributor in *Kirkus Reviews.* Writing in *School Library Journal*, Kathleen E. Gruver described the work as "an honest and complex depiction of a meaningful platonic friendship," and *Horn Book* critic Claire E. Gross reported that the "characters are unusually true-to-life as . . . they fumble toward fully formed identities and fulfilling relationships."

ing Spot interview. "So when I first started thinking about Bea and Jonah and realized their story was missing something, I decided to add the Night Lights as a kind of Greek chorus to their friendship."

The spark for *How to Say Goodbye in Robot* was ignited by a strange story about a mysterious former classmate that the author heard at her high school reunion. That tale challenged Standiford to look at her past with a fresh perspective. "It made me think about misunderstood people and the secrets they keep, and that was the genesis of Jonah," she stated to Canale. "I created Beatrice as an outsider who comes in and observes a tightly-knit, closed world, which was what school sometimes felt like to me. Because she's an outsider, she can see things in Jonah that no one else notices."

Confessions on Demand

Published by Scholastic Press in 2010, *Confessions of the Sullivan Sisters,* another tale set in Baltimore, concerns a large and well-to-do family whose members, including siblings Norrie, Jane, and Sassy, are dependent on the money provided by their domineering matriarch, Almighty Lou. On Christmas Day, a deeply offended Lou announces that one of her six grandchildren has insulted her, and she demands a written confession and apology by

New Year's Day. If the letter is not produced, Lou threatens to blot the entire family out of her substantial will. As it turns out, all three of the Sullivan sisters—Norrie, Jane, and Sassy—have done something that would upset their grandmother, making each of them a possible culprit.

Standiford tells her story using the girls' distinct, first-person narratives, through which readers discover the Sullivan sisters' various transgressions. Norrie, at seventeen the oldest of the trio, falls in love with a graduate student eight years her senior and plans to leave town with him on the night of a grand cotillion; Jane, a rebel who enjoys flouting rules, broadcasts her family's secrets over the Internet thanks to her scandalous blog, www.myevilfamily.com; and Sassy, an adventurous sort with an air of invincibility, believes she may have contributed to the death of Lou's fifth husband. "Standiford makes reading about Baltimore high society and the . . . Sullivans feel like a wickedly guilty pleasure," observed a contributor in *Publishers Weekly*.

Confessions of the Sullivan Sisters earned a strong critical reception. Ilene Cooper, writing in *Booklist*, described the novel as "a cleverly plotted romp," and a contributor in *Kirkus Reviews* similarly noted that "humor abounds in the inner workings of this interesting and unusual family." A number of critics praised Standiford's ability to create fully-realized characters. In *Voice of Youth Advocates*, Jennifer M. Miskec stated that "the female protagonists are deeper and more complicated than expected," and *School Library Journal* reviewer Robbie L. Flowers maintained that teens "will eagerly flip pages to hear the sins of the Sullivan sisters and love the tale each one spills." According to Jennifer Wermes in the *Journal of Adolescent and Adult Literacy*, the novel "touches on issues that teens care about: love, friendship, family, and wanting to be connected to others."

Versatility Is the Key

In addition to her stand-alone works, Standiford has published several series for young adult readers. Early on in her writing career, she contributed three works to "The Power," a young adult horror series, under the pen name Jesse Harris. Standiford's "Legally Elle Woods" series, targeted at middle-grade readers, is based on the popular literary and film character created by Amanda Brown. In *Blonde at Heart*, *Blonde Love*, and other works, Standiford offers an intriguing and amusing look at Elle's high-school years. According to *Booklist* critic Jennifer

Mattson, readers "will be entertained by the smart, likable girl's transformation from 'Planet Schlub' to 'Planet Glam.'"

Standiford's "Dating Game" series includes such titles as *Can True Love Survive High School?*, *Ex-Rating*, and *Parallel Parking*. The novels center around three high school buddies—Madison, Holly, and Lina—who start their own Web site, complete with a dating quiz, for the purpose of dispensing relationship advice to their schoolmates and arranging dates for those who need a little help. "Readers will care very much about the main characters," Melissa A. Palmer stated in a *Teenreads.com* review, and Linda L. Plevak, reviewing *Can True Love Survive High School?* in *School Library Journal*, remarked that the book's "soap-opera elements will appeal to those looking for a romantic read."

When she is ready to begin a new work, Standiford creates a computer file titled "Ideas" in which she lists possible titles, potential character names, sample first lines, and whatever else comes to mind as she brainstorms. Once her story starts to take shape, Standiford likes to build a loose outline of her plot. As the author remarked in her interview with Shannon on *Teenreads.com*, "Some books have complicated plots and require a more detailed outline. I always end up changing things as I write anyway. But I like to know what's going to happen so I can keep the story focused and sharpen every detail into an arrow that points to the end."

Asked if she had any advice for aspiring authors, Standiford told the *Manga Maniac Café* interviewer that "it's important to finish something." She also noted that it's important for young writers to shut off their internal editors and simply write an entire first draft. "It's like being a sculptor," Standiford explained, "Writing the first draft is making the clay. Once you have the clay, you can shape it and refine it into whatever form you like."

"I love that my job requires so much reading and writing, the things I enjoy most. And writing can sometimes feel like a form of problem-solving. When you find an answer, it's very satisfying."

—Natalie Standiford, in an interview with Naomi Canale.

With more than thirty works to her credit, Standiford has no regrets about her decision to become an author. "I once wondered whether I had the talent and drive to be a writer," she remarked in an interview on the *Figment* blog. "I had no way of knowing, and it felt like something out of my control. I've since learned that the drive is the important part, and I had it without being aware of it. Through all the obstacles and disappointments I've faced in my career (as every writer does), something has kept me going almost without thinking about it. I'm happy to know, now, that I can do it."

■ **Biographical and Critical Sources**

PERIODICALS

Booklist, March 15, 2005, Cindy Welch, review of *The Dating Game*, p. 1285; July 1, 2006, Jennifer Mattson, review of *Blonde at Heart*, p. 59; November 1, 2009, Courtney Jones, review of *How to Say Goodbye in Robot*, p. 32; September 1, 2010, Ilene Cooper, review of *Confessions of the Sullivan Sisters*, p. 98.

Horn Book, January-February, 2010, Claire E. Gross, review of *How to Say Goodbye in Robot*, p. 94; September-October, 2010, Martha V. Parravano, review of *Confessions of the Sullivan Sisters*, p. 95.

Journal of Adolescent and Adult Literacy, April, 2011, Jennifer Wermes, review of *Confessions of the Sullivan Sisters*, p. 547.

Kirkus Reviews, September 15, 2009, review of *How to Say Goodbye in Robot*; August 15, 2010, review of *Confessions of the Sullivan Sisters*.

Kliatt, May, 2005, Samantha Musher, review of *The Dating Game*, p. 30.

Publishers Weekly, November 25, 1996, review of *Astronauts Are Sleeping*, p. 74; February 14, 2005, review of *The Dating Game*, p. 77; October 26, 2009, review of *How to Say Goodbye in Robot*, p. 59; September 6, 2010, review of *Confessions of the Sullivan Sisters*, p. 41.

School Library Journal, August, 2001, Mary Ann Carcich, review of *The Stone Giant: A Hoax that Fooled America*, p. 172; August, 2005, Nicole Marcuccilli Mills, review of *The Dating Game*, p. 136; January, 2006, Linda L. Plevak, review of *Can True Love Survive High School?*, p. 143; May, 2006, Susan Riley, review of *Blonde at Heart*, p. 136; October, 2009, Kathleen E. Gruver, review of *How to Say Goodbye in Robot*, p. 136; September, 2010, Robbie L. Flowers, review of *Confessions of the Sullivan Sisters*, p. 165.

Voice of Youth Advocates, October, 2010, Jennifer M. Miskec, review of *Confessions of the Sullivan Sisters*, p. 359.

ONLINE

Baltimore City Paper Web site, http://citypaper.com/ (November 4, 2009), Lee Gardner, "Teen Slate: Natalie Standiford's New Young-adult Novel Brings Her Back to Baltimore."

Dreams Can Be Reached Blog, http://naomicanale.blogspot.com/ (April 16, 2010), Naomi Canale, "Interview with Author and Rock Star, Natalie Standiford."

Figment Blog, http://blog.figment.com/ (October 21, 2010), "Interview with Natalie Standiford."

Hiding Spot Blog, http://thehidingspot.blogspot.com/ (May 26, 2010), "Playing Favorites with Natalie Standiford!," interview with Natalie Standiford.

Manga Maniac Café Web site, http://www.mangamaniaccafe.com/ (February 25, 2010), interview with Natalie Standiford.

Natalie Standiford Home Page, http://www.nataliestandiford.com (August 1, 2011).

Teenreads.com, http://www.teenreads.com/ (December, 2009), Terry Miller Shannon, interview with Natalie Standiford; (August 22, 2010), Melissa A. Palmer, review of *The Dating Game*; Melissa A. Palmer, review of *Breaking Up Is Really, Really Hard to Do*; Melissa A. Palmer, review of *Can True Love Survive High School?*; Melissa A. Palmer, review of *Ex-Rating*; Terry Miller Shannon, review of *How to Say Goodbye in Robot*.

Ypulse Web site, http://www.ypulse.com/ (October 21, 2009), "Author Spotlight: *How To Say Goodbye In Robot* By Natalie Standiford."

Jude Watson

■ Personal

Actual name, Judy Blundell; born in New York, NY; daughter of a doctor and a homemaker; married Neil Watson (a museum director); children: Cleo. *Education:* Earned degree in English.

■ Addresses

Home—Katonah, NY.

■ Career

Author. Worked as a reader for Simon & Schuster and an editorial assistant at Silhouette, New York, NY.

■ Awards, Honors

Quick Picks for Reluctant Young Adult Readers, American Library Association, and Best Books for the Teen Age, New York Public Library, 2004, both for *Premonitions*; National Book Award for Young People's Literature, 2008, for *What I Saw and How I Lied*.

■ Writings

FICTION; AS JUDY BLUNDELL

(Coauthor) *Disappearing Act,* Skylark (New York, NY), 1994.
What I Saw and How I Lied, Scholastic Press (New York, NY), 2008.
Strings Attached, Scholastic Press (New York, NY), 2011.

"BRIDES OF WILDCAT COUNTY" SERIES

Dangerous: Savannah's Story, Aladdin Paperbacks (New York, NY), 1995.
Scandalous: Eden's Story, Aladdin Paperbacks (New York, NY), 1995.
Audacious: Ivy's Story, Aladdin Paperbacks (New York, NY), 1995.
Impetuous: Mattie's Story, Aladdin Paperbacks (New York, NY), 1996.
Tempestuous: Opal's Story, Aladdin Paperbacks (New York, NY), 1996.

"STAR WARS JOURNAL" SERIES

Captive to Evil, Scholastic (New York, NY), 1998.
Queen Amidala, Scholastic (New York, NY), 1999.
Darth Maul, Scholastic (New York, NY), 2000.

"STAR WARS SCIENCE ADVENTURES" SERIES

(With K.D. Burdett) *Emergency in Escape Pod Four,* Scholastic (New York, NY), 1999.

(With K.D. Burdett) *Journey across Planet X*, Scholastic (New York, NY), 1999.

"JEDI APPRENTICE" SERIES

The Dark Rival, Scholastic (New York, NY), 1999.
The Hidden Past, Scholastic (New York, NY), 1999.
The Mark of the Crown, Scholastic (New York, NY), 1999.
The Defenders of the Dead, Scholastic (New York, NY), 1999.
The Uncertain Path, Scholastic (New York, NY), 2000.
The Captive Temple, Scholastic (New York, NY), 2000.
The Day of Reckoning, Scholastic (New York, NY), 2000.
The Fight for Truth, Scholastic (New York, NY), 2000.
The Shattered Peace, Scholastic (New York, NY), 2000.
The Deadly Hunter, Scholastic (New York, NY), 2000.
The Evil Experiment, Scholastic (New York, NY), 2001.
The Dangerous Rescue, Scholastic (New York, NY), 2001.
The Ties That Bind, Scholastic (New York, NY), 2001.
The Death of Hope, Scholastic (New York, NY), 2001.
The Call to Vengeance, Scholastic (New York, NY), 2001.
The Only Witness, Scholastic (New York, NY), 2002.
The Threat Within, Scholastic (New York, NY), 2002.

"JEDI APPRENTICE SPECIAL EDITIONS" SERIES

Deceptions, Scholastic (New York, NY), 2001.
The Followers, Scholastic (New York, NY), 2002.

"JEDI QUEST" SERIES

Path to Truth, Scholastic (New York, NY), 2001.
The Way of the Apprentice, Scholastic (New York, NY), 2002.
The Trail of the Jedi, Scholastic (New York, NY), 2002.
The Dangerous Games, Scholastic (New York, NY), 2002.
The Master of Disguise, Scholastic (New York, NY), 2002.
The School of Fear, Scholastic (New York, NY), 2003.
The Shadow Trap, Scholastic (New York, NY), 2003.
The Moment of Truth, Scholastic (New York, NY), 2003.
The Changing of the Guard, Scholastic (New York, NY), 2004.
The False Peace, Scholastic (New York, NY), 2004.
The Final Showdown, Scholastic (New York, NY), 2004.

"LEGACY OF THE JEDI" SERIES

Legacy of the Jedi, Scholastic (New York, NY), 2003.
Secrets of the Jedi, Scholastic (New York, NY), 2006.

"LAST OF THE JEDI" SERIES

The Desperate Mission, Scholastic (New York, NY), 2005.
Dark Warning, Scholastic (New York, NY), 2005.
Underworld, Scholastic (New York, NY), 2005.
Death on Naboo, Scholastic (New York, NY), 2006.
A Tangled Web, Scholastic (New York, NY), 2006.
Return of the Dark Side, Scholastic (New York, NY), 2006.
Secret Weapon, Scholastic (New York, NY), 2007.
Against the Empire, Scholastic (New York, NY), 2007.
Master of Deception, Scholastic (New York, NY), 2008.
Reckoning, Scholastic (New York, NY), 2008.

"THIRTY-NINE CLUES" SERIES

Beyond the Grave (book four), Scholastic (New York, NY), 2009.
In Too Deep (book six), Scholastic (New York, NY), 2009.
(With Rick Riordan, Peter Lerangis, and Gordon Korman) *Vespers Rising* (book eleven), Scholastic (New York, NY), 2011.

"THIRTY-NINE CLUES: CAHILLS VS. VESPERS" SERIES

A King's Ransom (book two), Scholastic (New York, NY), 2011.

"PREMONITIONS" SERIES

Premonitions, Scholastic (New York, NY), 2004.
Disappearance, Scholastic (New York, NY), 2005.
(As Judy Blundell) *The Sight* (contains *Premonitions* and *Disappearance*), Scholastic (New York, NY), 2010.

FICTION; AS JORDAN CRAY

Hot Pursuit, Aladdin Paperbacks (New York, NY), 1997.
Firestorm, Aladdin Paperbacks (New York, NY), 1997.
Gemini 7, Aladdin Paperbacks (New York, NY), 1997.
Shadow Man, Aladdin Paperbacks (New York, NY), 1997.

Shiver, Aladdin Paperbacks (New York, NY), 1998.

Bad Intent, Aladdin Paperbacks (New York, NY), 1998.

Most Wanted, Aladdin Paperbacks (New York, NY), 1998.

Dead Man's Hand, Aladdin Paperbacks (New York, NY), 1998.

Felicity, Hyperion Paperbacks for Children (New York, NY), 1998.

Stalker, Aladdin Paperbacks (New York, NY), 1998.

■ **Adaptations**

Beyond the Grave was adapted as an audiobook, Scholastic Audiobooks, 2009; *What I Saw and How I Lied* was adapted as an audiobook, Scholastic Audiobooks, 2009.

■ **Sidelights**

When Judy Blundell got the call saying that her noir novel, *What I Saw And How I Lied*, had won the National Book Award, she was momentarily rendered mute. "I think Harold Augenbraum, the head of the National Book Foundation, thought I'd fainted," she said in an interview with Madelyn Travis of *BookTrust Children's Books* Web site. "He kept saying 'Jude? Jude?' I finally said, 'Harold, are you sure?' And he said, 'You're Judy Blundell, aren't you?'"

This is a fair question, actually. Blundell has written dozens of books under various pen names, including "Star Wars" novelizations and two entries in the "Thirty-nine Clues" series, both of which she wrote under the name Jude Watson. *What I Saw And How I Lied* was the first book she wrote using her real name.

"I was very underconfident when I was younger. I really felt that writers were these exalted beings, and it would just be way too much hubris for me to ever be one," she told Daniel Handler in an interview with *School Library Journal*, explaining her choice to use pseudonyms. Blundell noted that, Initially, she no plans to place her own name on the cover of *What I Saw and How I Lied*. As the author told Handler, "I really did not expect it to be a huge break for me, and I didn't think I was going to put my name on it. It was really my editor [David Levithan] who said, 'You need to put your own name on this book, because it's different.'"

Winning the National Book Award was not only a surprise, but, as Blundell told Sue Corbett of *Publishers Weekly*, a life changer: "One thing I learned was that I had been very comfortable with my anonymity. Writing under a pseudonym gives you a lot of freedom. I never had to worry about reviews. So at first I felt a little exposed, but it turned out to be a wonderful thing."

Blundell has also written another historical YA novel under her own name, *Strings Attached*, which deals with themes of love and trust, She told *Chronogram's* Nina Shengold that tapping into a teen voice is easy for her because "I'm very in touch with humiliation, despair, and hubris." Besides, she said in the same article, "I like drama."

It Started With a Broken Leg

The youngest of three children, Blundell lived in Queens, New York, where her father was a doctor

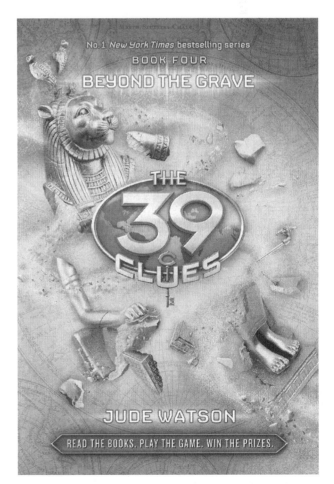

A prolific writer-for-hire, Watson has completed dozens of science-fiction and adventure novels, including *Beyond the Grave*, part of the "Thirty-nine Clues" series.

and her mother a homemaker. When she broke her leg at fourteen, her friends did not visit much—and she wasn't interested in them after she recovered. She remarked to Shengold in *Chronogram,* "I spent all that long summer alone. I developed a secret life. After midnight, I turned on the TV and watched movies all night: screwball comedies, drawing room comedies, dramas. I became a movie nerd. I fell in love with Cary Grant, idolized Irene Dunne. . . . That was the summer I became a writer, even though I never wrote a word."

"Writing on assignment, you learn to live in fear of having a reader put down your book, and you learn how important it is to keep a plot moving."

—Judy Blundell, discussing her work as a writer-for-hire under various pseudonyms.

History was one of Blundell's favorite subjects in school. "I liked reading about how people moved through their time on earth and how what was happening in politics and culture impacted them in a daily way," she told Donna Volkenannt in *Teenreads. com.* She majored in English in college, and went on to become a slush pile reader at Simon & Schuster where she slowly worked up her courage to become an author, writing a teen romance. Soon, she became a writer-for-hire, telling Shengold, "I don't know how many books I've written or how many pseudonyms I've used. I do know I have a basement full of cartons."

Many of her "Jude Watson" books are *Star Wars* spin-offs, such as the journals of Princess Leia Organa, Queen Amidala, and even Darth Maul. She's also the author of the "Premonitions" series about a teen psychic. She told Handler that she learned a lot from her life as a writer-for-hire: "Writing on assignment, you learn to live in fear of having a reader put down your book, and you learn how important it is to keep a plot moving," she said.

Then Came the Headache

Life was going along pretty smoothly at this point, Blundell told Leonie Flynn of the *Ultimate Book Guide.* "I was good at deadlines, didn't make a fuss,

so people came back and asked for more. I was Jude Watson and people liked my books—I thought that was enough," she said.

But when Levithan told her he wanted to see something of her own, she remembered the idea that had emerged one night. "Well, it all started with a really bad headache," she told Kristi Olson in *Teenreads.com.* "I woke up in the middle of the night with a pain in my head and an image of a girl sitting in a deserted hotel lobby playing solitaire." After taking some aspirin and returning to bed, Blundell could not get the image out of her mind, and she eventually formulated a tale about fifteen-year-old Evie Spooner, her mother and stepfather, and their complex relationship with a shadowy stranger. "As the story evolved," the author told Olson, 'I realized that what I was writing was really something that I'd been mulling over for a while—what do you do if you suspect that someone you love and trust has lied to you? I knew early on that Evie was going to come up against that somehow."

This idea grew into *What I Saw And How I Lied,* which a critic in *Publishers Weekly* called "a taut, noirish mystery coming-of-age story set in 1947." In the work, Evie lives in Brooklyn, New York, with her glamorous mother, Beverly, and her stepfather, Joe, a veteran of World War II. After Joe receives a strange phone call one evening, he makes an abrupt decision, taking the family to Palm Beach, Florida, for a vacation. Sequestered at a nearly empty hotel, the Spooners make the acquaintance of Arlene and Tom Grayson, another couple from New York who persuade Joe to go into the hotel business with them. Evie, meanwhile, finds herself entranced by Peter Coleridge, a handsome and charming ex-GI who, she learns, served with her stepfather in postwar Austria. Evie's budding romance with Peter disturbs both Joe, who seems to mistrust his old army buddy, and Beverly, who discourages her daughter's interest in the older man.

Matters become even more complicated when Joe's hotel deal falls though, largely due to anti-Semitism, and the Graysons are forced to depart town. Evie soon becomes suspicious of Peter's seemingly coincidental appearance in Palm Beach, and she discovers that he harbors a secret about his activities during the war, which involved guarding a "gold train," filled with treasure that the Nazis stole from Hungarian Jews. When Joe, Beverly, and Peter go out for a boat ride one day, only Evie's parents return, claiming Peter disappeared during a storm. After an investigation by local authorities, however, Joe is arrested for murder. "It is during the ensuing hearing that Evie learns that adults, even those closest to her, are not always what they seem," wrote *School Library Journal* contributor Sue Lloyd.

The book's homage to noir is apparent in its opening lines: "The match snapped, then sizzled, and I woke up fast. I heard my mother inhale as she took a long pull on a cigarette. Her lips stuck on the filter, so I knew she was still wearing lipstick. She'd been up all night." Even so, Blundell said she didn't set off to write in the genre. "Then once I had the story elements in place, I realized that I had incorporated some of the elements of film noir—the mysterious stranger, the blonde, the fact that nobody is telling the complete truth," she said to Olson. "There are certain tips of the hat to noir films in the book that some people have noticed, but if you've never seen a noir film in your life, you don't have to worry about it."

Evie might be from a different time, Blundell told Rita Williams-Garcia in a *National Book Foundation* interview, but her story is one today's teens can relate to: "She has to struggle to look at things as they are, and take a hard look at the reality of family stories that have been told and retold until they reach the status of myths. I think that process—of learning how to see your family and society from a clear and individual perspective—is part of every young person's journey."

What I Saw And How I Lied garnered a strong critical reception. "Readers can taste Evie's alienation and her yearning," a *Publishers Weekly* critic stated. "Using pitch-perfect dialogue and short sentences filled with meaning, Blundell has crafted a suspenseful, historical mystery," *Booklist*'s Jennifer Hubert noted in her review. Nicolette Jones, writing in the London *Times*, concluded: "Memorable and compelling, it is a book to grow up with."

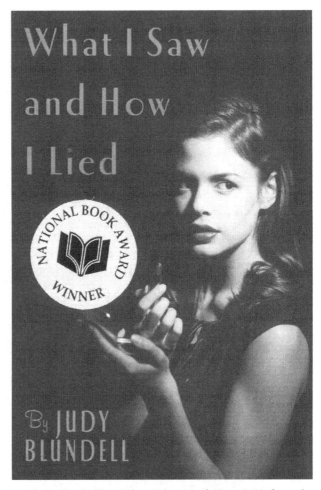

In the noir thriller *What I Saw and How I Lied*, set in 1947, a teen learns that her stepfather, who is accused of murdering an old army buddy, harbors a terrible secret.
(Cover photograph by Michael Frost. Copyright © Michael Frost. All rights reserved. Reproduced by permission.)

Uncovering More Lies

The process of writing *What I Saw And How I Lied* involved a tremendous amount of research. Blundell used the Internet extensively to look up original articles and transcripts and perused original editions from her mother's vintage newspaper collection. She also immersed herself in movies, magazines, and books of the 1940s. She even had her mother teach her the Lindy, a popular dance of the period. As she remarked to Handler, "My mother's in her 80s, and I realized that they had a different way of moving back then and a different rhythm in their speech. It's impossible to truly capture it, because I wasn't alive then, but just that act of learning the Lindy made me really think about the whole rhythm of a culture and how that changes during different eras."

In fact, it was while researching *What I Saw And How I Lied* that Blundell got her idea for her next novel, *Strings Attached*. While studying the post-war period, she told Sue Corbett in *Publishers Weekly*, she uncovered numerous stories of teenagers finding work in a job market that had opened up because of the war. "Teenagers had much more adult responsibilities," she remarked. "I found teenagers who were working, not just in factories, but as dancers or actors, kids who would save up what seemed to me like a pitiful amount of money and get on a bus or a train and go to New York. That must have been an extraordinarily scary and thrilling thing to do."

Set in 1950, the novel centers on Kit Corrigan, an aspiring dancer who leaves her Providence, Rhode Island, home and moves to New York City, where she lands a job in a quick-to-flop Broadway show. When her ex-boyfriend's father—a lawyer with mob ties known as "Nate the Nose"—offers her an apartment, clothes, and an audition for a glamorous job,

Watson, who received the National Book Award for *What I Saw and How I Lied*, once stated that the "postwar years were a time of great change in the United States—and that makes a great stage for a writer." (Copyright © 2010. Robin Platzer/Twin Photos. All rights reserved. Reproduced by permission.)

Kit jumps at the opportunity, but, as Paula Gallagher noted in *Voice of Youth Advocates* the teen "soon learns that making deals with a mobster comes with a price."

Once she begins working at the fabulous Lido nightclub, Kit is forced to do Nate's bidding, which includes taking delivery of mysterious packages and spying on Billy, her former boyfriend, as well as the gangsters who frequent the joint. Hopelessly entangled in Nate's web of deceit, Kit learns that one of the club's patrons winds up murdered, and she also stumbles onto a mystery from her own family's past, which may explain the disappearance of her Aunt Delia. "Evoking the glamour, grit, and gusto of the era, Blundell has produced a compelling narrative with well-crafted characters," Suzanne Gordon maintained in *School Library Journal.* A critic in *Publishers Weekly* also applauded the novel, calling it "first-rate historical fiction."

One of the key themes Blundell addresses in her work is the sexism of the era. According to Darcey Steinke, writing in the *New York Times Book Review,* "Girl Power as we know it did not exist in the 1950's and *Strings Attached* evokes a time when women often had to achieve their goals mostly through men." Even before getting too deeply involved as an informant for Nate, Kit learns that women often find themselves compromised; as she notes: "I wasn't very bright but I was beginning to get wise, just by keeping my ears open. I was beginning to realize how New York worked, how the men chased their secretaries or the Broadway dancers and brought them to discreet hotels or apartments they kept without their wife knowing."

Blundell said she hopes that readers of the novel, especially teenage girls, will learn something about how times have changed—and how they have not. "I think that young women today can see that they have many more options than they would have had in 1950," she said to Volkenannt in *Teenreads.com.* "They might know that intellectually, but I want them to *feel* it, how a young woman can find herself cornered. The power struggles Kit has, however, can still happen today. No matter how self-confident you seem, it can be hard to say no to someone who you want to please . . . or someone you're intimidated by."

Living With Dual Identities

Blundell lives in Katonah, New York, with her husband, Neil Watson, and their daughter, Cleo. She says she starts each day writing: "Before I've seen the newspaper, before I even talk to my husband, before my child is up, I reach for my laptop—I don't even have coffee," she told Flynn in the *The Ultimate Book Guide.* "Sometimes just for half an hour before I start the day—a little 'in' at the beginning of the day."

Her writing continues throughout the day, and in the evenings, too, sometimes even at her daughter's basketball practice. "Now that I'm a mom, I can work just about anywhere," she told *Teenreads.com.*

"I think that process—of learning how to see your family and society from a clear and individual perspective—is part of every young person's journey."

—Judy Blundell, in a National Book Foundation interview.

YA readers can expect more Blundell, but more Jude Watson, too: "I had such fun with *The 39 Clues . . .*" she commented to Flynn. "They're great fun to write, like really intricate puzzles. I put on my boy hat and get plotting. It's around that age that we lose boy readers, and I'm always looking for ways to keep boys reading—so one of the reasons I'd like to continue to write as Jude is because that's so important to me. And it's fun!"

■ Biographical and Critical Sources

BOOKS

Blundell, Judy, *What I Saw and How I Lied,* Scholastic Press (New York, NY), 2008.
Blundell, Judy, *Strings Attached,* Scholastic Press (New York, NY), 2011.

PERIODICALS

Booklist, November 1, 2008, Jennifer Hubert, review of *What I Saw and How I Lied,* p. 36; March 1, 2011, Ilene Cooper, review of *Strings Attached,* p. 59.
Books & Media, February 14, 2009, Kristin Kloberdanz, review of *What I Saw and How I Lied,* p. 3.

Bulletin of the Center for Children's Books, December 1, 2008, Elizabeth Bush, review of *What I Saw and How I Lied,* p. 150.

Canadian Review of Materials, October 18, 2002, review of *The Way of the Apprentice.*

Guardian (London, England), August 29, 2009, Philip Ardagh, "Puncture in the Postwar Fairytale," review of *What I Saw and How I Lied,* p. 12.

Kirkus Reviews, October 1, 2008, review of *What I Saw and How I Lied;* February 1, 2011, review of *Strings Attached.*

Kliatt, November 1, 2004, Olivia Durant, review of *Premonitions,* p. 26; March 1, 2006, Holley Wiseman, review of *Disappearance: A Premonitions Mystery,* p. 26; November 1, 2008, Janis Flint-Ferguson, review of *What I Saw and How I Lied,* p. 8.

New York Times Book Review, March 13, 2011, Darcey Steinke, "What Price Fame?," review of *Strings Attached,* p. 15.

Publishers Weekly, September 4, 1995, review of *Dangerous: Savannah's Story,* p. 70; September 29, 2008, review of *What I Saw and How I Lied,* p. 83; January 17, 2011, review of *Strings Attached,* p. 50.

School Library Journal, February 1, 1996, Jana R. Fine, review of *Dangerous,* p. 115; February 1, 1996, Jana R. Fine, review of *Scandalous: Eden's Story,* p. 115; March 1, 1996, Bambi L. Dunn, review of *Audacious: Ivy's Story,* p. 222; December 1, 2008, Sue Lloyd, review of *What I Saw and How I Lied,* p. 119; December 1, 2008, "Blundell Nabs NBA," p. 13; January 1, 2009, Daniel Handler, "The Great Unknown: Before She Snagged the National Book Award, Judy Blundell Was One of Publishing's Best-kept Secrets," p. 32; April 1, 2009, Sue Lloyd, review of *What I Saw and How I Lied,* p. 56; March, 2011, Suzanne Gordon, review of *Strings Attached,* p. 156.

Times (London, England), July 12, 2009, Nicolette Jones, review of *What I Saw and How I Lied.*

Voice of Youth Advocates, April 1, 1996, review of *Scandalous,* p. 31; June 1, 1996, reviews of *Audacious, Dangerous,* and *Impetuous: Mattie's Story,* p. 103; April 1, 1997, review of *Tempestuous: Opal's Story,* p. 34; February 1, 2009, Ava Ehde, review of *What I Saw and How I Lied,* p. 523; February, 2011, Paula Gallagher, review of *Strings Attached,* p. 578, and Christina Fairman, review of *Strings Attached,* p. 578.

ONLINE

Booktrust Children's Books Web site, http://www.booktrustchildrensbooks.org.uk/ (August 1, 2011), Madelyn Travis, "What She Saw," interview with Judy Blundell.

Chronogram, http://www.chronogram.com/ (May 27, 2011), Nina Shengold, "Million-Dollar Mommy: Judy Blundell Moves from Star Wars to Noir."

Judy Blundell Home Page, http://www.judyblundell.com (August 1, 2011).

National Book Foundation Web site, http://www.nationalbook.org/ (August 5, 2009), Rita Williams Garcia, interview with Judy Blundell.

Publishers Weekly Online, http://www.publishersweekly.com/ (January 20, 2011), Sue Corbett, "Q & A with Judy Blundell."

Scholastic Web site, http://www2.scholastic.com/ (August 5, 2009), profile of Watson.

Teenreads.com, http://www.teenreads.com/ (February, 2010), Kristi Olson, interview with Judy Blundell; (April, 2011), Donna Volkenannt, interview with Judy Blundell.

Ultimate Book Guide, http://theultimatebookguide.blogspot.com/ (July 7, 2009), Leonie Flynn, "Author Interview: Judy Blundell."*

Kurt Wenner

■ Personal

Born in Ann Arbor, MI; son of an college administrator father and a music teacher mother; married, wife's name Elizabeth; children: Anders (son). *Education:* Attended Rhode Island School of Design; attended Art Center College of Design; studied classical drawing in Italy.

■ Addresses

Home—Mantua, Italy. *Office*—Wenner Empire, Empire Entertainment Japan, Inc., 4-2-6-1F Toranomon, Minato-ku, Tokyo, Japan 105-0001. *E-mail*—masterartist@kurtwenner.com.

■ Career

Artist, designer, architect, and educator. Jet Propulsion Laboratory, National Aeronautics and Space Administration (NASA), Pasadena, CA, advanced scientific space illustrator, for two years; street artist, 1982—; illusionistic street painter, 1984—.

Conductor of conducted seminars and workshops for organizations, including National Gallery of Art, Smithsonian Institution, Disney Studios, Warner Bros. Studios, Toyota, and General Motors; Music Center of Los Angeles County, Los Angeles, CA, developer of art education program. *Exhibitions:* Paintings included in permanent collections in corporate offices, government buildings, hotels, churches, and museums.

■ Awards, Honors

Won several gold medals in European competitions; Kennedy Center Medallion, for outstanding contribution to arts education.

■ Writings

(With B. Hansen and M. Hospodar) *Asphalt Renaissance: The Pavement Art and 3-D Illusions of Kurt Wenner,* Sterling Publishing (New York, NY), 2011.

■ Sidelights

Kurt Wenner is an American-born illustrator, architect, and "Madonnaro" (street painter) who has gained international notoriety for creating three-dimensional works of street art that appear to sink into or emerge from the pavement on which they are painted. Wenner's marriage of classical art methods and subject matter with urban venues typically associated with graffiti or "street" art have allowed him to create a unique mode of visual expression that is both antique and modern.

"My interest in Renaissance classicism started with the simple desire to draw well," Wenner wrote on his home page. "I was struck by the vast difference between how students and teachers drew in the 20th Century and the way artists drew 500 years ago. It seemed to me that artists of the past had abilities far beyond those of today."

His unique combination of classical technique and modern setting led him to be featured in a documentary about street painters. Since then, Wenner has painted in some thirty countries, creating works in support of commercial campaigns and contributing his talent to activist efforts. He also holds the record for creating the world's largest street painting.

"Although I employ an arsenal of visual tools to create illusion, the classical language of form is the most vital. Classicism is vastly superior to other forms of realism for the creation of illusion, as it is based on human perception. Every stroke has the purpose of communicating form and space to the viewer."

—Kurt Wenner, in his artistic statement.

"I am a contemporary classicist who studies and researches lost, neglected or ignored ideas from historical aspects of western European art. I try to use them in an original way to make them pertinent to my time, and challenge my contemporary audience," Wenner told Claudio Parentela on the *eXTra finGer Blog*.

Success at Sixteen

Wenner was raised in the California beach town of Santa Barbara, and his interest in art came at an early age. Wenner notes that his childhood home—with its varied architectural styles, large villas, and creative, bohemian atmosphere—had a significant influence on his artistic vision. Artistically precocious, Wenner's skills allowed him to start his career while still in high school, painting his first commercial work at the age of sixteen.

"My first mural was for an ice cream store and manufacturer called McConnells Ice Cream," he remarked to Parentela. "It's a famous Santa Barbara institution. I portrayed the family of the owners in a composition that was a cross between the Last Supper and Alice in Wonderland." By the age of seventeen, Wenner was earning a living as a graphic artist.

Wenner enrolled in the Rhode Island School of Design to study with David Macaulay, a world-renowned illustrator and architecture expert whose book *Cathedral* was a significant influence on Wenner. However, the young artist did not find the education he was looking for in Rhode Island. "They told me I had no talent," Wenner said in an interview with Claudia Feldman in the *Houston Chronicle* in 2003. "They said I was excellent in a lot of things, but not drawing." His reception in New England eventually led him to California where he furthered his education at the Art Center College in Pasadena.

But it was Wenner's own intellectual pursuits that would have the most significant impact on his art and career. "The major subject I learned on my own was artist's geometry," Wenner stated in his *eXTra finGer Blog* interview. "This subject is perhaps the most important single component of our European artistic heritage, but in general it is taught badly, or not at all."

While in Pasadena, Wenner was invited by a physics teacher to create a science drawing for the famous Jet Propulsion Laboratory (JPL), which is located nearby. Wenner's drawing of an ion mass spectrograph won the attention of the Lab's management because none of the artists on staff had been able to capture the complex image with pen and ink. Wenner's success with the drawing ultimately won him a job at JPL, where he created artist's renderings of alien landscapes and the fantastic spacecraft of the future. The work Wenner did at JPL would prove to be indispensible to his development as an artist. "The images were created by hand from scientific data, landscapes of outer planets and future spacecraft. I can't even begin to describe what the experience taught me," he told Parentela.

From Outer Space to Italy

During his time at JPL, Wenner was exposed to some of the early examples of computer generated imaging (CGI), the technology that would ultimately

Wenner is credited with inventing an art form known as anamorphic or illusionistic street painting, as seen in this work that he created in Waterloo Station in London, England.

be embraced by the entertainment industry as the new standard for feature animation. The potential for this technology troubled Wenner. "It occurred to me that the tradition and significance of geometrical drawing and design would become lost with computer graphics in the same way that the tradition of classical drawing had collapsed with the invention of photography," he told Parentela.

Motivated by this realization and the success he had already achieved in his self-directed, non-traditional education, in 1982 Wenner left California to study drawing and architecture in Italy. He took self-guided courses in the works of Michaelangelo, Leonardo da Vinci, Raphael, and others, learning the techniques of the old masters by drawing from the original works. Wenner would sell his studies of the classics to museum employees and tourists in order to survive in Italy.

"For six months I spent eight hours a day drawing and learning from paintings and sculpture," the artist wrote on his home page. He added, "I spent many months looking through libraries and archives for texts written centuries earlier on the artistic subjects that most fascinated me."

Wenner employs both conventional and optical illusions in his art, such as this image of a bicyclist appearing to ride across a three-dimensional bridge, which appeared on London's South Bank.

Ultimately, one of the subjects that came to fascinate Wenner was the study of linear perspective and artistic geometry. These classical, highly technical processes for creating depth and balance in a work would become the trademark of Wenner's visual style. In particular, Wenner was drawn to anamorphic perspective, a technique that, according to the artist's blog, "gives the illusion of soaring architecture and floating figures in ceiling frescoes" that "create compositions that seemed to rise from and fall into the ground. In anamorphic perspective, painted forms appear as three-dimensional when viewed from one point in space."

But it was the confluence of these studies with a coincidental event that first connected Wenner to the form that has come to define his career. One day, Wenner came upon a street painter at work and asked him about his art. The Madonnaro told Wenner about his technique, and Wenner shared the contents of his own notebook.

Impressed by Wenner's work, and hungry for lunch, the street painter asked Wenner to complete a portion of his street drawing. "Working with the chalks came very naturally, and from that point on I've been street painting," Wenner told an *AgrinioArt* contributor in 2011.

Dazzling to the Eye

Taken by the new medium, Wenner began to focus wholly on street painting. Combining this experience with his previous study of anamorphic perspective, Wenner began to create his own, new approach to street art, continuing to draw influence from the art and architecture around him. "On some of the ceilings I noticed that the figures were elongated to appear normal from the ground. I was aware that my street paintings were subject to similar viewing circumstances—people looked at the work from an angle rather than straight on. This eventually inspired me to create a pictorial geometry specific to the street," he remarked to Parentela.

Wenner's new approach to illustration caught the attention of National Geographic and in 1985, the natural and historical society featured Wenner in a documentary about street painting called *Masterpieces in Chalk*. The film depicted Wenner's street painting work in Italy and Switzerland and received several awards, including the Blue Ribbon award at the American Film and Video Festival. Wenner credits the film for inspiring several street painting festivals around Europe.

As Wenner's technique became more demanding, the chalk of his first street painting experience revealed itself to be too dusty and temperamental for his evolving work. Wenner moved to pastels—eventually developing his own pigments to more accurately reflect his artistic vision. "I was fortunate because they still sold the necessary raw pigments in the hardware stores," Wenner recounted in his *eXTra finGer Blog* interview. "Although I studied old recipes for pastels, my final recipe was taken from an unrelated text dealing with marbling paper. My handmade pastels are stronger and more permanent than commercial products."

Wenner's unique style scored him a major breakthrough in 1989, when he was commissioned by the city of Mantua to create a street painting in preparation for Pope John Paul II's visit to the city. The work, depicting *The Last Judgment*, measured fifteen feet by seventy-five feet and was painted, under Wenner's direction, by thirty of Europe's finest street painters. The work took ten days to complete and was ultimately signed by the Pope himself.

After the breakthrough of *The Last Judgment*, Wenner's work has been commissioned and shown in a variety of settings and contexts. For example, one of his more dramatic works, *Dies Irae* from 2005, shows human figures in torment emerging from the flagstone town square or sitting on the edge of an illusory hole in the ground. Wenner's use of anamorphic perspective gives the viewer, when standing in the correct spot, the impression of a convex surface beneath the street. "I think the image 'Dies Irae' remains my favorite work because I learned the most from it," Wenner told Parentela.

A striking example of Wenner's commercial work was a commission from Dunkin Brands for the launch of the company's new fruit smoothies. The piece uses Wenner's techniques to create the illusion of a picnic area recessed in the surface of a public space, with bananas and strawberries in dramatic faux relief and the featured drink seemingly towering over the whole piece.

In 2010 Wenner lent his talents to the international activist group Greenpeace to support a campaign against genetically modified crops. The three-dimensional farm painting Wenner created measured three hundred eighty square meters and set the record for the world's largest image of its kind painted by a single person. The work depicts an organic farm and incorporates one million signatures collected by Greenpeace.

In his interview with Parentela, Wenner described the secret recipe that makes his art possible. "My own geometry is different from the 17th century works, and I have not published it. It combines a logical use of linear perspective with a projection

Inspired by "The Big Lunch," a celebration of community spirit held in the United Kingdom, Wenner completed this unique and dazzling work in 2010.

"Even as I'm creating a new part of the picture, I can see the finished parts are already fading. I'm not disappointed when it washes away because street painting is performance art; it's very much like attending a symphony. When the music ends everyone leaves with a memory of the music. My work is the same except one is left with a visual impression."

—Kurt Wenner, in an essay on his home page.

outward from the human eye. Other artists that emulate the three-dimensional pavement works use a more traditional geometry called 'quadratura' that does not involve complicated calculations. They do not understand that my geometry is unique."

■ Biographical and Critical Sources

BOOKS

Wenner, Kurt, B. Hansen, and M. Hospodar, *Asphalt Renaissance: The Pavement Art and 3-D Illusions of Kurt Wenner,* Sterling Publishing (New York, NY), 2011.

PERIODICALS

Daily Mail (London, England), August 20, 2009, Eddie Wrenn and Tamara Abraham, "Monsters Climbing through the Floors, Magic Carpet Rides through Fantastical Cities . . . Yes, It's the Return of the 3D Artist."

Houston Chronicle, June 9, 2003, Claudia Feldman, "Impressionism Unfolding: Artist Brings Classical Art to the Masses by Transforming His Canvases of Concrete into Masterpieces," p. 1.

ONLINE

AgrinioArt Web site, http://www.agrinioart.gr/ (May 24, 2011), "Exclusive Interview with Kurt Wenner."

The eXTra finGer Blog, http://theextrafinger.blog spot.com/ (May 26, 2011), Claudio Parentela, "Interview with Kurt Wenner."

Kurt Wenner Home Page, http://www.kurtwenner. com (August 15, 2011).

OTHER

Masterpieces in Chalk (documentary), National Geographic, 1984.*

Rita Williams-Garcia

■ Personal

Born April 13, 1957, in Queens, NY; father in the military, mother's name Essie (a domestic servant); married Peter Garcia (divorced); children: Michelle, Stephanie. *Education:* Graduated from Hofstra University; postgraduate study in creative writing at Queens College; studied dance under Alvin Ailey and Phil Black. *Hobbies and other interests:* Chess, playing Tetris, jogging, sewing.

■ Addresses

Home—Jamaica, NY. *E-mail*—info@ritawg.com.

■ Career

Writer and educator. Interactive Market Systems, New York, NY, manager of software distribution and production until 2005; Vermont College of Fine Arts, Montpelier, VT, faculty member of M.F.A. program in writing for children and young adults. Has also worked as a dancer and reading teacher.

■ Member

Authors Guild, Society of Children's Book Writers and Illustrators.

■ Awards, Honors

Notable Books for Children and Young Adults citation, American Library Association (ALA), 1991, for *Fast Talk on a Slow Track; Booklist* Editors' Choice selection, 1995, Best Books for Young Adults citation, ALA, and Coretta Scott King Honor Book selection, ALA, both 1996, all for *Like Sisters on the Homefront;* PEN/Norma Klein Award for Children's Fiction, 1997; National Book Award finalist, 2009, for *Jumped;* National Book Award finalist, 2010, Coretta Scott King Award, ALA, Scott O'Dell Prize for Historical Fiction, and Newbery Honor Book award, both 2011, all for *One Crazy Summer.*

■ Writings

YOUNG ADULT NOVELS

Blue Tights, Lodestar (New York, NY), 1988.

Fast Talk on a Slow Track, Lodestar (New York, NY), 1991.

Like Sisters on the Homefront, Lodestar (New York, NY), 1995.

Every Time a Rainbow Dies, HarperCollins (New York, NY), 2001.

Diamond Land (novella), Scholastic (New York, NY), 2003.

No Laughter Here, HarperCollins (New York, NY), 2004.

Jumped, HarperTeen (New York, NY), 2009.

One Crazy Summer, Amistad Books (New York, NY), 2010.

OTHER

Catching the Wild Waiyuuzee, illustrated by Mike Reed, Simon & Schuster (New York, NY), 2000.

Contributor of short fiction to anthologies, including *No Easy Answers: Short Stories about Teenagers Making Tough Choices,* Delacorte, 1997; *Second Sight: Stories for a New Millennium,* Philomel, 1999; *Period Pieces: Stories for Girls,* HarperCollins, 2002; *First Crossings: Stories about Immigrant Teens,* Candlewick Press, 2004; and *Pick-up Game: A Full Day of Full Court,* edited by Marc Aronson and Charles R. Smith, Jr., Candlewick Press, 2011.

■ Adaptations

One Crazy Summer was adapted for audiobook, Recorded Books, 2010.

■ Sidelights

Called "one of the finest middle grade and teen novelists of her generation" by *School Library Journal* blogger Elizabeth Bird, Rita Williams-Garcia is known for insightful novels that explore such hard-hitting teen issues as teen pregnancy, rape, genital mutilation, girl-on-girl violence, and child abandonment. Williams-Garcia's long-time editor, Rosemary Brosnan, writing in *Horn Book* on the occasion of Williams-Garcia winning the Coretta Scott King Award, a Newbery Honor award, and the Scott O'Dell Award, all in 2011, noted: "Rita is not an author who should be directed to write x, y, or z: she writes what her muse dictates, and this is how every book has come about. I trust her completely." Brosnan added, "Rita's books are not written quickly. Seven published novels in twenty-five years is not the hallmark of a prolific author. The charac-

ters have to become part of Rita; they need to talk to her before she can write." On her home page, Williams-Garcia observed of her novels: "I never tell my readers what to think or feel; I just pray that my writing inspires them to do so. My characters don't explain themselves at every turn because I want the reader to experience first-hand as they are reading."

"I never tell my readers what to think or feel; I just pray that my writing inspires them to do so."

—Rita Williams-Garcia, in an essay on her home page.

In highly regarded works such as *Fast Talk on a Slow Track, No Laughter Here,* and *Jumped,* Williams-Garcia draws on her experiences growing up in a New York City neighborhood, as well as on situations she has encountered as a teacher and as a dancer. Her Coretta Scott King Award-winning novel *One Crazy Summer,* written for younger readers, is equally informed by personal experience, viewing the 1960s and the Black Panthers from a child's perspective. Her young-adult novels depict African-American men and women living and coping with difficulties in an honest, uncontrived manner. "Williams-Garcia's portrayal of these urban black adolescents and their worlds feels genuine, neither sensationalized nor romanticized," declared *Horn Book* contributor Rudine Sims Bishop. "Her work is marked by an authentic rendering of the styles and cadences of urban black language, some touches of humor, and strong, dynamic characterization." Williams-Garcia's works have also been compared to books by such celebrated African-American writers as Jacqueline Woodson, Dolores Johnson, and Angela Johnson.

Growing Up with a Love of Words

Born in Queens, New York, in 1957, Williams-Garcia eventually moved to Arizona and then to California due to the demands of her father's military career. After her family settled in the California town of Seaside, Rita and her siblings spent their childhood playing outdoors a great deal. She explained to *Booklist* interviewer Hazel Rochman: "We were always doing things. My sister was an artist. My brother was into math. I loved words; I just thought that was normal. To characterize me as a kid, you could say that I was definitely a geek."

Williams-Garcia developed her reading skills early in life, teaching herself to read at age two by learning to associate letters with their sounds, partly through looking at billboards and partly through the efforts of her older sister, who would often share her books with her. By the time she entered school, Williams-Garcia was already an accomplished reader and a writer of poetry and stories, most of them involving her siblings.

Williams-Garcia was exposed to racial issues while growing up during the 1960s. She remembers discussing race relations and racism in the classroom in the aftermath of the 1968 riots and the assassination of Dr. Martin Luther King, Jr. At the age of twelve, she left California for Georgia for six months, then settled in Jamaica, New York, a section of the borough of Queens. In the sixth grade, she went looking for literature for young adults that featured black protagonists. She discovered biographies of historical figures, such as Harriet Tubman and Sojourner Truth, and a single novel, *Mary Ellen, Student Nurse*. Her teachers encouraged her to write for herself, and at the age of fourteen she published her first story in *Highlights* magazine.

After enrolling at Hofstra University, Williams-Garcia temporarily dropped writing for other activities. "In college, real life seemed to displace my need to 'make' stories," she commented on *Penguin.com*, "so I didn't write for nearly three years. (Real life was running my dance company and being political)." She declared a major in economics, auditioned for dancing roles in musicals, and performed community outreach work through her sorority, Alpha Kappa Alpha. In her senior year in college, Williams-Garcia enrolled in a creative writing class. In that class she combined her outreach work—teaching high school girls remedial reading—with her workshop training to pen an early version of the story that became her first novel, *Blue Tights*.

A Long Road to Debut Publication

Blue Tights, while partly based on Williams-Garcia's own experiences, is for the most part a conglomeration of the stories of many young women. The book tells the tale of Joyce Collins, an ambitious African-American who loves to dance and exhibits great talent. However, Joyce finds herself shut out of her school's European-oriented dance program because the dance instructor believes her full-figured body is not suited to ballet. Besides dealing with this great disappointment, Joyce has to come to terms with her home life—she has been raised by an often absent mother and a religiously fanatic aunt—and her identity. "A volatile combination of worldliness and innocence," Bishop stated, "Joyce seeks love and popularity in all the wrong places and with all the wrong people." "Williams-Garcia does not shy away from the harsh circumstances that define Joyce and her family," explained Susan Bloom in *Twentieth-Century Young Adult Writers*. "Aunt Em's severe treatment of Joyce stems from a horrific self-induced coat hanger abortion she suffered in her adolescence. Williams-Garcia provides less sensational, daily evidence of the grinding poverty that eats at this family." "Through her work with an African-American dance troupe," Bishop concluded, Joyce "discovers her own special talents as a dancer and achieves a new appreciation of her own self-worth."

It took Williams-Garcia several years to get *Blue Tights* published. While she worked on the book, revising and collating the stories she had assembled from her own life and the lives of her reading students, she went to work for a marketing company in Manhattan, mailing out manuscripts typed on an old typewriter in the company mail room. The manuscript of *Blue Tights* (originally titled *Blue Tights, Big Butt*), however, kept returning to the author with depressing regularity. Editors complained that the protagonist had a poor self-image and was too focused on her appearance. "The letters I got back from editors and agents were more or less on the same lines," the author explained to Rochman. "Can you make the girl older, about 17, if there's going to be any kind of sexual content in the book? Or, this is not a good role model; she's not positive; she doesn't have anything uplifting to offer to young African American women growing up; can you do something about her attitude? Can you do something about all these references to black culture? Readers aren't going to understand them. Can you make it more universal?"

Williams-Garcia continued to write and submit stories during the 1980s. In the meantime she had married and given birth to two daughters. After her job was cut during a company restructuring, she decided to pursue writing with more seriousness. She brought the *Blue Tights* manuscript to Lodestar Books, a publishing house known for its history of publishing challenging books. The novel was released in 1988 and won recognition from many reviewers. "By writing about urban black teenagers and a young girl who aspires to be a dancer," Nancy Vasilakis stated in *Horn Book*, "Rita Williams-Garcia incorporates a setting and a subject that she obviously knows well." "The novel vividly evokes Joyce's neighborhood and the rigor and joy of her dancing," commented a *Booklist* critic. "Joyce's understanding is believably paced and powerfully realized," declared a *Publishers Weekly* reviewer, "and her story is uplifting."

Facing a Harsh World

While *Blue Tights* gains its sense of optimism from its resilient protagonist, Joyce, *Fast Talk on a Slow Track* gains its uplifting tone from the way its main character deals with failure. Denzel, the smooth-talking valedictorian of his high school, attends a summer program for minority students at Princeton University. While he relied on his winning personal-

Williams-Garcia, who is known for tackling difficult subjects in her works, earned a National Book Award nomination for *One Crazy Summer*, which explores the Black Panther Movement of the 1960s. (Copyright © 2010. Robin Platzer/Twin Photos. All rights reserved. Reproduced by permission.)

ity throughout high school, Denzel soon discovers that those tricks no longer work in college. Ultimately, he is overcome by his sense of inadequacy and decides to abandon his chance for a Princeton education. Denzel turns to a part-time job as a door-to-door salesman to regain his self-esteem, and he experiments briefly with the world of black street culture. Finally, however, he bows to family pressure and resolves to attend Princeton, finding that, "with a little humility and some serious study, he *can* hack it," explained a *Kirkus Reviews* contributor.

The novel brought its author further critical praise. "Williams-Garcia writes just as authoritatively about teenage boys as she did about girls in her first novel," related Vasilakis in a review of *Fast Talk on a Slow Track* for *Horn Book*. "She understands the forces and fears driving a young man in search of his true self." In *School Library Journal*, Hazel Rochman observed: "Teens everywhere will be able to identify and commiserate with Denzel as he goes through his options, gains confidence, and matures."

The heroine of *Like Sisters on the Homefront*, fourteen-year-old Gayle, has her own set of problems and needs to gain maturity in order to cope with them. After she becomes pregnant for a second time (her first pregnancy resulted in a son, José, now seven months old), Gayle's mother takes the teen to an abortion clinic, then ships her off to the family home in Georgia. At first Gayle feels uncomfortable in the rural environment; she is away from her boyfriend and homegirls and has to cope with her uncle's disapproval, her aunt's insistence on proper child care for her young son, and her cousin Cookie's religious standards. She begins to change when her aunt gives her the responsibility of caring for her great-grandmother, Great, who is sick and near death. The relationship between Great and Gayle deepens as the old woman's condition worsens. Great "exhibits a strength of spirit and a stubbornness that Gayle recognizes in herself," noted Vasilakis in *Horn Book*. "Great understands Gayle, too. 'When you lay down your deviling,' she tells her great-granddaughter, 'you'll be stronger than those who lived by the rule all their lives.'" Great finally chooses Gayle to receive the Telling, the source of family history that keeps the family together.

"Strong-willed, self-absorbed, and impulsive, Gayle is not unlike the heroine of . . . *Blue Tights*," noted Vasilakis, adding that Williams-Garcia's protagonist is "imbued with a lively mix of naiveté and worldliness, particularly in sexual matters, that gives her characterization depth and vibrancy." "Painting Gayle as a hard-edged, high-spirited young woman clearly headed for either trouble or triumph, Williams-Garcia breathes life into what could have been a stereotypical portrait of a trash-talking, streetwise city teen," stated Deborah Stevenson in a review of *Like Sisters on the Homefront* for the *Bulletin of the Center for Children's Books*, "and while its scales are tipped in favor of a responsible life, the book is honest enough to acknowledge the pleasures of the other kind."

Realistic Tales of Urban Teen Life

Other novels for older readers include *Every Time a Rainbow Dies*, which features an odd, one-sided love story between shy Thulani, who stops a rape in progress, and Ysa, the victim who initially shows little gratitude to her savior. Still trying to recover from his mother's death, Jamaica-born Thulani is on the roof of his Brooklyn apartment building tending his pigeons when he witnesses a rape in the alleyway below. He arrives in time to save Ysa and thereafter becomes obsessed with this pretty young woman. But his affections are not returned in this "insightful, sensitive, and engaging tale," as *School Library Journal* reviewer Francisca Goldsmith described the novel. Finally, however, the pair form a tenuous bond and initiate a sexual relationship. "Well-observed and subtle, Williams-Garcia's latest novel artfully interplays harsh urban realities with adolescent innocence," wrote *Horn Book* contributor Nell D. Beram. Similarly, a *Publishers Weekly* writer felt that "this novel will hold the rapt attention of sophisticated readers." Further praise came from *Booklist* reviewer Hazel Rochman, who noted of this novel: "Without graphic language, [Williams-Garcia] portrays violence and anger in contemporary troubled teens who find courage and connection."

The author tackles another difficult theme in *No Laughter Here*, which focuses on a topic about which Williams-Garcia has strong feelings: genital mutilation. The author frames her topic in the relationship between two fifth-grade friends. Akilah Hunter and Victoria Ljike live in Queens, and when Victoria returns from a vacation with her grandmother in Nigeria a different, more subdued person, Akilah is concerned. As Victoria's inner turmoil becomes more apparent, her friend discovers that as part of her coming-of-age celebration, the ten-year-old American girl was given a clitorectomy. The author's handling of this potentially sensational subject impressed several critics. Noting that Williams-Garcia includes details appropriate for her middle-grade readership, *School Library Journal* reviewer Miranda Doyle wrote that the author "addresses . . . cultural issues and contradictions without overwhelming readers." While a *Publishers Weekly* contributor described the novel as "disturbing and poignant," the critic added that "the author

attempts to remain objective, showing how and why the ritual is still practiced in some cultures." Beram noted in *Horn Book* that *No Laughter Here* "will be an eye-opening book for most preteens," while in *Booklist* Gillian Engberg praised the author for balancing "what could have been strident messages with interesting contrasts" in a "skillfully told, powerful story." A *Kirkus Reviews* contributor called the work an "exquisitely written short novel [that] tackles an enormous and sensitive subject."

Jumped tells the story of three high school girls whose lives are changed by the threat of violence. Basketball player Dominique, frustrated after being benched by her coach due to poor grades, feels insulted when the vain, fashionable Trina cuts in front of her in the hallway at the start of the day, so she vows to beat up Trina after school. Trina does not hear Dominique threaten her, but bystander Leticia does. While Leticia does not want to intervene in the situation, her friend Bea urges her to do so. In chapters alternating the viewpoints of the three girls, Williams-Garcia portrays what each girl experiences as the day goes on and the hour of the showdown approaches.

Some critics thought Williams-Garcia had produced yet another realistic tale of urban teen life, with well-drawn, relatable characters. They "seem to leap off the page," related a *Publishers Weekly* reviewer, who saw this as an example of the author's "uncanny ability to project unique voices." In a similar vein, *School Library Journal* contributor Meredith Robbins commented that the girls all have "strong, individual voices," further noting that the author portrays each one in a nonjudgmental manner, making for a "thought-provoking tale without a clear-cut villain." To Jonathan Hunt, writing in *Horn Book*, there was a bit too much going on with each character, making it possible to lose sight of the key plot point. Still, he remarked, the novel provides "a piercing snapshot" of urban high school life. Some other reviewers had no such qualms. In *Booklist*, Daniel Kraus maintained that Williams-Garcia effectively depicts "the complicated politics of high school" and "subtly prepares the reader for the messy and gut-wrenching conclusion." A *Kirkus Review* critic added that the author "masterfully builds tension to the momentous ending."

Radicalism, from a Child's Viewpoint

Williams-Garcia targets middle-grade readers with her 2010 novel, *One Crazy Summer*. The "crazy summer" in question takes place in 1968, when eleven-year-old Delphine and her younger sisters, Vonetta

A greatly admired author who has received the PEN/Norma Klein Award for Children's Fiction, among other honors, Williams-Garcia (second from right) served on the "Diversity in YA Literature" panel at New York's Fordham University in 2011. (Copyright © 2011 School Library Journal. All rights reserved. Reproduced by permission.)

and Fern, fly from Brooklyn to Oakland, California, to be with the poet-mother, Cecile, who abandoned them as infants. Instead of being welcomed with open arms by their mother, the children are shuffled off the very next day to a center run by the Black Panthers, where they find a sort of home away from home.

Williams-Garcia noted in her Coretta Scott King Award acceptance speech, "Throughout my work, I've invited my mostly teen readers to ponder my offerings and form their own opinions. In my seventh novel I wanted to do something different. I wanted to share an era in which I had enjoyed my childhood—the late 1960s. Much to my delight and amusement, this is a historical period for eleven-year-olds today." Speaking with Bird, Williams-Garcia addressed the fact that little historical fiction has been written about the Black Panthers: "It's understandable that the Black Panther Movement wouldn't share the same national recognition and celebration as the non-violent campaigns of the Civil Rights Era. For many, the Panthers embodied their fears of black rage; this angry, militant image was the only face attributed to the party."

Williams-Garcia acknowledged that the Black Panthers in fact advocated revolution and were prepared to use violence in defense of their community. However, as Williams-Garcia explained to Bird, there was a socially conscious aspect to the Black Panthers, as well, and it was this aspect she wanted to focus on in *One Crazy Summer*. The author observed: "[The Black Panthers] began free breakfast programs, shoes and clothing drives, Sickle Cell Anemia testing. They advocated fair housing practices, spearheaded neighborhood clinics, legal aid for the poor, and they established Liberation Schools for children."

Narrated by plucky Delphine, the novel details the events of this turbulent summer in the United States, in the aftermath of the assassinations of Robert Kennedy and Martin Luther King, Jr., and the domestic unrest brought about by the Vietnam War. Young Delphine must become a second mother to her siblings, while the real mother, Cecile, reluctantly gets to know her daughters. And Delphine also begins to understand and even acknowledge her mother's need for freedom during these same weeks.

William-Garcia's novel won favorable reviews from many quarters. *School Library Journal* contributor Teri Markson wrote: "Emotionally challenging and beautifully written, this book immerses readers in a time and place and raises difficult questions of cultural and ethnic identity and personal responsibility." A *Publishers Weekly* contributor similarly commended the novel's "poetic language that will stimulate and move readers." Likewise, a *Kirkus Reviews* writer felt that the story of the three sisters' "resilience is celebrated and energetically told with writing that snaps off the page," while *New York Times Book Review* contributor Monica Edinger observed that *One Crazy Summer* "presents a child's-eye view of the Black Panther movement within a powerful and affecting story of sisterhood and motherhood." Further praise was offered by *Booklist* reviewer Engberg, who called it a "finely drawn, universal story of children reclaiming a reluctant parent's love." And Susan Dove Lempke, writing in *Horn Book*, thought that "readers will want to know more about Delphine and her sisters after they return to Brooklyn with their radical new ideas about the world."

Writing for African-American Youths

"I really don't think we deal with the complex issues of our young people's lives," Williams-Garcia told Rochman in discussing the importance of the books she writes. "We tell them about racism and those kinds of things . . . but then there's that real person who has to deal with the fact that he is not a symbol, he is not a model, he is a real, flesh-and-blood person who makes mistakes and has to keep moving and learning and accepting all these things as part of life. . . . It's what you come to know about yourself that is more important than any big thing that might happen to you."

In a later interview with a writer for the Web site *Brown Bookshelf*, twenty years after the publication of *Blue Tights*, Williams commented on the proliferation of stories about African-American youths. "We're here," she told the interviewer. "We're out on the shelves with our diverse stories. Characters don't bear the weight of having to represent all African Americans, or of meeting publishers' black quota for the year. We have a presence, yet there's still a need for even more stories and more writers to explore different genres." She noted that she has become more tolerant of stories written about young blacks by people from other populations "as writing from the other side has gotten better. Truer." She added: "More and more I see that we are not a people unto our selves. We make up a good deal of the American experience, culture and expression. I feel both loss and gain. This is the way of forward movement."

If you enjoy the works of Rita Williams-Garcia, you may also want to check out the following books:

Heaven, a 1998 novel by Angela Johnson that explores the meaning of family.

Jacqueline Woodson's *Locomotion* (2003), about a foster child and his caring teacher.

Walter Dean Myers's *Shooter* (2004), which centers on a violent episode at a high school.

In a *School Library Journal* interview with Rick Margolis, Williams-Garcia remarked on her goals as a writer: "I'm a happy person in general. I say to myself, 'If I can take care of my small area, then I'm making my contribution'—and I think my contribution is my stories. I'm always very hopeful about the generation that's coming up and the avenues that are opening up and how people are discovering that they can make an impact." On her home page, Williams-Garcia offered the following advice for aspiring writers: "Young authors must be hungry readers. Devour everything. Novels, nonfiction, poems, plays, comic books, graphic novels, articles. Listen to and observe the world around you."

■ Biographical and Critical Sources

BOOKS

Children's Literature Review, Volume 36, Gale (Detroit, MI), 1995.

Twentieth-Century Young Adult Writers, St. James Press (Detroit, MI), 1994, pp. 709-710.

PERIODICALS

Blackgirl, July-August, 2004, review of *No Laughter Here,* p. 4.

Black Issues Book Review, November, 2000, Yolanda Foster Bolden, review of *Catching the Wild Waiyuuzee,* p. 79.

Booklinks, January, 2007, KaaVonia Hinton, review of *Like Sisters on the Homefront,* p. 62.

Booklist, December 15, 1987, review of *Blue Tights*, pp. 696-697; April 1, 1991, review of *Fast Talk on a Slow Track*, p. 1561; March 15, 1992, review of *Fast Talk on a Slow Track*, p. 1365; February 15, 1993, review of *Fast Talk on a Slow Track*, p. 1053; September 1, 1995, Hazel Rochman, review of *Like Sisters on the Homefront*, p. 75; January 1, 1996, review of *Like Sisters on the Homefront*, p. 741; February 15, 1996, Hazel Rochman, interview with Williams-Garcia, pp. 1002-1003; March 15, 1996, review of *Like Sisters on the Homefront*, p. 1284; July, 1999, review of *Like Sisters on the Homefront*, p. 1934; November 15, 2000, Connie Fletcher, review of *Catching the Wild Waiyuuzee*, p. 651; December 15, 2000, Hazel Rochman, review of *Every Time a Rainbow Dies*, p. 809; December 1, 2003, Gillian Engberg, review of *No Laughter Here*, p. 668; February 1, 2009, Daniel Kraus, review of *Jumped*, p. 41; February 1, 2010, Gillian Engberg, review of *One Crazy Summer*, p. 61.

Book Report, March-April, 1992, Judith Garner, review of *Fast Talk on a Slow Track*, p. 42; January-February, 1996, Susan N. Bridson, review of *Like Sisters on the Homefront*, p. 42.

Bulletin of the Center for Children's Books, January, 1988, review of *Blue Tights*, p. 106; June, 1991, review of *Fast Talk on a Slow Track*, pp. 253-254; September, 1995, Deborah Stevenson, review of *Like Sisters on the Homefront*, p. 34; December, 2000, review of *Catching the Wild Waiyuuzee*, p. 166; February, 2009, Deborah Stevenson, review of *Jumped*, p. 264; February, 2010, Deborah Stevenson, review of *One Crazy Summer*, p. 266.

Children's Book Review Service, March, 1988, review of *Blue Tights*, p. 91; May, 1991, review of *Fast Talk on a Slow Track*, pp. 120; November, 1995, review of *Like Sisters on the Homefront*, p. 35; December, 2000, review of *Catching the Wild Waiyuuzee*, p. 54.

Dance, November, 1993, review of *Blue Tights*, p. 81.

Detroit Free Press, November 21, 2003, review of *No Laughter Here*, p. 5G.

Emergency Librarian, March, 1996, review of *Like Sisters on the Homefront*, p. 57; November, 1996, review of *Like Sisters on the Homefront*, p. 26.

English Journal, December, 1988, Elizabeth A. Belden and Judith M. Beckman, review of *Blue Tights*, p. 69; November, 1996, Alleen Pace Nilsen, review of *Like Sisters on the Homefront*, p. 131.

Horn Book, March-April, 1988, Nancy Vasilakis, review of *Blue Tights*, pp. 215-216; July-August, 1991, Nancy Vasilakis, review of *Fast Talk on a Slow Track*, p. 466; September-October, 1992, Rudine Sims Bishop, "Books from Parallel Cultures: New African-American Voices," pp. 616-620; November-December, 1995, Nancy Vasilakis, review of *Like Sisters on the Homefront*, pp. 748-749; May-June, 1998, review of *Like Sisters on the Homefront*, p. 18; March-April, 2001, Nell D. Be-ram, review of *Every Time a Rainbow Dies*, p. 216; January-February, 2004, Nell Beram, review of *No Laughter Here*, p. 93; March-April, 2009, Jonathan Hunt, review of *Jumped*, p. 205; March-April, 2010, Susan Dove Lempke, review of *One Crazy Summer*, p. 77; March-April, 2011, "And the Winner Is . . .," p. 151; July-August, 2011, Rita Garcia-Williams, "CSK Author Award Acceptance: One Crazy Road to Here," p. 86, and Rosemary Brosnan, "Rita Williams-Garcia," p. 94.

Horn Book Guide, fall, 1991, review of *Fast Talk on a Slow Track*, p. 160; spring, 1996, review of *Like Sisters on the Homefront*, p. 77.

Journal of Adolescent & Adult Literacy, March, 1996, review of *Like Sisters on the Homefront*, p. 516.

Journal of Reading, December, 1989, Carolyn Caywood, review of *Blue Tights*, p. 231.

Kirkus Reviews, December 1, 1987, review of *Blue Tights*, p. 1680; February 1, 1991, review of *Fast Talk on a Slow Track*, pp. 179-180; June 15, 1995, review of *Like Sisters on the Homefront*, p. 865; September 15, 2000, review of *Catching the Wild Waiyuuzee*, p. 1366; December 1, 2000, review of *Every Time a Rainbow Dies*, p. 1691; November 15, 2003, review of *No Laughter Here*, p. 1365; February 15, 2009, review of *Jumped*; January 15, 2010, review of *One Crazy Summer*.

Kliatt, May, 1998, review of *Like Sisters on the Homefront*, p. 18; January, 2001, Claire Rosser, review of *Every Time a Rainbow Dies*, p. 26; January, 2004, Michele Winship, review of *No Laughter Here*, p. 14

Language Arts, May, 2005, Lester L. Laminack and Barbara H. Bell, review of *No Laughter Here*, p. 402.

Library Media Connection, May, 1988, review of *Blue Tights*, p. 31; March, 1992, review of *Fast Talk on a Slow Track*, p. 42; September, 2004, Patti Sylvester Spencer, review of *No Laughter Here*, p. 69.

New York Times Book Review, January 17, 2010, Monica Edinger, "Seize the Day," review of *One Crazy Summer*, p. 12.

Publishers Weekly, November 13, 1987, review of *Blue Tights*, p. 73; February 8, 1991, review of *Fast Talk on a Slow Track*, pp. 58-59; July 31, 1995, review of *Like Sisters on the Homefront*, p. 82; November 6, 1995, review of *Like Sisters on the Homefront*, p. 68; December 2, 1996, review of *Blue Tights*, p. 62; November 10, 1997, review of *No Easy Answers: Short Stories about Teenagers Making Tough Choices*, p. 74; February 9, 1998, review of *Like Sisters on the Homefront*, p. 98; December 21, 1998, review of *Fast Talk on a Slow Track*, p. 70; January 8, 2001, review of *Every Time a Rainbow Dies*, p. 68; December 22, 2003, review of *No Laughter Here*, p.

62; February 2, 2009, review of *Jumped*, p. 50; January 4, 2010, review of *One Crazy Summer*, p. 47; November 8, 2010, review of *One Crazy Summer*, p. 35.

Reading Teacher, March, 1997, review of *Like Sisters on the Homefront*, p. 480.

School Library Journal, June/July, 1988, Gerry Larson, review of *Blue Tights*, p. 120; April, 1991, Hazel Rochman, review of *Fast Talk on a Slow Track*, p. 143; October, 1995, Carol Jones Collins, review of *Like Sisters on the Homefront*, p. 161; December, 1995, review of *Like Sisters on the Homefront*, p. 24; November, 2000, Kathleen Kelly MacMillan, review of *Catching the Wild Waiyuuzee*, p. 137; February, 2001, Francisca Goldsmith, review of *Every Time a Rainbow Dies*, p. 123; February, 2004, Miranda Doyle, review of *No Laughter Here*, p. 153; March, 2005, Kathleen T. Isaacs, review of *No Laughter Here*, p. 69; March, 2009, Meredith Robbins, review of *Jumped*, p. 158; March, 2010, Teri Markson, review of *One Crazy Summer*, p. 170; May, 2010, Rick Margolis, "Power to the People," p. 22.

Teacher Librarian, April, 2011, "Newbery and Caldecott Awards," p. 9, and "Coretta Scott King Awards," p. 15.

Tribune Books (Chicago, IL), March 14, 2009, Kristin Kloberdanz, review of *Jumped*, p. 3.

Voice Literary Supplement, May, 1990, review of *Blue Tights*, p. 41.

Voice of Youth Advocates, August, 1988, review of *Blue Tights*, p. 136; April, 1990, review of *Blue Tights*, p. 70; June, 1991, Jo Holtz, review of *Fast Talk on a Slow Track*, pp. 104-105; August, 1991, review of *Blue Tights*, p. 160; April, 1996, review of *Like Sisters on the Homefront*, p. 32; August, 1997, review of *Like Sisters on the Homefront*, p. 173; April, 2004, Jonatha Masters, review of *No Laughter Here*, p. 53.

Wilson Library Bulletin, March, 1992, review of *Fast Talk on a Slow Track*, p. S10.

ONLINE

Brown Bookshelf Web site, http://thebrownbookshelf.com/ (February 4, 2008), interview with Rita Williams-Garcia.

Cynsations Blog, http://cynthialeitichsmith.blogspot.com/ (March 27, 2009), Cynthia Leitich Smith, interview with Rita Williams-Garcia.

Penguin.com, http://www.penguin.com/ (December 4, 2009), "Rita Williams-Garcia."

Rita Williams-Garcia Home Page, http://www.ritawg.com (September 8, 2011).

Rita Williams-Garcia Web Page, http://comminfo.rutgers.edu/professional-development/childlit/AuthorSite/index.html (September 20, 1996), Susan Pais, Phyllis Brown, Ann Gartner, and Kay E. Vandergrift, "Learning about Rita Williams-Garcia."

School Library Journal Blog, http://blog.schoollibraryjournal.com/afuse8production/ (March 18, 2010), Elizabeth Bird, "SBBT Interview: The Remarkable World of Rita Williams-Garcia."*

Rick Yancey

■ Personal

Born in Miami, FL; married; wife's name Sandy; children: Jonathan, Joshua (stepsons), Jacob. *Education:* Attended Florida Southern College and Florida State University; Roosevelt University, B.A. *Hobbies and other interests:* Traveling, reading, puzzles.

■ Addresses

Home—Gainesville, FL. *Agent*—Brian DeFiore, DeFiore and Company, 47 E. 19th Street, 3rd Floor, New York, NY 10003. *E-mail*—rickyancey @rickyancey.com

■ Career

Author. Columnist and theater critic for Lakeland (FL) *Ledger*; Internal Revenue Service, revenue officer, 1991-2003. Also worked as a typesetter, convenience store manager, drama teacher, actor, ranch hand, playwright, and telemarketer.

■ Awards, Honors

Michael L. Printz Award Honor Book, American Library Association, 2010, for *The Monstrumologist.*

■ Writings

"ALFRED KROPP" SERIES

The Extraordinary Adventures of Alfred Kropp, Bloomsbury (New York, NY), 2005.
Alfred Kropp: The Seal of Solomon, Bloomsbury (New York, NY), 2007.
Alfred Kropp: The Thirteenth Skull, Bloombsury (New York, NY), 2008.

"MONSTRUMOLOGIST" SERIES

The Monstrumologist, Simon & Schuster (New York, NY), 2009.
The Curse of the Wendigo, Simon & Schuster (New York, NY), 2010.
The Isle of Blood, Simon & Schuster (New York, NY), 2011.

FOR ADULTS; UNDER NAME RICHARD YANCEY

A Burning in Homeland, Simon & Schuster (New York, NY), 2003.

Confessions of a Tax Collector: One Man's Tour of Duty Inside the IRS, HarperCollins (New York, NY), 2004.

"HIGHLY EFFECTIVE DETECTIVE" SERIES; UNDER NAME RICHARD YANCEY

The Highly Effective Detective, Minotaur Books (New York, NY), 2006.

The Highly Effective Detective Goes to the Dogs, Minotaur Books (New York, NY), 2008.

The Highly Effective Detective Plays the Fool, Minotaur Books (New York, NY), 2010.

The Highly Effective Detective Crosses the Line, Minotaur Books (New York, NY), 2011.

■ Sidelights

"I'm just a normal guy with a fascination for abnormal things." Author Rick Yancey is not afraid of exploring topics and imagery many writers would shy away from, as his statement in an interview with the *Dread Central* Web site shows. Having written for both adults and teens, Yancey's books cover a range of genres, from a memoir about a subject as dreaded as taxes, to gothic dramas, detective fiction, action-adventure fantasy, and gory horror. Some of his most popular works were written for a young adult audience, including the thrilling "Alfred Kropp" adventure series (filled with dramatic action sequences just begging for a Hollywood adaptation), and his acclaimed, award-winning "Monstrumologist" series, one of the most literate and bloody trio of horror novels published in recent years. When asked by online interviewer Stephanie Oakes why he was drawn to writing young adult fiction, Yancey said that he appreciated the ability to defy traditional literary boundaries: "The YA category does offer more freedom to explore genre-bending ideas. . . . That's the big thrill in writing for teens. You're not bound by any convention except the rules of good story-telling."

The Taxman Cometh

Yancey's voyage to best-selling author was not a straight path. Though Yancey claims he wanted to be a writer since he was young, it was only after many odd jobs, and more than a decade working for the federal government, that Yancey eventually achieved his dream. A native of Florida, Yancey first discovered his love and talent in writing as a middle-school student. In an interview with Vivian Lee Mahoney on her blog *HipWriterMama,* Yancey explained that he realized his desire to be a writer when a teacher asked him to compose a five-page story, and instead he turned in twenty-five pages. When he apologized for the length, his teacher responded that he should "never apologize for something you should be proud of." As a child, he read mainly sci-fi and fantasy novels, a love originally sparked by Terry Brooks's novel *The Sword of Shannara.*

A self-proclaimed "late bloomer," Yancey attended Florida Southern College and Florida State University before eventually graduating with a bachelor's degree in English from Roosevelt University in Chicago, Illinois. Though he dabbled in theater and as a playwright, Yancey found little success as an actor, and he began working a series of odd jobs, including teaching. Finally, in 1991, Yancey took a job with the Internal Revenue Service (IRS) as a field revenue officer, where he worked for the next twelve years.

Yancey's position at the IRS required constant interaction with people who were not happy to see him; as a field officer, it was Yancey's job to find people who were not paying their taxes and to make them pay. In a *Washington Post* online discussion Yancey noted that during his time at the IRS he had been "spat on, kicked, punched and called some names that would make a Marine blush. . . but it wasn't all bad. There was always the thrill of the chase and when I was able to 'get' the bad guys (and I worked a lot of bad guys) that was great fun." His position at the IRS, however, left little opportunity to undertake his dream of writing. It took several years before he began the pursuit again, encouraged by his wife, Sandy, a fellow revenue officer, who was one of the first people to suggest he should attempt writing a novel. His first book, a Southern gothic drama titled *A Burning in Homeland,* was published in 2003. National attention finally arrived, though, with the 2004 publication of *Confessions of a Tax Collector: One Man's Tour of Duty Inside the IRS,* a memoir of Yancey's time working for the government.

The Extraordinary Adventures of a YA Author

Yancey's success with his first books, written for adults, allowed him to quit his job and devote himself to writing full time. Soon after, Yancey inadvertently found himself writing for a young adult audience, a market where he has found his largest following. Yancey, a life-long fan of fantasy, had begun working on a novel about a thirty-something detective, but his writing suddenly took an unexpected twist when the protagonist discovered King Arthur's legendary sword, Excalibur. Yancey said in an interview on the *Bloomsbury* Web site that he was "flabbergasted" with the surprising direction the story had taken, but he decided to continue writing. The book did not quite work, however, and, at the suggestion of his publisher, Yancey wrote out his current protagonist (he would later use a similar character in a separate adult series, which began with *The Highly Effective Detective*), and added a teenage narrator named Alfred Kropp, transforming the book into a young adult series.

The Extraordinary Adventures of Alfred Kropp follows a lonely teenager named Alfred, who lives with his well-meaning but often misguided uncle, Farrell, after his mother dies of cancer. His uncle is hired to retrieve an allegedly stolen sword from a rich businessman, and Alfred finds himself enmeshed in a fantastical adventure with ties to the legend of King Arthur and his loyal Round Table knights. When Alfred and Farrell attempt to take the sword, they are confronted by a mysterious society devoted to protecting Excalibur. After his uncle is traitorously murdered by the man who tricked them into stealing the sword (known by several different names, including Arthur Myers, Mogart, or the codename "The Dragon"), Kropp joins forces with the remaining members of the society, heirs to Arthur's knights, in order to save the sword from Mogart, an unscrupulous former knight who hopes to use the powerful sword for his gain. Alfred meets Bernard Sampson, the heir of Lancelot, who had originally been keeping the sword safe until Alfred stole it, and who is eventually killed while attempting to retrieve the sword. After Sampson's death, Kropp convinces another knight, Bennacio, to allow Alfred to accompany him on the quest to wrest the sword from Mogart, and Alfred eventually discovers his ancestry and destiny are both linked to the legendary sword.

Yancey's novel blends elements of classic fantasy tales and contemporary thrillers, including high-speed car chases, and it immediately appealed to young fantasy and adventure fans. In a *BookBrowse* interview, Yancey noted: "I've always loved the Arthurian legend, and swordplay, too!. . . I wanted to write a great adventure story that combined my love for swords with the Arthur stories." When asked by Tom Ehrenfeld of the *800 CEO Read* blog about the similarities between Yancey's experiences with power in a large governmental organization like the IRS and Alfred's adventures with the powerful object Excalibur, Yancey explained, "Maybe the code Alfred discovers is the flip-side of

unspoken code I learned while working at the IRS. Which is that Power (as embodied by the Sword) is not something to be used to dominate and control, but a trust to guard and use only for good."

Generally, reviewers enjoyed Yancey's clever mix of fantasy, legend, and modern action-adventure, and found Alfred Kropp to be a likable and unexpected hero. Sarah Todd noted in *Publishers Weekly* that Alfred Kropp is really a coming-of-age tale about a teenager who "truly seems incapable of the task he's presented with," while another reviewer for the publication wrote that the author "deftly leavens the heavier plot elements with humor; this story of a 'bigheaded loser' is as funny as it is scary." A contributor for *Kirkus Reviews* praised Yancey's skill in balancing the tales of Camelot with cinematic-style action sequences, and noted that the plot was "expertly paced," adding that those interested in Arthurian legend "will get a kick out of watching this funny, self-deprecating teenager save the world."

"A former professor once said to me 'Art is how the soul breathes.' That's how I feel about writing. Between books, I'm an incomplete mess. In the middle of one, I'm a neurotic, distracted one."

—Rick Yancey, in a *Falcata Times* interview.

Yancey continued Alfred's adventures in two sequels, *Alfred Kropp: The Seal of Solomon* and *Alfred Kropp: The Thirteenth Skull*. The former takes place after the conclusion of the first novel, when Alfred finds himself trying to lead a normal life after saving the world and discovering he was a descendent of the Round Table's greatest knight, Lancelot. His world is thrown into disarray again when he is called upon to help retrieve a magical object stolen by Mike Arnold, an agent from the first novel who ends up double-crossing his organization, the Office of Interdimensional Paradoxes and Extraordinary Phenomena (OIPEP). The object, called the Great Seal, had originally been used by King Solomon to imprison fallen angels. In the wrong hands, the seal could prove disastrous, as it holds some of the Earth's most dangerous demons, who are not only evil but angry at having been trapped for several thousand years.

Though darker than its predecessor, *Alfred Kropp: The Seal of Solomon* contains the same mix of fantasy and adventure that made the first book popular. A reviewer in *Publishers Weekly* wrote that the "Hollywood action-flick pyrotechnics" will draw in "kids who might otherwise be playing video games," while Todd Morning explained in *Booklist* that Yancey is able to skillfully balance "action-packed scenes with tongue-in-cheek humor and occasional heart-on-sleeves sincerity." When how he creates his dramatic action sequences, Yancey told Mahoney in their interview that he generally acted out all of the scenes he could (it was "much more fun that way.")

The third installment of the "Alfred Kropp" series finds Alfred attempting to resume a normal life, this time with his new guardian, a former OIPEP operative. Quickly, Alfred finds himself on his own, facing a man seeking a mysterious object known as the "Thirteenth Skull" as well as revenge for the death of Mogart. In addition, Alfred encounters further pressure from the shadowy OIPEP organization, which wants the Seal of Solomon from him, and suspicion from authorities, who think he might be crazy. Though once again packed with action and fantastical happenings, *Alfred Kropp: The Thirteenth Skull* also displays the moral and personal growth Alfred has undergone over the three novels. All of the "Alfred Kropp" novels are notable for Yancey's portrayal of his protagonist, a young, awkward, everyman with few apparent skills and little self-confidence, but a remarkable past and heroic destiny. *School Library Journal* reviewer Samantha Larsen Hastings claimed the novel was filled with "numerous chase scenes. . ., flying bullets, betrayals, and more," and makes an ideal choice for "action fans and reluctant readers."

Men and Monsters: Drowning in a "Sea of Blood"

Though the "Alfred Kropp" books garnered praise and popularity, Yancey's biggest success in the young adult market came with the publication of his Michael L. Printz Award Honor Book *The Monstrumologist*. A dark, twisted, and gory horror novel, *The Monstrumologist* found critical and popular success with both teens and adults. *The Monstrumologist*, told in the style of a journal written years after the described events, tells the story of a boy named Will Henry, an orphan and assistant to the scientist Pellinore Warthrop, who has a singularly unique profession. Dr. Warthrop is a monstrumologist, a man who studies the "monsters that lie in wait under our beds," in which most rational adults have long abandoned belief. Henry's lonely life takes a terrifying turn one night in 1888 when a grave robber brings the doctor a gruesome find: a vicious, headless monster with its mouth

and eyes in its torso, wrapped around the body of a young girl who had recently been buried. Will soon finds himself aiding the doctor in hunting down and eliminating a colony of violent, man-eating monsters, called Anthropophagi, who have taken residence near Will's town of New Jerusalem.

With the aid of a sociopathic monster-hunter named Jack Kearns (a "monster who hunts monsters") and a frustrated town constable, Will and Dr. Warthrop must track down the source of the Anthropophagi, a species previously known only in Africa, and hunt the creatures. While the "Alfred Kropp" novels were notable for their cinematic-style action sequences, *The Monstrumologist* stands out for both its elegant language and unrelenting gore. Yancey does not shy from the graphic nature of the horror genre, even while writing for a young adult audience. In the service of Dr. Warthrop, Will Henry witnesses mutilated corpses and violent battles between humans and monsters, and he faces the dark nature of both animal and human souls.

"These are the secrets I have kept. This is the trust I have never betrayed. But he is dead now and has been for more than forty years, the one who gave me his trust, the one for whom I kept these secrets. The one who saved me . . . and the one who cursed me."

—Chapter one, *The Monstrumologist.*

Beyond the legendary and terrifying monsters, *The Monstrumologist* also explores Will's difficult relationship with his coolly distant employer and guardian. Will's father had been Dr. Warthrop's assistant before his tragic death, in circumstances possibly related to his dangerous profession. Dr. Warthrop claims that he cares for Will out of a sense of obligation, but, though both refuse to admit to a real emotional attachment, they have a deep dependence on each other, with Dr. Warthrop constantly claiming how "indispensable" Will is to him. Will's struggles with loneliness, his complicated relationship with Dr. Warthrop, and his attempts to come to terms with his parents' fate add a deeper emotional undercurrent to the novel.

When asked about the origin of his gruesome gothic horror novel in an interview on the blog *Monster Librarian,* Yancey explained that "some of the best stories come out of our primal instincts and primitive emotions," such as fear, and that he was inspired in part by a nightmare he had as a child in which he was being chased by a "faceless, huge, hulking shadow." The trauma of the dream, "the feeling of being doomed . . . with the clock ticking down until it caught me," remained in his memory for years. While writing the novel, Yancey decided he wanted a more scientifically plausible monster than was present in most horror and supernatural fiction. Yancey noted that "we were up to our literary eyeballs in vampires and the like," and wanted to find "a creature that was truly horrifying but could still have its feet (or claws) firmly planted in the natural universe." Simply by chance, Yancey discovered descriptions of the Anthropophagi, a race of cannibals that appear in literature as early as the writings of the Greek historian Herodotus, whose legend later morphed into that of a tribe of headless, man-eating beasts. Yancey knew that he had found his monster.

The Monstrumologist is not simply an exercise in horror, however, and much of the book's weight comes not from the monsters, but from the emotional connection of the characters. In his interview with Oakes, Yancey described Will and Dr. Warthrop as "the real guts of all the books. Horror only works to the extent that you care about what happens to the characters. . . . Great stories, even horror stories, have emotional resonance."

In addition to winning a loyal fan-base and the Printz honor, *The Monstrumologist* earned general critical acclaim. His novel has earned comparisons to H.P. Lovecraft, and reviewers note that the book will draw in fans of gothic horror. In *Booklist*, Daniel Kraus wrote that the novel has a "roaring sense of adventure and enough viscera to gag the hardiest of gore hounds," and may be "the best horror novel of the year." Some reviewers have expressed reservations that readers will be able to handle the extensive violence; a *Kirkus Reviews* critic commented that the "extremely violent and bloody carnage . . . may not rest easy with readers of any age." Prestigious awards and two current sequels have shown this concern to be misguided, as fans have embraced its dark mythology. In his interview with *Dread Central*, Yancey admitted that he had seen criticism in forums over the fact that the book is marketed at a young adult audience, but noted that what he "finds striking is no kid ever complains. Come to think of it, maybe that's not so surprising after all."

Yancey released a sequel to *The Monstrumologist* in 2010, titled *The Curse of the Wendigo*. Like *The Monstrumologist*, *Wendigo* bases its scares on a mythological monster, this time a cannibalistic one from Na-

tive American legend. Will again finds himself thrown into terrifying events when he and Dr. Warthrop are called upon to find John Chanler, a fellow monstrumologist who has disappeared pursuing the Wendigo, a fantastical creature that Dr. Warthrop does not believe exists, even after they find a seemingly possessed Chanler in the Canadian wilderness. After returning to New York, Chanler disappears and a killing spree begins, forcing Warthrop to confront his scientific beliefs that dismiss the existence of a creature like the Wendigo.

The Curse of the Wendigo again earned acclaim from reviewers, with Kraus in *Booklist* praising the fine literary horror novel Yancey created with *The Monstrumologist*, and claiming that *Wendigo* maintains the first novel's"high bar with lush prose, devilish characterizations, and more honest emotion than any book involving copious de-facings . . . ought to have." Amanda Raklovits wrote in *School Library Journal* that Yancey again blurs "man and monster . . . but it is the deeply complex relationship between the apprentice and master that will linger."

Fans of the series did not have to wait long for the third volume, as *The Isle of Blood* was published in 2011. Described by a *Kirkus Reviews* contributor as "[a]rticulately literary, horrifically grotesque and mind-bendingly complex," *The Isle of Blood* begins when a package made of human entrails and a mysterious (and horrifically dangerous) substance known as "pwdre ser" arrives at Will and Dr. Warthrop's home, sent by Jack Kearns, the psychotic monster-hunter who first appeared in *The Monstrumologist*. The package leads Warthrop on a quest to find its creator before Kearns does. The creator is the Typhoeus Magnificum, a monster greater, older, and more terrifying than any he and Will have faced before. Will and Warthrop are forced to examine their relationship when Warthrop leaves Will and takes a new assistant with him to seek out the Magnificum. When the assistant returns without the doctor, Will must decide if he will abandon his opportunity to lead a normal life and instead seek out his former guardian across the Atlantic, braving further terrors. The ramifications of Will's unorthodox lifestyle begin to reveal themselves, and, as with the other novels, the line between man and monster is not always clear.

Reviewers note that the emotional depth and horror level of the books has increased with each succeeding volume. A *Kirkus Reviews* contributor wrote that Yancey "deftly blurs lines between science and the supernatural." Liz Burns praised the book in a blog for *School Library Journal*, stating that *The Isle of Blood* was one of her favorite reads of the year: "Will Henry's journey, both physical and emotional, fascinates and scares me. Because monsters are real. Because this series keeps getting better and better."

Though *The Isle of Blood* was purported to be the last book in the series, having been reportedly dropped by the publisher, Simon & Schuster, a blogger launched a write-in campaign to save the series. The fan campaign drew the attention of several news outlets, including *School Library Journal,* and Simon & Schuster eventually agreed to offer Yancey a new contract, ensuring that Will Henry and Dr. Warthrop will continue their dramatically grotesque adventures for at least one more book. When asked about his experience writing the series, Yancey told *Bookshelves of Doom* interviewer Leila Roy that one of the things he struggled with most when he thought the series was ending was how attached he had grown to Will and Dr. Warthrop: "I did not account for the BIGGEST mistake I made with this series. Maybe the biggest mistake a creative writer (or any creative person) can make: I fell in love with my creation." He continued, "I vividly remember the night I wrote the final scene between them in *The Isle of Blood,* and I burst into extremely unmanly tears." In addition, Yancey noted that he had been heartened by the write-in campaign and the support of readers: "I am reminded why I dared to become a writer. Books do matter."

If you enjoy the *The Monstrumologist* series, you may also want to check out the following books:

Mary Wollstonecraft Shelley's classic tale **Frankenstein; or, The Modern Prometheus**, 1818.
The supernatural fiction of H.P. Lovecraft, including such tales as "The Nameless City," 1921, "The Lurking Fear," 1921, and "The Unnamable," 1923
The horror novels of Stephen King, including **The Shining,** 1977, and **The Stand,** 1978.

Yancey is an adventurous writer, and he is not afraid to take risks or allow his imagination to shape the plot naturally. In an interview with *Downright Creepy* contributor J.D. Prudden, Yancey explained that he generally does not like to outline stories, preferring instead to focus on his characters. As he told Prudden, 'Character creates plot." In addition, Yancey grows very attached to his books; in an interview on the *Bloomsbury* Web site, Yancey said that after finishing a novel he often goes through what he

calls his "postpartum depression," adding, "There comes a point in all creative endeavors when the thing you've created becomes something separate from you and takes on a life of its own."

With multiple critically acclaimed series, and a creative energy that cannot be bound by a single genre, Yancey has created a distinctive voice in young adult literature. For Yancey, though the end result is positive, the process of writing is not always painless, but it is often filled with emotion, a message that he passes on to aspiring writers. in his interview with Oakes, the author commented: "Trust that what move you, entertains you, fascinates you will also move, entertain and fascinate a certain percentage of your fellow humans. . . . Emotionally invest yourself in yourself in your characters and their lives . . . and others will share that emotional investment."

■ **Biographical and Critical Sources**

PERIODICALS

Booklist, May 15, 2007, Todd Morning, review of *Alfred Kropp: The Seal of Solomon,* p. 54; September 1, 2009, Daniel Kraus, review of *The Monstrumologist,* p. 92; September 1, 2010, Daniel Kraus, review of *The Curse of the Wendigo,* p. 96.

Kirkus Reviews, September 15, 2005, review of *The Extraordinary Adventures of Alfred Kropp;* September 1, 2009, review of *The Monstrumologist;* August 15, 2011, review of *The Isle of Blood.*

Publishers Weekly, August 29, 2005, review of *The Extraordinary Adventures of Alfred Kropp,* p. 57; October 10, 2005, Sarah Todd, review of *The Extraordinary Adventures of Alfred Kropp,* p. 6; April 2, 2007, review of *Alfred Kropp: The Seal of Solomon,* p. 57.

School Library Journal, November, 2008, Samantha Larsen Hastings, review of *Alfred Kropp: The Thirteenth Skull,* p. 139; March 2010, Amanda Raklovits, review of *The Monstrumologist,* p. 67.

ONLINE

800 CEO Read, http://blog.800ceoread.com/ (April 17, 2006), Tom Ehrenfeld, "Q&A with Rick Yancey—Taxes, Drama, and Honor."

Bloomsbury Publishing, http://www.bloomsbury.com/ (November 21, 2011), "Rick Yancey: Q&A on Alfred Kropp."

BookBrowse, http://www.bookbrowse.com/ (September 21, 2011), "An Interview with Rick Yancey."

Bookshelves of Doom, http://bookshelvesofdoom. blogs.com/ (August 16, 2011), Leila Roy, "Rick Yancey, on the *Monstrumology* situation."

Downright Creepy, http://www.downrightcreepy. com/ (April 27, 2011), J.D. Prudden, interview with Rick Yancey.

Dread Central http://www.dreadcentral.com/ (December 1, 2010), "Exclusive: Rick Yancey Talks *The Monstrumologist, The Curse of The Wendigo,* and More."

HipWriterMama, http://hipwritermama.blogspot. com/ (November 7, 2007), Vivian Lee Mahoney, "WBBT: An Interview with Rick Yancey."

Metropulse, http://www.metropulse.com/ (July 2, 2008), Jack Neely, "The Highly Effective Novelist," interview with Rick Yancey.

Monster Librarian, http://www.monsterlibrarian. com/ (November 21, 2011), "Interview with Rick Yancey."

Rick Yancey Home Page, http://www.rickyancey. com/ (September 21, 2011).

School Library Journal Blog, http://blog.school libraryjournal.com/teacozy/ (September 6, 2011), Liz Burns, "Review: *Isle of Blood.*"

Stephanie Reads, http://stephanieoakes.blogspot. com/ (September 22, 2011), Stephanie Oakes, "Interview with Rick Yancey."

Washington Post, http://www.washingtonpost.com/ (March 8, 2004), "Inside the IRS," online discussion with Rick Yancey.*

Author/Artist Index

The following index gives the number of the volume in
which an author/artist's biographical sketch appears: